POLAND
GENESIS OF A
REVOLUTION

POLAND
GENESIS OF A REVOLUTION

edited by
ABRAHAM BRUMBERG

Vintage Books
A Division of Random House
New York

First Vintage Books Edition, April 1983
Copyright © 1983 by Abraham Brumberg
All rights reserved under International and Pan-American Copyright Conventions. Published in the United States by Random House, Inc., New York, and simultaneously in Canada by Random House of Canada Limited, Toronto.

Grateful acknowledgment is made to the following for permission to reprint previously published material:

Institut Littéraire: "Alcoholism in Poland" was translated from the Polish original published in "PPN—Polskie Porozumienie Niepodległościowe" by Institut Littéraire, Collection Biblioteka "Kultury," 1978, vol. 294, pp. 123–30.

Spokesman: "The Gdańsk Agreement" is reprinted from *Solidarity—Poland's Independent Trade Union,* by Denis MacShane, published by Spokesman, Nottingham, England, 1981. Translation by Labour Focus on Eastern Europe.

Library of Congress Cataloging in Publication Data
Main entry under title:

Poland, genesis of a revolution.

Includes index.
1. Poland—History—1980–   —Addresses, essays, lectures. I. Brumberg, Abraham.
DK4440.P58 1983b   943.8′056   82-40111
ISBN 0-394-71025-8 (pbk.)

Manufactured in the United States of America

24689753

ACKNOWLEDGMENTS

A number of people have helped to make this book possible, but two above all: my editor at Random House, Klara Glowczewski, whose faith in its importance never wavered, and my wife, Josephine Woll, whose formidable editorial skills are reflected within its covers. To both of them—my gratitude.

CONTENTS

INTRODUCTION
The Strength of a Vision
Abraham Brumberg

Poland—Genesis of a Revolution is offered to the reader in the hope that it will help to clarify the mainsprings of that remarkable chapter in contemporary history known as the Polish "renewal," a chapter that began with a series of sporadic strikes in the summer of 1980, gave birth to the free and independent trade union Solidarity, and was halted by Polish armed forces on December 13, 1981. The purpose of the book is not to describe the dramatic developments of this period but, rather, to delve into its underlying causes, to examine the conditions that existed in Poland prior to the 1980 upheaval, to shed light on the forces of change and on the principal actors.

Part one consists of analytical essays and part two of excerpts from Polish books, newspapers, and official documents (see foreword to part two, p. 137). No doubt the essays overlap to some extent. It is difficult to write about the role of Polish workers, for instance, without mentioning their relationship to the country's intelligentsia. And any account of Poland's economic problems must inevitably cover some of the same ground as an analysis of the ruling party, whose policies were largely responsible for bringing those problems about. Yet I hope the reader will find that each essay illuminates a distinct part of a complex whole, and that the authors' varying approaches (some more historical, some more analytical) succeed in piecing together a story at once dramatic and significant—no less, in the long run, for other Communist countries in Eastern Europe than for Poland. And I hope, too, that the "Readings" will lend vivid substance to the subjects covered by the commentaries.

Perhaps this introduction can best serve the reader by focusing on a widespread perception that emerged in Poland on the eve of the 1980 upheaval—a perception all the more remarkable in that it cut across and transcended political and ideological differences, uniting even groups that were openly opposed to each other, and one that came to fruition in Solidarity itself. That perception regarded Poland as being threatened in its very fabric, as a society and as a nation, above and beyond any problems rooted in specific policies of the regime.

Certainly the problems that have beset Poland since World War II and that became especially pronounced during the reign of party secretary Edward Gierek (1970–80), stemmed from a variety of causes. Nowhere had the endemic Communist failure to erect an economic system at once rational, productive, and at least moderately equitable been so disastrous as in Poland. In addition to the doctrinaire insistence on extreme centralization, excessive investment in heavy industry, and concomitant neglect of agriculture and consumer goods, Gierek's policy of rapid industrialization—financed by Western banks and paid for by increasing exports of coal, copper, and other products—resulted in staggering debts, the decline of industries lacking in support infrastructures and unable to produce enough exports for a dwindling foreign market, and thus in the virtual paralysis of the country's economy. For a while Western credits benefited certain groups of the population and raised popular expectations. Yet the prosperity was deceptive, and policies that were to spawn a "new Poland" soon turned out to have contributed to growing impoverishment and mass discontent.

The abrogation of civil rights, the dogged refusal by the authorities to take society into their confidence or to permit open and honest discussion of the country's burgeoning problems and seek redress not by arbitrary action but by common effort, was galling not only to the intelligentsia—traditionally chafing under restrictions of speech and expression—but also to the increasingly sophisticated and educated working class. Censorship—the persistence of transparent mendacity and speciously optimistic propaganda in the public media—was an effrontery to human intelligence and dignity. A population of nearly 90 percent practicing Catholics found the regime's relentless discrimination against the Church and its believers particularly egregious. Students resented indoctrination in dogmas they knew no one believed in anymore, and the distortions of their country's true history, to which they turned ever more eagerly, as much to satisfy their intellectual curiosity as to find in it some guidance and inspiration. To all these grievances one must add yet another—the pervasive knowledge that Poland's rulers not only treated society with benign contempt, not only insisted on ruling to the exclusion of everyone else, but were revoltingly greedy to boot. The mounting evidence of huge economic and social benefits for a small elite, in a country fed on a diet of "socialist egalitarianism," was surely one of the major causes of the outbreak of public wrath that shook Poland in 1980 and ushered in the Solidarity movement.

Thus the reservoir of grievances that existed in Poland on the eve of the upheaval was enormous. And it is hardly astonishing that the various opposition groups that sprang up in the late 1970s all turned their attention to specific political and economic solutions, advocating them with increasing zeal and impudence in various "uncensored" (that is, in effect, illegal) journals, newspapers, books, and programmatic documents. Yet it would be a mistake to consider the plethora of diagnoses and recipes, however penetrating, as stemming from a concern with practical problems and pragmatic solutions alone. Something far more profound was at stake. Polish public opinion was animated not merely by a desire to correct, often drastically, specific wrongs, but by a much more ambitious and visionary goal: to restore, once and for all, the physical and spiritual health of a nation. The time was ripe to cure the "sick man of Europe," to relieve Poland of the accumulated ills of centuries of foreign rule, abortive insurrections, war, occupation, and, finally, an abhorrent and alien sociopolitical system. To be sure, even in the programs of groups that posited full national sovereignty as their ultimate goal—such as that of the Polish League for Independence[1]—the country's membership in the Warsaw Pact was not challenged, nor was the need for a "special relationship" with the Soviet Union that would take cognizance of Moscow's security interests. That relationship, however, would be based not on humiliating subservience, but on mutual respect between the two nations.[2] Thus the all-encompassing vision, however tempered by practical considerations, extended even to that sensitive and potentially lethal area of present and future Polish-Soviet relations. All in all, there was a consensus about the patient's alarming condition, and about the need for radical treatment no less than for a complete cure.

In the documents of such groups as the Social Self-Defense Committee (KSS/KOR), for instance, without doubt the most influential of all the opposition forces that came into existence in the second half of the Gierek era, political persecution, police brutality, and freedom of press and conscience are specific targets of concern. At the same time, many of KOR's writings suggest that such issues—and others, such as violations of legality, suppression of truth, and the persistence, within society at large and within the ruling elite, of intolerance, xenophobia, and anti-Semitism—were merely the outward manifestations of what KOR termed "the deteriorating moral condition of the nation."[3] The aforementioned Polish League for Independence (PPN), far removed from KOR ideologically, nevertheless shared with KOR its fundamental concern about the "normal, healthy development of the nation," and devoted a series of analytical surveys to such matters as education, family problems, the extent of alcoholism, and the like.[4] The various documents published by the Movement for the Defense of Human and Civil Rights (ROPCiO), which, not unlike PPN, placed considerable stress on Polish aspirations for independence and national sovereignty but which—unlike PPN—functioned openly, also demonstrate a concern for therapeutic measures only marginally related to ROPCiO's stated aims.[5]

Yet a third group, representing neither the generally left-oriented intellectuals who constituted the backbone of KOR nor the nationalists of PPN and ROPCiO, was the "Experience and the Future" club (DiP), which was made up of more than a hundred prominent intellectuals, many of them party members. Allowed to meet only once, in November 1978, DiP produced a series of papers that are fascinating not only for their searing indictment of the country's political, economic, and social problems, but also because they reveal that even Poland's "loyal opposition"—as it has aptly been called—was profoundly dismayed about what it saw as a malignant disease threatening Polish society. Underlying the criticisms contained in the two DiP reports published in the late 1970s—of the party's industrial and agricultural policies, of growing social inequities, of the *nomenklatura* system,[6] of stifling censorship—was fear of the effects of such phenomena on the mental and moral state of the Polish population. They called attention to pervasive "cynicism," "indifference," "collective psychosis,"

---

[1] Notes for the introduction and for part one appear on pages 297–314.

"the weakening of social bonds," the void "between the primary groups (family, friends) and the nation as a social totality," the "social pathology" resulting from the "erosion of the rule of law."[7]

What these few examples illustrate is that despite the diversity of views on specific issues, and a comparable diversity of ideological viewpoints among the many groups that were active in the 1970s, near-unanimity reigned on the perceived extent and nature of Poland's malaise. It should therefore follow that Solidarity—for sixteen months the voice of the vast majority of the Polish nation—would present a similarly holistic vision.

And indeed it did. In the programmatic document adopted by Solidarity in October 1981, the Poland of the future was envisaged as a model of "social, political, and cultural pluralism." It would not merely "guarantee basic civil freedoms and respect the principle of equality before the law"; it would also provide young Poles with the necessary conditions for "physical, mental, and moral development." "Submission and passivity," as well as hypocrisy and lies "in all areas of life," would be eliminated. The rights of the family and of the old, handicapped, and chronically ill would be protected, the environment preserved, alcoholics and drug addicts rehabilitated, workers given time off and "the opportunity to use it for cultural purposes." All this, of course, in addition to, or to enhance the overall goals of, democracy, freedom, and the right of society to shape and control its own political destiny.[8]

In the aftermath of martial law, and with the benefit of somber hindsight, such a program may seem extravagant. Nevertheless, what Solidarity strove for was what nearly all Polish citizens wanted. Palliatives and partial remedies were ubiquitously perceived to be inadequate; bailing out the ship of state in one area would not, by itself, prevent other leaks from springing or, ultimately, keep the ship from going down. Thus virtually the entire nation was in the grip of a well-nigh chiliastic passion, and Solidarity became its most articulate and powerful spokesman.

This book was conceived shortly after the emergence of Solidarity, took shape during Solidarity's arduous battles against its adversary, and went to the printer after the imposition of martial law in Poland. By the time it reaches the reader even more changes will have taken place, none of which can be predicted with any degree of certainty. What is certain, however, is that the issues depicted in this book remain not only historically valid but perhaps even more relevant today than in the past. The significance of Poland's "bloodless revolution," no matter what fate has in store for Poland in the immediate future, will endure—to a large extent precisely because of the strength of the nation's collective vision.

Part
1

COMMENTARIES: ISSUES AND ACTORS

1

IN SEARCH OF HISTORY
Jan Tomasz Gross

One of the most striking features of the movement of "renewal" that was ushered into Poland during the summer of 1980 was its profound and pervasive preoccupation with Poland's past and, most of all, with its recent history. It took the form of impassioned discussions in the press about events that had been either distorted or suppressed by censorship for more than thirty-five years[1] and the rediscovery of such figures as Józef Piłsudski and Roman Dmowski, both of whom had contributed, each in his own way, to the shaping of contemporary Polish political culture and political institutions.[2] It was reflected in the frantic pace with which memorial plaques were erected and unveiled—in Poznań, to commemorate the June 1956 uprising; in Warsaw, to commemorate the demonstrations of March 1968; in Gdańsk and Szczecin, to honor the victims of the December 1970 massacres; and in Radom, to pay homage to the striking workers of June 1976. All these attempts to link forever the present with the past may be readily observed today, yet they owe their genesis to the struggles of the 1970s, which most directly influenced the explosion of 1980, as well as to all the political unrest that has rocked the country since the Communist takeover in 1945.

Indeed, in the last two hundred years, every time Polish society coalesced and organized itself sufficiently to try to shake off the stranglehold of an unwanted state organization, it found it as necessary to conquer the past as to overcome contemporary institutions. In a series of almost instinctive efforts at self-preservation, Polish society has repeatedly resisted foreign-imposed masters not only by struggling against them but also by trying to come to grips with its own past, to understand its own sources of conduct, and to perpetuate its most important national traditions. This was true, for instance, during World War II, when the Polish underground press was intensely preoccupied with Polish history, especially with the nature of previous struggles for independence and freedom.[3] And it has been no less true in recent years. The reason for it is as basic to the history of Poland as it is to an understanding of the extraordinary events of the past few years: because of the peculiarities of Polish politics during the last two centuries, past and future are bound together for the Poles in a dialectic of liberation. To put it differently, since the 1790s every generation of Poles has found its present-day reality profoundly disappointing—and its past inspiring.

The Polish nation was deprived of political sovereignty for nearly 150 years—from the end of the eighteenth century until World War I. Thus, while the modern national identity was being forged in Europe, its most tangible symbol—the nation-state—was denied to the Poles. They strove to acquire their identity by armed uprisings, but failing repeatedly, they attained it spiritually, by an intellectual effort that transcended the oppressive reality of the present. This sublimation found its most important expression in the nineteenth century, during the Romantic Era, a period that saw the flowering of far and away the most illustrious literature in the history of Poland, and the emergence of values that to this day have shaped Polish political culture. A few words about the "romantic tradition" are therefore in order.

Take, as a point of departure, the Polish national anthem. Composed in the early nineteenth century, it tells the story of a romantic undertaking and begins with the words "Poland is not lost as long as we live." This perfectly straightforward assertion of patriotism reveals its complicated meaning only a few verses later: it turns out to be a statement made by Polish exiles in Italy who had formed armed detachments, the Legions, to march into their homeland and fight for its independence.[4] Whether or not they succeed, they assert, Poland as an idea—as a vision, if you will—shall continue to live in their minds. Subsequent generations of Poles—on their native soil, or in Western Europe, or later in the United States and Canada—similarly frustrated in their efforts to achieve independence, have intoned the words of this anthem, fully aware that by so doing, they are paying homage, above all, to an *idea*.

To be sure, the need for this definition of Poland as an idea was dictated largely by the logic of history. Poland lost its statehood in stages, its territory divided among its three powerful neighbors: Russia, Austria-Hungary, and Prussia. If the nation continued to exist, therefore, it was largely in the minds of Poles, and in a special way—as a spiritual entity, rather than as a geographical or political unit. To keep alive the idea of Poland as a nation, Poles developed a particular attitude toward their nation's history: instead of viewing it as a series of facts, such as dynastic successions, legislative acts, or some combination of extrinsic events, they proceeded to search for the meaning of that history.

This spiritualization of history permitted an imaginary escape from the oppression of foreign domination during the nineteenth century, but since no period of history made sense anymore in and by itself, its meaning—that is, all that was real about it—was embodied in an idealized sequence of past, present, and future events. The present was merely a link, a bridge, between what had been and what was yet to come. In a powerful interpretive gesture, the literature of Polish romanticism transformed the political predicaments of nineteenth-century Poland into a *figura* of Christ: Poland, enslaved and innocently suffering, was eventually to redeem the world. Romantic messianism, as developed by some of Poland's leading men of letters, attributed to Poland a universal, historical destiny—that of introducing into the world an era of liberty and happiness. To fulfill its destiny, Poland had to undergo purification by experiencing unspeakable suffering and injustice. In the words of the most influential poetic genius of the time, Adam Mickiewicz, "ibi patria, ubi male" ("Where my fatherland lies, there lies pain").[5]

Polish romanticism labored with the idea of freedom in a variety of ways. Because of the artistic genius of several poets and writers who lived and worked in this period—Mickiewicz, Słowacki, Krasiński, Norwid[6]—romanticism marked forever subsequent generations of Poles; romantic poetry and its various themes remained at the center of the Polish cultural heritage; and, in its own time at least, it directly inspired the popular political imagination. In the depositions of young Polish patriotic conspirators preserved in the records of tsarist police, the works of Mickiewicz and other romantic poets are mentioned in the same breath with strictly political texts, propaganda tracts, and various liberal-democratic emigré periodicals.[7] Romantic patriots made no distinction between poetry and political writings, and in a special way literature and politics have remained intertwined in the Polish tradition ever since.

The romantic hero is a rebel, a soldier-conspirator suffering for a cause, not unlike a creative genius, standing alone against the overwhelming material odds of the established order, whose power he is bound to break because he represents truth and justice. As if purposely turning upside down the cornerstone of realpolitik—the "might makes right" principle—justice and truth in the romantic vision are located outside the realm of power of the existing institutional order. Whether championed by a solitary genius or a group of committed, selfless men who will bear any sacrifice but not relent, justice and truth must fight an uphill battle to achieve recognition. The vision is, in a way, prepolitical. The conspiracy of freedom fighters is visualized as a mystical fraternity; patriotic initiation resembles a religious rite; the conspirators' catechism speaks of death and resurrection, of battling for people's souls and making converts, of christening and rebirth. Rebellion, it follows, emerges as a powerful, complex experience that transforms men's entire personalities. The religious metaphor clarifies it and, in a way, lends it legitimacy by pointing to the root common to both religious and patriotic fervor—a striving for righteousness. An association of patriotic rebels is likened to a religious order. Indeed, one could describe Polish romantic patriotism as a religion of freedom.

Romantic rebellion capsulizes generational conflicts as well. Youth is pitted against Age. Mickiewicz's "Ode to Youth" is probably the most famous artistic expression of this conflict.[8] And it describes the old order of society, not merely the political regime, as detrimental to the realization of freedom. Patriotic rebels are "new people" whose rank and distinction depend on "virtue, diligence, and sacrifice in the service of their country"[9] rather than on social origin. Napoleon, for example, embodied for the Poles the very essence of a romantic hero. Active patriotism was a great equalizer: joining a patriotic conspiracy was like entering into a new society.

Indeed, the theme of this dual liberation, political and social, runs through the Polish romantic tradition, as expressed in Krasiński's verse: "only one, only one miracle—Polish gentry with Polish people." The solution to Poland's predicaments, it seemed to some, could be worked out only in a joint effort of the gentry and the rest of Polish society. And advocates of this view pointed to several episodes from Poland's recent history, among them Kościuszko's insurrection of 1794, when peasant detachments won decisive battles for the Poles, and the enactment of the liberal Constitution of the Third of May, which so offended Catherine the Great's absolutist tastes that she was impelled to take over the Polish throne.[10] The link between the social emancipation of the lower classes and the political sovereignty of the Polish state was forged in Polish romantic thought, especially after the crushing of the November (1830) Uprising.[11] And independence and revolution have been intertwined ever since. The Polish emigration after 1831—the Great Emigration, as it is called in Polish historiography, because of its size and the intellectual quality of its participants—became the embodiment and carrier of the ideas of democracy and revolution in Europe. The Poles thought that "peoples" of Europe, rather than governments, would bring assistance and help to liberate Poland from its yoke, so they went to fight other peoples' wars of national liberation as if they were their own; "for your freedom and ours" became the watchword of Polish patriots.

This is obviously a rich tradition on which a twentieth-century movement of "renewal," of societal liberation, as it were, can draw heavily. Indeed, it can hardly be otherwise. Every schoolchild in Poland learns about the importance of the country's romantic authors. Not only literature textbooks but also history books—which everybody must read and study—eulogize the struggles for liberation. The Kościuszko insurrection and the November and the January uprisings are key subjects in all curricula.[12]

It so happens that all these watersheds in the modern history of the nation involve bloody confrontations with Russian imperialism. The lesson of this blood-soaked history is not lost on present-day Poles. All the uprisings were defeated by tsarist armies. Neither of the two other occupiers—Prussia and Austria-Hungary—followed policies as brutal, as fiercely designed to deprive Poles not only of political but also of cultural (and linguistic) identity, as those of the tsarist regime. Official historiography, which emphasizes the ostensible congruence of interests and historical alliance of Polish patriots and Russian Communists (who also fought against tsarist absolutism), is not terribly persuasive. The profound anti-Russian animus was passed from one generation of Poles to another, if only because it is easier to see a continuous line of conflict where two nations are pitched against each other than to absorb the rather subtle and meretricious idea that, at a certain point in history, class alliance superseded a conflict of nation-states. By far the great majority of Poles simply do not believe that Russian imperialism miraculously evolved after the October Revolution into something qualitatively different—i.e., "Communist internationalism." For many Poles, their recent family history contains some striking evidence to justify their suspicions.

During World War II Hitler's savage policies in occupied Poland affected almost every family of that country. About six million Polish citizens, half of them Jews—that is, virtually the entire prewar Jewish population—perished between 1939 and 1945. This was the highest of all nations' casualty rates during the war, greater than Yugoslavia's and double that of the USSR. Memories of those harrowing times have haunted the Polish population since 1945. The Communist regime installed in Poland after the war attempted to capitalize on this grief and sorrow. Desperately trying to establish its legitimacy, it repeatedly invoked the theme of Soviet liberation of Poland from under the German yoke. It continued to speak about the horrors of the war in order to remind the people that the German menace could be kept away from Polish borders only with the help of the Soviet army. The historical experience of World War II seemed to offer the best propaganda material to build up support for the new regime and its foreign sponsors, and to engage traditional Polish ethnic prejudices: to strengthen anti-German feelings while softening anti-Russian xenophobia. The Communist party tried to appeal to Polish nationalism in every way possible. In the late 1960s, for instance, it even engaged in covert anti-semitism in order to stir up people's chauvinism and thereby recapture their allegiance; unable to fulfill Polish national aspirations, the party played up to the darkest side of Polish nationalism.

But the whole attempt was marred by difficulties from the start, because the true story of Polish calamities during World War II had to be falsified in order to fit the propaganda image. In reality, much of the misery Poland suffered was jointly inflicted by Nazi Germany and the Soviet Union, especially in the early period of the war. An American diplomat comments dispassionately on this episode in the history of the Polish-Soviet relations:

> During the period of the German-Soviet Non-Aggression Pact the Soviet government, having in effect agreed with the Nazis on the destruction of the Polish state and the partitioning of its territory between Russia and Germany, naturally refused to recognize the Polish government-in-exile, established in London, which for obvious reasons could not accept the legitimacy of the partition. At the same time the Soviet police authorities proceeded to deport from the Soviet-occupied portion of Poland to the interior regions of Russia and Siberia, under conditions of extreme brutality and cruelty, people in the number of several hundred thousand—probably over one million. These people were, in the overwhelming majority of cases, guilty of no specific offenses whatsoever against the Soviet occupational authorities. . . . So appalling were the circumstances of their deportation and their subsequent treatment in the Soviet Union that a large portion of them, as much as 50 percent it is sometimes claimed, have never been heard from since. In addition to this, the Soviet authorities had taken into detention nearly 200,000 members of the Polish armed forces—men whose sole offense consisted, so far as one can see, in the effort to defend their country when it was attacked in 1939. And of these, nearly ten thousand officers—many of them reserve officers, doctors, lawyers, the cream in some measure of the Polish intelligentsia—had been individually executed in the Katyn forest, in the spring of 1940, by Soviet police detachments detailed for this purpose.[13]

As a result of this, George Kennan continues, in the concluding years of the war, while "Stalin's hostile actions toward the government-in-exile were no doubt partly attributable simply to Russia's improved military and political position, they were not fully explicable except in terms of an acute embarrassment, on the Soviet side, over excesses perpetrated by the Soviet police authorities against the Poles in 1939 and 1940, and a resulting determination that there should be in Poland in the postwar period no government that would have either the inclination or the ability to probe uncomfortably into the past and to make a public issue of these actions of the Soviet authorities."[14]

But after the war there was still more to hide from the Polish populace. There was the brazen cynicism and cruelty of Soviet inaction during the Warsaw Uprising in August of 1944 (nearly 200,000 people were killed in Warsaw by the SS while the Red Army, poised across the Vistula River, offered no assistance to the Poles and refused landing rights to Allied transport planes bringing supplies to the besieged insurgents). There were arrests, shootings, and deportations of whole detachments of the Home Army, as well as of members of the underground anti-Nazi network set up in occupied Poland and loyal to the Polish government-in-exile.

The balance sheet of World War II was, therefore, rather ambiguous from the Polish point of view. The Russians and the Germans split Poland in half at the outset of the war, with the Soviet Union eventually keeping the territories it had originally acquired through its alliance with Hitler. Stalin's regime inflicted numerous casualties on the Poles from 1939 to 1941, and in the latter part of the war the Red Army treated the Polish patriotic underground as an enemy force, arresting its leaders (suffice it to mention the famous Trial of the Sixteen in Moscow, in 1945),[15] imprisoning and deporting its members to the Soviet Union, and letting them be killed by their presumably common enemy. Expunged from the official record in People's Poland, the full truth about Soviet atrocities committed against the Polish civilian population and its armed forces was preserved only in the memory of thousands of families. And like all forbidden knowledge, its numerous versions were accepted uncritically by the generation born after the war.

Along with the romantic tradition and the recent history of Polish-Soviet (as distinct from Polish-Russian) antagonisms, one should also stress the institutional determinants of Polish attitudes toward Poland's Communist rulers. I have in mind here the traditional strength and role of the Polish Catholic Church and the traditional weakness and insignificance of the Polish Communist party.

Communism never carried much weight in Poland. Throughout the interwar years the Polish Communist party remained a small fringe organization, attracting its membership mostly from among ethnic minorities (Jews, Ukrainians, Byelorussians). The Polish-Soviet border war that had threatened the newly won independence of Poland in 1918 and that was settled only by the Treaty of Riga in 1921 nullified any appeal that communism could have had for the lower classes in Poland.[16] It became palpably evident that one could not combine loyalty to Polish statehood with an espousal of communist ideology. In Poland this was not merely an abstract, conceptual incompatibility, but a very real one, having been tested in practice during the Bolshevik offensive that was turned around only at Warsaw's outskirts in August 1920. Also, curiously, the Communist party did not fit into the pattern of Polish politics established in the latter half of the nineteenth century. In Poland, to the left of the political spectrum (with minor exceptions) were the socialists, who unflinchingly propounded national independence. On the right, the Polish nationalists took a conciliatory—indeed collaborationist—attitude toward Russia and opted for a constitutional solution of the "Polish problem" within the Russian Empire. This had consequences for interwar politics in Poland. At a time when nationalist appeals were becoming increasingly attractive all over Europe, the right in Poland could not castigate socialists as traitors to the national cause, nor did the claim of patriotism become the exclusive property of nationalists. Socialism and national independence were linked together, also symbolically, in the person of the most important political figure of the period—Józef Piłsudski. Communists could find no social base, even in the radical wing of the socialist movement in Poland.

As for the Catholic Church in Poland, the subject is treated elsewhere in this book. Suffice it to say that during the period of partitions the Church became a surrogate for the Polish state. With thousands of its officials deported to Russia, it shared in the fate of the nation as a whole. But it functioned throughout that period, nurturing the traditional, peasant patriotism of the ordinary people. It won the spiritual allegiance of almost the entire nation and shaped a peculiar entity with a distinctive mental-cultural outlook, revered by some, deplored by others—the Pole-Catholic.

These historical memories and traditions, then, are among the inspirations of the movement of renewal that gave birth to Solidarity in the summer of 1980. And, I believe, one ought to take them seriously. Over the past few years, Polish society has been exhibiting acute symptoms of rejection of a transplant brought into the country in an experiment in social engineering—that is, the imposition of a system of government alien to and profoundly abhorred by the majority of Poles. The essence of the "renewal" lay precisely in turning away from social experimentation. It is in history that the people of Poland search for the meaning of the present struggles and for inspiration in fashioning their future.

2

THE PARTY: PERMANENT CRISIS

Jack Bielasiak

The Polish revolution of 1980–81 had many causes, but one overriding concern: the relationship between the ruling Communist party and society. For sixteen months a broad social movement, made up of workers, intellectuals, peasants, and students attempted to emancipate Poland from the overbearing control of the Polish United Workers' Party (PZPR). Most Poles felt that thirty-five years of political misrule had brought the nation to the point of economic as well as political and social bankruptcy, and that any real solution to Poland's problems would require not merely changes in economic policy, but a change in the relationship between the political authority and the civil community as well. Fundamentally, what shipyard workers in Gdańsk and miners in Katowice demanded was Poland's right to organize itself.

Such a demand could not be ignored, and on August 31, 1980—in the face of a national challenge to its authority—the party was forced to grant sweeping concessions. At the same time it insisted on the recognition of its "leading role," a formula that in effect stood for the party's monopoly of power and was grounded in the assumption that as a representative of the "vanguard of society" it had a right to rule in the name of the people. The insistence on the "leading role" pitted the party against any attempts at meaningful autonomy and self-organization, and caused many of the disagreements between Solidarity and the PZPR after the August 31 accords. Even before August 1980, and certainly afterward, all disputes touched in some way and to some extent on the concept of the party's "leading role," from the November 1980 registration of Solidarity as an independent trade union to discussions on factory self-management and Solidarity's right to appoint factory directors, in effect bypassing the party's *nomenklatura* prerogatives.[1]

A CHECKERED PAST

Of course, 1980 was hardly the first time the party's position had been challenged; indeed, Poland's entire postwar history has been characterized by tensions over the role of the party and its domination of the country. Both because of the weakness of the Communist movement in prewar Poland and because that movement identified with the interests of the Soviet Union, Polish society was generally resistant to it, rejecting communism as a legitimate movement of social change.

The Communist Party of Poland traditionally pursued a policy that placed the interests of "proletarian internationalism" above the national aspirations of the Polish people. After World War I, when Poland became a sovereign state, the Communist Workers' Party (KPRP), as it was then called, advocated uniting Poland with the Soviet Union. During the Soviet-Polish War of 1920 the KPRP placed its hope for a socialist revolution in Poland on a Red Army victory; instead, Poles of all classes united against their traditional enemy, thus isolating the party even more. In the following years, Moscow's control over the party's policies became virtually unchallengeable, and the party's following in Poland eroded still further. Moreover, on top of its "internationalist" position, the party was weakened by internal divisiveness and tactical failures, most clearly revealed in its support of Marshal Piłsudski's coup d'état in May 1926. The party—by then called the Communist Party of Poland (KPP)—hoped that the coup would mark a leftward shift in government policies; instead, the regime became increasingly authoritarian. For its support the party paid in recriminations from the Comintern and the Kremlin, and the result was the complete submission of the KPP to Comintern directions. Increasingly, during the interwar decades, Poles regarded the KPP as an appendage of the Soviet Union and one, moreover, that could not provide any answers for specifically Polish circumstances. Other left-wing and socialist movements found a popular base among workers and peasants; the Communist party was never more than marginal. And the Kremlin, unwilling to acknowledge that its own intervention was in large part to blame, reproached the KPP for its weakness and ineffectualness. In the mid-1930s, Stalin launched a massive purge of Polish Communists that culminated, in 1938, with an official decree dissolving the Communist Party of Poland, physically eliminating most of its leaders, and thus essentially destroying it as an organized movement.

Only with, and because of, World War II did institutional communism re-emerge in Poland. Indeed, if the Nazi-Soviet Pact and the consequent division of Poland was one of the reasons for the decimation of the party in 1938, the German invasion of the USSR in June 1941 was one of the reasons for the party's resurrection. The Soviet Union needed to mobilize all forces against the Nazis, and that included—above all—the Polish Communists. In 1942, the latter reorganized themselves under a new name—the Polish Workers' Party (PPR). In effect, the Communists had two centers, one inside Poland and one in Moscow. As it turned out, the differences between them were formidable. The "Muscovites" were wedded to the idea of transforming Polish society entirely on the Soviet model. The domestic group, under the leadership of Władysław Gomułka, while also loyal to Moscow, nevertheless insisted on pursuing a distinctly "Polish way to socialism." This involved, among other policies, a rejection of forced collectivization and a greater degree of collaboration with other political groups. Stalin, profoundly suspicious of even the slightest manifestations of "deviationism," naturally supported the "Muscovites." In 1948, the latter triumphed. Gomułka was removed from his position as general secretary (on the grounds of "rightist-nationalist deviation"), and the offensive against all potential and real political rivals intensified. The Peasant Party was crushed, and the already truncated Polish Socialist Party (PPS) was forced to merge with the Communists in a new party, called the Polish United Workers' Party (PZPR).[2]

In the late 1940s and early 1950s the party pursued its aim of the "revolutionary transformation" of Poland with single-minded determination. Industry was nationalized, peasants were forced into collective and state farms, intellectual and cultural life was regimented, the Church was subjected to political discrimination and police harassment. The notion of accommodating popular demands, of coming to terms with certain endemic national traditions and institutions, was taboo. The party's fierce resolve to establish its "leading role" in all areas of life—that is, to control the society without granting any other social force the right to participate in and influence the political process—could not be challenged. The answer to any—even the slightest—sign of independent activity was to strengthen even further the party's apparat and all the coercive instruments at its disposal.

After Stalin's death in 1953, the Stalinist structure of power and the abuses of power—especially by the security services—came under increasing attack. Popular pressure, culminating in the workers' demonstrations in Poznań in June 1956,[3] was accompanied by internal party schisms on how to respond to that pressure; the danger of a total bankruptcy of the political system was so great that the party was forced to turn to its "deviationist," Gomułka, for restoration of political and social stability. Gomułka's personal authority and his earlier political program would, it was thought, restore national stability and at the same time safeguard the party's position. And in fact the nation gave considerable support to the new first secretary of the PZPR, largely in anticipation of further democratic changes. Such hopes were based on a misconception, or at least a kind of wishful thinking, that emphasized Gomułka's "Polishness" and downplayed his "communism." Gomułka did want to reduce popular pressures on the political system—but mainly in order to develop a "socialist" Poland. In other words, he saw his first task as that of strengthening the role of the party, partly through tightening up the party's political organization and partly—since it was unavoidable—through some form of accommodation with the aspirations of the people.

GOMUŁKA'S "LITTLE STABILIZATION"

Gomułka understood that Stalinist methods of coercive change had produced a confrontation between the party and society, and that repeating such methods would merely ensure renewed conflicts. The main thrust of his program, therefore, was to abandon the "revolutionary transformation" of society: he recognized workers' and peasants' grievances, significantly improved relations with the Church, provided better workers' representation in enterprises, and halted the forced collectivization policy, all with an eye to restoring the stability necessary for the establishment of a "new order." He devised a three-pronged strategy for consolidating the regime's position: strengthening his own personal authority, reinvigorating party membership, and reaffirming the party's functions in social and economic activities.

Within the party Gomułka juggled various groups, from his own trusted advisers (Ignacy Loga-Sowiński, Zenon Kliszko, and Marian Spychalski) to the conservative nationalist and anti-Semitic groups—the "Natolin faction" in the 1950s and later the "Partisans," led by Interior Minister Mieczysław Moczar—and (also in the late 1960s) Gierek's modernizing technocrats. On one hand, these factions neutralized one another; on the other, hostility among them escalated. Furthermore, since balancing these various factions tended to lead to no decisions at all on important policy issues—for fear that any innovation would damage the fragile "checks and balances" system—social and economic problems were ignored, and popular dissatisfaction increased.

Insofar as party membership was concered, Gomułka wanted to broaden and diversify the composition of the party, thereby integrating all sectors of the population and thus ensuring political stability. Action went forward simultaneously on two fronts: soon after he came to power, over 16 percent of PZPR membership—i.e., over 200,000 members—were expelled, and thousands of rank-and-file workers were recruited into the party. The "purification" process also reduced the professional staff of the party; over half of the apparatchiks went to work in state or mass institutions. This both consolidated Gomułka's position and enabled him to implement the desired shift from coercive social change to managed social change, because it got rid of the ideologically narrow, power-oriented bureaucrats and installed more personnel with technical, managerial, and professional qualifications.

During the 1960s, as more and better-educated professionals penetrated the party apparatus, recruitment among the rank and file continued: between 1959 and 1970 the party's size more than doubled (from 1,018,500 to 2,320,000). Throughout that period workers accounted for about 40 percent of the party's members and white-collar employees for about 42.5, percent, superficially suggesting a stable social composition within the party and equality between these two groups.[4] But when the figures are examined from a different vantage point, namely, what proportions of each group belonged to the party, the picture changes. In 1968, for instance, only 13 percent of all physical laborers belonged to the PZPR, while over 40 percent of engineers, technicians, and teachers were party members. Furthermore, workers were recruited in greater number partly to offset the fact that many of them left the party or were crossed off membership lists for inactivity. As a result the party was caught in a bind—precisely because it wanted to reinforce its "leading role," and needed better-qualified members to do so in an increasingly complex environment, it became less of a proletarian organization.

Gomułka wanted a party organization that reflected the major interests of society but that limited the participation of social groups in politics. As a result, soon after its rise to power, his regime embarked on a vigorous program of curbing the autonomy of any groups and institutions that were not part of the establishment (e.g., discussion groups that had sprung up in 1955–56), a program that eventually either eliminated them or brought them firmly under official control. In the fall of 1957 the outspoken student journal *Po Prostu* was closed down; a year later workers' councils were absorbed into "enterprise conferences of workers' self-management," in effect diluting and destroying them as genuine representative bodies. Youth movements had to submit themselves to directions—from the party; the Sejm's deliberative function gradually declined. Such moves sharply limited the possibility of independent action; instead of participating in—and thus broadening—the political process, groups were to be incorporated into a new institutional framework that legitimized the PZPR's superior position. The party did not have to resort to outright coercion in order to attain its objective: the use of "organizational" methods sufficed.

Of course, one consequence of the shift toward authoritarian politics was an erosion of popular support for the regime. And the less popular support the regime had, the more it feared destabilization. As a result, not only the "revolutionary transformation" of society, but even the evolutionary pattern of change, was abandoned. Increasingly, during the 1960s, the party leadership neglected severe economic problems in the country, thus contributing directly to its deteriorating condition.[5] As economic stagnation, social decay, and political inertia grew, tensions between society and the party, and within the party, mounted.

Intraparty differences surfaced on two levels: first, between the apparatus and "revisionist" elements within the membership; second, among the party elite, which splintered and split over specific policies and the course Polish development should take. In spring 1968 conflict erupted openly, eventually resulting in significant changes in the leadership and its policies.

Different kinds of people, with very different kinds of ideology, comprised each group. Revisionist Marxist intellectuals believed that the official Marxist ideology could be reformed, that the party could be democratized, and that its role within society could be reduced to that of a moral force, playing largely an "educational" role. Such a goal could only be achieved by introducing pervasive changes throughout the system—and an enlightened leadership, they believed, could implement such changes. The revisionists believed in working from within the party to influence the direction of change; their stance was open, and openly critical, vis-à-vis the party establishment. Two young socialists, Jacek Kuroń and Karol Modzelewski, in their *Open Letter to the Party*, issued in 1964, attacked the central party bureaucracy and its strangulation of rank-and-file influence on party decisions, subjecting the entire political system to what was essentially a Marxist critique. Similar criticism came from veteran Communist leader Władysław Bieńkowski and the (then) Marxist philosopher Leszek Kołakowski. The regime reacted swiftly and decisively, expelling such critics from the PZPR, and arresting its most vociferous critics; party intellectuals in turn protested, and by 1967 an open schism separated the Communist establishment from revisionist intellectuals.[6]

Even the ruling elite was riven, if not on the issue of how to respond to calls for liberalization—in that regard unified opposition reigned—then on issues of economic and social policy. The "pragmatists" (Gierek's group) advocated a bold program of economic modernization, based on professional expertise and sound management; their reformism hardly extended to the political arena, fearful as they were that popular pressure might undermine their program of economic rationalization. The "Partisans," led by veteran Communists who had been active in Poland during World War II, and far more nationalistic and conservative, criticized the Gomułka regime for its indecisiveness; they wanted to mobilize popular support by traditional national-chauvinistic means, with a dose of anti-Semitism and anti-intellectualism thrown in.[7]

Gomułka walked a tightrope above these two groups and eventually managed to silence the revisionists. But when authorities in January 1968 canceled the play *The Forefathers*, by the nineteenth-century poet Adam Mickiewicz (because of its embarrassing anti-Russian sentiments), and student protests spread, Gomułka's power tottered. The Partisans launched a major campaign against him in the guise of an offensive against "Zionist" elements in the party (already sanctioned by Gomułka by his own attack on a "Zionist fifth column" in June 1967, following the Arab-Israeli war), which rapidly deteriorated into an anti-Jewish, anti-"Muscovite," antirevisionist, and antiliberal witch hunt. It succeeded in making sweeping personnel changes at the mid-level of the apparat, and Gomułka preserved his position only by relying on the "pragmatists" and on provincial apparatchiks, who were rewarded with a greater voice in party affairs.

The 1968 upheavals had two major consequences. First, the liberal and revisionist elements within the PZPR were virtually eliminated from significant positions. More important, the revisionists, disillusioned by the wholesale attack on the intellectual community, ceased to believe that one could reform the system from within. They saw the 1968 attacks as evidence that the party cared exclusively about power, and that no meaningful political change was possible. Initially, and for some time, they therefore retreated into political passivity.

Secondly, 1968 caused a swing toward the modernizing, pragmatist faction within the party leadership. Its economic plan, based on a "technocratic" solution to national problems, emphasizing efficiency, restructuring the planning process, rationalizing the wage system, and increasing prices to shift consumption patterns from foodstuffs to durable goods, was adopted by the First Secretary; plans for its implementation were inaugurated in 1970. But the thrust of the proposed innovations favored the white-collar strata and penalized the working class, which would suffer most from the changes in wages, prices, and employment. The result, immediately after the announcement of price increases on December 12, 1970, was a storm of workers' protests, above all in Gdańsk and other Baltic ports. The government suppressed the demonstrations by force, but the effect of using Polish troops against the workers was so traumatic that it only intensified the political crisis. Just as Gomułka had come to power in 1956 through popular unrest, so fourteen years later did he lose power through popular unrest—the workers' open defiance of the regime's policies. On December 20, the Central Committee elected Edward Gierek as the new head of the party.

GIEREK'S FIRST YEARS:
PRAGMATISM AND CONSOLIDATION

The problems Gierek faced in 1970 were strikingly similar to Gomułka's in 1956. Once again economic reconstruction and social appeasement took priority for the party. But the reactions of the respective leaders differed—indeed, Gierek's policies, formulated after December 1970, were themselves a reaction to those of the Gomułka era, which were perceived as having contributed to a widening gap between the party and society, and to a growing conflict within the party. Gierek set about to reverse these tendencies: to stabilize economic conditions and to ensure party cohesion as a means of exercising greater control over society. While his strategy, involving new modes of operation and new party personnel, resulted in significant changes in the party's functions throughout the 1970s, it also had the unintended effect of further isolating the party from society and further exacerbating social conflicts in the country.

The new policies were inaugurated in February 1971. The Central Committee met to assess the new political situation in the aftermath of the workers' revolt. Policy failures were blamed on Gomułka's mistakes; the plenum committed itself to establishing a new mode of political rule. Since social tensions were viewed primarily as arising from economic dissatisfaction, the Gierek team embarked on an ambitious program of economic growth to improve the living conditions of the population. Better material conditions would, presumably, stabilize the political situation and legitimize (anew) the party. Ten months later the Sixth PZPR Congress approved Gierek's economic recovery program, which was based on a renovation of the industrial system and an increase in mass consumption. The theory was that economic productivity would improve while prices stayed frozen, hence living standards and wages and supplies would all increase. Gierek's slogan, "building a second Poland," would be implemented by a party capable of satisfying the material and social concerns of the nation, a party that would therefore be accepted as the leading institution in society. The new policy clearly represented a materialist concept of building socialism: it relegated to the background Marxist egalitarian and utopian values, stressing instead the party's practical approach, its ability to resolve the nation's problems and fulfill its needs.

Among the advantages of such a scheme was its full justification of the "leading role" of the party: in order to direct the modernization, the party needed the most effective instruments of power; in order for such policies to succeed, political authority had to be concentrated in the highest echelons of the party. Such a concentration of power reflected the Gierek view that the political factionalism of the Gomułka period was largely responsible for the party's inability to sustain a program of social and economic development.

The ruling apparat therefore sought to consolidate its own political position, first of all within the party. In June 1971 the party organizations of the 164 largest enterprises were placed directly under the supervision of the Central Committee staff, bypassing the normal regional chain of command. Ostensibly this would facilitate exchange of information between workers and the leadership—and thus forestall outbursts of discontent as well as improve efficiency. But the actual purpose was to facilitate direct control of major enterprises. Along the same lines, party functionaries gained greater control over local governments; administrative functions came under the direct supervision of the party—simply accomplished by fusing the posts of the party secretary with that of people's council chairman at all territorial levels. As a result of a series of such reforms, by 1975 the middle level of the organization was virtually eliminated and local communities were placed firmly under central control.

Gierek, himself former head of the powerful Katowice party organization, was only too aware of the provincial leaders' abilities to frustrate central commands. He wanted no repetition of the segmentation and fragmentation of political power, and to avoid precisely that he launched a comprehensive territorial reorganization that involved major shifts of party and state personnel. Thus local communes were consolidated, from 4,300 *gromady* to 2,380 *gminy* (districts); over 300 *powiaty* (regions) at the mid-level of the territorial structure were eliminated; and the number of provinces *(województwa)* increased from 22 to 49. By these means the new leadership eroded the local power base of political cadres, most devastatingly on the provincial level: former *województwa* were reduced both in size and in traditional cohesion. In short, in the two years from 1973 to 1975 territorial reform effectively curbed the political capabilities of local and regional administrative units in favor of central party authorities.

Further, the party expanded control over public and state institutions, again with the aim of strict supervision of mass organizations and social activities. An expanded *nomenklatura* list was issued in October 1972, representing an expansion of regime control over all aspects of people's lives.[8] At the same time, the party restrained activities of public organizations by centralizing their operations—under, naturally, party supervision. Such, for instance, was the result of establishing the Ministry of Labor, Wages, and Social Affairs in 1972: issues of employment, wages, and work conditions, formerly decided at lower levels, were resolved centrally. Not surprisingly, trade union organizations lost many of their prerogatives, and youth movements, which had previously represented diverse interests, were molded into one monolithic structure, the Union of Socialist Polish Youth.

Organizational constraints went hand in hand with ideological developments. Socialism was equated with economic growth, which could only be achieved through the party's definition of the common good and with its leading role in the country. Progress depended on unity. The PZPR's ubiquity in all areas of society was accompanied—and explained—by its primacy in society. To reinforce that connection the government chose the symbolic but significant act of revising the Polish constitution; changes in that supreme document would confer legal recognition on the party's dominance over society. Precisely for that reason the proposed amendments—affirming the "leading role of the Party," postulating Poland's "unshakable bond with the Soviet Union," and linking citizens' rights to citizens' obligations toward the state—provoked strong opposition, protests heated enough to force the regime to tone down the proposed changes. Still, the 1976 new constitution did recognize the PZPR as a "leading political force in society at the time of socialist construction."

Like Gomułka, Gierek also wanted to consolidate personal power as a means of stabilizing the political situation. He did so in stages, beginning with the elimination of Gomułka's supporters, from Zenon Kliszko, Marian Spychalski, and Ryszard Strzelecki (all of whom had been "Gomułka men" in the 1940s and held various positions in the late 1950s and '60s) down the line to lower members of the Gomułka elite. Making common cause with the Partisans, Gierek's technocratic faction succeeded in deposing virtually all of the former top-level men, replacing them with Gierek's close collaborators Edward Babiuch and Jan Szydlak, as well as with Partisan leader Mieczysław Moczar, who became a full member of the Central Committee's Politburo and Secretariat. Almost as soon as the Gomułka team had been thrown out, however, the alliance disintegrated, and the Partisan team was purged. Indeed, Moczar (who in May 1971 organized a conspiracy to oust Gierek) lost not only his Secretariat and Politburo posts, but also the chairmanship of the veterans' organization ZBoWiD, thus in effect losing his institutional power base. Within a fairly short time Gierek's clique had firm control over distribution of power within the party.

Gierek put a number of his supporters in charge of the security forces (with Stanisław Kania in the Central Committee Secretariat and Stanisław Kowalczyk at the Ministry of the Interior); their mission was to ensure the subordination of those forces to the party leader, and by and large they succeeded. He also dispensed political powers to individuals loyal—or obligated—to him, people like Zdzisław Grudzień, Jerzy Lukaszewicz, and Tadeusz Wrzaszczyk. Conversely, Gierek was on his guard against rivals, and acted to preempt any potential alternatives—such as Franciszek Szlachcic, who was moved from an important supervisory position in the early Gierek years, when he was considered number two man in the leadership, out of the Secretariat (in 1974) and out of the Politburo (in 1975). In between the two dismissals, his supporters lost their official positions as well.

The Seventh Party Congress, held in December 1975, acclaimed Gierek's supreme authority within the party. It was a Congress characterized by elite stability and continuity (with the exception only of Szlachcic's fall): several of Gierek's cohorts were promoted, others received membership in the expanded Central Committee. Among the ringing endorsements came one from Brezhnev, who had come from Moscow to praise Gierek as an "outstanding figure" of Poland and of the international Communist movement; Brezhnev's support no doubt explains some, at least, of Gierek's success in intraparty struggles. For the USSR, Gierek, reputed to be a pragmatic, capable individual, was doubly welcome: his economic recovery program would calm popular demands, and his political aim of restoring the party's primacy in society was above reproach. Moreover, he was infinitely preferable to Moczar, whose Partisan faction, with its nationalist and chauvinist bent, was regarded with some suspicion by Moscow. Gierek, on the other hand, made sure not to arouse Moscow's sensibilities, and continually payed obeisance to the "eternal friendship" between Poland and the Soviet Union.

Together with organizational reform and centralized leadership, Gierek's strategy involved one more goal: changing party personnel. Such a change was essential for several reasons. First, in order to proceed with a major economic and social reconstruction, the stagnant and often incompetent bureaucracy had to go. Otherwise any innovations would be strangled. Moreover, the rank and file of the party had been significantly affected by the December 1970 workers' protests; this, too, had to change. Finally, Gierek's program, both economic and political, required well-qualified personnel; without them neither modernization nor the eradication of social tensions was possible.

To this end Gierek, much as Gomułka before him, began with a purge. As early as April 1971 over 140,000 party members were expelled, largely individuals from the largest economic enterprises—they constituted a substantial part of the party's working class membership. Since the strike committees (of the December 1970 revolt) included many low-level party activists who had joined their nonparty counterparts during the demonstrations, they had to be replaced. In addition, to facilitate control over party members' activities, the Sixth PZPR Congress in December 1971 initiated annual interviews with one-third of the party's ranks, to be carried out by the staff of the central party organs. Members' cards would document their activities—this, too, facilitated scrutiny and control of the rank and file. The overall effect of these various reforms was to centralize control over recruitment of party members and increase supervision of member activity.

As for upgrading personnel qualifications, Gierek hoped to achieve this by emphasizing education and administrative experience. Incumbent party officials were pressured to improve their qualifications through reschooling that stressed managerial, administrative, and ideological skills—mainly in certain reactivated schools: the Higher School of Social Science (1971), the Management Training Center (1972), and the Institute for Basic Problems of Marxism-Leninism (1974). Besides offering higher degrees, these schools also provided a kind of continuing education or in-service training program, exposing party personnel to new developments or technological skills, encouraging contacts between them and expert professionals. The party would by these means gain apparatchiks with more education or experience in industrial management and local administration, better suited to implement the economic modernization program of the new leadership.

That program, the "economic miracle" promised by Gierek in the early days of his rule, required all the above-mentioned changes. According to the party's pronouncements, its success would satisfy people's material needs; the people would reciprocate by accepting both the political system and its elite. For four or five years Gierek's strategy seemed feasible: economic conditions improved, the standard of living rose. But these achievements could continue only in a climate of economic growth, and as the 1970s progressed such growth proved increasingly elusive.

DISINTEGRATION

The chimera of success nurtured its own destruction. Gierek's early strategy sought to combine socioeconomic development with continued political orthodoxy. Economic problems arose, requiring major innovations in political organization and economic management—but the existing political structures and arrangements could not be altered. Moreover, the pace of Gierek's modernization program, involving overinvestment in long-term projects and reliance on foreign credits, proved impossible to sustain after the 1973 oil crisis; the debt mounted, prices on imports rose, shortages increased, resentments multiplied.

The most logical answer—decentralization of decision-making, increased use of expertise—ran headlong into the stone wall of dogmas and ingrained habits. The regime would in effect have had to reverse the thrust of all its measures of the early 1970s, measures aimed at consolidating leadership and expanding party prerogatives. Moreover the party and state bureaucracies had too much to lose for them to welcome such a reversal—the successful recruitment of better-qualified personnel had led to higher rewards for that personnel. In short, the "pragmatism" of Gierek's leadership equaled, for the party bureaucracy, acquiring power and privilege. And opportunities for such acquisition had expanded significantly; the "new class" felt itself entitled to, and took, material rewards, power, and perquisites of all sorts. As the "Experience and the Future" discussion group put it, "Only members of the active political core of the party, its allied political groupings, and the administrative apparatus enjoy a privileged position in society. Their privileges extend to almost all spheres of life: access to status positions, real incomes, easier shopping, health, education, foreign travel—to say nothing of wielding power to a greater or lesser degree."[9] Political power manifested itself in conspicuous consumption, corruption, and abuse of privileges, while the worker class lived in steadily deteriorating conditions.

Any genuine structural reforms to improve the economy would, the elite thought, threaten its position, and protecting that position was its primary concern. Gierek's policies encouraged that view: the changes he initiated were aimed at strengthening the party's power, not assuring its adaptability to a changing social and economic environment. The party had a built-in bias toward maintaining its cohesion and cadre responsiveness to *its* needs, not the country's. Thus, even if individual experts, recognizing the growing national problems, attempted to propose solutions, no meaningful initiative was possible; the supremacy of political consensus and party domination doesn't leave much room for personal initiative.

The stifling of reform tendencies did not pass unnoticed. From the mid-1970s on, the public was well aware of the incompatibility of Gierek's policy: building "a second Poland" under the structural and political arrangements established in the first half of the decade could not work. The choice was clear: abandon the strategy of political consolidation, curtail the party's supervisory functions, decentralize management—or accept economic deterioration and its virtually inevitable social conflict.

The party, under Gierek's leadership, refused to recognize these alternatives. Instead it tried a third, a policy of "rationalization"—streamlining economic organization through reforms aimed at improving cost efficiency, but no structural decentralization. This meant, effectively, no more heavy subsidies of foodstuffs, the alternative to which would be price increases for a wide range of goods. Despite Gierek's awareness that the price issue was a very sentitive one, and might spark riots, he failed to take any measures to prepare Poland for the price rise. Thus, on June 24, 1976, when the new policy was announced, the working class once again refused to bear the burden of economic "improvements." Poland erupted, most notably in the town of Radom and the Ursus plant near Warsaw, and Gierek rescinded the price increases the very next day—from his point of view a lesser evil than the real possibility of losing power, as Gomułka had done in similar circumstances.[10]

Industrial unrest notwithstanding, not much changed. Gierek's team proceeded cautiously, preferring to muddle through economic difficulties while strenuously hoping that conditions would get better and people would calm down. Once again they tried to breach the gap between the party and society, launching a drive to expand and alter the make-up of party rank and file. Party membership increased, reaching 3,131,700 members in 1980, owing to a Polish-style "affirmative action" policy aimed at recruiting industrial laborers and fostering working class support. In fact, after years of a stable ratio of workers (40 percent) to white-collar personnel (44 percent), the trend reversed: by 1979, workers made up 46.2 percent of the party, white-collar personnel only 33 percent. However, the shift was largely cosmetic; as far as actual involvement in party affairs was concerned, not much changed. Since higher education and administrative experience were still deemed prerequisites for higher party positions, blue-collar workers didn't have much of a chance.[11]

Given the bureaucracy's desire to hold onto its power, it is not surprising that what substituted for meaningful economic reform was piecemeal tinkering. The "New Economic Maneuver," announced in December 1976 at a Central Committee plenum, was an example of such halfway measures. It involved reducing investments, increased supports to light industry and agriculture, a shift toward consumption—all with an eye to pacifying the population materially so as to regain popular support. It didn't work. What followed was a series of ad hoc responses to individual problems, not a cohesive program of change. Even in the face of open calls for structural changes and decentraliziation of management—by, among others, *Polityka*'s editor Mieczysław Rakowski—the Gierek regime continued to rely on its old, failed methods. At the PZPR conference of January 9–10, 1978, Gierek reiterated his line, denouncing economic inefficiency but excluding any innovative reforms to resolve the crisis. Command decision-making and party superiority were to be preserved at all costs, even in a Poland increasingly torn by economic and social strain.

Precisely because of that strain Gierek's monopoly of power began to disintegrate. His failure to grapple with national problems accentuated popular dissatisfaction and encouraged the rise of oppositional activities in society. More than that—in the wake of the regime's punishment of June 1976 activists, an opposition movement was born, and from 1977 on, opposition groups and dissident activities mushroomed. The Catholic Church became more active politically,[12] links were forged between dissident intellectuals and blue-collar workers.[13] Under the circumstances, the party overall and Gierek's leadership in particular sought social stability at all costs, even if that cost included toleration of dissident movements. Harassment occurred, of course, but no major steps were taken decisively to arrest the growth of opposition. Gierek's team was manifestly afraid: severe repression would lead only to further erosion of its power. At the same time the opposition could not dislodge Gierek: he and his regime were too well entrenched.

Thus, a stalemate ensued, marked by further party fragmentation on both issues: the opposition and the economy. A hard-line faction known as the "Hammers" reportedly advocated a tough line toward dissidents and a cohesive management policy for the economy, rejecting the Gierek policy of ad hoc solutions. Other party leaders wanted more flexibility and tolerance in economic and social management: the "Sickles" pushed for an end to the bureaucratic stranglehold and the participation of a broader part of the public in decision-making; such open-ended participation, they felt, would first resolve social alienation and then, in turn, allow for economic progress and modernization. In October 1977, for example, a group of former top party leaders—including Edward Ochab,[14] Jerzy Albrecht, and Jerzy Morawski—sent an open letter to Gierek criticizing the party's methods of political rule and demanding the introduction of more democratic procedures in party deliberations. On the other side, Tadeusz Grabski, then first secretary of the Konin province, took the floor at the December 1978 Central Committee plenum to attack the lack of direction in economic policy; he called for a more methodical approach to the operation of the national economy.

While "Hammer" and "Sickle" collided, the intellectual and professional wing of the party, increasingly shut out of policy deliberations, entered the fray, mostly by way of appeals to the leadership. One such was the call by Stefan Bratkowski, a prominent party journalist, at the meeting of the Polish Writers' Union in March 1979. Bratkowski advocated sweeping reforms throughout the system, including the removal of party control from economic management and public discussion.[15] Similar, if less forceful, appeals were made by Mieczysław Rakowski and the sociologist Jan Szczepański in 1980. Most significant among these efforts was the formation of the "Experience and the Future" group, referred to earlier, a specific forum for the exchange of views among experts from scientific, academic, and creative fields. Its purpose was twofold: to bring together talented individuals who could provide concrete solutions to Poland's problems and to bring together the political establishment and the intellectuals in a common effort. Because of the second, "Experience and the Future" rejected popular pressure as a means of forcing the political leadership to introduce change. Instead it tried to revive earlier revisionist ideas—change within the system. Revitalizing revisionism proved an immediate failure: the group's first and only plenary session took place in November 1978, after which the authorities intervened and the club was not allowed to meet again. It continued its work by compiling a survey of opinions about the state of the nation—which, ironically enough, was disseminated through the unofficial publications of the opposition movement.

The party, unwilling to make substantive changes that might jeopardize its privileged position, did its best to shunt aside all popular criticism. It did so by, among other means, scapegoating. Specific abuses could be criticized; party policy could not. Mistakes would be attacked—as being committed by organizations outside the party. At the Eighth PZPR Congress, in February 1980, the party and its leader were absolved of responsibility for the problems pervading Poland; instead, the cynosure of accusing eyes was Prime Minister Piotr Jaroszewicz, who was removed from the Politburo and the Council of Ministers.

Nevertheless, even Gierek's team realized that it was pointless to wait for a turnabout in Poland's economic fortunes; something more than passive resignation was needed to bring the country out of its downturn. It proposed a program of economic austerity: to streamline production, limit investments, improve work discipline and efficiency, curtail imports, stabilize wages and end price subsidies. Everyone was called upon to sacrifice for the good of the country: if all Poles got together and worked harder, the line went, Poland's economic difficulties could be resolved.

This campaign was meant partly to prepare the Polish working class for "rationalization"—that is, measures that would cut living standards. Under the direction of the new premier, Babiuch, an extensive campaign was launched in early 1980 to induce the population to accept the end of price subsidies. The lessons of 1970 and 1976 were clear: unexpected economic alterations would be answered with workers' unrest. So the government tried to avoid the familiar pattern by discussing, at length and in detail, what it saw as the need for economic austerity.

In an attempt to avoid confrontation, the first price increases, announced July 1, 1980, concerned meat products only. Further price changes were to be staggered, affecting different parts of the country at different times. But what might perhaps have worked ten years earlier did not work now. The impact of these increases—bound to hurt the average person while protecting the elite—was clearly perceived by the population. Strikes spread throughout the country; workers demanded higher salaries to compensate for the rise in prices. Once again, faced with a show of labor opposition, the regime had to back down. This time, however, the open defiance of government policies escalated rapidly to include demands not merely for economic rewards, but for institutional, political, and social changes as well. The unified strength of the working class forced the regime to recognize strikers' complaints: the result—the historic accords of August 31, 1980.

THE PARTY UNDER "RENEWAL"

While the purpose of this essay is to examine the events leading to the upheaval of 1980, a cursory look at the party and its behavior during the immediate subsequent period is revealing. The strikes that rocked Poland in July–August 1980 attested not only to the party's inability to govern the nation, but also to the fact that cosmetic changes would no longer suffice. Polish workers emerged from the confrontations of 1956, 1970, and 1976 with a clear understanding that promises of change issued by the party when its back was against the wall were invariably eroded in the aftermath of the crisis; repeatedly, the eventual result was party domination and neglect of popular demands. Because workers were no longer willing to accept such an outcome, the party could not solve the 1980 crisis merely by rotating personnel in top party organs or by making vague promises of future improvements. The shipyard workers in Gdańsk demanded a real change in the power relationship between the party and the working class as a guarantee of other economic and social improvements. They—and society at large—believed that the August 1980 accords signified a new compact between the party and the workers' movement, one that recognized society's right to organize itself, one that affirmed society's identity outside of party power.

What is so striking about the party's behavior in the post-August months is the familiarity of the response. Despite negotiations, despite concessions, the party consistently sought, just as it had in the past, to limit any challenge to its author-ity. It tried familiar tactics: pacification of the populace by blaming, and ousting, individual members of the Politburo who were targeted as scapegoats for eco-nomic mistakes; delays and vacillations in negotiations; intimidation of oppo-nents. The tactics also had a familiar goal: to preserve the party's monopoly of power. Thus, soon after the accords, the regime unilaterally demanded that Solidarity's bylaws include recognition of the "leading role of the party"—recognition that would formally subordinate the union to the power of the party. While a compromise was ultimately reached, the demand was characteristic, as were the repeated stalls and delays that resulted in the nonfulfillment of most of the twenty-one points of the agreement negotiated at Gdańsk.

The party deployed a similar strategy in coping with the demands of its restive and vocal rank and file, who sought decentralized party power, replacing the party hierarchy with local PZPR organizations, and grass-roots influence on policy formulation. Since the rank-and-file ferment was too extensive to suppress or even ignore, the party elite mixed calls for party unity with promises to democratize election procedures for party offices. It was a halfway, halfhearted measure meant to neutralize the rank-and-file movement by acceding to some of its demands without significantly altering the party's hierarchical structure. And when the Party Congress finally met, on July 14–22, 1981, the historic facts that for the first time elections for all high party offices were genuinely democratic and that the partly elite, at least at Central Committee level, qualitatively changed to include mostly workers and peasant activists were tempered by the limited effects of that democratization: the party after the Congress was still manipulated by the entrenched apparatchiks, who maintained their power over the rank-and-file membership.

For nearly forty years the Polish Communist party has ruled Poland, and for nearly forty years major segments of the Polish population have rejected the party's claim to political monopoly. Polish society, seeking to influence the development of Poland outside the confines of the PZPR's power and policy, has lacked institutions and channels through which it could articulate preferences and reach compromises. The party has consistently opposed establishing such institu-tions and channels, fearful lest its power erode. In turn, such intrasigence feeds popular discontent, a discontent nourished by the party's inability to meet popu-lar needs. The result has been twofold: noncompliance, open or covert, with party norms and accumulated resentment throughout the country.

Time and time again Poland has witnessed eruptions of social discontent that translated into political crises; in each case—October 1956, March 1968, De-cember 1970, June 1976, August 1980—the shortcomings of the system not only stood revealed by virtue of the upheavals: they were explicitly recognized by the political authorities. But despite promises to make significant changes, in each case the party leadership reverted to its old pattern of rule as soon as the immedi-ate crisis passed. In each case the party was forced to devise a new strategy, one that would both safeguard its monopoly of power and reestablish its institutional primacy. Precisely because of that monopoly of power, and the party's need to preserve it, nothing more than minor adjustments in party structure, policy, or hierarchy has ever occurred. Because the "leading role" of the party remains the cornerstone of party policy, and a symbol of the imposition of party will on Polish society, none of the various changes in the program, operation, or composition of the Communist party bridged the fundamental gap between the party and the nation. Such changes were, rather, tactical devices to maintain the party's power in the face of social onslaughts. The pattern—of nonaccommodation between the party and society—has repeated itself, but each time the gap widens more. Today, more than ever before, the Polish United Workers' Party is unable to guide society, impotent to resolve Poland's social and economic problems, and frustrated in its attempts to impose its monopoly of power on an ever more reluctant and defiant society.

3

ECONOMICS AND POLITICS: THE FATAL LINK

Włodzimierz Brus

It hardly seems necessary to emphasize the crucial role played by economic factors in precipitating the Polish revolution of 1980. Even during the so-called economic boom of the early 1970s, danger signals proliferated, most of which could easily have been detected by a practiced eye: the rapid rise in incomes in relation to the retail trade turnover during the 1971–75 period as compared with the preceding decade; the fall in output per unit of capital (particularly in construction and agriculture) from 1973 onward; and the alarming acceleration in external imbalances. Some of the basic elements in Poland's economic collapse will be examined below, but assuming that the fact itself is not in dispute, I shall first address the question of whether Poland differs so significantly from the other European members of Comecom (or CMEA, Council for Mutual Economic Assistance) as to constitute a special case. Affirmative answers to this question are frequently ideologically loaded and range from thinly disguised jibes about the Poles' allegedly traditional incompetence in managing their economic affairs (*polnische Wirtschaft* is the derogatory term common in both West and East Germany) to suggestions that their economic misery is a result of deviations from the true Marxist-Leninist line. The latter usually single out the regime's inability to collectivize agriculture or to enforce the "leading role of the party." Needless to say, these and other equally tenuous propositions do not lend themselves to serious scrutiny, based as they are on intangibles or on such dubious notions as "national character." However, a discussion of the broader issues affecting Poland's relative position within the Soviet bloc is clearly indispensable.

POLAND AND COMECON

The 1970s were, with few exceptions, not happy years for the entire world economy, and the price revolution in commodities has had long-term implications for both capitalist and Communist countries. There is, however, an obvious correlation between the degree of damage wrought by adverse circumstances and the overall state of an economy's health, as reflected in more general trends.

From this perspective Poland does not appear to be in stark contrast to Comecon as a whole. If we take the combined rate of growth of the national income (net material product) in the Soviet Union and among European Comecon members as the most aggregate indicator, we find that the downward trend is very marked: from around 10 percent annually in the 1950s to an annual 7 percent in the 1960s and 5 percent in the 1970s, with the decline steepening in recent years—6 percent in 1971–75 and 4.2 percent in 1976–80. With the exception of 1980, the rate of growth slowed in every consecutive year of the last five, from 5.9 percent in 1976 to 2.4 percent in 1979, with a slight improvement in 1980, when it reached 3 percent. The long-term trend was particularly pronounced in the Soviet Union, where, after the war, each consecutive quinquennium—excluding 1966–70—showed a diminishing rate, which from 1976–80 dropped to almost a third of that for 1951–55 (4.2 percent annually compared with 11.3 percent).

The picture was less clear-cut in the Eastern European countries during the 1970s because of the upswing in the first part of the decade (7.4 percent combined annual growth rate for six countries), but the latter part, 1976–80, showed a very substantial drop, to 3.7 percent (some 4.5 percent if Poland is excluded). The upswing of the first quinquennium must to a large extent be attributed to the net influx of external resources, reflected in a dramatic increase in indebtedness to the West: from US $4.5 billion in 1970 to $19.1 billion in 1975. In 1979 Eastern European indebtedness, excluding the USSR and the Comecon banks, was estimated at $47.5 billion. It might be of interest to note that by 1979 Poland, although much the biggest debtor in absolute terms, was not in the lead in terms of indebtedness per capita of the population: Hungary was first (with over $660 per capita), East Germany second (with $547 per capita), and Poland third (with $527 per capita). In relation to national income Polish indebtedness to the West was smaller than that of Hungary but greater than that of East Germany. Of course these indicators cannot be taken as a measure of a country's external position, since the ratio of foreign currency earnings and reserves to annual requirement of debt-servicing determines the degree of solvency, but they are illuminating in regard to the role played by external resources in helping to overcome internal difficulties.[1]

Despite the fact that these diminished rates of growth may look comfortable by present Western standards, especially in the midst of a recession, in the context of Communist economics they have to be regarded as worrying. To begin with, the slowdown is not the outcome of a deliberate policy to redirect resources toward improving the standard of living or protecting the environment. In fact, as a rule, deceleration goes against planning intentions, with results below and outlays above the plans. Efficiency indicators therefore look significantly worse than simple output figures: the so-called incremental capital/output ratios—i.e., the ratio of gross capital investment to increase in net material product—deteriorated in all Comecon countries during the 1976–80 quinquennium in relation both to the previous period and to the plan, which had tried to anticipate some of the increase in investment costs per unit of output. Conversely, actual increases in real incomes (particularly real wages) fell below the plans in all cases with the exception of East Germany; Hungary actually registered a fall in real wages in 1979 and 1980, while Czechoslovakia did the same in 1979.

Second, forced deceleration of growth in "supply-determined" economies exacerbates the perennial imbalances that plague them. This may seem paradoxical, in view of the conventional derivation of imbalances from an excessive rate of growth, but thus far the most effective method of dealing with imbalances under such circumstances has been the "flight forward." Without this possibility and with stronger constraints on the balance of payments, shortages spread, producing a kind of domino effect (or bottleneck multiplier, as some economists call it) between interconnected sectors. There have been clear symptoms of this in the USSR and in several other Eastern European countries.

All in all, there is little doubt that the Comecon economies are losing what was formerly held to be their strongest asset—the celebrated propensity for fast growth—and are gaining nothing in exchange, neither flexibility in supplying domestic or foreign markets, nor the capacity fully to satisfy rising consumer aspirations.

Obviously this brief discussion cannot do justice to the specific conditions of individual countries; it is not possible, for instance, to assess the efficacy of the "New Economic Mechanism" in Hungary simply on the basis of aggregate results, without taking into account the fact that during the 1970s Hungary was hit harder than any other Eastern European country by adverse change in the terms of trade. The German Democratic Republic may have suffered considerably, too, but its situation was alleviated by the special privileges of intra-German trade with West Germany, which facilitated access to the ECC (European Economic Council). Poland, on the other hand, did not lose from movement in the terms of trade in the 1970s compared with the previous decade, for by 1980 the index still—despite fluctuations—stood above that of 1970.

Any more detailed comparative analysis would require that other factors be considered. Nevertheless, even so perfunctory a background sketch is useful for our purposes and suggests—without by any means denying the gravity of the Polish economic disaster—that the Polish case should be treated as an extreme version of a more general problem. Individual differences notwithstanding, the entire Soviet bloc is displaying unmistakable signs of a serious economic malaise, which is becoming more acute as the "real existing socialism," to use Soviet terminology, gets more "mature and advanced." For explanations we must certainly look at the common systemic causes; we must also look at the consequences of the Stalinist development strategy that was imposed on the whole area. Together these have produced an economic and industrial structure ill adapted to modern requirements and scarcely susceptible to change.

THE PECULIARITIES OF THE POLISH CASE

Having examined some of the elements common to the entire socialist bloc, let us now turn to the second part of the question: what made Poland especially vulnerable to the Communist economic malaise?

To begin with, official statistics indicate that various aspects of Poland's economic performance have again and again fallen below the Eastern European average. True, after Stalin's death, during the "new course" and notably in the first two or three years after October 1956, Poland did comparatively well, especially in raising living standards. From 1959 onward, however, the picture changed: while the economy continued to grow at a steady annual rate of 6 percent well into the 1960s, the real incomes of the population rose so slowly that by 1970 Poland found itself worse off than any of its neighbors with regard to the index of real wages (119 to the level of 1960 = 100, compared with Rumania 146, Bulgaria 143, East Germany 137, USSR 134, Hungary 129, and Czechoslovakia 127).[2] Whatever reservations economists may have as to the accuracy of the official index numbers, there is no reason to doubt their *relative* validity. Taking the Polish figures at face value, the increase in real wages over the decade was a disappointing 1.8 percent annually—not even statistically significant, since it does not exceed the limits of computational error. This could hardly be regarded as a tangible improvement for workers, and the position of the peasantry remained more or less the same.

Small wonder, then, that Gomułka's attempt to increase food prices in 1970, combined with the prospect of several years of tight wages policy (the "new system of incentives"), provoked such strong protests in December of that year. The Gierek-Jaroszewicz government, which came to power after Gomułka's fall in December 1970, succeeded in reversing the trend for a short while. The rate of growth shot up to almost 10 percent annually in the first half of the 1970s, and by 1975 Poland overtook most of its Eastern European partners with respect to the index of real incomes. This brief interlude exacted a heavy toll, however, and the second half of the decade saw an accelerated downward slide, culminating in the virtual collapse of the economy on the eve of the August 1980 events.

The statistical record for over a quarter of a century thus seems to corroborate the point about Poland's poor economic performance relative to that of the other Comecon countries. Can this in any sense be correlated with the specific features of the Communist economic system in Poland?

After World War II, Poland was, among the Eastern European countries, the country most strongly opposed to communism. Later, the only attempt within a Communist party to resist Stalinization in a relatively open and coherent fashion came in Poland, in the form of Gomułka's "right-wing" and "nationalistic deviation" in 1948. Even when Stalinism was at its height in Poland, the pressure for collectivization of agriculture was unsuccessful. The collectivized area never exceeded 11 percent of the total arable land, and over 90 percent of the collective farms dissolved themselves after the 1956 events. Ideas of a market-oriented reform of the centrally planned economy, and of workers' participation in management, met with early, widespread, and persistent support in Poland. The position of the Catholic Church remained unique in the Communist world, while the degree of intellectual freedom and what might be termed "openness to the West" was generally higher than elsewhere. Perhaps most important, though, is the fact that two workers' revolts that had taken place in Poland before 1980 both resulted in bringing down the governments. The difference between 1956 and 1970 was enormous—great hopes dominated the former, while a rather desperate "lesser evil" attitude pervaded the latter—but there was one basic similarity: the expectation (and promise) of radical change in the way the system operated.

Surely by the 1970s the Communist leaders should have drawn two important lessons for the management of the economy: one, that the government's economic policies were subject to popular constraints; and two, that tangible reforms were needed to create any prospects of more favorable economic results. To illustrate the full import of these two points, let us take the example of agriculture, whose relevance to the Polish economic predicament can scarcely be overstated.

The power of popular constraints is clearly illustrated by the fact that the Polish Communist regime, when faced with the bitter opposition of the peasantry, was forced to abandon its all-out drive toward collectivization. To press on with it would have meant courting complete economic, social, and political disaster. But accepting the impossibility of collectivization was not enough: it should have been accompanied by a profound revision of the dogma that collectivization is the precondition for the modernization of agriculture. In other words, a consistent strategy for agricultural modernization on the basis of *private farming* ought to have been devised, comprising not only appropriate price and investment policies, but also measures pertaining to the structure and organization of related industries and trade on both supply and processing ends. Contrary to entrenched Communist dogmas, such policies would not have led to the "restoration of capitalism" in the country, although they would have to have made some allowance for private industry and trade, and would have provided a much more flexible version of planning and operating principles in the public sector than that prescribed by the prevailing centralized command model.

Unhappily, these lessons were never absorbed. Under both Gomułka and Gierek some positive measures vis-à-vis private agriculture were occasionally enacted, usually immediately after either a change in leadership or a particularly painful economic failure. But neither leadership ever embarked upon a long-term policy aimed at opening up the prospects of modern farming and offering a way of life acceptable to the young generation. On the contrary, the constraints on collectivization were perceived in terms of tactics, as provoking a need to change methods but not to alter the ultimate objective. The all-out assault on private farming was dropped in favor of a sort of prolonged siege, which would gradually make people realize that paths of development of agriculture on a private basis were virtually blocked, and that the only remaining avenue was that of state and collective farming. Under Gierek, development of state farming was strongly promoted, by such instruments as land, mechanization, procurement, and taxation policies, as well as by social policies, particularly pension entitlements.

An essentially analogous situation developed with regard to the functioning of the entire economy (the economic mechanism). By 1956 the deficiencies of the centralized command system—in which the country's entire economy (including the price structure) is directed from above—had been exposed, and a quite coherent set of feasible remedies involving decentralization and wider use of marked mechanisms had been proposed. The case, elaborated by a number of leading Polish economists within and outside the party, was so overwhelming that the government could not refute it even formally. But although economic reforms were recommended time and again in official documents, such reforms either remained on paper or were abandoned after initial halfhearted attempts to put them into practice.

The political system has probably had greater economic implications in Poland than elsewhere. The degree of submission to totalitarian controls was never of the same order in Poland as in the USSR and most other Eastern European countries. Popular political aspirations were revived in the wake of the 1956 upheaval, with all its promises of democratization. Hence, a degree of popular acceptance of, if not support for, state economic policies became indispensable for their success. This meant at the very least providing the society with some possibilties for influencing economic decisions, especially those affecting its welfare. Yet such possibilities were inconceivable without an improved flow of information, disclosure of genuine economic data rather than boastful claims calculated to produce widespread distrust and cynicism, the creation of mechanisms for popular discussions of policy alternatives, and so on. It also became necessary that the party stop selecting personnel only on political grounds and make better use of independent expertise. Nothing of this sort happened; instead, doctrinaire stubbornness increased the alienation of the regime from the people, eventually exploding in the 1980 crisis of confidence.

Poland's poor economic performance thus has its roots in the comparative weakness of the Communist regime and its inability to realize and react to that economic performance by embarking on reforms aimed at accommodating popular attitudes, beliefs, and aspirations. Perhaps this kind of policy would not have guaranteed better solutions of economic problems, what with the Soviet Union watching sullenly from the sidelines, but at least it might have offered a chance. While sheer incompetence played its part, neither greater authoritarian pressure nor spurious changes and pseudoliberal gestures worked—and the longer this went unrecognized, the more difficult it became to stop the rot. The Gierek decade of the 1970s amply bears this out.

SYSTEMIC FACTORS

The economic developments that immediately preceded and led up to the open crisis at the end of the decade have been well documented and analyzed by both Western and independent Polish economists, quite a number of them displaying foresight in spotting the danger signals long before they became obvious.[3] A detailed description of what actually happened can therefore be dispensed with. Instead I shall attempt to look at the 1970s from the viewpoint of the problems discussed above.

The beginning of the decade was clearly and profoundly affected by the shock of the December 1970 workers' revolt and its repercussions. While the new leadership seemed aware that its political credibility was very low, it nonetheless showed little inclination to introduce wider systemic changes. The soul-searching Central Committee meeting in February 1971 was mainly concerned with apportioning blame to members of the previous leadership accused of breaking the "true Leninist" principle of maintaining the party's links with the masses. Although the regime formed a special commission to review the economic and state systems, thereby tacitly acknowledging the political dimension of economic decisions, the extent of the postulated changes was minimal. The purpose of this body was to "modernize" the economic and state mechanisms—a term that in itself suggested that no profound structural changes were envisioned.

In practice the power structure remained essentially untouched in the immediate aftermath of December 1970. Those new elements—such as genuinely elected workers' committees—that had emerged at grass-roots level in the course of the shipyard strikes (particularly in Szczecin) were quickly eliminated. Promised consultations with the rank and file became purely formal, and lines of dependence from top to bottom of the hierarchy continued unabated, with the party apparatus retaining its superior position in the bureaucratic pyramid. Information channels were as controlled and manipulated as they had been before, with censorship allowing certain disclosures about past "mistakes," but suppressing any genuine criticism of present policies. Behind the eroded façades of "representative bodies"—Parliament (Sejm), local councils, party conferences and congresses, trade union organs, etc.—the *nomenklatura* operated undisturbed.[4] The one thing about Gierek's leadership might perhaps be credited with was occasionally abandoning the pretense of democracy: for instance, first party secretaries in districts and counties became *ex officio* chairmen of local councils, while local prefects were formally appointed and no longer pretended to be elected. The administrative reform that dramatically increased the number of provinces (*województwa*) from seventeen to forty-nine had the political effect of strengthening power at the center, especially the power of the first party secretary in relation to district secretaries.

Thus, nothing was done to circumscribe the propensity for arbitrary decisions on a macroscale. Pressure from below was not persistent enough, nor was it sufficiently directed toward radical change in political institutions, while the party, government, and economic bureaucrats continued to evoke official Communist ideology while exerting all efforts to maintain the status quo. Instead of making a genuine attempt to encourage popular participation, the regime tried to achieve legitimization through gestures such as the restoration of the Warsaw royal castle, or the removal of some of the obstacles to normalization of state-Church relations.

Whatever the overall impact of these moves, they certainly failed to create public trust in the government's economic policies. This failure was dramatically demonstrated in June 1976, when yet another attempt—similar to that of December 1970—was made to raise food prices. The measure was justified in economic terms, and in fact had been long delayed because of the government's political inability to face up to the harsh realities of life. It was, however, decisively rejected within twenty-four hours by massive workers' riots. As if forgetting the lessons of December 1970, the government once again did not submit its proposals to open scrutiny in advance. Had it done so, it might at least have worked out a better scheme of compensation than the one proposed and widely regarded as inequitable. The lack of any independent body to represent the interests of the population made negotations of a proper solution impossible, and the degree of mistrust was so high that the entire attempt came to be regarded as straightforward cheating. And while the government tried to deal harshly with those who had participated in the demonstrations, it retreated on the issue of price changes, even abandoning the idea of a modified version. Despite its survival, the political damage suffered by the regime was perhaps greater than that of 1970: in 1970 the upheaval came after a prolonged period of austerity, but in 1976 it came after a relatively substantial increase in personal real incomes and in social welfare measures. The events left the regime politically weaker (incapable, for instance, of quelling growing opposition activities) but still unable and unwilling to embark on a reform program.

The lack of political change adversely affected the economic sphere, both directly—through the poor caliber of central decisions—and indirectly— through its impact on the fate of economic reform. After Gomułka's fall in 1970, one of the first decisions made by the new regime was to abrogate the restrictive incentive scheme that, it was felt, compromised previous reform attempts.[5] It was stressed, however, that the intention was not to stop but, rather, to proceed with reform, enlarging its scope and making it more consistent. This made sense, as the existing command system was showing alarmingly diminishing returns in factor productivity, both in the input of capital, materials, energy, and labor per unit of output, and in the ability to meet the pattern of demand that resulted in growth of costly produced stocks side by side with painful shortages. Foreign trade considerations provided particularly compelling reasons for imposing economic calculation, flexibility, and inventiveness on a system hitherto operating on simplistic output-first principles, insulated from market pressures and paying scant heed to costs.

A number of such steps were in fact taken. Two measures introduced by the previous leadership were retained: a rather tame reform of producer goods prices and the reorganization of foreign trade. The latter meant a large direct involvement of industrial exporters and importers in transactions previously reserved exclusively for special foreign trade corporations, and an attempt at phasing out the notorious price-equalization mechanism, which had made the industrial exporter and importer immune to prices received and paid abroad. In its place exporters and importers were to operate under the system of a so-called transaction price—that is, a foreign-currency price converted into zlotys by an accounting rate of exchange for the respective currency area.

Second, in April 1972 the above-mentioned commission produced an overall blueprint for economic reform, euphemistically called "improvement of the system of planning and management." The reformed system was to go some way toward the application of market mechanism elements. Its chief features were that: (1) remuneration of employees and creation of decentralized development funds would be linked to progress in economic performance as measured by increase in value added (for wages and salaries) and profit (managerial bonuses); (2) direct targets, constraints, and physical allocation devices would be reduced to the following: (a) deliveries of "some" specific products; (b) minimum export quotas; (c) currency ceilings for imports from Western countries; (d) quotas for material inputs "allocated centrally"; (e) investment projects of "fundamental importance for the national economy"; (f) research projects linked to "key problems" of the national research plan. The reform plan also called for more flexible rules of price determination—that is, provision for managers to fix prices for internal turnover within a branch association of industrial enterprises, maximum prices for some items, negotiated prices for new products for a two-year period, and a gradual change in taxation with the aim of making producers more sensitive to changing market conditions.

It is clear, then, that even conceptually this was a limited reform that retained many of the features of the centralized model (direct obligatory targets and physical allocation of resources), while the actual degree of decentralization depended decisively on the current interpretations of vague notions of "some" products, projects, and so on. A significant feature of the intended system was that the new rights accrued not directly to enterprises but to huge industrial amalgamations (WOG—Wielkie Organizacje Gospodarcze, or Large Economic Organizations; hence the whole concept was called the WOG-reform), more easily controlled from above. Among other consequences, this type of devolution of economic decisions could not increase the scope of workers' self-management, channels for which were confined to the enterprise level; indeed, such organs of self-management remained equally moribund both before and after the reform was initiated. The huge pyramid of the state economic administration was left untouched both as far as the industrial ministries and the supradepartments of the party apparatus were concerned. (As a matter of fact, by the mid-1970s the number of ministries and "sectoral" vice-premiers directly overseeing the economy exceeded that of the early 1950s.) Moreover, because the reform was not introduced as a package, but gradually, bit by bit, there was an inevitable lack of coherence between coexisting old and new rules. This also made it easier to bring the process to a halt as soon as it faced its first hurdle, because the old system had by no means been dismantled.

And indeed, this is exactly what happened. The first "pilot units" started to operate at the end of 1972, but already by mid-1974 there were indications that the authorities were backpedaling. By 1975 the reform was for all practical purposes a dead letter, and although in 1977 the government tried to publicize its intentions of implementing a "modified" WOG-system, it was clear that another Polish reform attempt had failed without having been given even a fighting chance. The main reason advanced was the growing disequilibrium between domestic markets and foreign trade, which upset the conditions propitious for normal operation of the market mechanism and provided the more autonomous units with easy opportunities for profiteering and wage-push; the alleged answer had to lie in the reestablishment of central controls.

It is undeniable that shortages and the ensuing "sellers' market" created problems, and that by 1973–74 the favorable trend in Polish terms of trade came to an end (although even then the index stood above that of 1970). However, most of the tensions and bottlenecks were of the government's own making; the regime showed a complete disregard for the general conditions for successful economic reform. For example, the unprecedented influx of foreign funds was never considered as a source of reserves that would provide a firm foundation for the market equilibrium and hence facilitate the introduction of a new economic mechanism. In fact, the contrary was the case, inasmuch as these additional resources were obviously regarded as a golden opportunity to "deliver the goods" without changing the system. Fears that "marketization" might undermine the political monopoly of supporters of the "leading role of the party" principle must have played a part, even if, as the Hungarian example showed—because the Hungarian economic system had been reformed without the party losing control—the danger was exaggerated. Substantial vested interests, including material ones, were certainly a factor. As a distinguished American specialist once put it, "Active money would deprive many party functionaries of their present functions, powers and benefits."[6] Anyhow, whatever the balance of "objective" and "subjective" reasons, the fact remains that when the economy had to cope with growing difficulties, and desperately needed to make better use of its resources, not only was the economic mechanism not improved—it was reduced to a state of confusion.

THE AGRICULTURAL SECTOR

The last point that deserves mention in the context of systemic factors in the Polish economic crisis of the 1970s is agriculture. The general implications of an ideological bias against private farming, discussed above, need hardly be restated. But the link between the systemic consequences of this bias and the specific manifestations of the economic crisis of the 1970s should be explored.

The need for maximum possible utilization of the country's agricultural potential was more imperative than ever in this period because of the rapid increase in demand (particularly for meat) as a result of food prices having been frozen at the pre-1970 level, and because of the substantial growth in the population's income. In 1970–72, when the new leadership was still responsive to social pressure, a number of important policy measures favoring peasant farming were introduced: a sharp increase in prices paid by the state for agricultural produce, especially animal products; abolition of compulsory deliveries (from 1972); reform of the land tax; a greater emphasis on supply of producer goods for agriculture and extension of social security provisions. Even land-ownership policy seemed to have allowed for the possibility of improving the size structure of farms by enlarging private holdings: sales and grants to private owners from the State Land Fund (which absorbs land taken over from elderly peasants and abandoned or semiabandoned farms) increased from 24 percent of total land distributed for permanent use in 1970 to almost 39 percent in 1973.[7]

Partly through luck—favorable weather conditions—and partly because of these policies, the results in agricultural production were impressive. In subsequent years weather conditions were no longer so favorable, prompting the government to disclaim responsibility for the setbacks in agricultural production. That agricultural policies were directly related to performance is, however, illustrated—albeit negatively—by the developments in the mid- and late 1970s. On one hand, there came a renewed emphasis on "socialized agriculture" (state farms, collective farms, enterprises of the so-called Agricultural Circles). On the other hand, discrimination against private farming increased. This was particularly true for policies designed to affect its long-term prospects, such as investment, credits, supply of inputs (machinery, feed grain), and land. The percentage of land from the State Land Fund sold to the peasants dropped from 39 percent in 1973 to a mere 5.5 percent in 1975—that is, less than one-seventh of the total amount in 1973. A marked deterioration in output followed (though less propitious natural conditions cannot be discounted). After particularly calamitous results in 1975 and the annulment of price increases in 1976, another switch in policy occurred, but even in this period—perhaps in the rush to restore fallen meat production—state farms increased their share in livestock considerably.

The overall effect of Gierek's agricultural policies in systemic terms was a substantial shift in the relative positions of the private and the socialized (predominantly state) sectors, as the following data clearly show:

PERCENTAGE SHARES IN AGRICULTURE
(ROUNDED FIGURES)

| | 1970 | | 1980 | |
	PRIVATE SECTOR	SOCIALIZED SECTOR	PRIVATE SECTOR	SOCIALIZED SECTOR
Gross output	85	15	77	23
Marketed output	80	20	70	30
Net output				
(value added)	93	7	93[a]	7[a]
Arable land	86	14	75	25
Grain production	85	15	78	22
Cattle	83	17	73	27
Pigs	87	13	72	28
Meat production	84	16	65	35

SOURCES: *Polish Statistical Yearbook*, 1973, tables 5 (p. 96) and 1 (p. 256); *Polish Concise Statistical Yearbook*, 1981, tables 1 (p. 140) and 3 (p. 142).
[a]1979.

Despite the evident expansion of the socialized sector in arable land, livestock, and output, these figures amply demonstrate that the share in *net output* remained constant (actually it would even show a slight fall if not for the rounded figures). This discrepancy is most revealing, for it shows that the socialized sector uses much more material input per unit of output than the private sector: 2.5 times more in terms of value of machinery and equipment per 1 hectare of agricultural land; 2.1 times more fertilizers per 1 hectare; 1.5 times more feed grain per 1 kilogram of meat. The average capital-to-net-output ratio is 5–6 times higher in the socialized sector than in the private one, while in the enterprises of agricultural circles net output is actually negative. Of course, the produce from state farms plays a considerable role in supplies to the market, but at an excessive cost that further undermines the economy. This is demonstrably true in regard to the impact that expansion of animal production in state farms has had on the balance of payments. Fodder on private farms contains much less grain and other elements that have to be imported (potatoes still play a dominant role in feeding pigs); the shift, therefore, from private to state animal production generated a heavy and growing burden on foreign trade and became one of the major factors of the turnabout that occurred in the export/import balance in agricultural and food trade of the country. In the 1960s Poland was an overall net exporter in this group of products, to the tune of $650 million for the entire decade (cumulative, in current prices); in trade with the West the surplus was probably twice as high. In the 1970s the deficit in food and agricultural trade with the West alone reached a cumulative figure of over $4.5 billion ($3.3 billion if the catastrophic 1980 figure is excluded).

It should also be stressed that the performance of state farms was affected by the continuing system of command planning, which probably does more harm in agriculture than anywhere else.

THE "IMPORT-LED" DETONATOR

An expansionist strategy of "import-led growth" was superimposed on the already faulty political and economic system. In the 1970s the combination of the two generated adverse chain reactions accelerating over time and leading inexorably to the open explosion in the summer of 1980. Let us examine some of its principal features.

In one sense the entire concept of widespread use of Western credits for the modernization of the Polish economy grew out of the deficiencies of the system, which proved to be strongly inimical to innovation and which could hardly narrow the technological gap with the West. No remedy in this respect was expected from the Soviet bloc, perhaps justifiably, although the Polish perception could have been colored by traditional pro-Western bias and a condescending attitude to what was obtainable domestically or from its Eastern neighbors. In two cases at least, this bias is widely alleged to have led to costly mistakes: in the case of the French buses—Berliet—which were preferred to Hungarian Ikaruses; and in the more important case of the tractor deal with Massey-Ferguson, despite the availability of a good local solution with possible Czechoslovak cooperation.[8]

Still, the idea seemed attractive and reasonable: a massive injection of Western technology would create the necessary technological push, and credits would be paid off by selling abroad part of the gain in output. This would also help in restructuring industry by placing more emphasis on technologically advanced sectors like electronics and modern food processing and some branches of light industry. When the concept was first advanced in the late 1960s, it was linked (at least for a while) with the continuation of the austerity policy reflected in the ill-fated price rises and restrictive incentive schemes mentioned above. After December 1970, when the income part of the scenario proved unusable, "import-led growth" became even more attractive to the Polish authorities, because it opened up the prospect of combining investment expansion with a fast rise in living standards—the latter a highly desirable goal politically. The prospect of avoiding fundamental reforms must have made foreign credits look additionally advantageous to the ruling elite. Economic conditions in the Western markets seemed propitious: easy access to credits at low interest rates, Western firms eager to expand into Eastern Europe (especially under the banner of détente, which enlisted government support), and rising inflation carrying the usual promise of extra gains for the borrower.

Whatever the overall merits of the strategy, it soon became clear that the scale of the operation was absurdly excessive: 7.7 percent annual increase in gross investment in fixed assets was the rate envisaged in the 1971–75 plan adopted in June 1972, whereas in 1972 alone the actual figure was over 23 percent higher than in the previous year. The average rate for the whole quinquennium was almost 14 percent annually, and the total investment expenditure (in constant prices) in 1971–75 was almost twice as high as in 1966–70. The absorption capacity of the economy was widely overestimated, particularly in view of the existing, unchanged economic mechanism, which was not only cost-insensitive but also prone to investment overspending. Contrary to customary assertions that pressure from below (from ministries, local party "barons," etc.) was primarily responsible for the excessive strain in the investment programs, the Polish spending spree in the first half of the 1970s was mainly of the center's own making, albeit not without "reinforcements" from sectoral and local lobbies. The latter felt encouraged—or even pushed—to make bold investment initiatives, in accordance with the deeply ingrained Communist pattern in which lower-rung apparatchiks try to emulate, if not outdo, party leadership in zeal and ardor.

This applied equally to the involvement of foreign credits in investment projects: a kind of competition developed, and enterprises could conceivably be dubbed insufficiently progressive if they failed to press for Western equipment and know-how. There are known cases of foreign licenses simply being imposed on reluctant enterprises, and party documents of the time (the First Party Conference in 1973, even the Seventh Congress in 1975) were remarkable for their unclouded optimism. When the massive expansion got under way, no apparent provision was made for an adverse turn in events beyond the leadership's control, such as changes in Western markets or poor weather. This was an example of decisions made that on one hand ignored market considerations and on the other hand were not susceptible to political accountability. The country was led into a state of euphoria, with sycophants among economists proclaiming as outdated and defeatist many interrelationships and constraints that were, in fact, vital.

The scale of acceleration was closely connected with intensity of new investment initiatives. There was the usual consequence of excessive dispersal of limited capacities, sometimes resulting in horrendous delays in gestation periods that hindered timely repayments of foreign financial investments. There was also a considerable deterioration in the quality of central decisions, even by Eastern European standards. As indicated above, the massive stepping-up of the "import-led strategy" was not envisaged in the regular five-year plan (although the mere revision of the original plan took a year and a half to accomplish). The single largest project of the decade—the Katowice steel plant—which, together with supplementary projects, swallowed up 175 billion zlotys (over $5 billion at the official rate of exchange), was started, in 1972, without having been included in the original version of the plan.

A special term was invented, the "open plan concept," to cover the huge number of ad hoc decisions, frequently of crucial significance, made in a great hurry with barely any technical possibilities for proper scrutiny and coordination. This practice must have seriously undermined the main form of economic calculation available to a centralized system in the absence of meaningful prices—namely, the network of material balances. And supply imbalances would indeed have appeared very soon, if not for the relief function of credited imports. It is sometimes forgotten that Poland's huge trade deficit with the West was due not only to direct investment import but also to the import of raw materials, semifabricants, and components ("running import") indirectly connected with the former, and particularly to the excessive scale and the extraordinary rush of the investment drive. Imbalances made imports indispensable for keeping the economy going, and delays in completing projects prolonged the dependence on imported components. According to some estimates, no less than 40 percent of imports from nonsocialist countries in the course of the decade as a whole comprised the "running import" category, with the share rising to 60 percent and over in later years.[9]

In addition, another 20 percent of total imports from nonsocialist countries during the 1970s went into food (over 23 percent in 1978 and almost 29 percent in 1980). Thus the room for curbs shrank painfully. In the latter part of the decade, when substantial cuts could no longer be avoided, they became almost self-defeating because of the resulting decline in output, which in turn created fewer goods for export. Imbalances also grew because of the forced and—as usual—disorderly retreat in the field of investment. Apparently the early cuts applied in the first place to infrastructural sectors, thought inconsequential for output in the short-term (e.g., transport and electricity generation capacities), which almost brought the country to a standstill in the beginning of 1979, when winter proved to be unusually severe. The number of projects put into mothballs grew to huge proportions, resulting in a staggering figure of 821 billion zlotys frozen in unfinished projects (worth about 50 percent of the 1980 national income);[10] a portion of this has probably been irretrievably lost. Another victim that cannot be given proper pride of place here was the environmental complex, with some regions polluted to a degree rarely seen nowadays in Europe (Upper Silesia in the first place, but apparently even the historic city of Kraków).

The strategy of "import-led growth" frustrated the originally envisioned changes in industrial structure as well. Industry actually increased its share of investment expenditures, agriculture dropped (but from a much larger total), and within industry itself the initial swing in favor of light industry and food-processing industries was reversed. Traditional industries were on the whole able to maintain their position, particularly the iron and steel industry, which showed by far the greatest increase in capital allocations: 5.5 times more in 1978 than in 1970 in real terms, compared with 2.7 times more for industry as a whole.[11] This was obviously due to the special position of the Katowice steel plant, which came to be regarded as the symbol of misallocation in Poland. The governmental report cited above emphasizes that the steel plant's output was limited mainly to ordinary steel products, whereas the economy is undersupplied in higher-quality steels, which have to be imported. There are many more examples of frustrated attempts to improve the country's foreign trade position by modernizing the industrial structure.

In this connection it may be asked whether—or to what extent—Polish expansion of the 1970s was influenced by or at least coordinated with the Soviet Union and other Comecon members. No direct information on this score is available, and it might be conceivable that insofar as the Polish deals with the West did not involve intra-Comecon commitments, the matter was left to the Poles themselves. On the other hand, such a profound change in the original plans could hardly fail to influence those commitments; in addition, the expansion must have had links with military aspects of the economy. In the case of Katowice, both these factors undoubtedly played a role, particularly since construction of the plant involved the building of a special broadgauge railway line to the Soviet frontier. After August 1980, no mention was made of these problems in Polish sources, apart from general hints at the adverse consequences of adopting a Soviet development model within the structure of the Polish economy.

This discussion of the interaction of the political and economic system with the "import-led growth" bonanza would be incomplete if it failed to mention the moral aspect, which played such a prominent part in August 1980 and its aftermath. The connection seems quite tangible, its roots firmly embedded in disillusionment with the social and moral effects of Communist rule. After the bloody riots of December 1970, this disillusionment reached new heights. Dwarfed ideologically and incapable of embarking upon the road to genuine renewal, Gierek staked his political fortunes on the prospect of material success, especially for the bureaucracy. The party, state, and economic apparatus were already on the whole far removed from any traces of old-fashioned egalitarianism, and hardened enough by experience to eagerly accept *"enrichez-vous"* as the criterion of success. Greater dispersal of statistically registered incomes[12] may be regarded as a manifestation of this attitude, but not necessarily so, and certainly not the most important one. The universally acknowledged spread of corruption is another matter.

One ought to beware of exaggeration: corruption is not an exclusively Communist phenomenon, nor is Poland unique among Communist countries in this respect. The knowledge of corruption is to a considerable degree a function of the scale of disclosures, and from this point of view post-1980 Poland is far ahead of its neighbors. Having said that, and without intending comparisons, one must nevertheless stress the link between the growth of corruption and the conditions developing in Poland in the 1970s. The ideological and moral degradation of uncontrolled power was combined with increased opportunities for corrupt practices due both to gross imbalances in domestic markets and to the complex temptations of business dealings with the West; the state's desperate scramble for every piece of foreign currency and the resulting semilegal parallel circulation of Western money multiplied the opportunities for illicit gains.

Although this essay was confined to the antecedents of the 1980 upheaval, its conclusions about the close link between economic and political factors apply to subsequent developments as well. The failure to find a political solution to the mounting crisis during the period August 1980–December 1981 was the single major cause of the further rapidly accelerating decline of Poland's economy. The military takeover attempted to substitute the iron heel for a political settlement, but this could hardly provide the grounds for economic recovery. The dead weight of the obsolete political and economic system thwarted the utilization of the country's immense human and material potential even in conditions of relative plenty—and when considerable resources from the outside were at hand. There is no reason whatsoever to expect the same system to perform better under conditions of penury.

4

THE RICH AND THE POWERFUL

Aleksander Smolar

Of all the unsavory and unpopular features of the Communist system in Poland, perhaps none aroused more hostility and outrage, or contributed more to the outburst of discontent in the summer of 1980, than the existence of widespread social inequities; blatant disparities of income, social privileges, and material well-being between the bulk of the population on one hand and the small ruling elite on the other. To demonstrate the importance of these inequities one need not resort to elaborate statistical extrapolations or to esoteric sources; one open, official Polish source suffices. In August 1980, a public opinion poll was conducted by Warsaw's Center for Public Opinion Surveys and Programmatic Studies; the results were published in January 1981. "One of the sources of the crisis in confidence in the authorities was the acute sense of social injustice," the report stated. Eighty-five percent of the respondents, said the article, thought that social inequalities were "great or very great"; 86 percent considered differences in income "flagrant"; 61 percent considered it "unfair" to link privileges to high positions and demanded a leveling of incomes as well as limits on access to deficit goods like apartments and cars, and to privileges like special stores, vacation houses, sanatoria, and the like.[1]

How did this situation arise? Income differentials and social privileges are not, after all, an exclusively Communist phenomenon, and in no country do they meet with public approval. Yet seldom does lack of public approval, or resentment at inequities, engender mass revolts. Moreover, in a Communist country the distribution of positions, goods, and values—for the purposes of this essay referred to as social goods—constitutes one of the major tools of social control. How, then, did the principles underlying distribution of these social goods, which were designed as a means to stabilize the Communist system, turn into one of the major sources of its disintegration?

CONCEPTS AND REALITIES

In order to answer this question one must first examine the nature of the principles that have governed the distribution of social goods in Communist systems. One of them may be called—after Max Weber—sultanism.[2] It denotes, bluntly put, rewards granted on the basis of ideological and political loyalty. Sultanism eschews any considerations of performance; it bestows its rewards by way of individual privileges. It is characterized by arbitrariness, which is at once its source of strength and its weakness.

The most palpable expression of sultanism in Poland (as well as in other Communist countries) has been the *nomenklatura,* or nomenclature, the system whereby the ruling party controls appointments to various positions (estimated officially at about 100,000) in all areas of public life, from ministers to health resort staffs, from editors of national and provincial newspapers to fire brigade chiefs, bank managers, museum directors, and heads of local administrative bodies. A Central Committee document issued in 1972 (and discussed in greater detail below) defined the aims of *nomenklatura* as follows:

> For the party, nomenclature is one of the basic tools that guarantee that only people who are ideologically reliable, who are highly qualified, and who act in the social, political, and cultural interests of the country, will be called upon to fill management positions.

After sultanism, the second principle of distribution of social goods is effectiveness—or, to use official terminology, "to each according to his work." In other words, rewards are bestowed according to results. The criteria for measuring results may vary—from that of profit, plan fulfillment, or quality of the product to (in cases where results are difficult to measure quantitatively) a person's qualifications, degree of training, or professional standing. This principle occupies a prominent position in official propaganda as much because it is generally approved by society as because its application has proved to yield results in areas like the national economy, armaments, science, and education.

The third and final principle is that of egalitarianism. Its aim, presumably, is the achievement of social justice *par excellence,* and its criteria are as much at odds with the principle of effectiveness as—surely—with sultanism.

During the more than three decades of Communist rule in Poland, these three principles of distribution of social goods have often operated simultaneously, although at any given period any one of them may have dominated. Egalitarianism was initially implemented by the elimination (economic, not physical) of owners of industrial, trade, and farming enterprises. The authorities' intent was to reduce income differences, partly in order to broaden the party's mass appeal, partly in order to guarantee a minimum income to those strata of the population most affected by the policy of forced industrialization on which the regime, eager to follow its Soviet mentor, embarked almost immediately after consolidating its power. At the same time, sultanism was also implemented, with the aim of fashioning a cadre of ideologically sound people on whom the authorities could rely. As for effectiveness, its role in official propaganda has already been noted. Indeed, in the late 1940s and 1950s effectiveness officially governed promotion policies. Nevertheless, the higher one went in the hierarchy, the stronger was the influence of nomenclature. The effectiveness principle was additionally tempered by the distribution of various privileges to people of working-class and peasant background—that is to say, by egalitarianism.

The policies of admission to institutions of higher learning provide an apt illustration of the way all three principles—effectiveness, egalitarianism, and sultanism—worked at one and the same time. General selection rules favored applicants with outstanding knowledge and skills (the effectiveness principle). At the same time, a preference-point system was applied that favored entrants from working-class and peasant families (egalitarianism). Finally, parents who occupied high positions in the elite were able to pressure university authorities into accepting their offspring, regardless of their qualifications (sultanism).[3]

Other examples are equally apposite. In the domain of incomes, for instance, the government applied in principle the criterion of effectiveness—that is, results. In practice, however, income distribution was strongly influenced by egalitarian pressure. The sultanic principle was expressed in an arbitrary system of premiums and differentiated access to goods in permanent shortage. "Queuing" offers another illustration. The phenomenon of queuing has, of course, been caused by the perennial disequilibrium (excess demand) in several consumer goods markets. Effectiveness would fix prices at their natural level, in accordance with supply and demand. Egalitarianism would manifest itself in fixing prices at an artificially low level and rationing. The compromise between these two principles consisted in maintaining prices below their "natural" level on the one hand, and creating a priority system for access to food stores, or on waiting lists for cars and housing. Sultanism manifested itself in the creation of special markets for those who served the system best.

All these principles were meant to stabilize the system and win the regime a measure of acceptance. Effectiveness, it was assumed, would improve living standards and enhance economic development. Egalitarianism would satisfy a basic need for justice. Sultanism would assure the political integration and facilitate the construction of a communist society by creating and maintaining a permanent clientele loyal to the system and to the ruling elite. The last, of course, was always a source of popular resentment, and the party took various measures to appease and control that resentment. One way was by varying rewards and the relationship between different kinds of rewards. In most Western and Third World countries people with a high level of education enjoy a relatively high income and high prestige. In Communist countries in general and in Poland in particular the correspondence between distribution of different social rewards is limited. Greater prestige is balanced by lower salaries. There are groups with a low level of income but with a higher education and others with powerful positions but low prestige. This policy of "decomposition" (disaggregation) of social rewards was consciously introduced by the authorities as an instrument of conflict management and was clearly aimed at preventing popular discontent: the party hoped that by rewarding some individuals or groups with status, others with incomes, and still others with specific privileges, it could diffuse discontent.

In the late 1950s and 1960s, under the impetus of changes occurring in the USSR and other bloc countries after the Twentieth Congress of the Soviet Communist Party (February 1956), many Poles cherished illusions about changes in the USSR and in the Soviet bloc as a whole. After Gomułka's accession to power in October 1956, the party hoped to maintain the broad popular support it commanded at that time. Once secured, that support would presumably lessen the need for the *nomenklatura* and for political criteria in the distribution of social goods in general. Economic planning was to become gradually less centralized and less politicized, and as production of consumer goods increased, excessive egalitarianism and rationing would disappear and the system of privilege would become superfluous.

In other words, 1956 ushered in the expectation that Poland would eventually become a meritocracy. And indeed a series of changes after 1956 made such an expectation reasonable: the scope of the *nomenklatura* was narrowed, various privileges were drastically limited, marketplace distribution grew. Competence began to supersede faith or ideology, and the standard of living rose. But the change was for a number of reasons limited and short-lived.[4] In December 1970 the bubble burst.

THE 1970s

In December 1970 the government tried to raise prices. Such a price-rise would have substantially lowered the standard of living of a significant portion of the population. Moreover, the previous decade had seen a virtual stagnation of real wages and a very small rise in consumption: one study revealed that wages were considered inadequate not only by 79.3 percent of the poorest people but also by over half of the richest.[5] The result, then, was a workers' rebellion and Gomułka's fall.

Not surprisingly, given the events that brought him into power, Gierek gave the highest priority to increasing both wages and consumption. Material incentives would supposedly accelerate development and this in turn would guarantee improvements in the standard of living. For the incoming Gierek government, effectiveness and not the *nomenklatura* was to be the yardstick. And in fact, Gierek allowed discussions to appear in the press on the subject of discrimination against nonparty members.

Nevertheless, when we look at the data from the 1970s, what we find is evidence that workers' qualifications—education, training—were not synchronized with their earnings. Whereas in 1970 engineers and technicians earned 50 percent more than their blue-collar colleagues, by 1980 the difference was only 23 percent. In 1970 office workers earned 3 percent more than blue-collar workers; by 1980 they earned 16 percent less. People in such "nonproductive" fields as education or health care consistently earned less, despite their generally superior education. In any given enterprise, we find very little difference in earnings among the majority of workers, blue- or white-collar, until we reach the managerial staff, usually small in number, who earn considerably more owing to various bonuses and premiums. Thus throughout the 1970s there was no noticeable correlation between productivity or qualifications and compensation—despite official pronouncements. And when the authorities did increase the wages of a branch of industry or a professional category, they did so either because of strong public pressure or in order to placate workers in an industry—like mining—essential for their own needs. Criteria of efficiency hardly came into play.

Studies show that Polish society is imbued with an egalitarian ethos on the subject of compensation for labor. Lech Wałęsa summed it up: "I think that cleaning women, doctors, engineers are all people with stomachs that need food. And all these people are needed. When someone wants to study, we have to pay for his education. If someone has to work nights in a hospital, he should be rewarded. Someone else works in hazardous conditions—he too must be rewarded. This is the essence of socialism—since we all have the same stomachs, the solution must be the same."[6]

Such was hardly the view of the Gierek regime. Learning from Gomułka's mistakes, Gierek concluded that two things were necessary: more consumer goods and stronger authority, directed from above—which, of course, means strengthening the *nomenklatura* principle. In spite of propaganda to the contrary, then, the principle of effectiveness was in fact limited. And the result was an unprecedented expansion of nomenclature throughout the Gierek years. "In the current decade," said the editor of *Polityka* (now Deputy Prime Minister) Mieczysław F. Rakowski in an article published early in 1981, "we have seen a definite increase in the number of positions reserved for party members. The list of nomenclature positions has grown incredibly. It has gone so far that a retired teacher, who wanted to open a clubroom for retired people in a Warsaw borough, was told that the directorship of such a club was reserved for a party member."[7]

The importance of nomenclature was made explicit: one 1974 resolution of the party Politburo, for instance, spelled it out: "Proper cadre policies consist on the one hand of hiring people of high political and intellectual caliber for work in the ideological vanguard, and on the other of preventing politically alien or indifferent individuals from infiltrating ideological front institutions."[8] The resolution continues, linking education with this winnowing process: "Party organizations must have a direct influence on who is admitted to courses that prepare students for work on the ideological front"—that is, philosophy, sociology, economics, political science. Moreover, it calls for applying more stringent political and ideological criteria to such fields as pedagogy, history, and psychology: a recommendation was issued two years later (by the Council of Rectors of the University of Warsaw) to hire only party members for the mathematics and sociology faculties.[9]

Sultanism became not only more widespread, its character changed, too. Under Gomułka, while personal affiliations and connections did play a role in party politics, individuals generally gained or lost power within the apparat on grounds of political or ideological differences of opinion. Under Gierek, on the other hand, power politics predominated. The Polish sociologist Jan Szczepański termed it the "collegial" system of personnel appointments: for the sake of one's own security, one names to all important posts "good colleagues."[10]

In a sense the 1970s reflected the 1950s—but the image was a distorted one.

In both decades priority was given to principles of sultanism and effectiveness. But what in the 1950s stemmed from ideological and in a sense idealistic—however misguided—motives became in the 1970s expressions of cynical and self-serving pragmatism. Maciej Szczepański, then chairman of the Committee on Radio and Television, and a man close to Gierek, put it very bluntly in 1973: "If we [don't follow party directives,] we will lose our positions, because we will prove ourselves unsuited to hold power. We . . . derive our power from the regime; we must therefore effectively serve the interests and aspirations of the regime, and must take an active part in promoting and realizing its programs." At the same time Szczepański promised to give some consideration to living conditions because, to paraphrase his words, the leadership cannot ask workers to produce more work without rewarding them with "a better life."[11]

Not surprisingly, nomenclature guaranteed high incomes to those serving in the power apparatus, and the lack of any official statistics often gave rise to fantastic stories about the magnitude of these salaries. The data disclosed in 1981 show the figures were perhaps not all that extravagant: the premier and party secretary earned, officially, 28,000 zlotys each; the deputy premier—25,900; Central Committee secretaries and ministers—23,700, and so on down the line to district committee instructors, who earned 5,800–6,200 zlotys annually.[12]

However, nomenclature guarantees more than income. And the privileges attached to such jobs—awards of appreciation, "a little something in an envelope," annuities, retirement benefits, family supplements, special health-care benefits, access to spas and hunting resorts—are far more important. Again, because these privileges were kept secret, horrendous speculations proliferated. During the August 1980 strike the workers demanded, among other things, family supplements equal to those given to militiamen, for they assumed such supplements to be high. Deputy Premier Mieczysław Jagielski, in the course of negotiations, revealed that militiamen received 1,000 zlotys for a nonworking wife and 105 zlotys per child. He later amended the figures downward, to 300–400 zlotys for a nonworking wife plus a variable family supplement depending on salary. In other words, the workers who repeatedly demanded similar benefits had a highly inflated idea of the actual amounts involved in these supplements, largely because information on the subject had never been available to them.[13]

Inflated ideas notwithstanding, *nomenklatura* indeed serves its beneficiaries well. Such individuals have access to commodities that ordinary men can acquire only after years of waiting and self-denial: automobiles, apartments, almost all goods not available on the domestic market. They can circumvent certain laws: for instance, road regulations, duty on goods from abroad, or a leveling tax for earnings over 144,000 zlotys per year. On two occasions Prime Minister Piotr Jaroszewicz himself took advantage of these loopholes, exempting his son from paying duty on cars bought abroad.[14]

THE POWER AND USES OF CORRUPTION

In 1980 and 1981 the Polish press overflowed with descriptions of various kinds of privileges available to party members. Many are trivial, familiar to anyone with a knowledge of socialist countries. All, however, reveal the extent to which nomenclature has been transformed from a principle rooted in ideology to a principle pragmatic in nature and serving to strengthen the power of the authorities. The pervasive cynicism with which the party regards this principle was made shockingly clear by Katowice's party secretary and member of the Politburo, Andrzej Żabiński. In a closed meeting of party activists and police and security officials, Żabiński urged them to combat Solidarity by corrupting its leaders: "They have to taste power. Give them whatever office space they want, the more luxurious the better. I've always said, and say again, that every man can be corrupted by power; it's just a matter of time and degree."[15]

Żabiński's words show the flip side of sultanism. It not only rewards those in power; it can also be manipulated by the regime to reward various individuals or groups *outside* the power structure, thus acting as an antidote to discontent or opposition. Indeed, in June 1971 the Central Committee used sultanism in precisely this way and for precisely this purpose. In a delayed response to the workers' revolt in the Baltic seaports, the Central Committee implemented the following plans: so as to avoid falsification of information and to facilitate direct control, 164 of the largest industrial plants were subordinated directly to the Central Committee; a whole system of privileges was introduced, from wage increases, through educational opportunities in party-run schools (in effect, guaranteeing successful careers), to access to meat supplies.[16] Food distribution was manipulated in the same way: in 1976, the most "rebellious" town, Radom, was penalized when the Central Committee limited its supply of market goods and decreased its housing construction;[17] in 1980 twelve provinces were singled out for preferential food distribution, among them the "troublesome" ones of Gdańsk, Szczecin, and Bydgoszcz.[18]

From the point of view of nomenclature's beneficiaries, the system had two disadvantages. One was the insecurity of the privileges: a fall from grace in the 1960s meant a radical drop in living standards. (Roman Zambrowski, for instance, who was for twenty years a member of the ruling clique, lost his apartment after he was dismissed from both his job and the party in 1968.)[19] The other was the difficulty involved in passing those benefits down the line, to children or grandchildren. Naturally, attempts were made to correct both drawbacks. Throughout the 1970s the privileged group instituted a series of changes intended to increase the security of their positions, and to enable them to accumulate and even bequeath to heirs the rewards they received.

This evolution—or corruption—of sultanism is clearly manifested in two documents published in 1972. One formalized the principles of nomenclature, rationalizing, institutionalizing, and even bureaucratizing them. The document tries to define the hierarchy of positions and the assignment of jurisdictions, though the authorities formally reserve the right to fill positions under the jurisdiction of lower party organs. This attempt to organize an orderly hierarchy was surely intended to increase the sense of security of apparatchiks at various levels of government; to some extent it mandated independence of the central organs of power.

The second document involves pension rights of leading government and party workers and their families. It is an attempt to legalize "sultan" privileges and specifically contradicts the usual rules governing pensions and annuities. The age of eligibility is lower than usual, the amount of money higher; eligibility extends not only to close family members (parents and siblings) but to grandchildren as well. For this reason it is often called the "dynastic decree" in Poland.

The pension decree appeared shortly after Gierek took power, and not fortuitously. Given the experience of his predecessor, he and his regime had good reason to fear that their reign might come to an abrupt end, and one of their first considerations was how they might minimize material losses when they were deposed.[20] Hence the decree: not, surely, to legitimize privilege in the eyes of society but, rather, pragmatically to restrict future governing groups from depriving them of their rewards. Political defeat would no longer entail radical material degradation; losing power would not mean losing wealth or privilege.

According to data obtained in 1981, unlawful acquisition began at the top. Abuses concerning construction and acquisition of houses, villas, dachas, and property were committed by, among others, First Secretary of the Central Committee Edward Gierek, two Central Committee secretaries, 23 provincial committee first secretaries, 34 provincial committee secretaries, 7 vice-premiers, 18 ministers, 31 vice-ministers, and so on. Józef Klasa, former first secretary of the Kraków Provincial Committee, provided devastating testimony: "At the very beginning of the 1970s, and perhaps even a bit earlier, the government was infected with a 'fever,' known colloquially as 'Zarabie.' Wealthy Krakovians owned luxurious villas right on the Zarabie, and some comrades longed for them. We of the Executive of the Provincial Committee made our position clear: comrades holding high public office must refrain from acquiring [housing] shares and from house construction. We knew, of course, that members of the government would be offered, illicitly and at special prices, anything they wanted, even without asking for it. But the example came from the top, and so did encouragement. . . . I remember sometime in 1973 Piotr Jaroszewicz's spiteful remark: 'What is this, Comrade Klasa, are you pursuing some sort of separate policy? Are you forbidding the comrades to build themselves a place to relax after their hard work? Comrade Gierek believes in taking care of our activists.' "[21]

The pattern of housing corruption was simple. Construction was usually undertaken illegally, in off-limits rural or forest areas, and not infrequently in specially protected national parks. The builder (that is, the future owner) ignored legal restrictions and paid none of the appropriate taxes; he paid unnaturally low prices for land, and the entire infrastructure—roads, plumbing, electricity—was built largely or entirely at government expense.[22] Sometimes state agencies were involved in building villas for prominent individuals.[23] Very costly improvements were regularly made in apartments designated for government representatives, and when the tenants eventually bought the apartments—usually at very low prices—they were not charged for the improvements. Moreover, former tenants, who had been evicted from those villas or apartments to make room for the new owners, were generally rehoused by the government, despite regulations requiring the buyer to fulfill that obligation.[24] The laws pertaining to the size and character of summer resorts that could be constructed were routinely ignored—the official size limitation, for instance, of 110 square meters. And houses and apartments were often furnished—with everything from shoebrushes to color TVs—at state expense. In a number of cases there is even evidence that public roads, previously used by local population, were closed if they impinged too closely on newly constructed houses for the privileged (for example, in Myślenice, near Kraków, as described in *Trybuna Ludu,* March 17, 1981).

Of the new inordinately long list of abuses, the following are but a few examples:

· Edward Gierek "bought" a two-family house in Katowice. Construction costs amounted to 21 million zlotys; the Office of the Council of Ministers, the Katowice Provincial Committee, and other institutions paid for it. A greenhouse was added, at a cost of 1,500,000 zlotys. Together with his sons Adam and Jerzy he also acquired a house in Ustronie. Adam paid 200,000 zlotys for it; the rest—701,000 zlotys—was paid from the state treasury.[25]

· Adam Gierek and Zdzisław Grudzień (first secretary of the Katowice Provincial Committee) built a villa costing 27,200,000 zlotys. The inventory documents, however, put the price at only 4,100,000 zlotys—probably, as a journalist hypothesized, so that in a few years the house could be bought back from the state for a relatively low sum.[26]

· The first secretary of the Myślenice local committee, near Kraków, owned two apartments, in Kraków and Myślenice, and was in the process of building a third; he also had two additional houses in his wife's name.[27]

· Vice-Premier Tadeusz Wrzaszczyk received from the state several apartments, two single-family houses, some construction lots, and several cars for himself and his family.

· Maciej Szczepański, former chairman of the Committee on Radio and Television, was guilty not only of housing abuses: together with his assistant, also a member of the Central Committee of the Polish United Workers' Party, Szczepański "acquired" the sum of 2,900,000 zlotys. He created the Budorit agency, an organization exclusively devoted to performing personal errands for radio and TV notables. Its roster of 123 employees included 57 white-collar workers, 5 directors, and 25 managers.[28]

Not surprisingly, middle and lower-level apparatchiks followed the models set for them by those at the very top. Innumerable newspaper articles appearing throughout 1981 have revealed the generosity, to themselves and others, of various representatives of the government: Z. Chodyła, governor of Kalisz province, illegally distributed 180 coupons for private automobiles from 1976 to 1979; W. Lejczak, minister of mining and engineering, gave 7 houses and 54 apartments to persons not employed in his department; Adam Glazur, building minister, gave away as gifts washing machines, tape recorders, stereos, and radios;[29] and Roman Maloch, director of the Predom Mechanized Home Appliance Industry Union, gave two people prototypes of two mobile homes valued at 2,700,000 zlotys.[30]

These examples are not merely anecdotes. They indicate a transformation in the nature of the system, which became a peculiar hybrid of socialism and feudalism, with the central authority becoming weaker and the local authorities becoming stronger—a modification, in other words, of the operation of sultanism.

THE SECOND ECONOMY

Just as sultanism, or the nomenclature principle, was corrupted during the 1970s, so was the principle of effectiveness—and in both cases the aim was the same: to facilitate accumulation of wealth. In the case of effectiveness, corruption grew in what is called the parallel or second economy.[31]

In Communist countries the second economy is, essentially, a system of production and services parallel to the official system. Whereas black market production in a mercantile economy develops in opposition to official production, with goals like tax or insurance evasion or the manufacture of illegal products (like narcotics), in a centrally planned economy black market production is intertwined with the official economy. Sometimes its role is parasitic; this describes the illegal transfer to it of official capital, work, and raw materials. Sometimes its role is symbiotic: it often operates as a lubricant that allows the official economy to function. Certainly the second economy is essential: without it consumers' needs for both goods and services could not be satisfied. In the 1970s, as shortages increased and goods disappeared, the second economy developed to an unprecedented degree. Shortages create the black market; they encourage illegal price-raising by state workers; they give rise to the marketing of goods and services that are in principle free (illegal fees, for instance, received by teachers or hospital workers); shortages are the stimuli for illegal production and for the corruption of government agencies, which are constantly in search of spare parts, raw materials, and so on.

In a Communist country the second economy in effect bestows legitimacy on private entrepreneurship and reestablishes money as the universal equivalent of goods and services. But it exacts an enormous price, not only economically but morally and socially as well. It is a basic form of market corruption, and as such leads to social demoralization, to the justification of theft, to a rationale of success at any cost, to pervasive bribery, and the like. It leads to a polarization of wealth, a polarization that in turn provokes public outrage at the manner in which wealth is acquired, at the parasitic nature of the parallel economy, and at the ostentatious consumption of those who profit by it most.

Similar to the second economy, and in a sense connected with it, were the officially sanctioned foreign currency benefits created in the 1970s. Those who were willing to pay a somewhat higher price and able to pay in foreign currency could get virtually anything they wanted—without waiting in line. This dealt a body blow to any notion of egalitarianism, and crippled as well effectiveness as a criterion for reward. Queues, which in a way assured a fair distribution of goods, lost all meaning. Housing offers one salient example. In theory, individuals who registered with their cooperative and paid the appropriate deposit were to have gotten their apartments according to their place on the waiting list. However, as demand for houses grew, pressures increased to bypass the obligatory waiting list. From the mid-1960s through 1980 the number of apartments built by the cooperatives—which they could then distribute freely to those whose names were on the waiting lists—decreased sharply: from 66 percent in 1966–70 to 54 percent in 1971–75 and 38 percent in 1976–80.[32] Between 1976 and 1979 apartments built by the cooperative movements were distributed in the following proportions:

to local organs of state administration	22.2%
to work establishments	30.3%
to others, most likely central administration and party apparatchiks	10.5%
to the general cooperative movement	37.0%

No wonder, then, that members of the cooperatives had to wait for their apartments anywhere from seven to more than ten years.[33]

In 1971, the Council of Ministers established a set of priorities to govern cooperatives' distributions of housing, with top priority given to young married couples, to residents of substandard and overcrowded dwellings, and so on. But there were so many priorities, and so few apartments, that there resulted a plethora of arbitrary decisions that ignored the original basic criterion: waiting time. An inspection carried out in Gdańsk in 1979 revealed that up to 70 percent of the apartments awarded by work establishments went to people "not meeting the requisite criteria for the assignment of housing."[34] And one thing that replaced those "requisite criteria" was access to foreign currency.

"Locum," a special cooperative, was created: it guaranteed practically immediate sale of apartments for cash, especially for exchangeable foreign currency. In 1978, for instance, the plan foresaw the cash sale of 8,000 apartments, 35 percent of these for exchangeable foreign currency (Życie Gospodarcze, October 22, 1978). While the percentage, in terms of all the collective apartments built that year, is proportionately small—5 percent—its social impact and the indignation it evoked was immense. Indeed, the whole issue of foreign currency privileges aroused especially strong anger. The network of PEWEX stores, where both imported and domestic products were sold exclusively for foreign currency, grew enormously throughout the 1970s. At first found only in large cities, these stores were opened even in small towns—anywhere foreign currency could be extracted from the community. The PEWEX stores sold medicine and textiles, automobiles and building materials, alcohol and electronic equipment. In 1976, the last year for which official statistics exist, sales in these shops amounted to 2 percent of total sales. That same year foreign currency paid for almost 50 percent of all private cars sold in Poland—a fourfold increase in the space of five years. And it is a virtual certainty that this market expanded substantially in subsequent years.[35]

CONCLUSION

Great expectations ushered in the 1970s. It was thought that the party's control over distribution of wealth would be limited. The principle of effectiveness would dominate, while concomitantly the role of the principle of sultanism would diminish, based as it was on arbitrary decisions of the state and the party's system of privileges. The party would no longer need sultanism, or nomenclature, because it would earn legitimacy merely by satisfying the public's needs.

Indeed, the beginning of the decade seemed to promise the domination of effectiveness. But before long that promise proved a sham. Instead of rewarding competence, knowledge, and results, the state in effect increased the discrepancy between efficiency and its rewards. Inequalities increased instead of decreasing. Economic effectiveness declined; society disintegrated; the government, far from becoming more legitimate in the eyes of the society, became even less so. Poland became less and less stable, and people became more and more aware of rampant injustices.

As the principle of effectiveness lost currency, and as egalitarianism was discarded, sultanism—despite predictions to the contrary—grew in importance. Its growth in the 1970s had very different consequences from those of the 1950s, during the years of Stalinist terror. It still rewarded loyalty to the party; it still distributed wealth and positions; but this time the privileged groups were able to take full advantage of their power—the limitations that had existed in the 1950s were gone. In the 1970s the beneficiaries of the *nomenklatura* system could accumulate and pass on wealth; they occupied far more secure positions; their status within the apparat was accompanied by spectacular material benefits. (In a curious way the party, at the same time as it destroyed any real chances at popular acceptance, made itself accepted by necessity. That is, even as the people hated the authorities, they looked to them for the satisfaction of public needs—road- and industry-building, stocking the shops, caring for the poor. In a state-controlled society no one else could fulfill these functions.)

Had the party been able to enhance the efficiency of the economy and preserve a degree of discretion in exploiting its privileges, it might have limited, if not entirely averted, public indignation, which found an outlet in such vast destabilization in the summer of 1980. But the party leaders were powerless to fulfill public hopes and unable to moderate their own exploitation of power. The result was economic chaos, whose dimensions we can appreciate fully only today, and, simultaneously, an inordinate abuse of privileges—ostentatious, *nouveau riche* consumption, to say nothing of massive theft by the government.

A dictatorship based on a combination of superior force and ideology may perhaps evoke hatred and fear, but it may also result, among some people, in a grudging respect for or at least a fatalistic resignation to the ambiguous laws of the victor. The government that ruled Poland in the 1970s—an apparat that transformed itself into a kleptocracy, a party-encouraged "criminal bourgeoisie" resulting from the operations of the second economy, a leadership transparently weak and self-serving—evoked not fear, wonder, or even the seduction of victors' spoils, but contempt and moral indignation. At the same time that the new ruling class outdistanced any other Communist country in its increased privileges, it undermined the foundations of the very system to which its fate was tied.

5

THE INTELLIGENTSIA

Leszek Kołakowski

The term *intelligentsia* has never been imbued in Poland with a particular political connotation, as it has been in Russia. In prerevolutionary Russia, intelligentsia referred to people who were not only educated but who, if not actively
engaged in antitsarist political struggles, were at least opposed to the ideological
values of autocracy and stressed their own spiritual and political independence,
either on democratic or on revolutionary grounds. Loyal servants of the regime,
therefore, no matter how well educated, were not usually regarded as intelligentsia. In Poland this distinction did not obtain. The term *intelligentsia* stood for a
class of educated people who earned their living by their knowledge and skills;
among them were physicians, lawyers, and highly qualified engineers, as well as
intellectuals, writers, and the like. The very existence of a social stratum consciously defining itself in this manner has been a characteristic not merely of
Poland, but of Eastern and Central Europe as a whole. For the purposes of this
essay I will restrict my remarks to a smaller segment of the intelligentsia—those
whose social function has been to preserve, convey, and produce cultural (as
opposed to material and technical) goods—that is, teachers, artists, scholars,
clergymen, journalists, writers, and political leaders.

THE FORMATIVE YEARS

Two facts pertaining to the origins and character of the Polish intelligentsia
should be mentioned at the outset. First, the Polish intelligentsia not only grew
out of the gentry, but also succeeded in preserving many of its customs, values,
and traditions.[1] According to historians, the Polish nobility before the partitions
of the eighteenth century comprised about 12 percent of the total population. It
was thus a large, albeit highly differentiated class, with a fierce tradition of
personal freedom (within the class itself, that is), and a reluctance to obey laws
imposed by central authorities. Indeed, most historians consider this sense of
personal autonomy, often bordering on anarchy, as one of the causes of Poland's
inability to create a strong monarchy able to unite the country against the en-

croachments of its Russian, Prussian, and Austrian neighbors. The Polish nobility was also distinguished by its emphasis on the intrinsic equality of all its members in political and social matters. On the one hand, this tradition may have vitiated the idea of statehood in Polish life; on the other, it prevented Poland from ever producing despotic forms of government, and it certainly facilitated the spread of democratic ideas in the eighteenth century.

During the second half of the nineteenth century and later, the intelligentsia's ranks were swelled by people from Jewish, peasant, and petit bourgeois origins. Nevertheless, it was the traditional values of the nobility that continued to dominate the ethos of this growing social stratum—among them, the aspiration to provide spiritual leadership for the nation.

Second, and more important, is the fact that the intelligentsia as a distinct social body was being formed in the nineteenth century, in a period when Poland was robbed of its independence and Poles were resisting the oppression of foreign masters, including efforts to destroy Polish cultural identity. (One may argue that the Poles were to some degree fortunate in their misery, in that the southern part of their territory was annexed by Austria, where oppression was much milder and the scope of cultural autonomy much larger than in Russia or Prussia.) This coincidence shaped the functions and characteristics of the intelligentsia in various ways. Having been swept from the map of Europe as a political unit, Poland could survive as a distinct nationality only in a cultural sense. The role of classes whose function was to protect the cultural identity of the nation thus became crucial: teachers, priests, poets, novelists, historians, philologists, and philosophers embodied in their activity the idea of "Polishness," and this very idea became a substitute for the nonexistent state.

Under these circumstances, it was natural for the intelligentsia to concentrate its feelings and thoughts on national values and on the nation's predicament. The position of the Church as the guardian of the spiritual values of the nation was also reinforced, so much so that Catholic identity tended to merge with national identity. This tendency has persisted to the present, and is even more pronounced now than it was during Poland's independence between the two world wars. To be sure, the left-oriented Polish intelligentsia was often anticlerical: but only marginally anti-Christian. This was also true for the mainstream of the Polish socialist movement, the Polish Socialist Party (PPS), which had from its inception been strongly committed to the cause of Poland's freedom and to its national values. It should also be noted that in the nineteenth century it was the Western socialist movements and the European left in general that supported the Poles' struggle for independence, while the conservative forces, committed as they were to maintaining the post-Viennese order intact, registered little but indifference.

All this is not to suggest that the intelligentsia constituted a unified group. Throughout the nineteenth century it was rent by numerous conflicts, some over matters of strategy (such as whether Russia or Prussia was to be considered the main enemy), and some essentially ideological (such as whether the patriotic movement should appeal to the common cause of the entire nation or combine the national struggle with social goals—e.g., the emancipation of peasants and workers). There were groups—insignificant in the Russian and Prussian parts of the country, more important in Galicia—which proclaimed loyalty to the ruling powers. Later on a small Marxist party, the SDKPiL (Social Democratic Party of the Kingdom of Poland and Lithuania), disagreed sharply with the PPS, opposing the struggle for national independence as harmful to the class struggle.[2] Another strong tendency emerged after the unsuccessful insurrection of 1863; its adherents decided to repudiate conspiratorial struggles and to concentrate efforts on gradual economic and educational improvements. In the first years of the twentieth century, however, the traditions of armed conspiracy were revived, mostly within the socialist movement and its offshoots; they developed spectacularly during the 1905 revolution, culminating in the formation of the embryonic Polish army under Józef Piłsudski. When war broke out in 1914, the army was ready to take up the struggle for its country's independence from Russia.

Catholic loyalty among Polish intelligentsia was not universal, inasmuch as it included a large number of Jews who, though assimilated into Polish culture and contributing to its development, did not convert to Christianity. Poland also had a fairly strong tradition of Freemasonry. In addition, the cultural changes usually accompanying industrialization and urbanization processes—the weakening of religious feelings among educated classes and the growth of rationalism and of positivist philosophy—were increasingly noticeable during the second half of the nineteenth century.

FERMENT AND ATTRITION

The gulf between the intelligentsia—particularly its culturally creative segments—and the Church widened during the period of Poland's independence (1918–39). It may be argued that it was precisely the rigidity acquired by the Church during the Counter-Reformation in the seventeenth century that made it so effective in keeping alive Polish national identity during the subsequent centuries. Had it been more open and more tolerant, it would probably not have been capable of assuming this task. In independent Poland, however, its doctrinal inflexibility, its strong ties with peasant culture, and its aspiration to monopolize the spiritual life of the country repelled a part of the intelligentsia, among them a number of distinguished cultural figures. Various progressive and left-oriented organizations and periodicals emerged that were permeated with an anticlerical or atheist ethos, and that tried to combat the rising tide of jingoism and anti-Semitism. "Left-oriented" should by no means be equated with "Marxist." To be sure, Marxist currents had existed in Poland before World War I, but although they were represented by several outstanding personalities (including Ludwik Krzywicki, Stanisław Brzozowski, and Kazimierz Kelles-Krauz),[3] the mainstream of the Polish socialist movement could not have been called Marxist in any recognizable sense. Marxism persisted as a phenomenon of little significance and it failed to exert a noticeable influence on political and cultural developments.

As for the Communist party, which was made illegal in the 1920s, it, too, failed to make any significant inroads into the political and cultural life of the country. This was particularly true after the Comintern managed to "bolshevize" it and to eliminate people linked more closely with Polish cultural traditions. (It might be worth noting that the purges ordered by the Comintern in the late 1920s were not, apparently, altogether successful. Stalin remained profoundly suspicious of Polish Communists, finally ordering the dissolution of the party in 1938, as well as the arrest and execution of most of its leaders.) Nevertheless, a few writers identified themselves with Communist ideology (Władysław Broniewski was the best-known figure among them). In the last years before World War II, when the fascist menace hung over Europe and the political atmosphere in Poland became infected with nationalist extremism, a sort of broadly left-oriented intellectual movement began to emerge. It never embraced the bulk of the Polish intelligentsia, but it included a number of prominent writers and intellectuals who, though neither Marxist nor Communist—indeed, many of them were avowedly anti-Communist—joined in the effort to resist the mounting wave of obscurantism and chauvinism.

On the other hand, because Poland's independence had been won at the price of uncountable victims after almost a century and a half of bondage and was still fragile and permanently threatened from both the West and the East, national values kept dominating the minds of the educated classes. It was certainly this intensity of patriotic feeling that enabled Poland to develop a strong resistance movement under the Nazi occupation and to cling to its cultural identity under Communist rule. It was also, however, the source of its earlier and disastrous inability to handle the problems of national minorities (about a fifth of the population), and it infected Polish cultural life with a certain parochialism and narrow-mindedness.

This background explains in part some of the curious aspects of the post-World War II history of Poland's intelligentsia. The ravages it sustained during the war were enormous. Both the Nazis and the Soviets, who divided Poland between themselves in 1939, were bent on physically destroying the Polish elite. On the Soviet side the most savage—though hardly the only—example of this policy was the massacre of thousands of Polish officers in Katyń Forest in 1940. The Nazis, on their part, pursued a systematic policy of genocide: Jews and Gypsies were marked for total extermination; as for Poles, the Nazis resolved to deprive them once and for all of their intellectual and spiritual leaders, thus reducing the whole nation to the status of perpetual slavery.

STALINISM, POLISH STYLE

Communism was imposed on Poland against the obvious will of the overwhelming majority of the population, including the intelligentsia. After the Soviet and Communist-led Polish armed forces, formed in the USSR, entered Poland, they proceeded to destroy the remnants of the underground army that had fought the Germans during the occupation. For a few years Poland, especially in some rural areas, was virtually in the grip of civil war.

Yet, despite the cruelty of those years, Polish cultural life as it emerged from the ruins retained considerable vigor. At first the Soviet Union paid at least lip service to the Yalta and Potsdam agreements. Although the crucial areas of politics—security, army, and foreign affairs—were placed firmly under Communist control, some elements of political and cultural pluralism persisted: independent socialist and agrarian parties were allowed to function, Marxism was not declared the only (and compulsory) ideology, and no attempt was made to impose the standards of "socialist realism" on literature and the arts. The bulk of the Polish intelligentsia joined in the effort of rebuilding the devastated country—for patriotic rather than ideological reasons—and many who shared leftist or socialist traditions of old adopted the Communist faith. Apart from sheer careerism, various motivations were at work, several of them superbly described in Czesław Miłosz's *The Captive Mind*.[4] Some intellectuals saw in communism the continuation of the rationalist and humanist spirit of the Enlightenment, some were deluded by historico-philosophical speculations, others were repelled by the political ethos of prewar Poland or attracted to communism by the horrors of Nazi occupation.

It can be argued that such reasons affected only a small section of the intelligentsia. And yet, as one looks at the intellectuals who, since the late 1950s, have been active in the various kinds of democratic opposition and instrumental in shattering the ideological foundation of communism, one is struck by the high proportion of those who had either been members of the Communist party or were otherwise loyal to the regime. Among the writers of older generations, born before or during World War I, who had actually belonged to the party for a shorter or longer time we find people such as Jerzy Andrzejewski, Jan Kott, Mieczysław Jastrun, Julian Przyboś, Paweł Hertz, Adolf Rudnicki, Julian Stryjkowski, Adam Ważyk, Kazimierz Brandys, Marian Brandys, Igor Newerly; younger writers, born in the 1920s, included Tadeusz Konwicki, Wiktor Woroszylski, Witold Wirpsza, Jacek Bocheński, Jerzy Pomianowski, Andrzej Braun, Arnold Słucki, and myself. Many well-known writers who had never been party members manifested their political loyalty on various occasions in the early fifties, or were trusted enough to be given official appointments, some of them in the foreign service. These included Julian Tuwim, Antoni Słonimski, Jarosław Iwaszkiewicz, Konstanty Gałczyński, Czesław Miłosz, Irena Krzywicka, and others.

Similar lists can be made for other areas of artistic and intellectual activity, but to superimpose the situation of the 1960s and 1970s on the first postwar decade, and to maintain that communism in Poland lacked any support by intellectuals, would simply be wrong. It is true, however, that the support elicited by the authorities was frequently halfhearted or accompanied by moral scruples, misgivings, and guilty conscience: Soviet-type communism was so obviously incompatible with the Polish cultural legacy, and the Soviet version of Marxism was so primitive and boorish, that it was simply impossible for intellectuals bred in what were essentially West European civilizations to adopt it lock, stock, and barrel. In addition, full-fledged Stalinism in Poland lasted for a relatively short time—roughly from 1950 until 1954. For both these reasons it failed to become deeply embedded in the minds of Polish intellectuals who, from 1955, found it easy to free themselves from its impact. Whatever its damage, therefore, it was neither lasting nor irreparable.

Furthermore, Stalinism in Poland was on the whole somewhat less consistent by comparison with other East European countries. University professors in the humanities, for instance, who were expelled from their positions on ideological grounds—the sociologist Stanisław Ossowski and philosophers Maria Ossowska, Roman Ingarden, and Władysław Tatarkiewicz, for instance—were nonetheless kept on the payroll and were allowed to pursue their scholarly activities. Their books could eventually appear in print once the political climate improved. Attempts to impose Soviet doctrinal standards in, say, genetics or neurophysiology were short-lived and unsuccessful, and so was the pressure on the visual arts and music. Party leaders in the early 1950s, while attempting to cram Polish culture into the cage of Sovietism, were at the same time anxious to enlist the backing of the intelligentsia, and would thus frequently provide them with generous support (in the form of research centers and publishing houses); this in effect served general intellectual purposes and not just the "class struggle."

Indeed, everything in Communist Poland was clouded with a certain helpful ambiguity. Up to 1956 the Catholic intellectual movement suffered drastic oppression, yet it had never been entirely stifled. The party, trying to destroy the Church's independence and its moral authority, encouraged or organized various groups of "progressive Catholics," whose task—never successfully performed—was to split the Church from within. The most prominent among those groups was the association PAX. Headed by Bolesław Piasecki, the leader of a small fascist party in the 1930s, PAX enjoyed various privileges that enabled it to develop a relatively large industrial, commercial, and publishing activity, and it tried unsuccessfully to be accepted by the party as a partner in the government. Though ostensibly Catholic, PAX not only supported the official political doctrine unreservedly, but also often tried to be more consistently Communist than the party itself. It was strongly despised—perhaps more than the party—both by the Catholic intelligentsia and by all intellectuals opposing the totalitarian system. On the other hand, PAX ran a large publishing house and, enjoying some margin of freedom, printed many books by Western and Polish authors whose appearance in 1949–56 was unthinkable in any other Communist country. It is fair to say, therefore, that in spite of PAX's sinister political role, it nevertheless made a serious contribution to Polish cultural life.

By 1955, many writers, scholars, and artists began openly to criticize the political and cultural policies of Stalinism. This criticism came in the wake of Khrushchev's celebrated speech at the Twentieth Soviet Party Congress in February 1956 (never published officially, but circulated in print for "internal use" among party activists and soon known to the general public, thanks to the broadcasts by Radio Free Europe). Throughout the first half of 1956, the country was in the throes of a powerful political and intellectual ferment. The unrest culminated in the uprising and massacre of workers in Poznań in June 1956. Yet there was a perceptible difference between the patently anti-Soviet, anti-Communist, Catholic, and nationalist moods of a good part of the Polish population on the one hand, and the protests of intellectuals on the other. Among the latter a prominent role was played by people whom the party leadership soon stigmatized as "revisionists." Their critique (which had only a remote affinity with the movement so labeled and debated in socialist parties in 1898 and after) was an attempt to graft democratic values and intellectual honesty on the tree of communism, to get rid of the Stalinist legacy, to make communism compatible with popular feelings, to make its economic principles rational, and to shed the philosophical dogmas of Leninism—all while still preserving the "essence" of communism intact. To be sure, "revisionist" critics who had come from the party establishment still had some access to the mass media—a fact resolutely denied to all-out foes of communism. It is this that helps to explain, to some extent, the prominence of "revisionist critique" at that time.

In retrospect, it seems fair to conclude that the "revisionist" attack on Stalinism was at the same time both futile and efficacious. It was futile largely in the same sense that the movement later known as Eurocommunism was futile—namely, because of its incoherence; it could easily be proved that the totalitarian character of communism was not only perfectly consistent with, but clearly included in, its ideologically defined essence. To accept the revisionist idea of democracy, rationality, and truth would in effect amount to the dismantling of the entire machinery of Communist power—just as to take seriously the principle of equality among the members of the "socialist bloc" meant to destroy the very foundations of the Soviet empire. Yet revisionism was also efficacious precisely because of its inherently incoherent content. By appealing, in its attack on Stalinism, to the stereotypes of the same doctrinal tradition, it contributed to the internal corrosion of Communist ideology and initiated a movement that would in time cause its collapse. Certainly the revisionist movement, which found a large number of adherents within the ranks of the party intelligentsia, could not last very long. As it turned out, it was eventually compelled—as a result both of its own logic and of historical events—to reject communism entirely.

FROM DISARRAY TO DISINTEGRATION

The convulsions that shook the Communist world in 1956 assumed the most dramatic forms in Poland and Hungary. The Polish party, thrown into disarray by factional struggles and ideological uncertainty, was incapable of coping with the mounting social unrest. It launched various measures designed to appease the society (such as an amnesty for political prisoners, reforms of the security apparatus, and promises of economic reform), but it failed to stop the gradual disintegration of the system. It was saved by the presence of Władysław Gomułka, the former first secretary, who, after several years in Stalinist prisons, had gained the reputation of a patriot and even—oddly enough—that of a liberal. Gomułka's return to power in October 1956 was hailed as a major breakthrough and as a giant step toward a renewal of communism, especially because the Soviet rulers were opposed to his reinstatement and accepted it only reluctantly when Polish leaders stuck firmly by their choice. For a brief time Poland lived in a state of almost universal enthusiasm and hope. The bulk of the intelligentsia—whatever their ideological views—shared in the popular illusions.

This comedy of national unity could not have been but ephemeral. The "Polish October," far from being the start of a "renewal," turned out to be the beginning of its end. Whatever had been gained in terms of cultural liberties, civil rights, relaxed censorship, workers' councils, and the like, had predated Gomułka's reign, and the "Polish October" initiated a process of the recapture of power by the shattered party apparatus. The Hungarian uprising, the Soviet invasion, and its official endorsement by the Polish leadership all occurred within a few days of Gomułka's return to power, thus dashing the expectations of a democratized communism. The subsequent fourteen years were marked by the party's slow but unceasing efforts to suppress the cultural life of the country by gradually tightening the vise of censorship, closing down—or "reorganizing"—various literary and political journals, dissolving discussion clubs, and limiting the intelligentsia's contacts with the West. As for the party's catastrophic economic policies, they were designed to satisfy both ingrained dogmas and the leadership's thirst for more and more power.

Still, the Stalinist order could not be restored: the injuries it sustained could not be undone. As time went on, the chasm between the ruling party and the intelligentsia steadily widened. During the Stalinist period, as noted above, the leaders—though employing various forms of coercion to impose Soviet standards on Polish culture—had attempted, often successfully, to woo, flatter, and bribe some segments of the intelligentsia. (It must be noted, however, that a small group remained genuinely committed to the communist idea.) Under Gomułka, these attempts were largely given up. Apart from Gomułka's personal narrow-mindedness, ignorance, and deep-seated suspicion of intellectuals, the party had fewer and fewer ideological commodities to offer. Marxism and the Communist doctrine were becoming increasingly irrelevant to national problems, preoccupations, and fears. The party itself, in trying to legitimize its power and receive some kind of popular hearing, appealed more and more to *raison d'état* and to Poland's geopolitical predicament, rather than to the doctrinal promises of a glorious communist future and the principle of proletarian internationalism.

This made the internal revisionist critique gradually less important, even though the remnants of revisionism persisted for several years. Most of the party intellectuals and almost all those who were active in the revisionist movement in the mid-1950s were expelled from or left the party in the 1960s. The party's repressive cultural policies provoked various acts of collective and individual protest. The most famous of them was the protest letter, signed by thirty-four outstanding writers and scholars, delivered to the Polish government in March 1964. Its signatories included Antoni Słonimski, Maria Dąbrowska, Leopold Infeld, Tadeusz Kotarbiński, Maria Ossowska, Jerzy Turowicz, Jerzy Andrzejewski, Wacław Sierpiński, Władysław Tatarkiewicz, Edward Lipiński, and Aleksander Gieysztor. This was followed some years later, in January 1968, by the Warsaw writers' condemnation of the party's decision to terminate the performance of Adam Mickiewicz's play *The Forefathers,* because of its anti-Russian overtones (its target was the Russia of Nicholas I).

This process reached its zenith in March 1968. The brutal police attack on a peaceful student meeting at Warsaw University was followed by a massive wave of arrests and trials; a thorough purge of the universities, publishing houses, and journals; and a vitriolic press campaign. A number of professors and junior teachers, many of them former party members, were dismissed from their posts (among them Bronisław Baczko, Włodzimierz Brus, Maria Hirszowicz, Stefan

Morawski, Zygmunt Bauman, and myself). The campaign had a strongly anti-Semitic character, and the party propaganda of this period often vividly resembled that of the Nazis. Although it was Gomułka who inaugurated the anti-Semitic campaign, its unexpected magnitude and violence were largely the work of a party faction trying to unseat the existing leadership.[5]

The events of March 1968, the year that also saw the Soviet invasion of Czechoslovakia, can be seen as the ultimate break of the Polish intelligentsia with the party and its ideology, the latter hardly noticeable by that time except for its anti-Semitic component. Revisionism, too, received its final burial. It had lingered on among some students, largely thanks to the influence of Jacek Kuroń and Karol Modzelewski, young intellectuals who in 1964 circulated a comprehensive analysis of the social, economic, and cultural situation in Poland. This criticism—for which the authors were sentenced to extensive prison terms (they were released just before March 1968, only to be rearrested and sentenced yet again)—was still based on contrasting Marxist principles with the highly developed class system of Soviet-type societies. But the thousands of students who demonstrated against police brutality and cultural regimentation did not think in Marxist or communist terms. They wanted to get rid of the intolerable burden of Communist mendacity and oppressiveness.

Their efforts were not crowned with instantaneous success, yet neither were they in vain: March 1968, despite all persecutions and repressions, finally liberated Polish culture from the ties with the Communist system and its ideology. There was nothing left to "revise" anymore, and nobody was ready to expect any improvement from one or another party faction. The party's anti-Semitic campaign, while resulting in the exodus of almost all remaining Polish Jews, failed to yield the expected results among workers, though the latter remained largely passive and failed to support the intelligentsia's struggle.

At the end of 1970, the workers' revolt, followed by massacres in Poland's northern cities, brought about the collapse of Gomułka's government. The intelligentsia, still paralyzed and intimidated by the 1968 pogrom, offered little or no help. Gomułka, who had been swept into power on a wave of quasi-unanimous enthusiasm, ended his career, to general relief, in a cloud of humiliation and hostility. In the party itself there was nobody to defend him (a curious contrast to the fate of the Hungarian leader János Kádár, who, having earned in 1956 the well-deserved reputation of a Quisling—a simple agent of the Soviet invaders—managed to achieve, after several years and thanks largely to his economic policy and relatively nonrepressive rule, a measure of qualified approval).

The new party leadership in Poland under Edward Gierek tried to acquire a shaky legitimacy by renouncing some of the most deleterious economic policies of its predecessors and by promising an era of prosperity. Between 1971 and 1974, some economic improvements did in fact take place. But Gierek's policies also resulted in massive and unprecedented corruption in the party and state apparatus. With the growth of cynicism, ideological criteria lost whatever significance they may still have had; this was true as much for the intelligentsia as for the population at large. No one believed in the old Communist dogma anymore, and in fact no one was expected to believe in it, even though its tenets were occasionally repeated for ceremonial purposes.

THE NEW PHASE: OPEN STRUGGLE

The new phase of social unrest and intellectual opposition coincided with the beginning of the end of Gierek's artificial economic boom.[6] In December 1975, a group of fifty-nine intellectuals issued a statement protesting the proposed amendments to the Polish constitution, which, by formally legalizing the "leading role of the party" and the country's allegiance to the "socialist bloc," in effect legitimized Poland's national and social unsovereignty. The statement, however, went beyond this immediate target and included a comprehensive attack on the suppression of all civil freedoms in the Polish state: freedom of speech and education, of religious worship, and of work. Coming after a period of passivity, the statement was the first open act of democratic opposition to totalitarian—albeit inefficient and clumsy totalitarian—rule. The new intellectual ferment was still in swing when it coincided with the workers' protests and strikes of June 1976. This time the harsh repressive measures against the strikers, including beatings, torture, and arrests, did not succeed in intimidating the population but merely heightened the social tensions and contributed to the strengthening of opposition to the regime.

In September 1976, a group of intellectuals decided to establish a body whose goal would be to mobilize public opinion in defense of the persecuted workers. The Workers' Defense Committee, known by the acronym KOR, included about thirty people, ranging in age from twenty-five to ninety. Among them were writers (Anna Kowalska, Jerzy Andrzejewski, Stanisław Barańczak, Jerzy Ficowski, Jan Józef Lipski), lawyers (Aniela Steinsberg), scientists (Jan Kielanowski, Piotr Naimski, Mirosław Chojecki), historians (Wacław Zawadzki, Adam Michnik), priests (Rev. Jan Zieja) and actors (Halina Mikołajska). A few were former party members (Jacek Kuroń, Jerzy Andrzejewski) and some were former social democrats (Antoni Pajdak, Ludwik Cohn, Edward Lipiński, Aniela Steinsberg). Disdaining any conspiratorial activities, KOR gradually developed into an open antitotalitarian opposition movement. In spite of police harassment, innumerable arrests, beatings, and intimidation, it attracted hundreds of people of different ages and professional backgrounds, willing to engage in the struggle.

KOR systematically collected documentary evidence about repressions and abuses of power in the country, developed a communication network among workers in a number of industrial centers, published underground journals exposing the illegality and arbitrariness of the police regime, and organized the financial, legal, and medical help for the victims of persecutions. KOR (later renamed Social Self-Defense Committee—KSS/KOR) refused to draw up a comprehensive political program or to be transformed into any kind of party; it considered the idea of human rights a sufficient basis for its activity, the scope of which gradually expanded. Its aim was to encourage sundry civic initiatives in trade-unionist, cultural, and political areas, in order to restore the centers of civil society that had been devastated by the regime. Largely as a result—and sometimes parallel with—KOR's efforts, a number of uncensored newspapers and journals emerged—literary, political, and professional—and other opposition groups were formed, some with a pronounced political profile, others (such as the Movement for the Defense of Human and Civil Rights—ROPCiO) of a more general nature. A large group of scholars and intellectuals initiated unofficial academic courses in areas especially distorted by political taboos and ideological dogmas—current and recent history, political economy, sociology, and political science.

Until 1976, though very few of the Polish intelligentsia identified themselves with the political system in which they lived (and virtually none among those who enjoyed moral or intellectual authority), very few were engaged in active public opposition either. The majority despised and hated the regime but avoided head-on conflicts. The ruling party, of course, had at its disposal many instruments of political, physical, and, above all, material pressure to force people to obey; these pressures worked very effectively on some (i.e., journalists and lawyers) and less so on others. From 1976 onward an increasing number of scholars, writers, teachers, lawyers, and students were shaking themselves free of fear of repression and venturing into oppositional activity of one kind or another. There was a general feeling that all spheres of national life were in deep crisis; the feeling spread, affecting even many of those who belonged to the ruling class and had a vested interest in keeping the existing power system intact. It was becoming evident that the entire system had gone bankrupt   economically, socially, ideologically—and that it had no self-restorative mechanisms.

It was inevitable that, with the increase in political activity and the proliferation of uncensored publications, some of the old divisions and traditional thought patterns should come back to life. To be sure, it was no longer possible to fit them into the standard categories of ''left'' and ''right''; these labels had lost all recognizable meaning. All of the opposition groups stressed their commitment to democratic values and to the cause of Poland's sovereignty. The differences among the various political currents were not focused on the validity of these general ideas. The various groups differed, rather, in the distribution of emphasis, in their political idiom and phraseology, in the tradition they appealed to, in strategic and tactical suggestions. And even though the prewar party ideologies could not, of course, be resurrected—many old issues had become irrelevant to the new conditions and many new ones had emerged—some mental structures survived in new divisions.

On the whole, certain trends in the intellectual movement were closer to the social-democratic idea (most people from the KOR milieu and many that were to become advisers to Solidarity belonged to this category); others (the Movement for the Defense of Human and Civil Rights—ROPCiO; and the KPN—Confederation of Independent Poland) stressed their attachment to national values and to the tradition of patriotic struggles. A variety of former ideological patterns could be detected in the uncensored press: social-democratic, liberal-conservative, radical nationalist (the dissident Communist or Marxist varieties such as Trotskyism or Maoism were conspicuously absent). The names of Józef Piłsudski and, to a lesser extent, of Roman Dmowski, the leader of the National Democrats, returned to prominence, and their respective ideas, merits, or mistakes became objects of lively discussion. Some opposition groups refused to elaborate comprehensive political programs and to be transformed into political parties; others tried precisely that. Most had been operating openly for years; some, however, preferred to work in anonymity in order to be free from all tactical considerations; this was true of the group calling itself PPN (Polish League for Independence), which published several important and lucid historical and political studies. Another body, set up in 1979 and operating under the name "Experience and the Future" (DiP), included a number of intellectuals who discussed Poland's predicament from "within the system," as it were; the group included party members and people close to the Establishment. They produced several devastatingly critical analyses of the social and economic situation in the country, even though they accepted both the principles of the socialist system and Poland's membership in the Soviet bloc.

The presence of the Church was of enormous importance at this time. It had remained the only independent source of moral authority in a sick society. Though the bishops and priests, under the leadership of Cardinal Stefan Wyszyński, avoided direct political pronouncements, many of them not only sympathized with the democratic opposition but actually helped or participated in it. The Catholic press, though subject to a particularly vicious censorship, was an enclave of truth, whereas the state-controlled public word, poisoned by the mass of official lies, was believed by no one. In fact, the party leaders, perceiving that their credibility was utterly lost, often canvassed for the Church's help when they desperately tried to avoid the outbursts of popular wrath. The Church never encouraged violent expressions of protest, yet it was firm in defending human rights—not only the rights of the Church itself—and in denouncing violations of these rights. It suffered various restrictions, pressures, and chicaneries but nevertheless appealed to the people to maintain calm—occasionally, perhaps, with exaggerated cautiousness—when social tensions were becoming dangerous and threatened the social structure with collapse.[7]

During this period the old conflicts between secular and Christian culture became largely irrelevant. Both because non-Catholic segments of the democratic opposition realized the irreplaceable value of Christian moral tradition and its fundamental historical importance in preserving human and national dignity under the totalitarian regime and because of changes in Catholic mentality and education, the Enlightenment's appraisal of Christianity lost meaning. Obscurantism became virtually monopolized by the ruling party, second only to the means of production and state power. And thus, in the seventies, there began to emerge a tacit alliance of the intellectual opposition, the Church, and the workers: this was the background of the 1980 eruption or, at any rate, of the basis for the course it would follow.

THE LEAP FORWARD

The strikes occurring in the summer of 1980 were by no means caused by KOR's activity. They were rooted in the economic and social disasters that the power system had produced, and they were organized on the spot by embryonic independent workers' unions. Yet KOR's influence on the way the workers voiced their grievances and articulated their demands was certainly essential. For four years KOR had worked on organizing a communications network, making contacts with workers in various factories, printing and distributing their journals and leaflets; the uncensored (thus "illegal", in the authorities' eyes) weekly *The Worker* ran off 20,000 copies before the major strikes took place; one has to live in a Communist country to appreciate properly this incredible achievement. KOR's people were active in various cities from the beginning of the strikes, helping and advising the workers.[8]

It is a matter for speculation as to why the show of unity that was finally achieved in the Solidarity movement had failed to materialize earlier. It seems, however, that the alliance of workers and intelligentsia is not a phenomenon that occurs, as it were, in the nature of things; rather, it happens only in exceptional circumstances, as priorities and values are bound to be somewhat different for each of these two classes (insofar as the word "class" is aptly used). In a Communist country, where the main aim of the power machinery is to prevent all spontaneous forms of social communication and to replace them with state-imposed artificial structures, such an alliance is, of course, much more difficult to achieve; it requires a coincidence of various social tensions of unusual force. And popular revolutions normally have an anti-intellectual aspect; this aspect has been almost absent in the Polish revolution. Some strains and frictions reflecting conflicting values became detectable in Solidarity, but not on a scale that would make them seem important. One could see from the very beginning of the 1980 summer strikes that the workers were perfectly aware of the fact that the fight for cultural liberties was an essential part of their cause, and that this cause would be lost if they did not list among their grievances a number of specific political demands: freedom of speech and print, an end to the party's monopoly of the mass media, abrogation of various restrictions imposed on the Church, release of political prisoners. It was obvious from the outset that the workers' revolt was not only against poverty and wretched work conditions: it was essentially a revolt against the rule of lies. There is a great demand among workers for truthful historical literature. The desire to live in truth and dignity was perhaps the most powerful driving force of the explosion in Poland.

It is plausible to argue that the cooperation of these three forces—the workers, the Church, and the intellectuals—is the first condition on which the success of the revolutionary process in Poland depends; the ruling party will certainly do everything possible to break this alliance from one side or another.

The above remarks had been written before military dictatorship was established in Poland. By sending thousands of workers and intellectuals to camps and prisons, by trying to destroy both the workers' unions and any independent intellectual activity, the Jaruzelski regime—despite its intentions, to be sure—has given impetus to the convergence of the fundamental needs and desires of both the workers and the intelligentsia. Never before has the clash between the vested interests of the party, police, and military bureaucracy, defending their privileges by massive violence, and all the aspirations—cultural and economic—of Polish society been revealed so glaringly.

Communism in Poland has thus been reduced to a reliance on guns, and there is something quite natural in this culmination of its history. The chances of a compromise have been eradicated by military despotism; Polish culture and, indeed, Polish society will continue to live and to survive in a long struggle against the entire political structure, now stripped of all ideological adornments and compelled to appear for what it is: naked coercion. In some respects, however, the outcome of the struggle is likely to be more successful, not only by comparison with the years under German occupation but with the years preceding the summer 1980 upheaval; restored dignity cannot be killed with police clubs.

6

THE WORKERS

Alex Pravda

In the summer of 1980 Poland saw the rise of a workers' movement more extensive, better organized, and more successful than any of the other protest movements that had punctuated the country's history over the previous quarter of a
century. Sporadic work stoppages in July were followed in the second half of
August by a wave of strikes spearheaded by workers in the Baltic ports. Under
the pressure of so massive a challenge, the authorities conceded demands ranging
from wage increases through the establishment of free trade unions to the release
of political prisoners and the relaxation of censorship.

Whatever the future brings, the protest of 1980 will remain remarkable for
three firsts in the history of Communist states. It was the first mass protest in the
era of so-called developed socialism—or perhaps termed more accurately, socialism with a consumerist face—and it demonstrated the contradictions inherent
in an attempt to build popular support on the basis of "premature consumerism"[1] within a traditional, and inflexible, Communist party system. For the first
time in a Communist state, workers' self-assertiveness went beyond violent,
fragmented, and short-lived protests to emerge as a well-organized, unified labor
movement.

Finally, 1980 brought an unprecedented expansion and politicization of workers' demands. Instead of pressing only for material security and improvement,
strikers asked for institutional change, for the establishment of self-governing
trade unions independent of the party and government. Political demands did not
stop at representation and participation. For the first time in Eastern Europe,
workers were in the very forefront of the struggle for civil liberties, a cause that
is commonly, and perhaps mistakenly, regarded as being of greater concern to
intellectuals. Not only did the events of 1980 confound Lenin's contention that
spontaneous working-class protest founders in economistic "trade unionism";[2]

This essay is a revised and abbreviated version of an article that originally appeared in the April 1982
issue of *Soviet Studies* (Glasgow). The author wishes to acknowledge his debt to Archie Brown,
Włodzimierz Brus, and Zvi Gitelman for their helpful comments, and to the Center for Russian and
East European Research at the University of Michigan, the National Council for Soviet and East
European Studies, and the Nuffield Foundation for their generous financial assistance and support.

they also cast doubt on notions of working-class authoritarianism. Focusing on these pioneering aspects, this article examines the roots of the revolt of 1980, the form the protests assumed, and the demands they projected.

THE ROOTS OF THE 1980 REVOLT

The unrest of 1980 was a product of the confluence of three classic crises: a crisis of distribution, a crisis of legitimacy, and a crisis of participation. Much of workers' discontent stemmed from economic performance and the way material wealth was distributed. Their readiness to protest was conditioned by a decline in the legitimacy of a leadership incapable of either managing the economy or controlling powerful corporate interests. Willingness to challenge the regime openly was increased by mounting frustration with a bureaucratized system of representation and participation.

The Hazards of Premature Consumerism

Economic factors were crucial in precipitating the 1980 upheaval. Increases in the price of meat triggered the first wave of strikes; economic issues quantitatively dominated strikers' demands, and, in retrospect, most Poles attributed the crisis to government mishandling of the economy.[3]

To a great extent, the discontent fueling blue-collar protest in 1980 was the result of the boom strategy launched by Gierek in 1971 in a bid to make consumption the spur to growth and political support. This strategy seemed logical enough, considering that Gierek had come to power in the wake of a workers' protest against an attempt to raise food prices and after a long period of stagnating living standards. Large credits from the West made possible a rapid and sizable growth in income and consumption that was premature in relation both to popular expectations and the economy's real capacity. Having set consumer expectations and consumerism on an upward spiral, boom turned into recession in the later 1970s, opening a widening gap between demands and economic performance. In an important sense, therefore, the protest of 1980 was produced by disappointed rising expectations.

To understand how this happened we must look at the evolution of popular economic attitudes through the 1970s. During the first half of the decade, Gierek's strategy seemed to operate successfully. In 1975 three out of every four Poles thought that their living standard had improved in recent years—hardly surprising, since wages had rocketed while food prices remained almost frozen. Burdened by a growing price subsidy bill, the Polish leadership in June 1976 announced a 60 percent increase in the price of basic foodstuffs, assuming that new-found prosperity would have made workers more tolerant of price hikes. To its surprise, workers responded by immediately launching protest strikes in industrial centers throughout Poland; in a few cities, notably Radom, protests led to violent clashes with security forces.[4] The events of June 1976 confirmed that

TABLE I

PUBLIC ASSESSMENT OF RECENT DEVELOPMENTS IN MATERIAL CONDITIONS/
LIVING STANDARDS (Responses in Percent)

	MID-1975	MID-1979	FEB. 1980	JULY 1980	SEPT. 2, 1980
Improved	77	56	52	35	29
Remained unchanged	15	25	27	29	17
Deteriorated	3	16	18	32	50
No opinion	5	3	3	4	4

SOURCE: Ośrodek Badania Opinii Publicznej (Center for Public Opinion Studies), Poll No. 16, 1980, "Summary of Results," p. 3. The poll was based on a national representative sample of the adult population.

the material improvements brought by the boom, while widely appreciated, had not reduced the workers' deeply rooted anxiety about price levels. Even though the government withdrew its proposed increases in the wake of the protests, the crisis irretrievably damaged the public confidence in Poland's economic prospects that had been built up in previous years. Indeed, the strikes revealed the underlying fragility of that confidence. As table 2 shows, the level of optimism about the country's economic prospects fell by half following the June 1976 protests, never to recover the plateau reached in the early 1970s. Such volatility was symptomatic of an unevenness in popular perceptions of the benefits of the boom, which is obscured by the favorable overall figures shown in table 1. A majority of Poles thought that 1970–78 had seen a slight rather than a substantial rise in living standards—the 10 percent reporting a marked improvement being offset by those whose situation had deteriorated (see table 3). Since this essay seeks to trace the economic roots of a *blue-collar* protest, it is interesting to note the considerable disparities between the assessments of different social groups. If we look at table 3, members of the intelligentsia emerge as the clearest beneficiaries of the boom strategy; workers come out as the least advantaged. And within these groups it is those in the highest income brackets who have done best and those in the lowest who have been hardest hit. True, living standards had apparently improved overall, but to many it seemed that the rich had become richer and the poor poorer.

This mixed verdict in part reflected the prematureness and imbalance of Gierek's consumerism, which generated economic discontent on two scores. Promises of unprecedented prosperity aroused consumer expectations that the economy failed to fulfill. For instance, a doubling in the number of private cars between 1970 and 1975 only served to increase the workers' desire for automobiles.[5] Imports from the West further inflated consumer demand, while freer contact with capitalist countries highlighted the contrast between Polish and West European living standards. Such disparities were particularly evident to workers in the foreign trade sector—interestingly enough, it was the workers in export industries who launched the protests in 1980.

TABLE 2

PUBLIC ASSESSMENT OF THE ECONOMIC OUTLOOK (Responses in Percent)

	1973–75	LATE 1976	1977	MID-1978	MID-1979	FEB. 1980	MID-SPRING 1980	JULY 1980	SEPT. 2, 1980	MID-SEPT. 1980
Will improve	app. 60	30	15	45	39	44	33	22	70	64
Will remain unchanged				30	33	36	33	35		21
Will deteriorate				10	15	9	21	29		5
No opinion				15	13	11	13	14		10

SOURCES: Center for Public Opinion Studies, Poll No. 16, 1980, p. 3; M. Wojciechowska, "Nastroje," *Kultura* (Warsaw), November 6, 1980, p. 9; and J. Kurczewski, "W oczach opinii publicznej," *Kultura*, March 1, 1981, p. 9.

TABLE 3

SUBJECTIVE ASSESSMENTS OF FAMILY LIVING CONDITIONS IN THE 1970s (Responses in Percent)

SOCIAL CATEGORY	IMPROVED CONSIDERABLY	IMPROVED SOMEWHAT	REMAINED UNCHANGED	DETERIORATED SOMEWHAT	DETERIORATED CONSIDERABLY	OTHER
Economically active, including:	11.2	52.3	22.1	9.2	3.1	2.1
Workers	6.6	51.6	26.5	9.2	3.4	2.7
Intelligentsia	16.8	50.3	18.3	7.8	4.0	2.8
Peasants	11.7	56.7	17.2	10.3	2.7	1.4
Peasant-workers	11.2	52.7	25.4	8.3	1.8	0.6
Pensioners	9.0	37.4	27.0	18.4	6.0	2.2
Economically active, by per-capita monthly family income:						
up to 1,000 zlotys	8.0	50.6	21.3	12.9	6.1	1.1
1,001–1,500 zlotys	5.4	54.6	26.2	9.6	2.3	1.9
1,501–2,500 zlotys	11.4	51.1	22.7	8.9	3.2	2.7
2,501–3,500 zlotys	13.9	60.9	15.3	6.7	1.9	1.3
3,501–5,000 zlotys	23.7	46.2	20.4	6.5	1.1	2.1
5,001 zlotys and above	27.3	27.3	36.4	3.0	—	6.0

NOTE: The following question was asked: "Have your family's living conditions (*warunki bytu*) improved overall in the years 1970–78?"
SOURCE: Results of the research project *Moja sytuacja rodzinna* (My family situation) conducted by the Social Opinion Research Center of the Institute of Fundamental Problems of Marxism-Leninism of the Central Committee of the Polish United Workers' Party, given in L. Beskid, "Potrzeby ludności w świetle badań społecznych" (The population's needs in the light of social surveys), *Nowe Drogi* (Warsaw), No. 6, 1980, p. 142.

Besides creating new sources of discontent, the boom strategy also compounded older problems. Disproportionate investment in capital projects meant that the development of light industry, agriculture, health, and housing were neglected by comparison. Though food consumption grew, supplies remained erratic and were rated as poor by a majority of Poles in the late 1970s. Housing was given high official priority, yet its share of investments dwindled and construction plans went unfulfilled, thus lengthening waiting lists for accomodation.[6] What exacerbated the workers' dissatisfaction, particularly among the young ones, with housing, as well as with consumer goods in general, was not so much that living standards had fallen but that availability of goods failed to meet the workers' rising expectations. Thus beneath what appeared to be general public appreciation of the benefits of the boom, there lay deepening dissatisfaction with the regime's inability to furnish basic requirements and growing disappointment with the blatant shortcomings of Gierek's "consumerist" policy.

The public's ambivalent attitude toward the economic successes of the early 1970s made it all the more vulnerable to the recession of the second half of that decade. Growth rates slowed sharply after 1975, and foreign indebtedness mounted. Of greater relevance to workers was the concomitant slowdown in pay growth and the growth of inflation, which resulted in a decline in real wages in 1978 and 1979.

Exactly how Poles viewed this reversal in economic development is critical to any assessment of the economic roots of the upheaval. The public opinion data in tables 1, 2, and 4 shed some light on this issue. Overall, popular perceptions of the economic situation from 1975 to mid-1980 did reflect the pattern of decline (tables 1 and 2). However, actual downturns took some time to register in public consciousness. Thus the decline in real wages over the preceding eighteen months notwithstanding, in mid-1979 a majority of respondents thought that material conditions had improved (table 1); while 50 percent considered the economy to be in poor shape, few were pessimistic about its prospects (tables 1 and 2). The time lag between the actual decline and the public's perception of that decline may account for the dramatic shift between February and July 1980 in popular assessments of recent, current, and future developments. During these crucial months immediately preceding the protests, the number of Poles doubled who asserted that their living standards had deteriorated, while positive assessments of the economy halved (tables 1 and 4). By July 1980 a decisive majority

TABLE 4

PUBLIC ASSESSMENT OF THE ECONOMIC SITUATION OF THE COUNTRY
(Responses in Percent)

	MID-1979	FEB. 1980	JULY 1980	MID-SEPT. 1980
Good	48	50	28	9
Bad	45	46	65	86
No opinion	7	4	7	5

SOURCE: Center for Public Opinion Studies, Poll No. 16, 1980, "Summary of Results," p. 3.

had reached the conclusion that the economy was in a perilous state (table 4). More important as an indicator of public confidence was the deepening pessimism about the country's economic prospects—for the first time since the 1960s, pessimists outnumbered optimists (table 2).

What emerges forcefully liom the public opinion data are the destabilizing effects of discontinuous economic development. Just as the speed and imbalance of Gierek's attempt to meet consumer demands created expectations that bred discontent, so the rapid succession of expansion and recession produced by the boom strategy had a profoundly disruptive impact on a population accustomed to steady and predictable economic development. Triggered in part by a relatively sudden realization that the country was in the throes of a deep economic crisis, the 1980 upheaval was largely generated not by material pauperization but by a widening gap between rising expectations and falling performance.

Legitimacy, Social Justice, and Confidence

If economic developments fueled popular discontent, they also increased workers' readiness to protest. Nowhere is economics more likely to spill over into the political arena than in Communist states. For not only are economy and polity structurally linked, but in recent years the public has been increasingly enjoined to identify economic with political performance. Confronted with the task of boosting the popularity of a regime notoriously lacking in public support, Gierek mortgaged political legitimacy on economic achievement more heavily than any of his East European counterparts.

That Poles actually considered the government, rather than economic circumstances, responsible for economic performance is suggested by their asessment of the country's prospects (see table 2). The marked upturn in optimism between mid-1979 and February 1980 may have reflected widespread anticipation that the Eighth Party Congress would produce a viable program for economic recovery. Public disappointment was, therefore, all the greater when the Congress (February 11–15, 1980) produced only blanket reaffirmations of current policy and issued exhortations for more productivity and warnings of coming austerity.[7] Hence, perhaps, the sharp fall in public confidence in Poland's economic prospects after the Congress. By the same token the dramatic upsurge in optimism in September 1980 following the agreements between government and strikers suggests that most Poles thought that economic recession might be checked by a new leadership ready to accept structural change.

Apart from the damage wrought by disappointing economic performance, regime and leadership legitimacy was also adversely affected by two aspects of the boom strategy: evident loss of central control and the burgeoning of inequality. Were one to single out one factor conditioning workers' support for Communist regimes, it would be an expectation of protection from instability, uncertainty, and insecurity by a strong welfare state.[8] Gierek gambled on being able to compensate Polish workers with greater prosperity for any erosion of certainty and security. In any event the gamble failed, not just because the boom strategy proved incapable of generating sufficient improvement, but also because it undermined the image of central control.

Coming after a long period of relative price stability, the 30 percent jump in prices between 1975 and 1979 must have severely shaken workers' confidence in such control. Amid reports of failing exports and mounting indebtedness, growing public and semipublic criticism of economic mismanagement by the government further bolstered the idea that the leadership had lost control over its own strategy. Also, it became increasingly obvious that if any steering was still being done, the tiller had been relinquished by the political leaders and was now in the hands of large corporate interest groups, made up mainly of the large economic organizations (WOG), the major ministries in each region. As the party itself later acknowledged, "various departmental and regional pressure groups" had exercised a "decisive influence" over investment policy.[9] If at the time the complete picture remained hidden from public view, enough could be seen, even at the factory level, of the burgeoning corruption. Inflation only reinforced the widespread belief that privileged groups were profiteering at the expense of the ordinary working man. Along with bureaucracy, cliques, and corruption, special concessions for the privileged were perceived as central to the country's malaise and almost as important as overall economic mismanagement in generating the 1980 crisis.[10]

But pressure groups, corruption, and cliques were only part of a larger picture of growing social inequality and privilege that undermined the legitimacy of the regime. For Polish workers looked to the government not only to provide welfare and security, but also to ensure a minimal level of egalitarian social justice. Since most workers considered Polish society too stratified even under Gomułka, it was hardly surprising that the 1970s brought deepening dissatisfaction on this score. As has already been noted, the boom strategy disproportionately benefited high-income groups. The workers felt themselves slipping in the hierarchy of access to material resources, even as they watched top salaries rise, stretching differentials beyond acceptable bounds. Whereas most workers considered as just a maximum to minimum ratio of between 1:3 and 1:5, differentials of 1:14 were common in industry in the late 1970s.[11] Particularly objectionable to the workers was the conspicuous extension of privileges to the favored few. With the influx into the Polish economy of massive funds and luxury imports from the West, the elite's *nouveau riche* life style flourished. Anxious to secure the support of key groups considered vital to the success of his economic policy, Gierek in 1972 granted all party and government officials, including the police, special allowances and tax exemptions.[12] The vehemence with which strikers attacked the granting of such benefits in 1980 testifies to the depth of feeling this issue aroused.

Loss of confidence in the authorities' ability to manage the economy, control bureaucratic elites, and ensure social justice was compounded by poor communication between leadership and labor. Gierek had taken office on a platform of building a new relationship of trust between party and workers. Claiming that failure in communication had been a key cause of the 1970–71 crisis, the new First Secretary set about making "consultation" the hallmark of his leadership. In the early 1970s he toured hundreds of factories, reminding audiences of his own proletarian past, his sympathy with the working class, and his vision of "the new Poland." Initially such personal appearances may have impressed workers used to very distant political leaders—Gierek's face-to-face debate with Szczecin strikers in January 1971 certainly made an impact. But by the mid-1970s such visits had degenerated into public relations exercises, carefully orchestrated, with officials addressing hand-picked, "safe" audiences. And whatever trust remained was all but destroyed by the attempt to spring price increases on workers in June 1976 without warning, let alone proper consultation. Despite the violent protests that this move precipitated, the leadership, almost incredibly, tried the same technique in 1980. Although the Polish public had been warned of the need for a general reduction in food price subsidies, it was given no advance notice that certain categories of meat would be transferred to commercial shops—thereby commanding higher prices—a move that triggered the first work stoppages. The confusing and covert manner in which these price increases were introduced infuriated the workers, who interpreted the move as an insult to their intelligence and dignity.[13] Isolated from the workers and closely identified with mismanagement, weakness, elitism, and injustice, the Gierek group had little credibility or legitimacy left by 1980. Most workers simply discounted Gierek's late August appeal for an end to protests and few mourned his political demise.

Participation and Representation

Problems of participation and representation contributed to the unrest of 1980. These problems should be considered in the context of enterprise as well as of national politics. The fact that the national labor protest of 1980 was centered in the industries underscores the close links between enterprise and polity that exist in Poland and that are inherent in the structure of all Communist states. By anchoring themselves organizationally in factories and seeking to inject a political element into all aspects of work and all authority relationships, Communist parties politicize industrial relations. Just as shifts in industrial relations impinge on national politics, so national policy decisions directly affect the situation within factories. In Poland throughout the 1970s developments in enterprise politics placed mounting pressure on worker representation and participation at a national level.

ENTERPRISE POLITICS. Economic changes in the 1970s broadened the scope for conflict between labor and management. With the growth of material incentives, workers' earnings became more dependent on management discretion and performance. Differences over pay and the distribution of bonuses emerged as the most common causes of contention. Industrial relations were also affected by the changing complexion of both labor and management. Most of those who entered the factories in the 1950s and early 1960s came from peasant families. As first-generation factory workers, they generally appreciated the apparently higher rewards offered by industry, and if many found it difficult to adjust to the demands of factory life, their lack of experience and their continued attachment to the farms they had left behind reduced to a minimum any active attempt to shape their work conditions. By the late 1970s, the younger generation of workers made up 40 percent of the nonagricultural labor force. Better-educated and more accustomed to the conditions and rewards of industry, these second-generation workers were also far more critical of the status quo and more concerned than their elders had been with exercising some influence over the factors that affected their income and environment.[14]

Facing this new generation of workers was a new generation of managers: two-thirds of the directors in office had less than ten years' experience.[15] More highly educated than their predecessors, many of these new directors maintained an authoritarian style and were insensitive to the human factor in production. Also, they were separated from the work force by greater social distance; unlike the previous generation, they had not come up in the ranks from the shop floor. To be sure, this was not true of all new directors; the situation varied greatly from factory to factory, much depending on local conditions and personalities. Nonetheless, on the whole—as borne out by surveys conducted in 1960–80—one out of every three workers looked upon industrial relations as a source of conflict.

The system designed to mediate and resolve such conflicts was woefully inadequate. Semi moribund arbitration commissions dealt with two or three disputes per year. Workers' councils had effectively ceased to exist by 1959, having been absorbed by the Conferences of Workers' Self-Management, whose only function was to discuss production problems and which lacked any influence over management other than that wielded by their constituent trade unions and party organizations.

On paper, the trade union councils were endowed with sufficient powers to enable them to fulfill their designated role as protectors of workers' legal rights. In fact, they were hamstrung by their other function—to promote production. The unions' "dual representation" was based on an assumption that workers' interests were inseparable from those of management and production. In reality, however, the relationship between the two sets of interests was far from symbiotic, let alone synonymous, and when faced with a conflict, unions tended to favor production and management over labor. Thus union councils devoted very little time to improving working conditions, housing, and pay, and to representing members in disputes with management—all issues that the workers themselves thought should be the legitimate concerns of unions. Instead of defending workers' rights, union officials turned a blind eye to infractions by the management. No wonder that only a small minority of workers considered unions effective representative or participatory bodies.[16]

The weakness and ineffectiveness of unions shifted the onus of institutional representation of workers' interests onto party organizations. The situation was not without its paradoxes. Although party officials were considerably more powerful than their union counterparts, they, too, were generally aligned with management. The party committee secretary's first responsibility was to make sure that the factory ran smoothly and that production plans were carried out. This entailed a collaborative rather than an adversary relationship with management, so that only rarely did party secretaries back workers against the director. Rank-and-file party activists, however, were often torn by divided loyalties. Many of them were trusted by the workers and sided with labor rather than with management.[17] As a result, the party organization became a popular repository for workers' complaints. This is clearly indicated by the data in table 5. The absence of any reference to the union council is eloquent testimony to that body's actual role in industry.

TABLE 5

INDUSTRIAL WORKERS' OPINION OF THE MOST EFFECTIVE WAYS TO PRESS THEIR DEMANDS, 1972–74

	RESPONSES (IN %) OF WORKERS EARNING MORE THAN 5,000 ZLOTYS PER MONTH	RESPONSES (IN %) OF WORKERS EARNING UNDER 2,000 ZLOTYS PER MONTH
Use workers' self-management bodies	81	54
Take demand to party organization	79	48
Take concerted action (*"solidarne wystąpienia"*)	67	24
Complain to management	66	55
Avoid carrying out work directives	28	22
Leave work or		26
take day off	19	20
Lower quality of work performance	14	11
Cause damage	12	13

SOURCE: L. Gilejko, in A. Wajda (ed.), *Klasa robotnicza w społeczeństwie socjalistycznym* (The working class in a socialist society) (Warsaw, 1979), pp. 274–75 (survey of 3,000 industrial workers conducted in 1972–74).

The surveys conducted in the 1970s also reveal that large numbers of workers considered informal direct methods the most effective way to get things done. True, some workers preferred to act individually; the majority of higher-paid, skilled workers, however, opted for collective action.

Each successful use of collective action further reduced the viability of official institutional channels and strengthened the cohesion of the skilled, higher-paid blue collar groups who most frequently used such methods. The very success of informal participation also helped to make other groups feel excluded. Unfamiliar with the rules of the game, and enjoying neither access to formal channels nor the knowledge and industrial muscle necessary for pressure tactics, younger workers often remained outside the informal if customary arrangements characteristic of enterprise politics. At the same time, they were the ones most acutely affected by pay differentials, housing shortages, and the gap between expectations and economic realities. Add to this the fact that their expectations for real participation were higher than those of older workers, and it is hardly surprising that young workers—who constituted about 40 percent of nonagricultural labor—figured very prominently in the 1980 strikes. They had no vested interest in preserving the existing system of participation and everything to gain by its change.

Also alienated from both formal and informal participation was a different and far smaller group: the radical worker activists. Frequently ex-members of union or party factory committees, they were highly critical of the institutional channels available to represent workers' interests. They regarded informal methods as no more than stopgaps and pressed for alternative representative institutions. In early 1978 radicals in Katowice, Gdańsk, and Szczecin set up Free Trade Union Committees and mounted a campaign for the election of independent-minded representatives to local union councils as well as for the eventual establishment of free trade unions. Though few in number, radical workers were influential in organizing workers' protests. Attempts to suppress these "trouble makers" only increased their popular standing. Clashes between management and radical workers heightened tension and later played a key role in the 1980 protests: demands for the reinstatement of a free trade union activist, Anna Walentynowicz, sparked the August stoppage at the Lenin Shipyard in Gdańsk, which rapidly became the spearhead of the whole 1980 labor movement.

Not that management invariably took a tough stand against radical activists, or against all those who used informal methods of participation. Reasons for such forbearance are not difficult to find. In the first place, informal methods smoothed the course of industrial relations. Worker pressure could also be used as leverage to help extract additional resources from hierarchical superiors unresponsive to more orthodox methods. A director able to argue that supply shortages or poor equipment would definitely produce industrial conflict increased his chances of obtaining the necessary materials. Nevertheless, while such leniency may have temporarily eased tensions within the enterprise, in the longer run it created further uncertainty, because blue-collar participation came to depend largely on the local director's attitudes; the realities of enterprise politics undermined the credibility of formal institutional channels. Finally, a major destabilizing effect of informal participation was the creation of a widening gap between workers' access in factories and their say in national politics. And it was on the national level, of course, that all the major decisions affecting workers' interests were made.

NATIONAL POLITICS. If notions of dual representation hampered institutional participation within an enterprise, they presented more formidable obstacles at the national level. Here party and trade unions recognized as legitimate only those "working-class" interests that were so defined by the political leadership. Even though official notions often had little in common with the actual interests of the workers, they were given precedence by the bureaucrats who controlled both organizations. Admittedly, Gierek did attempt to gather more information about workers' actual desires and grievances, but this seems to have had little impact on government policy.[18] The fact that more workers were now in the party may have given it a more respectable social profile, but it did little to enhance its credibility among workers. According to a party-commissioned poll in 1976, only one in every five industrial workers thought that the party represented their interests.[19]

By giving party organizations in the largest industries direct access to the Central Committee apparatus and encouraging them to think of themselves as key links in the policy-making chain, Gierek raised their expectations. In practice, party activists found that they exercised little influence; when they did pass on the demands of their constituents, their reports were often treated as "hysterical outbursts."[20] By blocking attempts to articulate workers' real interests, the party apparatus inadvertently promoted the cause of working-class radicals. The party's tactics also antagonized the most popular and energetic of the Communist activists, many of whom sympathized with the strikers in 1980.[21] Far from reducing pressure on representative and participatory institutions, Gierek's attempts at reform thus bred frustration among party activists and reinforced workers' faith in direct action as the only way of asserting themselves against incompetent rulers who were leading the country to disaster.

1980: ANATOMY OF REVOLT

In addition to the sheer number of workers involved—approximately 12 percent of the entire nonagricultural labor force—the 1980 strikes were remarkable for their nonviolence, self-assurance, organization, and worker solidarity. Unlike previous protests, they were peaceful and orderly. Indeed, the strikers managed to impose law, order, and sobriety on their members more effectively than the authorities did. There was a new confidence, too, in the strength of labor—as Wałęsa told one reporter, the government had to grant the workers' demands if it wished to govern, because the workers could go on striking for five years.[22] And although such self-confidence and efficient organization may have been far from universal, this was largely offset by the emergence of unprecedented solidarity between industries and the various regions in which they operated. Whereas the best organized of previous protests—in 1970–71—had been confined to specific enterprises, those of August 1980 were coordinated by regional Interfactory Strike Committees in Wrocław, Jastrzębie (Silesia), and most notably in Szczecin and Gdańsk. This, of course, constituted a powerful weapon against the authorities' attempts to fragment the workers. What is more, the two Baltic committees were at the forefront of a movement that not only united Polish labor, but also commanded overwhelming public support.[23]

What explains the remarkable show of strength, organization, and solidarity of the Polish workers in 1980? To start with, it is important to remember their make-up and the material resources that were available to them. The concentration of almost two-thirds of the industrial labor force in enterprises of more than 1,000 employees certainly facilitated collective action. Outstanding among such factories were the giants employing 15,000 or more, built as flagships of socialist industrialization, only to become bastions of protest. The basic equipment in these companies—such as public address systems and broadcasting facilities—made communication within and between plants easy. More important, their strategic position in the economy ensured that when they were occupied by strikers, the authorities and the public alike paid urgent attention. Furthermore, since the key industries were located within closely defined geographical areas, tight-knit, homogeneous working communities were created in which workers in the largest local enterprises were naturally regarded as leaders. But these factors alone do not suffice to explain the unprecedented power and unity that developed in 1980. Three other sets of factors were important: the response of the authorities to workers' protests; religious and intellectual influences; and the impact of collective experience and identity.

The Authorities' Response

All protests are limited forms of warfare in which the morale and strategy of the combatants are mutually conditioned. The inept way in which the political authorities handled the 1980 strikes had an important effect on how workers' action developed. The only effect of attempts to pacify strikers by immediately meeting their demands and offering unsolicited wage increases was to provide financial incentives for other workers to go on strike. Threats were made against strike organizers but were rarely carried out, thus further reducing the authorities' credibility while hardening the protesters' resolve. The party's Central Committee instructed its local organizations to combat the strikes, and a few of them tried to do so. Most party organizations, however, kept a low profile and some even disintegrated.[24]

Of key importance to the spread of the strikes in 1980 was the authorities' unwillingness, or inability, to use force against the strikers. Perhaps one of the reasons was the memory of the massacres of Baltic port workers in 1970–71, with all the disastrous political consequences those events precipitated. Whatever the reasons, the refusal to use force encouraged the workers and enlarged the number and geographical extent of the strikes. Not only did the absence of coercion ensure the peaceful course of protest action; it also provided vital time for workers both to organize and to coordinate their protests within and between factories. The party's decision to use political means to resolve the crisis also encouraged the complex organization of the protest movement; willingness to negotiate with strike committees entrenched them more firmly as valid representatives of their plants. And this in turn provided a model for workers in other parts of the country to follow.

Not that the authorities' behavior was a direct cause of the organizational achievements in 1980. To a far lesser extent than in previous protests did workers merely react to government moves; in 1980 they set the pace, and their determination made the authorities seem more like supplicants. The principal causes of workers' confidence, organization, and unity lay, rather, in the intellectual, material, and psychological resources on which they could draw.

Religious and Intellectual Influences

Publicly, the top hierarchy of the Catholic Church adopted a typically cautious line during the protests, thus evoking unfavorable reactions from some workers.

Behind the scenes, however, Cardinal Wyszyński reportedly played a key role in strengthening the strikers' hand in negotiations. At the local level, Catholic priests boosted workers' morale by holding open-air masses in occupied factories and generally identifying themselves with the strikers. In so doing priests followed a long tradition of the Church supporting those fighting for their human rights. After the repressions following the June 1976 protests, this support had taken a more concrete form, in financial aid for the families of workers who had been imprisoned or dismissed from their jobs, as well as public campaigns for their release and reinstatement. In a country where the overwhelming majority of the population are practicing Catholics, the support of the Church gave the strikers a moral sanction, the impact of which can hardly be overestimated. Catholic intellectuals also contributed to the strike movement in Gdańsk by providing expert help and advice during negotiations with the government commission. This, too, was but the most dramatic manifestation of an established pattern: for years Catholic intellectuals had been active in the struggle for political and civil rights.

In Gdańsk, and to a lesser extent in Szczecin, advice was provided by more radically inclined intellectuals associated with the Flying University (the system of academic courses set up by a group of independent scholars in 1978), and the Social Self-Defense Committee, formerly the Workers' Defense Committee (KSS/KOR). For political reasons members of KOR maintained a low profile during the actual negotiations, yet they had made an important contribution to the workers' attempts at organization and the development of their strategy. *Robotnik* (The worker), a newsletter produced jointly by blue-collar radicals and KOR intellectuals, had long urged workers to adopt the tactics that proved so successful in 1980.[25] The most important intellectual influence of the workers' movement was thus of an indirect kind, mediated through worker activists. It was instrumental in helping workers realize their own strengths and to learn from their own experience.

COLLECTIVE EXPERIENCE AND IDENTITY. In a sense, the success of the 1980 movement hinged on the fact that while authorities failed to learn from the past, workers showed a remarkable capacity to do so. Thus, for example, the best-organized strikes occurred in industries with long histories of protest. Every industrial conflict enlarged the pool of workers who had some experience in organizing, or at least participating in, protest action, and this was true even though activists were dismissed or transferred after each incidence of protest. Typically, the key leaders of 1980—Wałęsa in Gdańsk, Jurczyk in Szczecin— had long records of protest involvement.[26] Experience in the Free Trade Union Committees also provided encouragement to think audaciously and concentrate on organization. These committees had "educated" a small but critical number of young activists who later emerged as front-rank leaders in Gdynia, Gdańsk, and Warsaw. It was through the Free Trade Union movement, too, that older activists from different industries first met and established the contacts that laid the foundations for interfactory collaboration in 1980.[27]

The traumatic experiences they had shared created a bond among these worker activists and a supportive environment for future action. Memories of police repression in 1970–71 and after 1976 conferred a halo of special authority on those, like Wałęsa or Świtoń, who had suffered for their dissidence.[28] This loyalty—the sense of collective identity and consciousness—had grown steadily in the 1970s, particularly among young second-generation industrial workers, who felt the social walls surrounding them becoming ever more impenetrable. And it had in turn been reinforced by a growing awareness of the power of protest. True, in 1970–71 and in 1976 workers had suffered defeats—and casualties. But on both occasions they had, in effect, forced the authorities to back down. In retrospect it is clear that these earlier conflicts had contributed significantly to the workers' self-confidence.[29]

Last but not least, solidarity based on labor consciousness was enhanced by a national identity. The frequent singing of the national anthem, the ubiquitous presence of Polish flags, the statements by strike leaders that they regarded themselves as Poles first and foremost, the appeals to national unity, and the emphasis on apposite events in their country's history all testified to the fact that the workers saw themselves as representing the ordinary Polish people against the privileged, bureaucratic elite who had betrayed the dignity and interests of the nation. In the past, striking workers had frequently found themselves either isolated from or even at odds with other social groups. By 1980, their cause was also the cause of the whole country, and as such a patriotic one.

Demands

The fact that strikers used the power of organized labor to press for political as well as material gains gives 1980 a significance transcending that of size and commonality. Ultimately, the stability of all Communist states depends on the ability of the leadership to keep workers indifferent to issues of political power—and in this respect the failure of Poland's leaders was monumental. In addition, the workers' politicization helped to dispel a number of conventional notions—for example, that workers are basically interested only in their economic plight and that they seek and favor an authoritarian figure or structure that relieves them of the need to weigh issues and make decisions concerning their own lives.

Three categories of demands became prominent in 1980: for economic gains, for more adequate representation, and for recognition of civil liberties. Economic demands came first, with the workers calling for higher wages and an abrogation of price increases. These were soon linked with demands for the redistribution and improved management of economic resources. By August, demands for institutional representation were being made, along with calls for civil liberties, which in fact were given top priority. Thus material concerns did not supersede political demands; rather, what emerged was a confluence of demands pertaining to material, institutional, and human rights. This reflected the combination of factors that had produced the crisis in Poland in the first place. Furthermore, since the demands were compiled in a democratic fashion—that is, by freely elected strike delegates—they manifestly expressed the views and grievances of an overwhelming majority of industrial workers. The fact that the Gdańsk Agreement[30] was adopted by strikers throughout the country is further proof of the popularity of these demands. Let us, then, take a look at each category in turn. THE ECONOMY. Initial demands for the withdrawal of meat price increases, articulated in some of the July strikes, was an issue that never attained the prominence it had had in 1970 and 1976. From the outset, workers placed great emphasis on a demand for higher wages, first pressing for an increase of 5–10 percent, which soon rose to 10–20 percent and in August topped the 50 percent mark. What lay behind this shift from an essentially defensive posture, in which only a rollback or equalization of acknowledged increases was called for, to such an assertive stance? To begin with, pay increases were a tangible and popular objective that proved relatively easy to attain. Indeed, rapid settlement of early claims by management and local officials anxious to curb the spread of strikes encouraged the escalation of wage claims. Mounting inflation also focused workers' attention on wages: by the late 1970s nearly all workers felt, quite rightly, that their incomes were being eroded by rising prices.[31] Hence the emphasis on "compensatory" increases and the shipyard workers' call for index-linked pay—a Western-type labor response to a situation resembling capitalistlike "stagflation." Most of the wage demands hardly qualified as strictly compensatory, however; they clearly manifested the phenomenon of rising expectations and aspirations. Despite a 45 percent rise in real wages from the mid-1960s to the mid-1970s, the gap between the pay that workers received and the pay they felt they deserved remained unchanged, at just over 40 percent; by 1979 it had grown to nearly 50 percent.[32]

Alongside demands for more money, demands for its redistribution underscored to what extent rising material expectations supplemented rather than supplanted traditional egalitarian values. This double-barreled alignment of consumerism and egalitarianism made workers' demands particularly formidable. Strikers pressed for redistribution to reduce both privilege, on the one hand, and deprivation, on the other. The pervasive resentment of privilege produced demands for the elimination of the hard-currency PEWEX shops and of the special benefits enjoyed by officials. At the same time the workers insisted on upgrading the lowest subsistence level. Much more than they had in previous protests, they sought to help those worst off by pressing for across-the-board increases or increases that favored the lower-paid. Calls for the rationing of scarce commodities and for improved housing and welfare provisions also reflected these egalitarian concerns. Szczecin strikers demanded a guaranteed social minimum, a demand aimed directly at alleviating the plight of the large minority of workers—24 percent, according to a 1979 study—living below that level.[33] Some of these demands echoed the vested interests of groups in the vanguard of protest. On the whole, however, they stemmed from a strong and long-established tradition of worker concern for egalitarian social justice.

A concern with equity also prompted demands for a more distinct and rational structure of pay to replace the tangle of the existing system—i.e., "prescriptive-managerial demands." Three issues emerged. First, strikers demanded that priority be given to the needs of the working population when resources were allocated. They insisted that only surpluses should be exported; they called for a major shift of investments from capital goods to consumer goods in order to correct the imbalance of the 1970s. Second, they pressed for greater managerial efficiency, arguing that directors and administrators should be appointed on the basis of their qualifications rather than for reasons of loyalty and political reliability, as had so often been the case in the past. Finally, the strikers called for the free exchange of information and opinion on the economy, demanding that the government produce a proposal for thoroughgoing economic reform.

This was a remarkable development, mirroring changing perceptions of what was wrong with Poland. Research dating from the early 1970s suggests that the younger generation of workers tended to attribute the country's problems to structural defects rather than to the shortcomings of the working population—such as laziness or drunkenness—that preoccupied their parents.[34] The economic crisis of the late 1970s merely confirmed their view that the system itself was at fault. This perhaps explains why workers seemed so receptive to the reforms favored by their intellectual advisers: decentralization, rationalization, market mechanisms. Admittedly, reconciling economic rationalization of prices and employment with workers' traditional security and welfare concerns posed problems. But potential incompatability was eased by the workers' insistence on reserving the right to criticize and oppose any reforms they perceived to be in conflict with their interests.

REPRESENTATION. In the first strike wave, Lublin railwaymen demanded free trade union elections. In the second, the demands escalated into calls for the establishment of new independent unions equipped with the right to strike. The first of the now famous "twenty-one points" of the striking shipyard workers in Szczecin and Gdańsk concerned free trade unions: in the end only the government's reluctant acceptance of the principle of free trade unionism opened the way to the general accords that ended the protest. Though Poland and Eastern Europe had seen previous movements for free trade unionism, never before had independent unions served as *the* rallying cry of a mass labor movement. Why did Polish workers in 1980 insist so strongly on new unions, and what kind of unionism did they envisage?

No doubt, members of the Free Trade Union Committees helped to influence the formulation of the Baltic demands.[35] Certainly, the idea of free unions answered a widely felt need of the rank and file; dissatisfaction with formal institutional channels had, as noted above, led workers increasingly to resort to direct action. But while strikes were effective as a means of challenging decisions or pressing urgent demands, they were clearly inadequate instruments for defending and promoting workers' interests on a regular basis. As one Gdańsk striker declared, it was ridiculous that every time workers wanted to make themselves heard they practically had to stir up a revolution.[36] And even if protests could trigger changes in political leadership, the experiences of 1956 and 1970 showed that such changes brought no lasting improvement in workers' representation and participation at the decision-making level. This could be achieved only through strong institutions that would represent workers' interests.

None of the existing representative bodies, however refurbished, seemed to fit the bill. Better local council and parliamentary representation could not ease problems with a given enterprise and did not even figure in workers' demands until the 1981 Solidarity program evolved. Nor was a democratized Communist party deemed a solution: there were no calls for party democratization during the 1980 strikes.[37] The movement for party reform came only after the agreements and was confined to rank-and-file party members; in the summer of 1980, the party, with its primary interest in production, was not regarded as a vehicle for workers' interests. For different reasons, workers' councils also failed to attract the popular attention they had enjoyed in earlier worker protests.[38] The sorry plight of their predecessors—which arose in 1955–56 and were effectively emasculated by 1958—made the very idea of worker participation in management highly suspect; it wasn't until 1981 that the call for workers' councils surfaced again.

This left the unions. The early calls for free union elections signaled grassroots support for a reform of the existing union movement, an option not unnaturally favored by government negotiators in August. But experience taught strikers to insist on wholly new and independent unions; they had learned from previous attempts to invigorate old unions, which had come to naught. Rather than simply exchange old unions for new, the Gdańsk leaders pressed for the establishment of independent trade unions coexisting with the old ones. This was based on the assumption that not only would competition help to prevent degeneration of the new organization, it would also break the monopolistic representation of workers' interests that was central to the traditional bureaucratized system. While the old unions would continue to serve workers' interests by promoting production, the new Solidarity movement would defend workers' "rights, dignity, and interests" above and before all else.[39] In effect, the demands for unions that would first and foremost defend and promote their interests and only secondarily promote production expressed a nineteenth-century concept of adversary unionism. And central to this notion was a union independent of the "company," whether the "company" took the form of management, ministries, government, or party.

The emphasis on full independence explains Solidarity's reluctance to accept the "leading role" of the Communist party and the decision that officials of other organizations would be ineligible for election to Solidarity offices. It also explains why the strike leaders in Gdańsk pledged that their unions would be apolitical—this despite the essentially, inherently political role they would have to play. The paradox was glaring, for how could the unions press policy recommendations on the government, or make the authorities keep their promises, except by playing a major role in the political arena? But the leaders of Solidarity meant to avoid turning the union into a political party or a challenge to the socialist system. They envisaged the unions as exercising "social control" from outside the existing institutional apparatus of power. And the notion of "social control," whatever controversies it may have generated among the labor movement leadership, reflected general worker preferences. A growing number of workers, particularly the young, wished to exercise more influence over policies affecting them; few, however, appeared to want direct participation or power as such. So independent unions, strong enough to defend workers' interests but disclaiming responsibility for economic or social policy, seemed an ideal solution.

CIVIL LIBERTIES. If the demand for free trade unions gave the events of 1980 a strong political thrust, the calls for freedom of speech and opinion made the protests a force for general democratization. Not that strikers pressed for a re-

form of the whole political system: proposals for judicial, electoral, and parliamentary reform appeared only in the Solidarity program adopted at its congress
in October 1981. What workers spontaneously championed in 1980 were civil
liberties. These were central to four of the first five demands advanced by the
Gdańsk Interfactory Strike Committee: the right to strike; the broadcasting of
information about the protests; compliance with constitutionally guaranteed freedom of speech and press; and the reinstatement and release of all those who had
been dismissed or imprisoned for their personal convictions.[40]

Never before in Communist Poland, or anywhere in Eastern Europe, had
workers so forthrightly espoused civil rights. In Poland, typically, intellectuals
had fought for civil liberties while workers had pursued material gains. After
1976, intellectual dissidents had shown more interest in workers' grievances, and
made strenuous efforts at joint actions with the workers, but without much success. Conventional wisdom usually cites worker indifference, or even antipathy,
to the concerns of intellectual dissidents as the reason for the lack of collaboration between the two groups, and pinpoints as the cause of that indifference the
working-class propensity for authoritarian rule.[41] But the events of 1980 showed
workers' attitudes toward freedom and democracy to be quite different. How,
then, can we explain the apparent turnabout of 1980; what were the sources and
quality of worker support for civil rights and liberties?

Certainly, intellectual dissidents played a role in promoting the libertarian
cause among strikers. KOR reportedly asked the Gdańsk strikers to intervene
with the government on behalf of KOR members who had been arrested or
imprisoned. But similar demands figured prominently at Szczecin, where intellectuals played no significant role. Fundamentally, workers' personal and collective experience of harassment and imprisonment was far more important than any
intellectual advocacy of civil liberties. Moreover, emotional attachments were
reinforced by practical considerations. A legal right to strike would remain extremely fragile unless it was buttressed by a supporting frame of civil rights.
Similarly, workers' insistence that censorship should be limited to clearly defined areas was prompted not only by a concern for free discourse, but also by a
realization that freedom of speech was essential for the solution of economic
problems, as well as for the existence of an independent labor movement. The
lesson of past experiences was clear: free trade unions could not operate effectively in a country where constitutional liberties were systematically violated.

The climate of struggle in 1980 strengthened the bonds, both rational and
emotional, linking workers to civil liberties. Yet the struggle against an authoritarian regime alone did not create worker sympathy for those rights. Such sympathy, encouraging the commitment to civil liberties, stemmed as well from the
traditional stress Polish workers placed on individual freedom and dignity, which
in turn might be linked with their Catholicism. The basic doctrinal teaching on
the inviolability of human rights was driven home for them by a long history of
state attempts to restrict the civil rights of the Church.[42] The younger generation
especially, less concerned than their parents with basic material and physical
security, was more critical of bureaucracy and authoritarian power and more
optimistic about the advantages of democratic influence and pressure from
below.[43] Their attachment to civil liberties seemed to be grounded as much in

democratic conviction as in libertarian sentiment. And it was this generation, which had come of age under what in official Communist jargon is called "developed socialism," that furnished most of the leaders in 1980. Their commitment to a democratic, freer, and more efficient society largely gave the movement its political thrust and momentum.

THE SIGNIFICANCE OF 1980

The protest movement of the summer of 1980 was certainly a distinctive Polish phenomenon: in an important sense it was part of a Polish pattern of politics aptly described as a "party congress every five years and a political catastrophe every ten."[44] It is nevertheless true that Poland's problems, while more visible and more urgent than those of her neighbors, are not different in kind, and that the key aspects of the 1980 movement bear directly on relations between workers and regime in all Communist states. Hence the anxiety displayed by Poland's neighbors throughout the period of "renewal," and hence, too, the chorus of approval that greeted Wojciech Jaruzelski's coup in December 1981.[45]

The fact that Solidarity was born in Poland—that the strikes of summer 1980 occured in Gdańsk and Gdynia—underlines the importance of political culture, tradition, experience, and leadership in shaping development. Polish Catholicism and nationalism, as noted earlier, greatly nourished the solidarity and popular support of the 1980 labor movement. Much of the determination of strikers stemmed, too, from a long tradition of successful—or, at least, impressive—protest actions. Moreover, the behavior of the Polish leadership demonstrated the role political management of discontent can play in generating and shaping the course of protest. Gierek's policies and responses are an object lesson for any Communist leader on how *not* to handle intellectual and worker dissent. The 1970s showed that alternating between permissiveness and halfhearted repression impairs the credibility of the regime and reinforces dissent. In a sense, the tough line on dissent typically taken by Communist regimes helps to explain the absence in other Communist countries of labor movements similar to Poland's.

To be sure, a tough line can backfire. The events of 1980 showed how coercion can radicalize labor protest and strengthen workers' espousal of civil liberties. Repression was the very stuff of which the memories and myths sustaining solidarity were made; shared suffering forged stronger links between workers and intellectual dissidents than abstract discussion. Furthermore, had the regime suppressed intellectuals or working-class radicals even more than it did, it would still have been unable to prevent the emergence of critical ideas and protest action among Polish workers. For what made Poland's labor movement so formidable and so significant was its self-mobilized nature. True, intellectual groups influenced some key leaders. But the young worker activists who came to the fore in Solidarity had educated themselves—and came to adopt radical positions—mainly by learning from experience.

This generation of workers, mostly in their twenties and thirties, provided both the vanguard and mainstay of the 1980 upheaval. And while they were obviously influenced by specifically Polish developments, they have a great deal in common with their counterparts in other industrially advanced Communist states. Thus the events of 1980 have more than a merely Polish significance. The protests, as mentioned earlier, were the first to come from the generation that had matured under "developed socialism." That they came from young workers, rather than students, reflected the greater impact of educational, economic, social, and political development on the industrial proletariat. And a number of traits characteristic of this new generation are just as evident among other East European workers as among Poles.

First, these workers, raised in the climate of post-Stalinism, tend to be less afraid of their rulers than their parents were. Second, better-educated and expecting greater job satisfaction than their parents, they are more concerned with improving and influencing their environment. And their concern reflects as well a greater attachment to basic socialist principles (of egalitarianism, for instance), which makes them more critical than were their parents of the defects of "real existing socialism." Third, as second-generation workers, with higher qualifications but fewer opportunities for upward mobility than their parents had, this generation tends to share a stronger identity and seeks improvement more through collective than through individual action. Finally, brought up on regime promises of plenty, they are not merely grateful for the welfare and security so appreciated by their elders; they expect more pay and a higher standard of living as well.

Until the mid-1960s, East European workers were preoccupied primarily with security and welfare benefits salvaged from the turmoil of "constructing socialism." As long as the regime provided such benefits—a welfare wage, fully secure employment, a lax work pace, and low differentials—workers were prepared to accept a passive political role within an authoritarian structure. The arrangement may be envisaged as an unwritten social compact, one on which the political stability of Communist states hinged and in large part continues to depend. Since the late 1960s, however, the growing need for economic efficiency has made such benefits increasingly costly to the state. Communist regimes have therefore attempted to change the terms, offering workers more money and goods in exchange for harder work and more flexibility on price levels and income differentials. Instead of accepting these new terms, workers throughout the region have added expectations of material improvement to their stock of welfare-security demands.[46] The situation is analogous to the growth rings that form a tree trunk. Security-welfare concerns are like the innermost ring of workers' concerns. The second ring comprises expectations of higher pay and better living standards. Polish developments show how a third ring—concern with economic efficiency—can emerge from the second and link up with a fourth—demands for genuine representation. Finally, the events of 1980 suggest that under certain conditions a fifth ring—concern for civil liberties—may further expand the scope of workers' demands.

Furthermore, the 1980 upheaval indicates the conditions under which such demands may be advanced by a labor movement. It forms a textbook illustration of how discontinuous and imbalanced economic development can foster a gap between expectations and performance. And while Poland may be in more dire economic straits than any other Communist country, its pattern of development is not atypical: in the late 1960s and early 1970s all Communist states went through a period of rapid growth accompanied by a new emphasis on consumerism, and all have suffered recently from slowing growth and stagnation. In varying degree, too, all have adopted "premature consumerism" as a strategy, though the slower general pace of growth affected expectations less dramatically in other countries than it did in Poland, just as more careful management in those countries has allowed them to avoid the depths comparable to the Polish recession. But the gap between popular expectations and economic performance exists. Typically, in East Germany, Czechoslovakia, and the USSR, that gap has been papered over by further increasing already massive price subsidies. Polish developments underline the dual danger of shoring up the social compact in this way: high subsidies perpetuate the workers' inflexibility on prices and encourage unrealistic expectations; they can also place an insupportable burden on the economy and thereby force the government to attempt sudden, large price increases with politically destabilizing consequences.

If economic parallels between Poland and the rest of the region are obvious, parallels connected with legitimacy and equality are even more important. It was these issues that focused the workers' resentment on the regime and that were the catalysts for transforming economic discontent into political protest. The workers' perception of distribution and social justice was linked to their attitudes toward the legitimacy of the regime. And while Poland has produced perhaps one of the most unequal of Communist societies, in recent years there has been a general crystallization of social stratification and an entrenchment of privilege throughout the entire East European Communist bloc. Rapid economic growth, Western imports, and second (that is, illegal) economies have swelled the conspicuous inequalities between the ruling bureaucrats and the workers, and have further vitiated the relationship between effort and reward. All the available evidence suggests that the kind of egalitarianism manifested in Poland is also part of the workers' ethos in other Communist countries. And such egalitarian principles of social justice can serve as the basis for a new labor identity and solidarity arising in opposition to privilege and corruption. Should Communist regimes allow the current *embourgeoisement* and growth of privilege to continue, they may find themselves confronted with ideological backlash of the most ironic type—workers pressing for implementation of principles of equality and the dignity of labor that they have "salvaged" from Marxism-Leninism.

The fact that after sixteen months of "renewal" Solidarity was throttled and the gains achieved by workers taken away from them by tanks and bayonets in no way invalidates the long-range implications examined in this essay. For the conditions that gave rise to the protest remain, and sooner or later the movement is bound to reassert itself, perhaps even more strongly than before. The pressure for greater representation and participation will continue, and attempts to reduce it by paltry concessions—thus making sure that it does not escalate once again into a direct challenge to the "leading role" of the party in all areas of public life— may prove even less viable, what with the workers' memory of astonishing political victories on the one hand and the inability of the government to offer any meaningful economic rewards on the other. Whatever steps the regime of

Jaruzelski (or his successor) may take, the lessons of 1980 will not be lost on it. And the lessons are that the new working class is a repository of revolutionary potential; that it is capable of organizing itself, formulating demands, and acting upon them; that it is at once the creature and adversary of the Communist system; above all, that it is no longer a pillar of continuity but a force of change.

7

THE CHURCH

Christopher Cviic

A picture taken in a Gdańsk shipyard on August 17, 1980, at the height of Poland's "summer of discontent," showed the workers on their knees receiving communion at an open-air mass at the shipyard gate. The picture, which was subsequently published in scores of newspapers and magazines throughout the non-Communist world, intrigued and puzzled many in the West. Even in traditionally Catholic countries like France or Italy, workers do not regularly go to church and would certainly never dream of having a mass said in their workplace, especially in the middle of a strike. Indeed, one of the Catholic Church's bitter regrets, regularly voiced since the nineteenth century, has been its loss of support among the working class. And where an attempt was made to retrieve the loss—France, for instance, in the 1940s and 1950s—the results were deeply disappointing. Idealistic worker-priests, sent out to win the working class back to the Church, failed; quite often, in fact, they ended up by becoming Marxist militants and leaving the Church themselves. Why, then, should the Polish Church, regarded by "progressive" Catholics as an embarrassing, ultraconservative anachronism in the era of reform ushered in by the 1962–65 Second Vatican Council, prove to be the sole exception? And why should it prove able not only to maintain the Polish workers' allegiance, but even to emerge as their close ally in the struggle for independent trade unions? As with much of Poland's current situation, the answer lies in history.

CHURCH AND NATION

The Catholic Church's involvement in Poland's peaceful revolution of 1980–81 is only the latest example of a long involvement in the country's affairs. In A.D. 966 Mieszko, Poland's first ruler, had himself baptized. The year before he had married Dubravka, a Bohemian princess, thus allying himself with a neighboring Slav country that had been Christian for some time. His elder son, Bolesław, conquered Silesia, Pomerania, and the Ukraine, founded the archdiocese of Gniezno, and secured political and ecclesiastical independence for Poland.

For centuries Poles considered their kingdom the outpost of Western Christianity and themselves the defenders of Christendom. But the identification between Poland and Catholicism became particularly close during the period between 1795 and 1918, when Poles lived divided under three empires, the German, Russian, and Austrian. This was an era of constant, sometimes violent, struggle to preserve the nation's identity, which the occupying powers were trying to suppress. Like the Catholic Church in Ireland, the Polish Church came to be regarded by the people as the chief guardian of the nation's culture and language and thus, also, of its identity. In the part of Poland that was under German rule, the Church opposed the policy of forcible Germanization. At the height of Bismarck's *Kulturkampf,* in 1874, the archbishop of Poznań, Cardinal Mieczysław Ledochowski, was imprisoned for opposing the introduction of German into religious instruction. Similar resistance was offered by the Church to the policy of systematic Russification pursued by the tsarist regime in its part of Poland.

Along with the rest of the population, the Church suffered reprisals by the occupying powers, which included the expulsion of religious orders and the confiscation of Church property. During this period, perhaps inevitably, the Polish Church learned that in time of political and social upheaval those institutions fared best—and stood the best chance of survival—that were most deeply rooted in the nation's history and traditions; in other words, that in the prevailing circumstances rigid conservatism might be a sounder recipe for survival and continuing effectiveness than supple reformism. From the partition period, too, the Church learned that it did not need temporal power to support and sustain it, and that it could even remain aloof from the secular rulers provided that it remained institutionally strong and in touch with the nation's feelings.

From 1918 to 1939, during the existence of the First Republic, the Church lost the support of a large part of the intelligentsia, which was put off by the Church's traditionalism, exclusivism, and (unfortunately, among large segments of both the hierarchy and lower clergy) intense anti-Semitic prejudice.[1] But it retained its hold over the masses, particularly the peasantry, who constituted the bulk of the Polish population. Relations between the Catholic Church and the state were not as close in independent Poland as they were, for example, in Salazar's Portugal or in Austria under Dollfuss and Schuschnigg. Nonetheless, the Church succeeded in maintaining a privileged position in Polish society, as much under the various governments in the early 1920s (when most bishops supported the extreme right-wing National Democratic Party) as under the so-called *sanacja* regime of Marshal Józef Piłsudski (1867–1935), which came to power in a military coup in 1926.[2] The close links between the Church and the secular authorities benefited both partners, but they contributed to the deep suspicion in which the hierarchy was held by many Polish liberals, alarmed by the pseudofascist direction in which the regime was heading.[3]

During World War II, the Catholic Church in Poland suffered together with the rest of the population. The hierarchy and the clergy found themselves, almost without exception, on the side of the national resistance movement. Under Nazi occupation thousands of Catholic priests and a number of bishops were imprisoned. About a third of all the clergy were executed by the Germans or died in concentration camps. A number of priests and seminarians studying for the priesthood fell in the 1944 Warsaw Uprising, in which the late Cardinal Stefan Wyszyński, then not yet a bishop, acted as a chaplain to the resistance forces.

Thus the Communist regime, which the Soviet Union installed in Poland in 1944, could hardly accuse the Catholic Church of collaboration. Furthermore, the country over which the new regime presided was more solidly Catholic than ever before. Interwar Poland had within its borders a number of minorities (Byelorussians, Germans, Jews, Ukrainians) who were for the most part also religious minorities—i.e., non-Catholics—and who formed a high percentage of the population. By the end of the war most of Poland's prewar Jewish population of 3,350,000—or 9.7 percent of the total population—had perished in Nazi death camps. Only some 50,000 had survived, with perhaps another quarter of a million in prewar Poland's eastern territories, which the Soviet Union annexed in 1945.[4] In the new territories that had belonged to Germany before the war, 3.6 million Germans had already fled or been evacuated by the Nazis before the arrival of the Soviet army in 1945. Another 3 million were expelled between 1945 and 1950. Their place was taken by the ethnic Poles repatriated from areas taken by the Soviet Union in the east. During the years between the wars more than 10 million of the Polish population had belonged to the national minorities. After 1945, they numbered only 500,000.

FRICTION AND COMBAT

In September 1945, the Polish government canceled the 1925 concordat with the Vatican on the grounds that the Vatican had refused to recognize the new regime and continued to support the government-in-exile. But the regime refrained from a direct confrontation with the Catholic Church, nor did the Church give it justification for such a confrontation. From the beginning the Church had accepted the establishment of Communist rule in Poland as one of those de facto situations that needed to be neither approved morally nor opposed openly. The Church avoided doctrinal disputes with the Marxists and did not object to major reforms such as the nationalization of industry and banks and the land reform. In foreign policy, the bishops warmly supported Poland's demand for official recognition by the West (and the Vatican) of its title to the former German territories in the west and north that Poland had held since 1945. Only once did the Church offer an open political challenge to the regime: a pastoral letter read from all the pulpits during the runoff to the January 1947 election. The letter urged all Catholics not to vote for any party that was against Christian ethics and the teaching of the Church—that is, the Communists. But a combination of electoral manipulation and police terror managed to ensure a Communist victory anyway, and so this Church gesture proved without effect.

As time went on, the Catholic Church, a large, independent organization with a network of parishes and educational establishments and with enormous moral authority in the country, became more and more of a hindrance to the Stalinist regime's plans for a complete monopoly in all spheres of public life. An excuse for a harsh crackdown was provided by a Vatican decree of July 1, 1949, excommunicating members, supporters, and followers of Communist parties.[5]

The document was carefully worded: it prescribed exclusion from the sacraments for "conscious and voluntary membership in the party, support for it, and the reading and dissemination of its publications." The harsher penalty of excommunication (on the ground of apostasy) was reserved for those Catholics who "espouse the doctrine of materialistic and anti-Christian communism." The government in Warsaw responded by passing, on August 5, 1949, a decree about liberty of conscience and political opinion; implementation of the Vatican decree in Poland became a crime punishable by law. This was followed by the suppression of a number of still-existing privileges: Church land, previously exempt from the land reform, was nationalized, and income from it was used by the state to pay the salaries of priests and bishops; Caritas, the Church's main charitable and welfare body, was removed from Church control; heavy censorship restricted Catholic publications to purely spiritual and ecclesiastical matters; religious instruction in schools was discontinued and chaplains were withdrawn from prisons, hospitals, and army units. A propaganda campaign was launched against the Vatican, depicting it as the Western "imperialists'" ally in the Cold War; and when the bishops refused to support regime-sponsored "peace campaigns" and to sign propaganda appeals against nuclear weapons, they, too, came under heavy attack.

To weaken the church from within, the regime made use of PAX, a body set up in September 1945 by Bolesław Piasecki to promote cooperation between Catholics and Communists in building socialism. Piasecki, who before World War II had led a small and extreme nationalist party (modeled on the Italian fascist party), during the war fought against the Germans and then the Russians. Captured by the Soviet army, he was sentenced to death by a Soviet court in February 1945. To general surprise, he was soon released; moreover, furnished with full official support and ample funds, he was allowed to launch PAX. The bishops' attitude toward Piasecki was from the start one of utmost reserve and mistrust, but in doctrinal matters he pursued an ultraorthodox line, thus forestalling any Church moves against him or his organization. By and by, he even managed to attract some support among the laity and clergy, both for PAX and for the regime-sponsored "patriotic priests'" association that he had also helped to launch. His main instrument of influence was a large publishing business, which issued a daily newspaper, a number of magazines, prayerbooks, and Bibles, as well as books by Polish authors and translations of well-known Western authors (including Graham Greene, Evelyn Waugh, Heinrich Böll, Giovanni Papini, François Mauriac, and Jacques Maritain) not otherwise available in Poland. He gathered around himself a number of able young people, most of whom were anxious to get on but were unwilling to join the party.[6]

On April 14, 1950, Catholic opinion in Poland and abroad learned with some surprise that an understanding (*porozumienie*) had been reached between the government and the Polish bishops.[7] The latter were now led by Monsignor Stefan Wyszyński, since the end of 1948 archbishop of Gniezno and Warsaw. In the document the Polish episcopate acknowledged the supreme authority of the state in all secular matters. In exchange the Church was guaranteed autonomy in the religious sphere and confirmation of existing privileges, notably the promise not to abolish religious instruction in schools, the continued existence of the

Catholic University of Lublin (the only one of its kind in postwar Eastern Europe), and the free and unfettered functioning of existing religious orders; article 5 of the document described the Pope as the "authoritative and supreme authority" in matters of "religion, morality, and church jurisdiction"; on other matters the bishops promised to be guided by "Polish *raison d'état.*" And the bishops further promised to instruct parish clergy in the countryside not to obstruct the "development of the cooperative movement"; they pledged themselves ready to punish under canon law priests guilty of "underground and antistate activities."

Both sides had tactical reasons for supporting the "understanding." The Church hoped to avert in Poland the sort of persecution that had led, for example, to the banning of religious orders in Czechoslovakia and Hungary. The regime probably wanted to neutralize the Church on the eve of the five-year plan and the onset of collectivization. But the uneasy truce ushered in by the 1950 deal lasted only a year and a half. After the October 1952 elections for the Sejm (Parliament) the anti-Church offensive began again. A number of priests were arrested on trumped-up spying charges. In February 1953 the regime arrogated to itself the right to make and unmake ecclesiastical appointments. In September a bishop and his three priests were given heavy sentences for alleged "antistate and anti-people's" activity. The episcopate, under heavy pressure from the government, condemned the four men, but Wyszyński—a cardinal by then but unable to travel to Rome to get the red hat—refused to join the condemnation, and was arrested and interned on September 29. By the end of 1953 all priests and bishops had taken the oath of loyalty to the state as required by the February decree.

TRUCE AND CONSEQUENCES

Three years later Wyszyński was released, and in December 1956 he negotiated a revised version of the 1950 agreement that nullified most of the 1953 changes.[8] The Church again had the right to administer its own affairs: the state reserved the right only to "influence"—that is, veto, but not make—Church appointments. Religious instruction in schools was reinstated, Church-appointed chaplains were allowed to return to prisons and hospitals. The government agreed to the appointment of five new bishops for Poland's western territories, and priests and nuns expelled from those territories were allowed to return. The bishop who had been sentenced for alleged "antistate" activity was released, his sentence quashed for "lack of proof." Wyszyński himself had been released from internment at the order of Władysław Gomułka, the man who only days before had himself been reinstated as party leader and whom the Church clearly regarded as a lesser evil than the earlier Stalinist group that had run Poland since 1949. The Church, like the rest of Poland, felt relief that a Soviet military intervention had been averted and that Poland had been spared Hungary's fate. This mood was reflected in a sermon the Cardinal gave in his cathedral in Warsaw in December 1956:

> We have had enough conflagrations in our fatherland. We want peace, both religious and social. We are tired of all these struggles and want to say to ourselves: the time

has come at last to work for ten years in peace; it is high time they stopped mustering armies of heroes and shedding blood on Polish soil; we should work in peace to create a better future, a better house for the fatherland. . . .[9]

Gomułka, for his part, was happy to have the Church's endorsement. He needed it. It was to that endorsement, tacit but clear, that he owed the massive majority obtained in the January 1957 election by the party-sponsored and controlled Front of National Unity. As a gesture toward the Church, the government allowed a group of Catholic intellectuals close to the hierarchy to be elected to the Sejm and to form their own group, Znak (The Sign). Znak began as a group of writers, academics, and journalists, former members of a prewar intellectual and student movement called Odrodzenie (Renaissance), which after the war grouped around the weekly *Tygodnik Powszechny* and the monthly *Znak,* both published in Kraków. Their inspiration was French Catholicism, particularly figures like Emmanuel Mounier, father of French "personalism" and editor of the influential monthly *Esprit,* and Jacques Maritain, the famous Thomist philosopher and author of widely read works on religion and politics.

Both Kraków publications had been closed down in 1953, after *Tygodnik Powszechny* had refused to publish an obituary of Stalin on its front page; both were placed under PAX, which then resumed their publication for three years without informing readers of the change in ownership. When Gomułka came back to power in 1956, former editors were allowed to resume publication of both *Znak* and *Tygodnik Powszechny.*

The group was also allowed to found Clubs of Catholic Intelligentsia (KIK) in five cities: Warsaw, Kraków, Poznań, Wrocław, and Toruń. The leading figures in the Znak parliamentary group were Jerzy Zawieyski, a Catholic playwright, and Stanisław Stomma, a lawyer who had been barred from practicing during the Stalinist era. They were joined by two former PAX members— Tadeusz Mazowiecki and Janusz Zabłocki—who broke with Piasecki when the Vatican formally banned PAX in 1955. Znak's financial support came from the sale of its publications and from income provided by a small firm called Libella, producing cosmetics and haberdashery, that the government allowed it to run. Under Gomułka, PAX lost much of the influence it had enjoyed under the earlier regime, not least because it had associated itself, during the period of party infighting, with the anti-Gomułka Natolin group in the party. But even after 1956 it was allowed to continue its activities, a fact that many Poles attributed to PAX's strong Soviet backing, dating to the time Piasecki spent in a Soviet prison in 1945 and the deal he was presumed to have made with the KGB at that time.

By 1958 the pendulum had swung the other way, and the political truce between the party and the Church was at an end. Strict censorship was reimposed and all information about the Church eliminated. The authorities began to accuse parish priests of using the pulpit for anti-Communist propaganda. In July 1958 the police raided the Jasna Góra monastery in Częstochowa, Poland's main national shrine, and claimed to have found political pamphlets; the monastery's prior was arrested and given a suspended prison sentence. Heavy taxes, which parishes were unable to pay, were reimposed. In the western territories the government refused to hand over to the Church ecclesiastical buildings, instead charging the Church rent for their use. Local authorities refused to permit the building of churches in large new housing estates. And in 1961, religious instruction in schools was made illegal.

The Church responded vigorously when in 1961 the government issued an order requiring the new catechism centers, to which religious instruction had been transferred, to register with the authorities. Cardinal Wyszyński forbade parish priests to do it. In the parishes, local congregations often attacked tax collectors. Fierce resistance was offered to demolition gangs sent to raze churches built without permission. In 1957 the Cardinal launched a nine-year campaign in preparation for the approaching millennium of Polish Christianity in 1966. The novena for each year until the millennium was given its special theme, and The great millennium novena culminated in 1966 in the renewal of vows of loyalty made in 1656 by King John II Casimir to God and the Virgin Mary after a handful of Polish soldiers managed to defend the monastery at Częstochowa against Swedish invaders. Every diocese and every parish was involved in this vast evangelical effort, whose principal feature was a series of "festivals of faith" held throughout the country to strengthen the link between patriotism and faith. The government tried to sabotage the Cardinal's program by, among other things, staging a rival program of celebrations of the "millennium of Polish statehood." Not infrequently, Church and state celebrations took place in the same place on the same day—as, for example, happened in Poznań on April 17, 1966.

Relations between the Catholic Church and the government had already been exacerbated when in November 1965 a group of Polish bishops attending the Vatican Council sent a "letter of reconciliation" to the German bishops, inviting them to the millennium celebrations in Poland the following year. The authorities attacked the Church for encroaching on their preserve—foreign policy. Cardinal Wyszyński's passport was impounded. And the government continued to make political capital out of the Vatican's reluctance to give its official blessing to Poland's title to former German territories in the west and the north, recognition the Polish Church had pressed for ever since 1945. (Although Pope John XXIII had, more than ten years earlier, acknowledged Poland's right to these territories, the Vatican did not act officially until June 1972, after the West German Bundestag had ratified the Polish–West German treaty of December 1970 in May 1972.)

TRIUMPH OVER ADVERSITY

Church-state confrontation continued throughout the 1960s right up to the time of Gomułka's fall from power in December 1970. Almost certainly, it was the Church and not the regime that benefited from the clash. Years of Communist rule had generated a variety of political, social, and economic discontents. The country's continuing subjection to Soviet domination and visible Soviet military presence were constant irritants. The increasingly authoritarian way in which the regime continued to exercise power—especially after the gains and promises of the "Polish October" of 1956—bred frustration and hostility. Private farmers resented first of all the collectivization of agriculture and then, once it had been scrapped by Gomułka, the authorities' neglect of and discrimination against the private sector in agriculture. Almost all Poles resented being bombarded by official propaganda in a press that hardly ever told them anything about what was really going on in their country. *2 / 7381*

In this sort of situation the Church, simply by virtue of being there—an organization independent of government control and engaged in a conflict with the government—absorbed all these discontents and became an outlet for them. At the very least, the fact that it did not tell lies, though it could not always say what it wanted, made people listen to it.

But the Church, under Wyszyński's astute and imaginative leadership, became more than a mere outlet for the nation's growing opposition to the Communist regime. Through its catechism program it maintained its influence on the religious and moral development of generation after generation of children and youngsters. It imbued them with ethical norms and invited them to use these as a yardstick by which to judge their society—and their government. In other Communist-ruled countries, where the Church has lacked access to the young or has, for historical reasons, been isolated from large sections of the population, growing revulsion against communism, its corruption, authoritarianism, and, above all, its systematic lying, gradually turned into cynical conformism or resignation, followed by internal withdrawal. In Poland, because the majority of the people identified themselves with the Church's traditional values of patriotism and integrity, its moral authority with the population grew steadily.

At the same time the authority of the regime declined, climaxing in the student demonstrations of March 1968 and the ensuing vicious crackdown. The alienation between the ruling party and the intelligentsia was almost complete. Disillusioned intellectuals, party members and those outside the party alike, began to look at the Church with new eyes—not simply as another totalitarian institution, poised to gobble them and their souls, but as a valuable source of inspiration and, increasingly, an ally in the struggle against the ruling dictatorship. The fact that the Church did not appear as a direct participant in the power struggle enhanced its moral position in the eyes of the population.

The Catholic Church's involvement in the events of 1968 was modest. On March 11, the five Znak deputies in the Sejm—Konstanty Lubieński, Tadeusz Mazowiecki, Stanisław Stomma, Janusz Zabłocki, and Jerzy Zawieyski—protested to the prime minister, Józef Cyrankiewicz, against the treatment of the students by the authorities and demanded "steps to relax the political situation," above all by "putting an end to brutal police action."[10] Their parliamentary "interpolation" was rejected a month later (though the constitution prescribed an answer within seven days). On March 21, Cardinals Wyszyński and Wojtyła wrote to Cyrankiewicz on behalf of the episcopate demanding the release of arrested students, an end to "drastic" methods of investigation and punishment, and more truthful reporting rather then "tendentious expositions" in the press.[11] "A truncheon is never an argument in a free society," wrote the cardinals; "it rouses the worst associations and mobilizes public opinion against the existing order." Their letter was ignored: a few days after receiving it, the government launched a wide-ranging purge of institutions of higher learning. (It should be noted, however, that on the subject of the anti-Semitic campaign, which had been going on since the 1967 Arab-Israeli war and had been intensified after March 1968, the official Church remained silent, regarding it as a "quarrel among Communists.")

The informal alliance formed in March 1968 between the Catholic Church and Poland's opposition was further strengthened when publications close to the Church helped dissidents who had been forbidden to write in party-controlled publications. *Tygodnik Powszechny,* the weekly organ of Znak (edited by Jerzy Turowicz) and *Więź,* an intellectual monthly (edited for the Warsaw Club of Catholic Intelligentsia since 1958 by Tadeusz Mazowiecki) opened their columns to the opposition intellectuals, some of Jewish descent, and allowed them to write under pseudonyms.[12] Adam Michnik, who as a student played a leading part in the March 1968 demonstrations and was much reviled in the official press, summed up this new, more favorable view of the Catholic Church by the Polish left in a book published abroad several years later. He wrote: "For many years now, the Catholic Church in Poland has not been on the side of the powers-that-be, but has stood out in defense of the oppressed. The authentic enemy of the left is not the Church, but totalitarian power, and in this battle the Church plays a role which it is impossible to overestimate."[13]

THE CHURCH ON THE RAMPARTS

Subsequent events have confirmed the validity of Michnik's judgment. And the Church's role as champion of those battling for human and civil rights developed gradually after that first modest intervention in 1968. The path followed by the Church was not, to be sure, without its zigzags and contradictions. After the riots in Poland's northern ports in December 1970, in which the security forces killed a (still-disputed but certainly large) number of workers, the bishops issued a strong statement that was read in the churches on January 1, 1971. The nation's life, it said, could not "develop in an atmosphere of intimidation." It upheld "the right to freedom of conscience and freedom of religious life, together with full normalization of relations between the Church and the state; the right of freely shaping the culture of one's own nation, according to the spirit of the Christian principles of the coexistence of people; the right to social justice, expressed in fulfilling just demands; the right to truth in social life, to information in accordance with the truth, and to free expression of one's views and demands; the right to material conditions which ensure a decent existence of the family, and of each individual citizen." The statement also supported the citizen's right not to be "insulted, harmed or persecuted in any way."[14]

At the same time Church authorities went out of their way to demonstrate to the new Gierek regime that they were not seeking a confrontation. Indeed, they went so far as to call upon the workers to go back to work and preserve Poland's "social peace." On March 3, 1971, Cardinal Wyszyński and Prime Minister Piotr Jaroszewicz held a meeting that received a good bit of publicity in the regime press. On the one hand, regime representatives reiterated their desire for "full normalization of relations with the Catholic Church," and the Church was granted a few permits to build new churches. On the other hand, circulation of nonregime Catholic papers continued to be severely restricted, censorship remained as strict as ever, seminarians continued to be called up for military service, and efforts to cause new splits in the Catholic ranks in Poland and between the Polish Church and the Vatican were intensified.

The Church, while fending off these new pressures, did not forget the need to widen its support among the people. In 1969, a festival of religious songs called Sacrosong was started, attracting large crowds of young people. The early 1970s saw a further strengthening of the so-called Oases movement, which had begun in 1954 as a series of summer retreats for young people, held by priests. Eventually the movements cam to embrace not just schoolchildren and university students but also parents. By the mid-1970s a network of local groups had been established throughout Poland. Small groups met each week for prayer and Bible study while also helping parish priests with their tasks. These activities brought the Church into frequent conflicts with the authorities. Heavy fines were imposed on organizers of summer retreats and on farmers who had given permission for their land to be used for these camps. Hundreds of churches were built without permission throughout Poland by local people. After the regime refused to give out building permits, violent clashes occurred. The Church also clashed with the government over the government's plans for educational reorganization, which would have resulted in children in rural areas being bused to large schools in district centers and kept there all day, thus missing religious instruction in their parishes.[15]

Two events sealed the Church-dissident alliance in the mid-1970s. The first was the regime's proposal to amend the 1952 constitution. The proposed amendments were to spell out the "leading role of the party," make specific reference to Poland's "unshakable and firm bond" with the Soviet Union, and make citizens' rights conditional on their "honest fulfillment of duties." Widespread opposition ensued. The Church made its specific objections to these amendments in the form of two memorandums to the goverment in January 1976.[16] Cardinal Wyszyński and Cardinal Wojtyła attacked the constitutional proposals in separate sermons. On February 10, 1976, the proposed amendments were, nevertheless, adopted by the Sejm with minor modifications, but the leader of the Znak group, Stanisław Stomma, abstained. His punishment was to be struck off the list for the next election in May. The constitutional debate provoked a split in Znak. Some of its leading members like Mazowiecki had already left the parliamentary group before (or had been eased out). In 1976, after Stomma's resignation, the control of the group passed completely into the hands of progovernment figures.

In another move calculated to demoralize those members of Znak who refused to toe the government line, control of the private firm that financed many of the movement's activities (including its publications) was handed over to the proregime faction, which came to be known as Neo-Znak. This group, led by Count (!) Konstanty Lubieński, was also given the premises of the KIK in Poznań. In September 1977, after Lubieński's death, Neo-Znak's leadership passed to Janusz Zabłocki, head of the (similarly proregime) Center for Social Studies (ODiSS). In December 1977, Zabłocki was elected to the presidium of the party's main umbrella organization, the Front of National Unity (FJN). But supporters of the old Znak rallied around the remaining KIK clubs (such as the one in Warsaw) that had not been taken over. *Tygodnik Powszechny* and *Więź* continued to come out and, amazingly, to maintain an independent line. The authorities, which had by that time become preoccupied with other challenges, left them relatively undisturbed. Meanwhile, Neo-Znak continued to be used for propaganda exercises aimed at Western Catholics.

The other event that brought the Church and the new opposition in Poland even closer together was the wave of unrest that followed the introduction of higher prices for meat and other products in June 1976. On July 16 the bishops appealed to the authorities not to dismiss workers who had demonstrated to protect themselves and their families against exorbitant price increases—increases that were introduced (and subsequently rescinded) by the government.[17] In a sermon on September 26, Cardinal Wyszyński said that it was "painful when workers must struggle for their rights from a workers' government." In a sermon on December 7, he said that he had a list of thirty-four workers who had been "brutally manhandled" by the police while under arrest.[18] On November 28, collections were held in Catholic churches in Poland to help workers who had been arrested or dismissed, as well as their families. On April 14, 1977, the Cardinal referred in a sermon to the "overwhelming tragedy of exhaustion suffered by our miners, who, under pressure from propaganda machinery, have hardly one free Sunday in a month, as not until after three consecutive Sundays have been used for mining might the fourth turn out to be free."[19]

The government, sensing its growing weakness, sought to appease the Church by concessions. More permits were issued, for example, for new churches to be built. The government shelved its 1973 plan for an educational reform that the church took such exception to. Seeking to broaden his political support with Catholics at home, First Secretary Edward Gierek called on the Pope in the Vatican on December 1, 1977. A month or so earlier he had met—for the first time—Cardinal Wyszyński and had assured him that the party and the government wanted to preserve religious freedom. But the Church refused to be persuaded into silence and passivity by these gestures and the minor concessions that had accompanied them.

Throughout 1978, the bishops hammered at the government over the issue of censorship, which they bluntly called a "weapon of the totalitarian state." The bishops offered their support to the Flying University, a system of unofficial lectures on Polish history, religion, politics, literature, and other subjects that many top Polish intellectuals regarded as being taught in a partial, incomplete, or downright mendacious way at the state universities. In Kraków, Cardinal Wojtyła allowed city churches to be used for these lectures, which the police did their best to disrupt when the lectures were held in private homes. Cardinal Wyszyński defended these lectures to the government.

THE POPE'S DIVISIONS

Just as the authorities were preparing another major offensive against the dissidents and the Flying University, news came on October 16, 1978, that Cardinal

Wojtyła had been elected Pope. The election of a Polish Pope completely transformed the religious and political situation in the country. The Catholic Church's
prestige was enhanced, and public interest increased dramatically. Religious
processions and pilgrimages attracted even larger crowds than before. Catholic
believers became even bolder than in the past. A public petition to allow the
Church access to radio and television attracted nearly a million signatures. All
this while morale in the ruling party slumped and the credibility of Gierek's
regime was further eroded by serious economic problems, notably shortages of
food and other consumer goods.

The Pope's visit to Poland in June 1979 had a tremendous impact not just
in the religious but also in the political arena. "The *pays réel* has suddenly
emerged into the open and shown its new-found pride and sense of identity," a
Catholic editor in Kraków told me (I was in Poland at that time), "while the *pays
légal* looked on with chagrin and dismay." Stalin's old question about the Pope's
divisions was quite openly and accurately answered (for Poland at least) in a
hand-painted poster I saw on the railings beneath the altar at which Pope John
Paul II celebrated mass at the Jasna Góra monastery in Częstochowa. The poster
offered the Pope "3,000 divisions of our beating hearts." The visit was a triumph of organization for unofficial Poland, because order was kept in
Częstochowa and elsewhere, and very efficiently, by men from the parishes; the
militia looked on. It was during the Pope's visit that non-Communist Poland
learned its true strength and at the same time gained new recruits. I remember
seeing in my hotel in Kraków a group of Communist officials who, thinking that
they were unobserved, drank the Pope's health at the moment of his arrival in the
city.

The visit was, in a true sense, a dress rehearsal for the events of 1980. The
content of the Pope's message to Poland was well understood, despite the fact
that he went out of his way to avoid a direct confrontation with the regime. To
the workers of his old archdiocese, who came to greet him on June 9, 1979, at
Mogiła, near the new industrial town of Nowa Huta, the Pope said pointedly that
Christ would never approve that "man be considered merely as a means of
production." (Indeed, ever since the first strikes occurred in July 1980, the Pope
has continued to voice his approval for the independent trade union Solidarity
and to stress that Poland must be allowed to solve its own problems—that is,
without Soviet intervention. In January 1980 he received a Solidarity delegation
led by Lech Wałęsa amid signs of total support.)

At home in Poland several months before the summer strikes, the bishops kept
urging the government toward a more liberal policy. In their statement on February 29, 1980, they asserted that only "through free organizations and a free
exchange of opinions is it possible to achieve much-needed national unity." The
workers, the statement went on, "have the right to form their own organizations,
and social and economic problems should not be solved by just one group."[20]
On May 7, the bishops called for an end to the "recently intensified reprisals"
against people holding nonconformist views and demanded a "climate of social
peace and mutual trust" between the authorities and the society at large. The
bishops noted a recent increase in the number of "incidents of police repression," which, they said, hampered efforts to achieve social peace and exacerbated existing tensions.

On August 15, 1980, Cardinal Wyszyński made his first indirect reference to the strikes in a sermon in Częstochowa. He said that Poles were "asking for bread in a tactful way, in a way full of dignity." He also prayed for the "spirit of freedom" and the "right of self-decision." Two days later, on August 17, he delivered a sermon in which he said that the strikers were seeking "legitimate civil freedoms" and also appealed for "calm and honest work." (The regime distorted his words by quoting them selectively and out of context.) To clear any misunderstandings caused by Wyszyński's August 17 sermon (and another one he gave a few days later)—especially by his appeal to workers to work, which was widely perceived as a concession to the authorities—the episcopate issued a long statement on August 27 that declared that the observance of "inalienable rights of the nation" was a "precondition for the return of social peace and order." They also called for a number of freedoms along the lines of those demanded by the workers, even including a right to independent trade unions. The statement, in analyzing the root of Poland's crisis, pointed to grave errors made over the years by Poland's rulers.[21]

On August 25, seven intellectuals, including Catholic laymen Tadeusz Mazowiecki, editor of *Więź*; Bohdan Cywiński, former editor of *Znak* magazine in Kraków; and Andrzej Wielowieyski, head of the Warsaw Club of Catholic Intelligentsia, flew to Gdańsk to advise the strikers on legal, economic, and other matters and to help them draft agreements with the government. The local Catholic intelligentsia club in Gdańsk was turned into an advisory center, providing legal, financial, organizational, and technical advice to people planning to set up independent trade unions in their workplaces. The same happened in other major towns. In an interview with *Le Monde* on September 9, 1980, Mazowiecki described his own and his colleagues' role as follows: "If we have helped them at all, it was in giving expression to what was within them so as to find the balancing point between emotion and reason. That is the role which the independent intelligentsia should continue to play." On December 8, Solidarity's National Coordinating Commission appointed Mazowiecki editor of the union's weekly paper, *Tygodnik Solidarność,* whose first issue appeared on April 3. Bohdan Cywiński, another Catholic activist, became one of the two deputy editors.

A NEW CHAPTER—AND NEW TRIALS

A discussion of the role of the Church in contemporary Polish history, especially during the events immediately preceding and following the fateful summer of 1980, is incomplete without at least a few remarks about the position of the Church during Poland's "renewal" and some speculations about its role following Jaruzelski's military *Putsch* of December 13, 1981.

First, a brief look at the proregime Catholics. Clearly, they were significantly affected by the Pope's visit in 1979, the political upheaval sparked off by the strikes of 1980, and above all by the emergence and spectacular growth of Solidarity. The vicissitudes of PAX are particularly interesting. Sometime after the death of Bolesław Piasecki, the organization's founder, in January 1979, his successor, Ryszard Reiff, began to seek a rapprochement with the Catholic hierarchy. In June 1980, on the eve of the first wave of strikes, he was received by Cardinal Wyszyński. In September 1980, PAX came out in support of Solidarity and of economic and political reforms in general. A month later, four top members of the movement, all glaringly proregime figures, were removed from PAX's presidium. The PAX daily, *Słowo Powszechne,* got a new editor and became a firm proponent of the "renewal," publishing, throughout the many months of freedom, some of the most illuminating accounts of and commentaries on the burgeoning struggle between the unions and the government. PAX's role up to December 1981 was markedly in contrast to its role in previous upheavals—in 1956, when it tried to prevent the return of Gomułka by playing on the fears of Soviet intervention, or in 1968, when it was in the vanguard of the anti-intellectual and anti-Semitic campaign.

However, martial law and the ensuing "new reality" put an end to this salutary chapter in PAX's history. Ryszard Reiff, who in the autumn of 1981 was indefatigable in calling for a new "national accord" between the party and society, was dismissed from his position, as were those of his closest followers. A new leadership took over, throwing its full support to Jaruzelski's regime. Thus once again PAX resumed its traditional role as a loyal defender of the status quo.

As for Neo-Znak, it was never infected too much by the "renewal," and indeed was manipulated by the regime in time-honored fashion. In January 1981, with the explicit backing of the party, a new organization, calling itself the Polish Catholic Social Union (PZKS), came into being, under the leadership of Janusz Zabłocki. It comprised Neo-Znak and ODiSS (which had meanwhile changed its name to the Christian Social Association—ChSS). The PZKS began to form its own Catholic intelligentsia clubs, with the transparent aim of rivaling and splitting the independent (and steadily mushrooming) KIKs. This diversionary move of the regime, however, proved ineffectual: while PAX, as a result of having embraced the "renewal," attained a new credibility, Zabłocki's group remained altogether marginal, as much in the eyes of society at large as in those of the Church. The fact that one of PZKS's leaders, Jerzy Ozdowski, received a ministerial portfolio in the spring of 1981 did not help matters. True, Zabłocki, a Sejm deputy, manifested an altogether unusual degree of defiance by protesting the imposition of martial law. However, the PZKS as such soon followed in PAX's footsteps, thus further forfeiting its claim to speak on behalf of Poland's Catholics.

The position of the Church, of course, was quite different. On September 7, 1980, Solidarity received its formal blessing from Cardinal Wyszyński during a visit paid to him by Lech Wałęsa. The Church played a direct and active role in the campaign for the recognition of the farmers' union, Rural Solidarity, whose registration was finally allowed by the government in April 1981. According to the Cardinal's close legal adviser (also a Catholic layman), Dr. Romuald Kukołowicz, the Cardinal personally played a prominent role in bringing about Rural Solidarity, not least at top-level meetings with the new first secretary, Stanisław Kania, and Prime Minister Jaruzelski. He also dispatched Kukołowicz to three important centers of farmers' agitation for a union to assist them in negotiating agreements with the government. The bishops' conference issued no less than three statements in February and March 1981, all mentioning approvingly the demands for a farmers' union.

The Church also found itself directly involved in negotiations to settle the particularly difficult industrial strike in Bielsko-Biała in February 1981 (which involved workers' allegations of official corruption and industrial mismanagement by local leaders whose dismissal they demanded). An agreement was finally reached, with three Catholic bishops (including Bishop Bronisław Dąbrowski from Warsaw) acting as guarantors. But on the whole the Church showed throughout the first year of Poland's peaceful revolution a preference for keeping some distance from day-to-day developments, a preference that has been continued by Archbishop Józef Glemp, Wyszyński's long-time secretary who, after the latter's death in May 1981, became his successor. Lech Wałęsa, too, has repeatedly stressed the need for the Church and the union to follow their separate paths. A document prepared for distribution to foreign unions stated clearly that Solidarity "identified itself with no ideology and no religion." The document continued:

> It is true that, among the Union's symbols, those of the Catholic religion are especially prominent. This reflects the great respect which our society, most of whose members are Catholics, has for the moral authority of the Church. But the Union itself, as a social movement, is secular. It acknowledges Christian values to the foundation of European culture, but it is not politically related to the Church nor does it consider the Catholic social doctrine to be its program.[22]

A similar formulation is contained in the "programmatic declaration on national culture" adopted at Solidarity's first national congress in Gdańsk in October 1981 (and published in its weekly paper on October 23):

> Mindful of the fact that Christianity introduced us to our wider homeland, Europe; that Christianity has crucially determined the shape and substance of Polish national culture for over 1,000 years; that in the most tragic times our nation has found support in the Catholic Church; that our ethics have been determined primarily by Christianity; and, finally, that Catholicism is the living faith of most Poles, we take the view that the process of national education must make honest and suitably extensive provision for the role and place of Christianity and the Church in the history of Poland and of the world. At the same time, we declare ourselves in favor of the state's neutrality toward world views in all domains, above all in that of national education and culture. We view this neutrality as guaranteeing the tolerance in which our forefathers took pride.

An enlightened view, completely in accord with the thinking of modern French Catholicism, which has had a deep influence on the Polish Catholic intellectuals active as Solidarity's advisers. Also (one hopes) a final break with the old view that "a Pole is a Catholic," an identification that has so long been abhorrent to all liberal spirits in Poland, Catholic no less than non-Catholic.

So much—in brief—for the positions of Solidarity and the Church during the "renewal." But what of the future? An important clue may well have been provided by Father Józef Tischner, a Kraków theologian and close friend of the Pope, who attended the Solidarity congress in September–October 1981. In a BBC interview conducted on November 12, 1981, Tischner summed up the view of the Church in the following words:

> The workers in Poland are a great force and we know why: their number and their determination. But this force could also be a blind one. The Church gives the workers not only courage and self-confidence in crucial moments—it is also the voice of reason. Take, for instance, the Solidarity congress. People were nervous and exhausted after discussions lasting 12 or 13 hours. The next morning would start with a mass which would calm the atmosphere and put things into perspective. The authorities see the creative and moderating role of the church. This bestows great responsibility upon the priest. He should not influence the discussions or the decisions of Solidarity, but he can point out the context in which the discussions are taking place. If, for instance, you tell the Solidarity congress that a similar gathering took place at the end of the 18th century, and that it led to the creation of the famous Polish constitution of May 3, 1791, then the participants feel a sense of dignity and of historical continuity. And it is precisely the Church that can communicate this sense of history, not only because of its own thousand-year-old history, which coincides with that of the country as a whole, but also because our Marxists often behave as if world history began with the October 1917 revolution. And it is this sense of belonging to great traditions that can be so uplifting.[23]

If liberalization had been allowed to continue and the achievements of 1980–81 had been consolidated within the framework of the rule of law and a measure of multiparty democracy (under whatever name), the Church itself would have been affected. Differences within the Church itself, among the bishops and also between some of the bishops and some of the lower clergy, which have always existed but have been largely suppressed in the interest of unity in the face of a common enemy, would have emerged more clearly. A "peacetime" Church would have been able to afford to relax—something Cardinal Wyszyński's "Church in the trenches" could not. But the differences would have revolved principally around theological, moral, and generally Church-oriented issues. Above all, it is unlikely that the Church would have succumbed to the temptation of a more direct and formal involvement in politics. For by now the essential principle of modern Catholic pluralism—that it is the Church's business to propagate its teachings and to urge believers to act upon them, without telling them exactly how and what policies to choose—has been widely accepted in Poland. By the same token, society and, in the first place, the free trade unions, while maintaining their spiritual links with the Church and openly acknowledging their debt to its social doctrines, would probably have continued to shape their daily policies and strategies quite independently of the Church. This certainly was the pattern throughout 1980–81, when Solidarity incorporated the rituals and symbols of Catholicism on important and solemn occasions (e.g., strikes, demonstrations, and formal gatherings), at the same time basing its course of action on what it felt were pragmatic considerations, frequently even against the advice occasionally proffered by the priests or members of the Church hierarchy.

But liberalization has not been allowed to continue; and among the hopes that were so brutally crushed by Jaruzelski's troops on December 13, 1981, was also the hope that the Church would finally be allowed to assume a more relaxed and "peacetime" position. Instead, the Church has been forced to come out "from the rear" and revert to its traditional role of protector and defender of the nation. At the same time, the regime's efforts to enlist the Church's support in establishing "law and order" also increased—with mixed results. It is obviously impossible to predict precisely what policies the Church will pursue in its attempt to remain at one with the fundamental aspirations of a defiant society while also seeking (as it has done throughout the ages) to attain social peace and national reconciliation. One thing, however, is certain: in the new chapter in the history of Poland the role of the Church will no doubt be prominently inscribed.

8

ANTI-SEMITISM: A TRUSTY WEAPON

Tadeusz Szafar

On Sunday, March 8, 1981, more than 3,000 Polish students and young intellectuals gathered on the Warsaw University quadrangle to commemorate the thirteenth anniversary of a singularly traumatic experience in the recent annals of Polish history: the so-called March events of 1968, when demonstrations by young people demanding greater intellectual freedom were brutally suppressed by the police and other armed representatives of "People's Poland." The 1981 meeting was cosponsored by the independent student associations of Warsaw University and of the Academy of Catholic Theology, and by the independent self-governing labor union Solidarity. While the authorities' tolerance of the meeting illustrated the distance traveled by the country since the summer of 1980, the joint student-worker sponsorship seemed to suggest that the split between the two social groups most interested in changing the status quo in Poland was by then becoming a thing of the past.

The official Communist newspaper, *Trybuna Ludu,* reporting the mass rally in a two-sentence item on a back page, devoted twice as much space to a rival political event taking place simultaneously in another part of the city. Several hundred elderly men gathered near the former building of the Ministry of Public Security to "recall violations of legality during the so-called cult of personality, when many citizens had been victimized." It was pointed out, *inter alia,* that an active part in those earlier occurrences had also been played by some people who later became teachers at Warsaw University and had been expelled from the institution in 1968.[1]

From the same news item, widely distributed by the official Polish wire service PAP, readers learned for the first time about an organization that called itself the Grunwald Patriotic Union. The name was startling, though not chosen at random: in 1410, in the battle of Grunwald (also known in German and Western historiography as the battle of Tannenberg), allied Polish and Lithuanian armies had inflicted a crushing defeat upon superior forces of the Teutonic Knights. In the twentieth century, half a millennium later, this medieval feat of Polish arms had been seized upon by the jingoistic National Democratic Party (*endecja*) as a vivid symbol of pan-Slavic solidarity in the face of the ever-present German threat—for some obscure reason enhanced by the even greater danger perceived to be posed by the Jewish ethnic and religious minority. The anti-German, pro-Russian Grunwald symbolism was later usurped by Polish Communists at a time when, with Stalin's blessing, they were trying hard to project a "patriotic," nationalistic image. The anti-Semitic component of this image was then deliberately dimmed, though never totally suppressed.

USES OF THE PAST

The World War II Holocaust wiped out, at once and forever, the largest and most vital Jewish community in Europe, but oddly enough it did not eradicate anti-Semitism in Poland. Of three and a half million Jews who had lived there before the war, some three million perished in Nazi extermination camps (and in the Soviet *gulags*); over 90 percent of the survivors preferred to leave their native country, associated in their minds not only with an unprecedented genocide but also (though hardly of its own volition) with a new social system, hostile to Jewish spiritual values and alien to their traditional way of life. By the late 1950s, the Jewish minority in Poland—or, rather, Poles of Jewish origin—dwindled to some thirty to forty thousand—1 percent of their prewar number, one-tenth of 1 percent of the country's population. Political anti-Semitism, however, by itself a phenomenon fairly recent in Polish and European history, had not disappeared or even faded in proportion.[2] On the contrary, under Communist rule it gradually acquired respectability and legitimacy, never enjoyed before outside the *endecja*. It became, as a matter of fact, the choice method of camouflaging internecine struggles within the ruling party. Even the physical absence of Jews from the Polish scene did not materially change the picture. In this respect it can be said that Poland has indeed been unique.

In the early postwar years, when the situation in the Soviet-occupied, Communist-ruled country verged on civil war, political anti-Semitism was openly resorted to by some extreme right-wing opponents of the regime. The traditional stereotype of "Żydo-komuna"—an almost untranslatable invective lumping together Jews and Communists—which was then still tacitly cherished by parts of the Church hierarchy, deliberately exploited (and exaggerated) the presence of a handful of Jewish Communists, fellow travelers, or just survivors in the higher and middle levels of the party, state, and police apparatus, and the Soviets, too, sometimes showed an ostentatious preference to people deemed unsusceptible to the lures of Polish nationalism.[3] Even so, some elements of the Communist apparat were inclined to make use of anti-Jewish prejudices, endemic in the most backward strata of the population. The whole truth has not yet been revealed about the instigators of the 1946 Kielce pogrom, when a rumor that the local minuscule Jewish community had planned to kill a Gentile boy in order to use his blood in the baking of Passover matzohs—that old medieval "blood libel"—led to an orgy of mass murder.[4] And only Stalin's death stopped the slide to overt Communist anti-Semitism, already heralded by the Slánský trial in Czechoslovakia and by the Kremlin "doctors' plot." Poland seemed next in line for a purge.[5]

The first major attempt to use political anti-Semitism openly, as an argument in the power struggle inside the party, ended in dismal failure. In 1956 the so-called Natolin faction (named after the country house near Warsaw where it would meet), denounced by its antagonists as Stalinist but in fact composed of ardent followers of Khrushchev (and in turn enjoying his wholehearted support), tried, but managed neither to seize control nor to bar the way to Gomułka's return to power. This happened despite (or, perhaps, because of) the extensive use the Natolinists had made of anti-Semitism in their oral propaganda: at that time the tightly controlled mass media were dominated by opponents of the Natolin faction, and were thus virtually inaccessible to it. In fact, that was the one and only period in the pre-1980 history of Communist-ruled Poland when the press, reflecting the prevailing mood of the population, not only advocated reforms of the system, but even waged open warfare against anti-Semitism in its reshaped, Communist version. The Natolin insistence on "national regulation of cadres" (i.e., a purge of Jewish activists) and on spurious "Jewish" identification of their antagonists from the Puławy faction (also named after the locality where its members would meet)—in particular those who had spent the war years in the Soviet Union and had played an active role in imposing a Stalinist rule of terror in Poland—misfired. It found some echo among the recently promoted party, state, and police apparatchiks, but next to none in the wider public: whatever bore the "made in USSR" stamp, as the Natolin-style anti-Semitism obviously did, was deeply suspect. All the cases of allegedly spontaneous outbreaks of anti-Jewish popular feelings, meticulously checked by the then very numerous foreign press correspondents in Poland, were either denounced as baseless rumors or bore unmistakable stigmas of crude police provocation (for instance, the desecration of the tombstones of the great German socialist leader Ferdinand Lassalle and of a prominent Jewish historian, Henrich Graetz, in the old Jewish graveyard at Wrocław).[6]

In one respect, however, the Natolinists' attempts to unleash an anti-Semitic campaign did not prove entirely fruitless. For it was then that the pattern was set: to discredit opponents, whatever their ethnic origin, as Jews who were responsible for all or most of the crimes committed in Poland during the Stalinist period.

How strongly this stereotype still survives can be gauged by the fact that at the Grunwald gathering mentioned earlier, the names of the "Polish patriots" who had been allegedly "tortured, sentenced, and executed" at the hands of the "Jewish-Stalinist" clique in the early 1950s were solemnly read and honored. Subsequently, Polish mass media published several protests against so cynical an exploitation of the memory of victims of Communist terror by the executioners' spiritual heirs; an open letter to the editor of *Kurier Polski,* for instance, was signed by eighty-six victims of the non-Communist, anti-Nazi Home Army, whose survivors had been singled out for especially brutal treatment under Stalinist rule.[7] Of special poignancy, however, was a letter written by a relative of one of the victims to the editor of the weekly *Polityka:* for all the relaxation of censorship, the writer obviously was unable to offer any details about him—except his name—Colonel Józef Jungraw. The fact that he had been one of the nineteen senior officers of the Polish armed forces shot on Moscow's orders by the Informacja (Polish military counterintelligence) was not mentioned. Moreover, since none of the culprits had ever been punished, or even exposed, the victim's relative could only assure the readers that she knew the names of the investigation officers, the prosecutors, and the judges who had sentenced Colonel Jungraw, and that all of them "had been Poles, without the slightest admixture of alien blood."[8]

SCAPEGOATS AND DEVILS

The general claim that somehow a handful of Jewish Communists and security officials were to blame for all or, at least, most of the Stalinist crimes in Poland, that Poles, whatever their role, had been but innocent victims of the terror, and that the Soviets had had nothing to do with all this—the Natolin faction's original contribution to Polish political culture—was embraced by, and further developed by Gomułka during his second term of office (1956–70)—this despite the fact that this canard had been used against him. The circular letter of the party's Central Committee issued shortly after Gomułka's return to power, April 1957, did, in fact, stress the need to combat anti-Semitism as an ideology alien to communism—but it was never widely publicized. Gomułka's liberal emigration policy allowed many Jews disenchanted with communism to leave the country; among them were almost all those "repatriated" from Soviet *gulag* camps and from Siberian exile as part of the post-Stalinist "thaw." On the other hand, Gomułka's retreat from his reformist promises, and the subsequent active campaign against the "revisionists" (more often than not Jews and intellectuals) hurt not only veteran Jewish Communists but also liberal intellectuals, whether of Jewish origin or not.

Faithfully following the trend earlier introduced in the Soviet Union, Gomułka considered certain professions as too sensitive for Jews. After the initial purge, carried out under the pretext of getting rid of "Stalinists," he quietly introduced a policy of three "don't's": "don't hire, don't fire, don't promote" Jews (or, rather, increasingly, Poles of Jewish origin, since most of those who regarded themselves as Jews had seized the opportunity to emigrate). While on the one hand a slightly higher concentration of intellectuals of Jewish descent in research institutions, higher education, and mass media was still tolerated, on the other the whole subject of Jews was carefully avoided: in the 1960s, Jewish contributions to Polish history, the history of Jews in contemporary Poland, anti-Semitism were all topics hardly, if ever, mentioned in public.

The policy of ignoring both the role of Jews in Poland and of the still firmly entrenched anti-Semitic prejudices, combined with popular disenchantment with the increasingly authoritarian and repressive Gomułka rule, created a fertile breeding ground for a new, ambitious party faction, bent on making use of anti-Semitism in its drive for power. Headed by Interior Minister General Mieczysław Moczar (whose ties with the Soviet security police were an open secret), the faction came to be known as the Partisans—because of their alleged(and frequently exaggerated) role in the anti-Nazi underground during

World War II, which presumably rendered them more "genuinely Polish" than those Communists (the "Muscovites") who had spent the war years in Russia, and who in the late 1940s were put in some of the leading positions of the party and the government apparat. The Partisans' tactic was to stress even more strongly than Gomułka the nationalistic and patriotic elements of the new ruling ideology. In doing so, however, they were faced with considerable difficulties: the traditional mainstream of Polish nationalism had to be ruled out, because of its anti-Russian direction. The anti-German card had been preempted by Gomułka himself, and besides it was losing importance with the increased stabilization of postwar Europe and the decreasing fears of German revanchism. Only anti-Semitism was left—always available as a means of "mass mobilization," and particularly attractive to those elements in the Communist establishment craving an outlet for their frustrations. By the mid-1960s, Gomułka endorsed the Soviet pro-Arab and anti-Israeli policies, and after the outbreak of the Six-Day War in the Middle East in June 1967, attacked the "Zionist" (read: Jewish) "fifth column" in Poland.[9] Thus the general climate in the country became even more propitious for a new anti-Jewish witch hunt, which the Moczarites hoped would bring them eventually to power.

In March 1968 the interfactional struggle inside the Polish United Workers' Party (PZPR) reached its apogee. For obvious reasons, most Western observers concentrated on the openly anti-Semitic overtones in the shrill propaganda of the "police faction" (as the Moczarites were often called) and on the tragic experience of its victims—hunted, slandered, dismissed from their jobs, and finally forced to leave the country of their ancestors. In fact, liberal intellectuals, for any number of reasons considered an obstacle in the Partisans' drive to power, were also subjected to abuse. But not even they were the real target: anti-Semitic and anti-intellectual prejudices and biases, particularly widespread in what Djilas has so aptly termed the New (ruling) Class, were shamelessly exploited to pave the road for a changing of the guard at the top of the PZPR and of the state.

The hysterical (though meticulously orchestrated) witch hunt brought the Moczarites to within a hairbreadth of success. Still, victory was not to be theirs. The passions unleashed resulted in the promotion of the "racially pure" supporters of the "anti-Zionist campaign" and in the expulsion of over half of the Jewish (or Jewish-related) survivors from their jobs and the country—as well as the intimidation of numerous liberally minded intellectuals. But Moczar remained where he had been, and Gomułka, aided and abetted by Moscow's fear of the Czechoslovak contagion, managed to retain power.

A few years later Moczar again assumed an active role behind the scenes in an attempt to use the December 1970 workers' revolt in the Baltic ports to topple Gomułka and to enthrone a new party leadership under Edward Gierek. Again the policy was only partially successful: Gierek came to power, but Moczar himself, together with most of his supporters, was purged shortly thereafter. Nevertheless, the faction neither disappeared from the political scene nor gave up the use of anti-Semitism in promoting its political plans. Since there were virtually no more Jews, or Poles of Jewish origin, left in positions of power in the party and state apparatus, and very few among the creative intelligentsia, the anti-Jewish campaign took on a somewhat new form: along with the whispered propaganda that Stalinist (cum "Zionist") Jews were still in positions of power, came the assiduously propagated image of the corporate Jew as the enemy and the external threat to the Polish nation (often portrayed—the pathological imagination is fathomless—as working in cahoots with West German revanchism). Soon yet another element appeared on the scene: numerous "scholars" set about to rewrite Polish history in a narrowly nationalistic, xenophobic, and overtly anti-Semitic spirit. To be sure, the mass media were at first relatively unaffected by this outburst of historiographical zeal, but eventually their arguments (never, let it be noted, refuted by genuine scholars) began to infiltrate publications aimed at the general reader and to influence the younger generation, thirsty to learn more about its country's past and usually immune to direct Communist indoctrination. Roughly between 1973 and 1978, the presses were so busy as to give the impression of a well-orchestrated campaign.[10]

To cite one example among many: a one-volume history of Poland, compiled by a team under the editorship of Professor Jerzy Topolski, was published in 1976, with a printing of 140,000 copies. It was beautifully produced and lavishly illustrated. Designed to provide the general reader with a comprehensive survey of the nation's past, from prehistoric times to the present day, it was unreservedly praised by reviewers. The party's theoretical monthly, *Nowe Drogi,* devoted a special scholarly symposium to it. It may therefore be justly regarded as an official exposition of the views held by Poland's rulers in the 1970s.

About the one-thousand-year-old coexistence of Poles and Jews the reader of *The History of Poland* was told next to nothing; he found, instead, a most sympathetic treatment of the *endecja.* He was told, for instance, that in the late 1930s, when the government of Marshal Piłsudski's epigones had "supported the emigration of the Jewish population to Palestine," *endecja* in turn had called for "the boycott of Jewish trade and a restriction on the number of Jewish students." "None of these slogans," concludes the author (Antoni Czubiński) on a note of unmistakable regret, "led to a solution of the overpopulation issue."

A solution of sorts was later provided by Hitler, but, for obvious reasons, the author is most reticent when dealing with the Holocaust. In two different chapters, he fleetingly touches on the fate of Polish Jewry. While ignoring Jewish suffering and heroism (in nearly 1,000 pages, only seventeen lines are devoted to the fate of the Jews under the Nazis!), he carefully blurs the difference between the Nazi policy of genocide and the terror that had also claimed three million Polish (non-Jewish) victims. The fate of the survivors of the Holocaust is not even mentioned: the chapters dealing with the postwar period simply note with satisfaction that "the population of Poland underwent a process of national homogenization," because "immediately after the war the non-Polish population in principle returned to their native countries."

By the same token, there is no mention whatsoever of anti-Semitism under Communist rule; the March 1968 events are dismissed in two short sentences: "In the spring of 1968 the party was confronted with another assault by various antisocialist forces, including revisionists. With the support of the working classes, these forces were routed."[11]

All this propaganda notwithstanding, the Gierek leadership, having gotten rid of Moczar and his most vociferous followers, quietly put an end to active discrimination against Jews and intellectuals—mainly, one supposes, to improve Poland's image in the West on the eve of a massive quest for foreign credits. But no public discussion was ever allowed about the March 1968 events, which were as painful for the intelligentsia as the December 1970 massacre in the Baltic ports became for the Polish working class. Both continued to be treated as nonevents, thus exacerbating popular dissatisfaction with a system that treated truth—present and past—in so cavalier a fashion.

A NEW PHASE

By the mid-1970s, the "Gierek economic miracle" finally collapsed. The 1976 constitutional amendments and the June 1976 workers' protests against arbitrary price hikes gave rise to somewhat more open opposition, an activity that for the first time threatened to unite workers and intellectuals against the regime.[12] Using brutal police force against the striking workers, the party leadership stopped short of suppressing the intellectual dissent and the *samizdat* publications; instead, it tried once again the well-tested weapon of political anti-Semitism—albeit on a much more modest scale. The smear campaign, directed mainly against the Workers' Defense Committee (KOR) in order to provoke worker distrust of allegedly Jewish troublemakers, was conducted by word of mouth rather than in the media, as it had been in the 1960s, and was never officially sanctioned by the authorities. Still, the propaganda against the world-wide "anti-Polish Zionist conspiracy" and the anti-Semitic distortions in popular books, articles, and even movies dealing with recent Polish history acquired a momentum of their own and were deliberately stepped up in the latter half of Gierek's rule.[13]

The internal security forces, the main power behind the 1968 anti-Semitic campaign, were the first to beat the same drum immediately after June 1976. Even the early issues of the KOR *samizdat* publications quoted specific cases of policemen and other officials warning workers against KOR as an "espionage organization whose purpose was to slander Poland." KOR was allegedly "composed of traitors and Jews paid by Israel and West German revisionists," and workers' protests could therefore serve only the interests of Radio Free Europe and "the Jews."[14] In an effort to produce additional ammunition, the PZPR Central Committee's Ideological Education Department published in January 1977 a booklet, "for internal party use only," entitled *Topical Problems of the Class Struggle*. It claimed that the centers of the "anti-Polish subversion organized by the imperialists" had been joined, after 1956 and 1968, by émigrés of "cosmopolitan" views who had left Poland ostensibly for Israel, but who in fact spread out all over Western Europe and the United States offering their services to anti-Communist and Zionist organizations; they "included revisionists and Zionists who [had] attacked the party's policy in March 1968."[15] The booklet provided a long list of names of Polish intellectuals, the great majority of them Jews or having "Jewish connections."

By the first half of 1977, the mass media, too, began to engage in anti-Semitic propaganda. A particularly noxious case in point was an attack on Jewish religion by the notorious Communist hack Władysław Machejek.[16] Significantly, Machejek's magnum opus, a four-volume novel written to prove his thesis that all the troubles and misfortunes of postwar Poland had been caused by Jewish Stalinists who had infiltrated the Polish Communist movement and had cruelly persecuted its national-patriotic core, was quickly released for publication.[17]

If to the Communist Machejek the Jews were to blame for the crimes of Stalinism, the PAX Catholic writer Jan Dobraczyński blamed the Trotskyites. The Roman Catholic Church, he argued, should therefore beware of any support for Polish dissidents: "Thirty-odd years after the war," he wrote, "Jews constitute the great majority of the movement of the so-called Troyskyites. The Trotskyite movement in Western Europe is very active and there can be no doubt whatsoever that it supports and assists the propaganda of those who undertake all kinds of protest actions in socialist countries. There can be no connection between this dissent and Catholicism."[18]

Dobraczyński's "warning," however, should not be seen as a simple reverberation of March 1968, when the PAX movement joined forces with the Moczarites (as it had done, back in 1956, with the Natolin faction) in an attempt to rouse the country against the "Jewish conspiracy." The situation was no longer the same. After the workers' revolt of June 1976, the authorities decided—albeit with reluctance and against the opposition of the hard-liners (including PAX)—that an all-out campaign against the burgeoning dissident movement was fraught with serious political dangers. The decision to tolerate the intellectual opposition, while using the secret police to thwart any collaboration between the intellectuals and the workers, resulted in the emergence of a "second Poland"—the *pays réel* as opposed to the *pays légal*—with its uncensored press and lively discussions, strikingly bright against the bleak background of the official "propaganda of success." Even in the intellectual underground, however, the ideological discussion of such problems as the nature of modern nationalism and its abuse by the Communists (including the perennial question of anti-Semitism) was couched in historical terms. On the surface, the arguments concerned the *endecja* tradition in Poland's past, as well as the more recent March 1968 events. In fact, they dealt with some of the most pressing contemporary political issues.

As could be expected, the first to recognize the importance of these issues were the young intellectuals who had rallied around KOR. Some of them had already been active before 1968; many others received their political baptism of fire during the student protests in March of that year. Whatever their ethnic background, the campaign of 1968 was a traumatic experience they had to overcome. Hence the importance of a questionnaire sent out shortly before the tenth anniversary of March 1968 protests by the KOR *Biuletyn Informacyjny*. Its editors asked about thirty writers, scholars, and student activists to evaluate "the results of the events of March 1968 and their role in Poland's most recent history." The responses were then published as a symposium by one of KOR's "uncensored" quarterlies, *Krytyka*.[19] While paying proper due to the anti-Semitic slogans of the "police faction" and its allies, most respondents concentrated on the fundamental political and sociological implications of the campaign—that is, how the campaign reflected the nature of the Polish political system (authoritarian, narrow-minded, chauvinistic) and why it managed to arouse passions of people who were otherwise opposed to the regime (that is, the problem of latent anti-Semitic and xenophobic sentiments within the population at large). By discussing issues that had hitherto been either taboo or maliciously distorted by the official media, the participants in effect on the one hand engaged in a collective catharsis and on the other scored an important victory against the institution of censorship.

Significantly, the new spirit of open discussion affected young Catholic intellectuals as well, especially those at the Catholic University in Lublin. Indeed, some Catholics had tried to come to grips with the issue as far back as 1973, when a number of Clubs of Catholic Intelligentsia (KIK) had initiated more or less regular "Weeks of Jewish Culture." In 1977–78, their uncensored press turned its attention to the previously mentioned official discussions on Polish history, consistently denouncing its narrowly nationalistic interpretation, and in particular the disparagement of the Jewish contribution to Poland's social, political, and cultural life.[20] When the KOR followers, joined by liberal and Catholic intellectuals, initiated the informal educational courses of the Flying University, the problems of nationalism and communism in Poland's past and present figured prominently both in the lectures and in the ensuing discussions.

The same critical attitude, however, was not evinced by other dissidents who had joined the political opposition under the banner of the defense of human and civil rights. Many of them were, in fact, inspired mainly by an old-fashioned nationalism, not all that different from the one so dear to the hearts of the PAX ideologists. Although, as far as can be ascertained, not once did their uncensored publications (e.g., *Opinia, Droga, Bratniak, Gazeta Polska,* et al.) openly endorse the Communist-style (or even PAX-style) anti-Semitism or xenophobic chauvinism, nevertheless, their attachment to *endecja* traditions, their supercilious attitude toward the March 1968 events—which they regarded as a purely internecine party struggle—and their frequent hints alleging "foreign" influence inspiring the KOR opposition movement seemed to indicate that at least some of the poisonous indoctrination had indeed sunk in.[21] The uncensored publications of the democratic opposition and of Catholic intellectuals did not miss a single opportunity to denounce such conscious or unconscious lapses by people claiming to reject all aspects of totalitarianism in the name of human and civil rights.

Quite apart from the ideological and political discussions among the various oppositional groups—discussions totally ignored by the official mass media—a public reappraisal of the March 1968 events became inevitable once the massive workers' strikes of July–August 1980 had brought about not only another personnel change in the PZPR leadership and the government, but also far-reaching alterations of the whole social fabric. At least three members of the newly elected Politburo had twelve years earlier actively engaged in the anti-Semitic and antiintellectual campaigns (Mieczysław Moczar, Stefan Olszowski, Andrzej Żabiński). Even the new first secretary, Stanisław Kania, was himself guilty, at least by association.[22] Their very presence there was a symbol of the resilience—and continuity—of certain political traditions of the PZPR. On the other hand, the unprecedented victory of the strikers, crowned by the creation and official recognition of the independent labor union Solidarity, had enormously

intensified the process of spiritual emancipation of the intelligentsia, well under-
way since 1975. With the relaxation in the fall of 1980 of strict party controls
over political and cultural life, and in particular of media censorship, an open
discussion of the past became inevitable.

Significantly, it was the academic world, sorely affected by the purges carried
out after 1968 under anti-Semitic and aniliberal slogans, that first seized the
initiative. In September–October 1980, in the Polish Academy of Sciences, at
Warsaw University, and in other schools of higher education and scholarly institutes, faculty committees were spontaneously formed to redress wrongs committed twelve years earlier. Although the practical effects of their activities were
undoubtedly negligible (by that time most of the purged professors and lecturers
that were still living had either eached retirement age or had long ago found other
intellectually rewarding posts in foreign universities), the very fact that they were
able to restore contact with former colleagues in the country or in exile (and, too,
that the authorities did not try to prevent or even conceal such contacts) was by
itself convincing proof of the changes that had taken place in Poland.

WHAT NEXT?

This essay (and the book as a whole) deals primarily with developments immediately preceding—and only tangentially with those following—the momentous
summer of 1980. It might, therefore, seem proper to end the story here. Yet what
happened during the sixteen months of Solidarity's "self-limiting revolution"—particularly with regard to the politics of anti-Semitism—is so significant for an understanding of the roots and nature of this period that a brief review
of the events of 1980–81 is in order.

In the first months of the social upheaval, the radical changes in the spiritual
atmosphere of the country did not escape the notice of some of the leaders of the
erstwhile "police faction," including Moczar himself. In an obvious effort to
divest himself of his poor reputation—especially in the eyes of the West—
Moczar, in his first major public speech after his return to active political life,
paid tribute to the slaughtered "three million Polish citizens of Jewish descent
who lived among us on Polish soil and, together with us, created our history and
made a great contribution to our culture and science."[23]

Yet Moczar's belated discovery of the Jewish chapter in Polish history was
apparently not to the liking, either, of some of his faithful supporters, who felt
that anti-Semitism had not yet outlived its usefulness in settling the score with the
opposition, and with those inside the party who were inclined to make
concessions. In late 1980 and early 1981, therefore, allusions to the actual or
alleged Jewish origins of some of the KOR activists and Solidarity advisers kept
appearing in some newspapers and periodicals. Such allusions appeared even—
either intentionally or inadvertently—in a provincial Solidarity bulletin,[24] and
the subject sometimes came up in some statements by local trade union leaders.
In addition, there was a spate of "anonymous" anti-Semitic leaflets, posters,
and booklets (some of them carefully and professionally printed and widely
distributed all over the country).[25] All these scurrilous attempts at inflaming

anti-Jewish passions were firmly and methodically denounced by Solidarity—in particular, whenever such attempts involved their own ranks and publications—as well as by a growing number of independent and Catholic intellectuals. Moreover, the censorship was at that time largely inoperative, and in any case would not have interfered with open denouncement of anti-Semitism in the independent press and in those mass media in which followers of the "renewal" had gained the upper hand. Consequently, the so-called Jewish question appeared to gain importance out of all proportion to the other problems the crisis-ridden country had to cope with. In contrast to earlier attempts at exploiting anti-Semitism, it was at least clearly demonstrated that society at large was no longer susceptible to this kind of demagoguery. For the first time since the imposition of Communist rule, some of the more shameful episodes in the postwar history of Poland were openly discussed, including even the 1946 Kielce pogrom.[26]

Still, by the first quarter of 1981, the anti-Semitic campaign assumed an organized form, culminating in the previously mentioned founding of the Grunwald Patriotic Union. The reason for this and related phenomena is not difficult to fathom: in the country as a whole, and in the party rank and file, too, sympathy for Solidarity was growing by leaps and bounds; the pressure for democratization of Polish political life directly threatened the entrenched party, and government apparatchiks were fearful of losing their power, their jobs, and their privileges. The "hard-liners" then began to fight back: by again attacking the intellectuals for engaging in antisocialist activities; by accusing journalists of wallowing in unbridled criticism and pessimism; and, finally, by seizing upon the wretched (and largely discredited) triad of "Jews-Zionists-Stalinists." In the summer of 1981, when food shortages, especially of meat, began to overshadow all other complaints of the working population in Poland, Grunwald had its scapegoats ready: you never saw a Jew in line before an empty shop, it claimed, because all of them (100,000 in the whole country, according to Grunwald's count) received specially privileged meat rations, amounting to 3.7 kilos prime kosher beef per person.[27]

The formation of Grunwald could be said to mark the beginning of a new phase: for the first time since the Communist seizure of power, an openly anti-Semitic organization was officially sanctioned and even publicly commended by a leading member of the party's Politburo.[28] The facts that the association's claim to have 100,000 members was a patent falsehood[29] and that "by openly propagating anti-Semitism"—as was pointed out by Warsaw's sole remaining Yiddish newspaper—it in effect violated the Polish constitution did not seem to matter. Unlike Solidarity several months earlier, Grunwald had no difficulty in obtaining legal registration, and its activities (such as they were) met with no restrictions on the part of the authorities.

The emergence of Grunwald was greeted with a wave of bitter denunciations, emanating as much from Solidarity as from many liberal-minded intellectuals and prominent Catholics. The popular Warsaw daily Życie Warszawy, for instance, published an "open letter" (dated March 19, 1981), initially signed by 124 well-known intellectuals, with the total number of signatures eventually growing to 622. The letter protested against proliferation of "illegal publications inciting racial hatred" and concluded that "behind many activities are concealed personal interests of individuals and groups attempting to nip the renewal process in the bud, and to do away with the restorative social tendencies, thus distracting public opinion from the genuine culprits of evil and distortions.''

Similar protests were voiced by the Polish PEN Club, the Catholic Intelligentsia Clubs, radio and TV journalists, the Polish Academy of Sciences, and other organizations. A well-known Communist writer from Kraków, a surviorr of Auschwitz, Tadeusz Hołuj, published in the local party daily an open letter about Grunwald. Recalling the shameful anti-Jewish witch hunt in 1968 in terms quite exceptional for the official Polish press even in 1981, Hołuj appealed to the party's Control Commission to initiate an inquiry in order to find out whether actual deeds of party members within Grunwald (and not merely their verbal declarations) were compatible with the ideological principles of the party.[30] In a similar vein, a prominent historian of contemporary Poland, Professor Jerzy Holzer, writing in a PAX weekly, analyzed the March 1968 events as an attempted pogrom of Polish culture, carried out behind the smoke screen of an anti-Zionist campaign: ''March [1968] represented a powerful manipulation of the consciousness of large segments of the population. Anti-Semitism played an essential role in this manipulation. From time immemorial, the hidden Zionist enemy of Poland's welfare was allegedly responsible for all Polish misfortunes. Attempts to ascribe to ourselves all our successes and to people of Jewish origin all the possible offenses were an outrage not [only] against the Jews, but against the entire Polish nation.''[31]

The party leadership, itself deeply divided, tried at first to avoid an unambiguous taking of sides for or against Grunwald, but the Soviet press eagerly endorsed the new wave of ''anti-Zionist'' propaganda.[32] The hard-line elements in the party, and especially in the lower and middle levels of the party apparatus, were quick to take Moscow's cue. Organized factions, starting with the so-called Katowice Party Forum, began to mushroom all over the country under different names, more often than not simply parroting the anti-Semitic slogans of the allegedly nonparty Grunwald. It became clear that what was at first regarded as merely a lunatic fringe in fact enjoyed the support of a sizable group within the party elite, and that anti-Semitism was again being used—both against Solidarity and as an instrument of intraparty struggles. The strength of the hard-liners—in the party, if not in society at large—was confirmed in late May 1981 with the appearance of a new weekly magazine, *Rzeczywistość,* with a large print run at a time when newsprint was in very short supply and when other publications were being drastically cut or eliminated altogether. *Rzeczywistość,* ostensibly published by a party club, Warsaw '80, numbered among its contributors not only some of the leading lights of Grunwald, but also party stalwarts such as Ignacy Krasicki, who back in 1968, both under his own name and under various aliases (e.g., Wacław Szafrański) had distinguished himself for his virulent ''anti-Zionist'' diatribes and who now became an ''expert'' on the alleged imperialist, counterrevolutionary, and Zionist inspiration of the Solidarity movement. It was another attempt to drive a wedge between the workers and the intellectuals who had joined independent trade unions. One of the most prominent among them, the world-famous historian Professor Bronisław Geremek, was at first referred to by his original surname, Lewartow, to indicate his Jewish origin,[33] and later openly accused of Zionist sympathies and a virulent "anti-Polish" animus. Another proponent of this strategy was the notorious hard-liner and an activist of the "old" (i.e., run by the Communists) trade unions, Albert Siwak, who at the Ninth Party Congress in July 1981 was elected not only a delegate of the Warsaw party organization but also a member of the PZPR Central Committee and the Politburo. An obscure magazine, *Fermentacje,* published by Siwak's unions, reprinted in several issues some excerpts from the notorious anti-Semitic forgery "The Protocols of the Elders of Zion."[34]

The "creeping militarization" of political and public life in the summer and fall of 1981 brought into prominence extreme Communist hard-liners, drawn almost exclusively from among regular army officers and internal security people. Their ideology included, naturally, a strong dose of anti-Semitism, preached day in and day out by the official organ of the armed forces, *Żołnierz Wolności,* and—in an even less concealed form—by other army publications. To no one's surprise, the coup of December 13, 1981, ushered in a new chapter in anti-Semitism, too: anti-Jewish propaganda was intensified. Significantly, once the independent trade unions and the liberal intellectuals had been silenced by the imposition of martial law, opposition to anti-Semitism—as to other facets of neo-Stalinist Communist ideology and policy—disappeared overnight from public life. It is no coincidence—as Marxists like to say—that Grunwald was one of the very few organizations neither dissolved nor even suspended by Jaruzelski's regime.

One additional aspect of the problem needs elucidation: as the cynical exploitation of anti-Semitic prejudices by Communist hard-liners, both civilian and military, was reaching an unprecedented pitch, most of the so-called party moderates preferred to ignore it. In view of past experiences, this seems almost incredible. Again and again, during the crises that had shaken postwar Poland, clear and irrefutable evidence has abounded that the objective of anti-Semitic campaigns had never been simply to get rid of Jews—or, for that matter, liberal intellectuals, of whatever ethnic background—but to weaken and undermine the "reformist" elements of the party itself. Anti-Semitism, with all its odious implications, has proved to be the classic tool of diehard Communists bent on achieving or consolidating power, on tightening the screws of dictatorship. In 1980–81 this elementary fact of life was even more obvious than in 1956 or in 1968–70, if only because by no stretch of the imagination could any "pernicious" Jewish influence be discovered in a country that was now virtually *Judenrein.* Most Polish liberal intellectuals, whether secular or Catholic, understood this and did their best to oppose the campaign. So did the vast majority of the Solidarity leaders and advisers.[35] Most of the Communists did not—and that includes the so-called moderates, many of them already purged by the supposedly "military" government, others passively awaiting their turn. Why? There is no truly satisfactory answer to this question—unless we search for it, perhaps, in the common roots of the two contemporary brands of totalitarianism, communism and fascism.

A leading Polish hard-liner recalled with approval a once widely repeated piece of Gomułka's down-to-earth wisdom: the former party leader, toppled from office in December 1970 but later partially restored to grace for his incorruptibility (no bribes, no villas, no pornographic videotapes), used to compare the "dogmatist" deviation to flu, but "revisionism" to tuberculosis—and advised the party to treat them accordingly.[36] The meaning is clear: those who make use of anti-Semitism to prevent the party from sliding into the morass of "revisionism" are motivated by good intentions, and even if going too far—introducing military occupation, for instance—do not cease to be "our kind of people." The history of the Communist movement in Poland is eloquent testimony to the endurance of Gomułka's obiter dictum: comrades suffering from flu need not worry—the military surgeon's knife is not likely to touch them.

9

POLAND AND
EASTERN EUROPE

George Schöpflin

In 1980, as Poland entered the tenth year of the Gierek era, it became increasingly clear to the close observer of Eastern Europe that yet another upsurge of mass discontent was in the offing. Much less predictable was what form it would take and how the country's rulers would respond. One thing was certain: specifically Polish features were of paramount importance. Hence an examination of these features and a comparison with the situation in other Eastern European countries may shed light on why Poland became the scene of the 1980–81 "renewal." It must be stressed that while some of the factors were present elsewhere, it was the particular combination of these factors that resulted in the wave of strikes in the summer of 1980 and in the subsequent radical redistribution of power in the state and society. The first part of this chapter, then, will compare the principal actors in the Polish events—the Church, the ruling elite, the workers, the peasants, and the intelligentsia—with their counterparts in other East European countries.

RELIGION

Roman Catholicism is the oldest and most effective system of ethics and authority in Poland and as such claims a secure place at the top. Despite its appearance of being universally identical, with the same institutional framework and values wherever it exists, the Roman Catholic Church is, of course, nothing of the kind: a moment's reflection on the Church in, say, France and Ireland will show how misleading this appearance can be.

What has differentiated the Polish Church from the Church in other Roman Catholic countries in Eastern Europe has not just been its immense institutional strength and ethical vigor. The Polish Catholic tradition has generally tended to regard the individual not as subordinated to the Church but as complemented by it. From the post-Reformation period onward, political and religious thought in Poland has tended to merge, and this has had a crucial impact on political identity, especially since the emergence of modern nationalism at the beginning of the nineteenth century. In effect, religion and a sense of nationhood fused, with the result that the religious value of individual conscience was imported into the Poles' political value system. The final suppression of Polish sovereignty in 1831 helped to crystallize this set of attitudes, for the Church and its teachings became a surrogate for the state and the nation, thus intensifying the relationship between religious and political values. The imposition of an alien system on Poland after 1945 once more thrust on the Church the role of society's independent conscience; paradoxically, this process was facilitated by the weakening of the Church's secular power in the interwar period—the only time when the Polish Church was closely identified with the state rather than with society. In this sense, the Communist takeover has delayed the secularization that one would have predicted for Poland, based on analogous developments in other industrializing societies. As a result. Polish society was permeated with religious-political values that were to have crucial and far-reaching consequences in August 1980. The self-confidence of Polish society was unquestionably boosted by the visit of the Pope in 1979, but over and above that, the role of religion should be seen as one of the means of reaffirmation of individual existence. To quote one of Poland's gifted youngd philosophers and historians, Marcin Król: "The social function of religion, of religious observance, and of the emotions in the realm of the sacred were to constitute a single system of infallible values, which could be relied on in a world of universal mistrust. Religion was the sole source of emotions and thought that were real, authentic. . . . What played a crucial role was the consolidation of religion into a system of values, emotions, and authentic thought (not just of a religious but also of a patriotic character, for example)."[1]

Nowhere else in Eastern Europe, Roman Catholic countries included, does the Church play this kind of role—with the exception of Croatia and, relatively, Slovakia. There are sound reasons for this, derived from both past history and more recent developments. In the Roman Catholic areas of Czechoslovakia, Hungary, and Yugoslavia, Roman Catholicism is considerably weaker than in Poland, even insofar as a religious observance is concerned. In the conflict between society and the state in Czechoslovakia and Hungary, the Church has not been able to muster the kind of spiritual élan that is so prevalent in Poland. In the former Austro-Hungarian lands, the Church was subordinated at a fairly early stage to the state and was never thereafter able to reassert its claim to autonomy, in either spiritual or secular matters. From the Austro-Hungarian period on, stipends—salaries for clerics—were paid by the state.[2] Indeed, in interwar Czechoslovakia, the ruling authorities regarded the Roman Catholic Church with deep suspicion as having been rather too close to the Hapsburgs for its own credibility as a genuine Czech institution. In neither Czechoslovakia nor Hungary is society quite as monolithically Roman Catholic as in Poland: in both countries the Protestant churches have good claim to be the heirs and guarantors of the national tradition, much as the Catholic Church is in Poland.

In Bohemia-Moravia, in any case, secularization was well advanced even before the Communist takeover, the consequence of a high degree of industrialization as well as of a suspicion of the Church because of its former relationship with the Hapsburgs.[3] Secularization seems equally far advanced in Hungary, where recent surveys of religious observance returned results below 50 percent. To these factors must be added the history of the postwar conflict between Church and state. While in Poland the Church lost its power but gained authority, in Czechoslovakia and Hungary the Church lost both. It found itself badly placed to act as the conscience of the nation and was ill served by its leaders, particularly Cardinal Jozsef Mindszenty, who was completely unable to muster the kind of flexibility that might have strengthened the prestige of the Church after the war, when it was still relatively powerful in parts of the country. His successor, Cardinal Laszlo Lékai, was not able to achieve very much with this legacy. In Czechoslovakia, Cardinal Josef Beran's position was simply too weak to enable him to play a role similar to Wyszyński's in Poland. As a result, the authorities in both Hungary and Czechoslovakia found it relatively easy to limit the influence of the Church.

In Croatia, the prestige of the Church declined as a result of its association with the state. Above all, its uneasy and sometimes ambiguous position toward the wartime fascist independent state of Croatia left it morally exposed to the charge that it had condoned genocide. During the postwar years, the Croatian hierarchy worked hard to reestablish itself and did so with some success, but for all that, its authority did not match that of the Polish Church; and for what it was worth, the regime, which derived its authority in part from an indigenous revolution, was acceptable to a considerable part of the Croatian population. Only in Slovakia did the position of the Roman Catholic Church begin to approach that of Poland, although the Czechoslovak authorities had ensured that the Slovak (as well as the Czech) hierarchy would be as small as possible, and every kind of obstacle was placed in the way of parish priests and believers.

Consequently, in the area of religion, despite initial similarities, the situation in Poland and other East European countries differed markedly. In Poland, it seems fair to suggest, the balance of authority, though not of power, had shifted appreciably away from the state; and the Church was well placed to increase its own claim as the principal moral authority in society. In other East European countries neither of these circumstances obtained: the state either retained its claim to authority or was able to keep challengers out of the arena. Alternatively, the Church lacked the strength to issue such a challenge (Croatia being the nearest to an exception).

THE ELITE

Before a revolution from below can succeed, its actions must meet with minimum of resistance from the rulers, and this only arises when a ruling elite is already demoralized and has lost some of its will to rule. This certainly happened to the Gierek leadership in 1980, but it was not unprecedented in the Communist world. In Hungary in 1956 and in Czechoslovakia in 1967–68 something very similar took place—the morale of the elite collapsed. The factors that brought this about in Poland, however, were very different from those events: in Hungary and Czechoslovakia Erno Gerö and Antonin Novotný put up a good deal of resistance before going down to defeat. In Poland, not only did Gierek take his holidays in July 1980—surely a case of hubris, if ever there was one—but after his return in August, he caved in remarkably quickly.[4]

The swift demise of the Gierek regime was characteristic of an elite with a transparently weak claim to legitimacy, and one whose resilience had slowly been eroding as a result of its failure to face up to political challenges. The Polish elite seems to have a curious facility to become completely isolated from society and to learn nothing from the past. By 1980, Gierek had obviously not the least idea of what was going on in the country at large. The irony of this clearly emerges when one reads the attacks Gierek made on Gomułka in 1971 for the same failing, together with his solemn promises that under his leadership the party would not be severed from the people again. If one contrasts this with the determination shown by János Kádár or Erich Honecker to stay in touch, Gierek's apparent determination to cut his own political throat seems even more difficult to comprehend.

Closely allied with isolation was the arrogance of the Polish elite, especially as expressed in material terms. Because the elite—bureaucracy, police, intelligentsia—had access to a higher standard of living than the masses, they scarcely noticed that the bulk of the population was very much worse off than they, and, even worse, that for most Poles the standard of living had declined sharply and perilously in the late 1970s. In addition to the arrogance, which manifested itself much more provocatively than it had in the past in the response to the strikes in the summer of 1980, a burgeoning corruption enveloped Poland in the 1970s. There seems to be something of a causal nexus between the sudden influx of large sums of money, especially money that had not been truly earned, and the corruptibility of an elite. The last few years of the Shah's Iran provides another illustration of this tendency. In Poland, the corruption was profound, destroying ethical values in those involved and, in consequence, their sense of judgment. This played a crucial role in sapping the elite's will to rule. Finally, the Polish rulers were singularly receptive to their own propaganda of success. The all-pervasive censorship and a determination to out-Pangloss Pangloss left the political decision-makers incapable of seeing problems, let alone taking effective action. A Western banker who visited Poland in the spring of 1980 recounted how the country's economic and financial experts had a very clear idea of the disastrous state of the Polish economy; the politicians refused to acknowledge that there was any urgency in the situation at all.

In most of these respects Poland was unique in Eastern Europe: nowhere else had the morale of the elite deteriorated to such an extent. The precise causes of the collapse, however, are very difficult to pinpoint. Isolation from society was evidently not a sufficient cause on its own. The Czechoslovak leadership was at least as cut off from Czechoslovak society as was its Polish counterpart, yet it managed to meet the challenge of Charter 77—the human rights movement launched by a group of Czech intellectuals in 1977—by successfully restricting its political impact and preventing the ideas of the charter from taking root in society. The Czechoslovak leadership's recognition that the maintenance of economic well-being was a key component in political stability was clearly a crucial factor. Hungary provides another contrast. As in Poland, the Hungarian economy performed badly in the late 1970s—in 1979, real wages fell by 2 percent—yet the leadership was able to prevent this potential danger from developing by creating a political atmosphere that prevented the Hungarian workers from coming to the conclusion that only direct action—taking to the streets—would be of any use in bringing about a change in conditions. This was done by ensuring that supplies were maintained, however expensive these might be; by persuading Hungarian society to accept a measure of austerity; and by blocking the fledgling Hungarian opposition from forming links with the working class.

The problems faced by Yugoslavia in the aftermath of Tito's rule were just as serious as in Poland. These included a much weaker leadership, which lacked the unique personal authority of Tito, an inflation running at 30 percent, and an ethnically heterogeneous society with a plethora of internal disputes that could threaten the country's stability. Yet the one thing that cannot be said about the Yugoslav leadership is that it lost its nerve, despite the buffetings to which it was exposed in the months following Tito's death. The explanation of this self-confidence must lie in the sense of legitimacy shared by the leadership and society, which derives from the fact that Yugoslavia's Communist revolution had been a native one and not a foreign import. Furthermore, the Yugoslav leadership has understood the importance of not becoming isolated from society and, while insisting on its exclusive right to rule, has done so by paying heed to popular aspirations.

The only East European leadership that bears any resemblance to Poland's is that of President Nicolae Ceausescu of Rumania. He has successfully emasculated all possible contenders for power and has created a leadership entirely dependent on him; if he were to be removed, the chances of anarchy in Rumania would be high. Much of what Poland suffered afflicted Rumania, too: a low standard of living (although without the experience of a period of prosperity), corruption, isolation of the elite, and a personal, quixotic quality in the exercise of power. No wonder that Ceausescu's initial reaction to the events in Poland was in some respects even more shrill than that of his sturdily pro-Moscow neighbors. True, in his speeches in September 1980 he clearly served notice that a Soviet military intervention would be unacceptable to Rumania. On the other hand, he broke one of his oldest rules—never to criticize the internal affairs of another Communist party—by in effect charging the Polish leadership with irresponsibility.[5]

Ceausescu's great fortune was that the competing value system of religion, which offered Polish society an indispensable reference point in which to base its claim to autonomy, was largely absent in Rumania. Religion has been nationalized—the Rumanian Orthodox Church is largely a "transmission belt." National traditions have been in effect appropriated by the Communist government.[6] The intelligentsia, which might have developed alternative concepts of political organization, had been (with some minor exceptions) co-opted. The only choice open to Rumanian society appeared to be anarchy, which, given that country's traditions, would have been violent. Rumania, let us recall, was the scene of the last peasant jacquerie in Europe in 1907.[7]

THE WORKING CLASS

The reactions of the Polish working class to the policies of the regime were shaped as much by the forces already discussed as by its own experiences. In this respect, the most striking feature of Poland's postwar history is that, on the whole, mass action by workers did not result in the kind of bloodletting that the East Germans and Hungarians underwent or in bleak repression, such as the one imposed on Czechoslovakia after 1969. The riots in Poznań in June 1956 were followed several months later by a wave of liberalization, only gradually canceled and reversed by Gomułka in the years that followed. The events of 1970 proved to be a further stage in the political maturing of the Polish workers. The December uprising was suppressed; but the fall of Gomułka meant that the workers had the power to remove a leadership blatantly contemptuous of their interests and to force the authorities to rescind precipitous increases in food prices.

For a time, the implications of the new state of affairs (which might be characterized as marking the advent of authoritarian, as distinguished from totalitarian, rule in Poland) seemed to be perceived not only by the workers but also by the authorities. The workers were reluctantly and tacitly accepted as having a kind of an offstage voice in Polish politics, and the party acted as if it understood that it could no longer rule so as to totally exclude society from its plans. In addition, it seemed to realize that internal stability was predicated on a continuous price freeze. The events of 1976, however, proved once again that the party's capacity to learn from experience was limited at best. As for the workers, their self-confidence, if anything, increased. And with the growth of self-confidence came also a militant aversion to manipulative tactics and a pervasive distrust of the government in general. By the end of the 1970s, the distrust clearly meant that workers were determined not to accept official promises without legal and institutional safeguards.

This self-confidence did not exist anywhere else in Eastern Europe. In Hungary, the limits set by the failed revolution of 1956 were still holding, even though the generation directly traumatized by the suppression of the revolution and the repression of the 1956–61 period was ceasing to be the dominant section of the working class. In Czechoslovakia, the events of 1968 were even closer in time, and Czechoslovak society seemed to accept economic well-being as a compensation for its loss of broader political prospects. In East Germany, where four-fifths of the population are able to see West German television and have access to a wide range of information about Poland, the workers not only remained quiescent but to some extent even began to move in some way toward supporting the status quo.[8] The explanation for this must be sought in the lingering memories of the 1953 uprising, the continued presence of twenty Soviet divisions on East German territory, and the relatively high standard of living achieved by East Germans, which they would surely have been loath to give up.

In Yugoslavia, the situation was far more complex. To begin with, a significant proportion of Yugoslav workers go abroad for short periods—to work in Western Europe or Australia, for example—with the result that a potential source of conflict and unrest is diminished. In addition, despite the galloping inflation, the administrative structure of Yugoslavia—especially the devolution of economic decision-making to the commune and enterprise level—has given workers some genuine access to power, thus narrowing the gap between the state and society that has existed elsewhere in Eastern Europe. Finally, national cleavages crisscross Yugoslavia, and this both makes the situation more dangerous and helps to take the heat out of certain socioeconomic problems by providing alternative focuses for loyalty.

The Rumanian working class had the most cause to follow the Poles. It had suffered deprivation for two decades, as consumption levels were squeezed in pursuit of high and not very effective investment. But apart from stoppages, like the one at Tîrgovişte in 1980,[9] there is little evidence that the Rumanian workers had reached the level of cohesion where they would form organizations and pursue sustained action against the authorities. The reasons lie in the general backwardness of Rumania—the country with the lowest standard of living in Comecon—and the immaturity of its working class. The great majority of them are ex-peasants, not long away from much worse drudgery on the land and thus satisfied with the meager improvement in conditions represented by urban life. That satisfaction may well wear off, but the Rumanian leaders have some time in hand; for the moment, any unrest could be dealt with by police methods.

Much of the above was borne out by the immediate response of East European societies to the developments in Poland. Contrary to what some Western observers suggested, the Polish workers' action did not meet with universal sympathy and approval. In fact, there was considerable evidence of fear, anger, and even contempt: fear that the hotheaded action of the Poles would jeopardize everyone else's hard-won gains; anger that the Poles had made such a mess of things and were thereby endangering the stability of Eastern Europe; and contempt for the supposed laziness and incompetence of the Poles. It does not take long for negative stereotypes to rise to the surface in Eastern Europe.

A generally sympathetic Hungarian worker was asked if he thought that the Polish events would have any repercussions in Hungary. "We are at least as badly off as they are," he responded. "I don't think that [the events] can have much of an effect. It could be that we'll have to put something in the kitty to make up for those few billions that [the Polish leaders] wasted. We'll be seeing something like this modern style of begging. Of course, not just the Hungarians, but all the socialist states. In my view, there will be no other effect. Maybe, we'll get more extra shifts to work."[10]

THE PEASANTRY

It is clear that one of the proximate causes of the Polish crisis has been the country's inability to feed itself. This brings us directly to the question of the peasantry. As a rule, peasants and farmers tend to be politically inactive. As long as the state provides tolerable minimum conditions for agricultural producers, they will seldom rebel. It is only when they see their political or economic position seriously threatened by the state and no other ways open for bringing pressure to bear that peasants take to the streets. In Poland, this quiescent attitude was reinforced by the experience of the failed collectivization of the 1950s, which left many private farmers, especially the older generation, grateful for being left alone. By the mid-1970s, however, Gierek succeeded in doing something unprecedented in Communist history: he managed to mobilize a section of the peasantry into active opposition against the regime.

The origins of this lie in two factors. One was the failure of the party to accept the continuation of private production in agriculture in the long term, which had resulted in underinvestment and a lingering uncertainty—on the part of the regimes as well as of the peasants—about the future of the private sector. The fears of the peasants were intensified by creeping nationalization of the land, which brought the proportion of the land in private ownership down from 84 percent in 1970 to about 78 percent in 1975. The second factor was the degree of control exercised by state administrators, particularly at the *gmina* (district) level, over farmers. This was so far-reaching and so intrusive that the net combination of low procurement prices, low investment, and state interference persuaded many farmers, quite understandably, to cease producing for the market and to revert to something like self-subsistence. The results were disastrous. By 1979, the estimated gap between supply and demand in meat was about 25 percent. It was hardly surprising that in 1980, many Polish peasants decided that regardless of the cost, they would press for an independent trade union of their own.

None of this applies elsewhere in Eastern Europe. Only in Yugoslavia is there still a sizable private sector, and the Yugoslav peasantry remains satisfied by state and local policies. Elsewhere, the bulk of the land is collectivized or is directly under state control in the form of state farms. The most noticeable feature of collectivized agriculture is that, astonishingly, it has tended to satisfy peasant aspirations. The dog that did not bark in Czechoslovakia in 1968, when it really had a chance of so doing, was the peasantry—there was no pressure for decollectivization at all.[11] In Czechoslovakia, Hungary, and East Germany, where the proportion of agricultural producers has been declining sharply to West European levels, the peasantry has shown no inclination to attack the existing order; on the contrary, the agricultural sectors of these countries produce, although perhaps not too efficiently, generally enough to prevent the food import bill from becoming too excessive. Thus the complex of problems that helped to destabilize Poland—not enough food and a dissatisfied peasantry—is not to be found anywhere else in Eastern Europe.

THE INTELLIGENTSIA

One of the functions of the intelligentsia is to think independently, to offer alternative ideas about the future, to criticize the present, and to interpret the past. A regime that can offer its intellectuals minimum conditions for pursuing these tasks can generally count on their loyalty and even perhaps their creativity. For communist systems, however, it has been difficult to live with the criticism of the intelligentsia because the leadership is claimed to be the sole interpreter of the one source of all knowledge and wisdom—Marxism-Leninism. This helps to explain why since 1956 and 1961 Communist leaders have sought a limited accommodation with intellectuals, particularly the technical intelligentsia needed for its skills in "constructing socialism." In return for loyalty, the state offered intellectuals some room to maneuver, to pursue their tasks—a great improvement on the enforced conformity of the Stalinist era.

The Polish variant of this dispensation that emerged in the 1970s was different from those in other East European countries in one important respect: by the late

1970s, the intelligentsia had begun once more to claim a role autonomous of the state and to reject co-optation. The principal reason for this was the evident disintegration of state and society—above all, of the economy—and popular resentment at Gierek's comfortable passivity. Moreover, the intelligentsia's mounting determination to question the way in which Poland was being governed signaled its dislike of being ignored not merely in matters of broad policy, but even in much more readily immediate or mundane matters such as the plans for the Katowice Steel Works, where objections and arguments against it were simply dismissed by the authorities.[12] The activity of KOR and ROPCiO was only the most visible end of the spectrum of dissatisfaction. It is at this point that the relationship between the intelligentsia and the Church took on a special significance. Unlike the role played by religion for the workers, the intelligentsia's interest was in the Church as a competitive framework of institutions, which the state was never able wholly to subdue.

In other East European countries, the relationship between the party and the intelligentsia never reached this form of political contest. In each case, some local factor inhibited the intelligentsia, which might have had reasons as cogent as the Poles had, from making a similar impact. In East Germany this was owing primarily to the residual commitment of many East German intellectuals to Marxism and the view that however unpleasant some aspects of the German Democratic Republic might be, it was still the only socialist German state. The competition from West Germany as an alternative focus of German politics has always posed a danger to the regime, because it represents another, equally viable center of loyalty for East German society. Hence the East German intelligentsia has never dared to stray too far, and the party has found it relatively easy to contain the ad hoc protests that have emanated from intellectuals. In Czechoslovakia, the authorities, relying on the effect of the post-1969 trauma of Czechoslovak society, felt safe in defusing the challenge of Charter 77 with police and propaganda methods. Their efforts have been largely successful. The charter's call for a dialogue was ignored; chartists have been harassed, tried, imprisoned, or expatriated without any risk of serious popular reaction. The bulk of Czechoslovak intellectuals, sensing perhaps that they could not rely on broader support, remained passive—and this has been quite enough for the regime.

In Hungary, it was the mechanization of co-optation evolved after 1961—a successful attempt by the regime to persuade its intellectuals that it represented the least undesirable system that Hungary could hope for—that has been the means of keeping the intellectuals quiescent. Encapsulated in this is the trauma of 1956, with its failed hopes and restricted horizons, together with the effects of the second terror (1956–61).[13] Despite growing evidence by the late 1970s that the Kádár system differed from those in other countries only in the subtlety of its manipulative methods and that it restricted the intelligentsia's access to decision-making almost as much as any other East European regime, the equation continues to hold. The small opposition that emerged in 1977 has limited itself to activity among other intellectuals, and its agenda contains nothing more subversive than alternative theoretical visions of the organization of society.

In Rumania, the intelligentsia has been, if anything, even more subservient, and it has accepted its peripheral role with hardly a murmur. With some exceptions, it has sought no right to criticize or to present alternatives. Indeed, a large number of intellectuals have actively entered Ceausescu's service, especially by identifying themselves with the party's promotion of a nationalist ethos. The Rumanian tradition of conformity and pursuit of hermetic, abstract philsophical speculation, the absence of links with other groups in society as close, as, say, in Hungary or Poland, have made it much easier for the party to co-opt the intellectuals. In Bulgaria the pattern has been similar, albeit without the tradition of abstract philsophical speculation.

POLAND: MODEL FOR EASTERN EUROPE?

In the preceding sections of this chapter, I have attempted to provide at least a partial answer to this question by stressing the specific features of and developments in Poland, and by suggesting that there were (and are) comparatively few direct parallels in other East European countries. However, a discussion of prospects of political change must also take other factors into consideration. Indeed, there are grounds for arguing that, potentially, the Polish disease is contagious—if not immediately, then in the long run. The crucial assumption in this argument rests on the fact that East European states and societies have all started from the same base line. They were all forced to adopt virtually identical (that is to say, alien) political systems, and although the evolution of these systems has varied from country to country, a number of trends have been common to all. This is what has made the Polish upheaval such a problem for the rest of Eastern Europe.

Essentially, no East European country has succeeded in broadening its political system sufficiently to allow a wider section of the population access to power over decisions taken in its name—this at a time when popular aspirations for greater control over one's environment are growing throughout the world. Naturally, these aspirations can be deflated by force, as Czechoslovakia demonstrates, but the effect of such a use of force eventually wears off, and then pressure from below is too likely to reassert itself, possibly more powerfully than before.

In this respect, the existence of an independent trade union movement is bound to exercise a fascination for other East European societies, where many people have come to feel the need for a better protection of their interests than the present system provides. The right of society to organize itself without intervention and direction from above is a part of the political tradition of many of these countries, as illustrated by previous crises (Hungary, 1956; Czechoslovakia, 1968). The chances are, therefore, that in the long run the Polish experiment will serve as a point of reference elsewhere in Eastern Europe, possibly somewhat in the way that religion played that role in Poland.

What one society adopts from another, is, of course, tempered by other factors. One of these is whether society A, the model, is seen favorably in society B, the imitator. It is relevant, therefore, to examine the stereotype of the Pole in other East European societies; for the more positive the stereotype, the greater the attraction of the Polish example. The picture is a mixed one. In both East Germany and Czechoslovakia, for instance, Poland's image has been rather negative. In East Germany this is compounded of traditional anti-Polish sentiments evidenced in contemptuous expressions like *polnische Wirtschaft,* or *polnische Ordnung* (both of which may be translated loosely as "the way the Poles run things") and resentment at the thousands of Poles who had streamed over to the German Democratic Republic for shopping expeditions in the 1970s.[14] In addition, the East German leadership was deliberately fostering an anti-Polish mood in 1980–81 by blaming economic difficulties on dislocations caused by Polish events. The intensification of the campaign to rehabilitate Prussia provided a set of symbols with an unmistakably anti-Polish coloring.[15] Finally, the East German population itself, fearing that it would lose substantially if Poland collapsed, proved receptive to the campaign fostered by the regime—so much so that in April 1981 the East German Lutheran Church felt impelled to "express dismay that old prejudices are being revived at times" and to call for prayers for "our Polish neighbors."

Perhaps the image of things Polish was never quite as unfavorable among Czechs as among East Germans (and is much more positive among Slovaks). Nevertheless, the initial response in Czechoslovakia to Polish events was cautious, at best neutral, and generally tinged with anxiety lest the outcome of the crisis result in increased hardships for the Czechoslovak consumer. Mixed with this there was probably a measure of *Schadenfreude* stemming from the lingering resentment with the part played by the Polish armed forces in the occupation of Czechoslovakia in 1968; that, added to a whole complex of historical quarrels between Czechs and Poles, helped to explain the cool reception accorded to the Polish events by many Czechs and Slovaks. This may well have been compounded by a sense of cultural superiority, not unlike that of the East Germans—the feeling that the Czechs had nothing to learn from the Poles. Over and above this relatively negative attitude on the part of Czechoslovak society, Czechoslovak perceptions must have also been influenced to some extent by the vitriolic anti-Polish campaign waged by the party leadership, most notably by the hard-liner Vasil Bilak.

By contrast, the image of the Poles among Hungarians has been much more positive—and so has, accordingly, been the response of most Hungarians to the Polish events. To judge from the interviews published in Hungarian *samizdat,* workers were intensely interested in the strikes and their aftermath, and were generally very sympathetic to Solidarity. Among the intelligentsia, reservations were far more in evidence, perhaps conditioned by a fear that Hungarian workers, inspired by the Polish example, might set off a chain of events leading to a repetition of the 1956 bloodbath. The Hungarian leadership showed itself to be more sophisticated than its counterparts in East Germany and Czechoslovakia, and refrained from engaging in abusive polemics. In Rumania and Bulgaria, contacts with Poland had always been few and far between, so the reactions of both the people and their leaders were not based on any existing stereotypes. Perhaps because of their geographic and psychological remoteness, Bulgarians seemed to be relatively unconcerned about the momentous developments in Poland; so were the Rumanians—although there is some evidence that by and large the popular response in both countries was fairly positive. To be sure, as the situation in Poland kept deteriorating, and as Solidarity became increasingly radical, the leaderships of all East European countries adopted a harsher and more menacing stance. Yet these can scarcely be taken to reflect the attitude of their respective populations.

The foregoing was written before the imposition of martial law in December 1981, and in full awareness that the Polish "renewal" might eventually be aborted. The military *Putsch* was, of course, greeted with relief by the East European regimes, hopeful that a virus that had threatened to spread throughout the bloc has now been successfully eliminated. Yet in the long run these hopes are likely to prove illusory, much as Jaruzelski's faith in the efficacy of power is likely to sour. Which is to say that the attraction of Solidarity—with all the qualifications outlined in this essay—may well outlive the measures taken against it.

Above all, there has been no indication that the satisfaction of the East European regimes is tempered by any awareness of the magnitude of their own problems. On the contrary, they seem content to relapse into a comfortable conservatism, more than ever determined to ignore the challenge of political change facing that part of the world in the 1980s.

Part 2

READINGS

FOREWORD

The excerpts from newspapers, journals, and books that appear in these pages are all related to the topics covered in part one. With a few exceptions (such as a few items under the heading "Censorship"), they do not belong to the category of "documents," either official (government decrees, instructions, and the like) or unofficial (e.g., programmatic statements by oppositionist groups or letters of protest). Documentary materials of this sort are, of course, of immense importance, but most of them have already appeared in print and are accessible to the English reading public. For this reason, I tried to select items such as articles, essays, discussions, and interviews that are likely to convey a vivid sense of the reality of Poland in the 1970s—the economic and social conditions, the issues (political, religious, ideological) that preoccupied ever larger segments of the intelligentsia, the way in which society's aspirations and grievances were articulated, the nature and impact of government policies. Obviously the "Readings" neither exhaust the range of possible subjects nor do justice to their complexities and nuances. Yet, taken together, they provide an insight into a remarkable period of contemporary history, and thus into the forces that contributed to the genesis of Poland's "bloodless revolution."

Some of the items have been slightly abbreviated. Except for specific journal citations, all the footnotes are mine.

Sources

Biuletyn Informacyjny (News bulletin) (Warsaw), official organ of KOR
Bratniak (The fraternalist), published in the 1970s by the Young Poland Movement (RMP), a nationalistically oriented group with headquarters in Gdańsk
Czarna księga cenzury PRL (Black book of censorship of the Polish People's Republic), 2 vols., published by *Aneks*, London, 1977
Głos (The voice) (Warsaw), an independent sociopolitical monthly established in 1977 by a group of writers connected with KOR
Krytyka (Criticism), a political quarterly associated with KOR and representing, according to its editors, the traditions of the PPS (prewar democratic Polish Socialist Party)
Kultura (Culture) (Warsaw), an official political and literary weekly
Kultura (Paris), an influential émigré monthly, published in France under the editorship of Jerzy Giedroyć since the late 1940s
Placówka (The outpost), an uncensored peasant periodical
Res Publica (The republic), an independent quarterly of mildly conservative and traditionalist views
Spotkania (Encounters), according to its masthead, "an independent journal of young Catholics," published in Lublin
Zapis (The record), an independent literary monthly, one of the first uncensored publications, established in 1977
Życie Literackie (Literary life), a weekly, published in Kraków, under the editorship of Władysław Machejek

NOTE: All the uncensored periodicals (identified by an asterisk) listed above ceased publication in December 1981.

Economic and Social Problems

The items in this section pertain to some of the major afflictions of Polish society, that led to the 1980 upheaval—*e.g.*, the monstrous mismanagement of the country's economy and the resulting economic decline; the growth of "cronyism," graft, corruption, and social inequality; and finally, one of the most alarming symptoms of social decay—alcoholism.

All these problems became increasingly manifest during the Gierek era; yet to discuss them openly and honestly became, at the same time, commensurately more difficult (see section on censorship). Which is why much of the most damning evidence appeared not in the official press but in the various journals and newspapers published by oppositionist groups. Thus the article "Things I Have Known," by the journalist Józef Kuśmierek (who had never, incidentally, been associated with any dissident activity), appeared in a KOR publication, immediately becoming a *succès de scandale*. Yet the official Polish press, too, would frequently come up with a revealing insight, such as the humorous portrait of a con man—"Dyzma," by Jerzy Urban, at the time of its publication a leading contributor to the weekly *Polityka,* subsequently General Jaruzelski's assiduous press spokesman. Other matters could be discussed only in publications designed for a limited audience. This is true of the survey of alcoholism in Poland, which became widely known only after its publication by an anonymous political group known as the Polish League for Independence.

As for the last item, "Privileges," it, too, is typical of the complexities and contradictions of Polish life. It appeared openly in Poland,. but not until a year after the emergence of Solidarity, and (as the editorial preface points out) not without considerable opposition on the part of the censors. The picture of social stratification presented in this article pertains largely to the 1970s, yet much of it remained relevant during the country's "renewal." The regime's reluctance and/or inability to deal with this problem clearly contributed to the burgeoning social and political conflicts of that period.

THINGS I HAVE KNOWN

Józef Kuśmierek

Unfavorable weather conditions have become an inseparable part of our economic life, and so—to counterbalance them—have constant overfulfillment of plans and completion of capital projects ahead of schedule, always accompanied by heroic dedication and self-sacrifice on the part of those responsible. It is high time to eliminate the bad weather and self-sacrifice from our everyday vocabulary, reserving them for occasions when their use is fully justified.

We know the conditions in which we have existed as a people and a state for a thousand years. Maximum and minimum temperatures, summer and winter rainfall, the water level in our rivers, wind velocity—all have been recorded for the past two hundred years. Since 1851 this has been the duty of specially appointed officials. All the data have been carefully collated and are the subject of research by specialists in various branches of science. This research provides a basis for standard procedures in the building industry, communications, energy, and the armed forces. Specifications for lubricants and oil, brake fluids used by motor transport, oils in transformers, substances to protect freezing have all been carefully worked out. There exist special agencies to determine whether in view of the prevailing climatic conditions new materials and substances should be authorized for general use, and whether old ones can still be used in new technologies or new building systems.

All this, and the experience of centuries, provides us with guarantees against the caprices of nature, which can be unpleasant at times but need never be catastrophic. We have been recording for the past thirty years the power of both electricity and the turbines that generate it. We know the area and volume of the dwellings that we have to heat, the capacity of the installation, and the necessary input of energy to maintain the temperature required for health and safety.

This whole system has been evolved and given the force of law because no one can take lightly the normal functioning of the life of a nation of 35 million people, or of its health. One cannot simply toss a coin to decide whether next winter will be mild and gentle, whether normal temperatures or—which can always happen—abnormally low temperatures will prevail. Unfortunately, in none of the areas mentioned here, and in some others not mentioned, have these rules been observed for a long time.

At the beginning of every winter, whether mild or harsh, the mass media use the offensive phrase "winter has taken us by surprise." Some are, perhaps, surprised to find that snow falls between December and March, that temperatures drop below zero, that winds blow, and that the roads are icy. The majority of the people are not surprised—witness the fact that we buy toboggans and skis for our kids, that we take our winter clothing out of mothballs, and that those who feel the need for it equip themselves with a tan in the summer months, obedient to the urgings of those very same mass media.

Every—literally, every—winter it turns out that two-thirds of the snowplows and sand scatterers are unserviceable. To scold the caretakers of dwelling houses for failure to clear sidewalks is a mockery of common sense, as can be seen from the lists of registered buildings and the numbers of paid caretakers and of householders, provided for in the budgets of our towns. There is something insulting in this business of shifting onto all of us the blame for the results of "surprised by winter." Modern meteorology and a really experienced farmer, skilled in observing and recording natural phenomena, can predict either with a high degree of probability or indeed with complete certainty what the coming winter will be like.

At a press conference, I think in 1973, the then Vice-Premier and Minister of Mines and Power announced—and reporters present at the conference made much of it—that "Polish power stations have reached for the first time a level of output at which reserves exceed peak demand." At the same conference we were also told about the government's decision to build two big new power stations, Polaniec and Northern Oder, so as to create the basic condition for the regular growth of our whole economic life at the rates provided for in the plan. According to the decrees published at that time, the two stations were to begin operating in 1975 and reach full capacity in 1978.

It was the ambition of the senior officials in the Ministry of Mining and Power, and of those in charge of Energoprzem at Kraków and the Enterprise for the Construction of Power Stations and Works at Szczecin, to reduce the time spent on building the two stations to thirty-six months instead of fifty to sixty months, the previous time span. Their calculation was simple: building in thirty-six months would be more expensive, but the earlier linkup of the station to the network would more than cover the higher investment cost in the short term, and the construction firms with all their equipment would be able to move on to their next site fifteen to twenty-five months earlier. Work on the two buildings began with a flourish. Hundreds of hours and tons of concrete and thousands of tons of steel were sunk into the foundations; the necessary equipment and skills were assembled; sidings and unloading platforms were built.

Then, in 1974, work at both sites was interrupted. At Opole the work came to a complete stop: those in charge switched to the construction of Swinoujście III, leaving behind a "No entry to unauthorized persons" sign and some boarded-up huts. Billions of zlotys that were supposed to bear interest in the form of heat and light for Opole in 1975 remained imprisoned in the ground. The most important of the managerial staff were transferred to other jobs, but a pretense was made that something was happening, and that the first megawatts would be produced, as our television triumphantly announced . . . sometime after 1980. This involved cancellation of the order for boilers for the two stations, which were to have been built in Racibórz, postponement of the expansion of Dolmel at Wrocław, and withdrawal of orders from Zamech at Elbląg. We'll build Polaniec in record time, our officials boasted: Work there will be completed in 100 months, and at Opole in 120.

I was not "surprised" by what happened on New Year's Eve this year because on my way back from Racibórz, immediately after this decision had been taken (which meant suicide for our economy), I talked for several hours with a brain trust of experts in our power and electrical engineering industries. "We don't like to think what will happen to our country after 1977," said the most important members of that group. Well, they need not have worried about thinking of the future: all, to a man, have been relieved of their posts.

The effects made themselves felt before 1977. Other agencies, which were not informed of the decisions on energy, rapidly developed their potential, reporting every twenty-second of July that new enterprises had been set in motion and old ones modernized. "Limitation" of power for old and new plans began as early as 1975, and a year later artificial fertilizer factories, agriculture, and the service industries suffered power cuts. In 1977, when power cuts became general, and not only in winter months or at peak hours, the two power stations should have been producing 7,000 megawatts. This, mind you, according to a government decision!

On September 2, 1978, the Chairman of the State Energy Council, Professor Kazimierz Kopecki, testified that "the losses suffered by the Polish economy as the result of power cuts must be reckoned in the region of 20 billion zlotys a year." Polaniec, built at a forced pace, would have cost 18 billion. The absence of Polaniec deprives us of the value of one new power station every twelve months.

II

Of all the shortfalls that plague our economy it is the lack of reserve capacity in transport that has brought us to the brink of economic chaos and ruin.

The prewar experience of highly industrialized countries showed irrefutably that rail transport was becoming less important than road transport. The experience of the last war showed that road transport lends itself to more uses than any other mode of transportation. Every war yields lessons for the peacetime economy, as Hannibal showed when he first blazed what is now the most attractive tourist trail across the Alps. Had it not been for Napoleon and his Continental Blockade, who knows whether we should not still have been sweetening our tea with cane sugar? The war of 1939–45 proved that the heavy truck is the finest form of transport.

When the decision was being taken to build what is today a rather large automobile industry, someone should have asked what sort of vehicle would, if not compete, then at least cooperate, with the railway, while eliminating horse-drawn transport from the towns. . . .

At the Unification Congress* we hailed the first five vehicles from Starachowice as a great achievement. It was the result of continuation of the prewar ideas and efforts of our designers.

The three-tonner was a miracle of automobile engineering before 1939, although even then many European and American firms were producing an increasing number of seven-, ten-, and fifteen-ton vehicles. Delight in Starachowice's success clouded our vision of the motor industry's future. The new vehicle was a good one for military needs, but too small and too light for intercity transport, and too big for use as a delivery van inside towns. When I discussed the matter with designers at Starachowice in the sixties, I was told that our four-tonner Star would fill a gap left by the European automobile industry. I was assured that all the big firms were going over to the production either of big trucks or of pickup delivery vans carrying up to one and a half tons. I did not find these arguments very convincing. If such experienced firms as Fiat, Mercedes, Berliet, Volvo, Leyland, and even little Steyer were switching to trucks over ten tons, perhaps it was because they had a better notion of market demand than our ambitious but still immature team at Starachowice. We did indeed fall into a hole left by the European automobile industry: our Star, now a six-tonner, is an orphan in the homeland of European trucks.

It is a fact that no one produces anything like it, but it is also a fact that no one wants to buy it. We may sell or donate a batch of Stars to a Third World country, and that is all. Although it has grown up to be a six-tonner, it is now, as before, undoubtedly too big for an urban delivery vehicle and decidedly too small for a motor vehicle to supplement rail transport.

The mistake was soon spotted, and it was soon decided to design and build trucks in Jelcze, called originally Żubr and now Jelcz. The defect of this vehicle at birth was the Wola engine. It was quickly decided to buy a license for the production of the Leyland engine, which was then still up to European standards. But whether with the Wola or with the Leyland engine, Żubr remained at the lower limit of big trucks, laboriously pushing its way from its original six to its present ten tons. Still, the license for a good engine had been bought, it went into production in Mielec and Andrychów, and . . . something extraordinary happened.

Twice I performed the triangular journey from Starachowice (where the new version of the engine as adapted for the six-tonner was tried out) to Mielec (where extra horsepower was squeezed out of the Leyland, since it was correctly foreseen that the end of cooperation between Skoda-Karossa-Jelcz in 1970 would create a need for an engine for a large bus) and Andrychów, where the Leyland engine, admirably suited to a six- to seven-ton vehicle, was already being produced under a license. Proof of this is the cooperation between Andrychów and Sanok, which preferred the Andrychów to the Starachowice engine for the buses it built. What, then, was the "extraordinary" thing of which I spoke? Well—not

*In December 1948, following a period in which the Workers' (i.e., Communist) Party had consolidated in power and succeeded in weakening the PPS (Polish Socialist Party)—largely by arresting many of its leaders on charges of "counterrevolutionary" and "anti-Soviet" activity—the two Marxist parties merged into one: the Polish United Workers' Party. The merger in effect turned Poland into a one-party state.

one of the designers at Mielec or Andrychów visited Starachowice, or took any interest in what was going on there. The Starachowice people were equally incurious. It was an extraordinary thing because all this was happening in enterprises belonging not just to the same ministry but to the same combine. So that, "officially," the only person who knew what was going on in all three factories was myself, a newspaperman.

Then at last came a period of rapid growth, and with it the need to transport containers to help out the railways, to satisfy the growing demand for urban and intercity bus services, to service export trade. . . . And we, although we had a considerable potential frozen in the motor industry, were and still are forced to buy for hard currency Espano-Suizas, Berliets, Steyers, Fiats, Volvos, Tatras, Mercedes, Majiruses, Hungarian Icariuses, Yugoslavian Sonoses, and even the Rumanian International, which in spite of a name so pleasing to our ears nobody wants. . . . There is no country on earth on whose (quite respectable) highways you can see so many types and makes of vehicles circulate as on Polish roads. The service garages could not be happier. The Central Wrecking Yards have a high turnover. Every one of the vehicles bought so dearly in foreign currency goes to the wrecker's yard after 200,000–300,000 kilometers because spare parts are unobtainable. If it comes to that, our homemade Star, Jelcz, and the more recent Berliet are doing no better.

We cannot call it a "surprise" that motor transport, which forges ahead rapidly everywhere else in the world, is in a bad way in Poland . . . or that we have a payments deficit with capitalist countries.

III

I have been a reporter for thirty-five years. I have never spent a single day at an editorial desk. I avoid brainwashing at training and briefing sessions. I have always written about what I have seen, heard, and checked for myself, what I could write about with full responsibility. This sense of responsibility has sometimes meant that I have had to burst open the doors that the censors had stupidly slammed on obvious truths, and to pay for it by being kept out of print and out of employment.

I have some experience, and I know about the function of information, the role of the press and propaganda.

The mistake of our propaganda stems from the erroneous assumption that society is hostile to the changes initiated after the war. This leads to hysterical demands for constant and loud approbation of the regime and its policies. For the past thirty years no one among those in charge of our propaganda has recognized that the public cannot live in a state of uninterrupted euphoria and feverish enthusiasm.

It is infantile if not downright idiotic to think that by harping on and endlessly invoking past successes we can ever mobilize and win the support of the public. Successes are the result of work and effort on the part of society, and are neither a miracle nor an extraordinary achievement for which the regime can claim exclusive credit.

It is absurd to praise the railroad men for overfulfilling their norms when everybody is acutely aware from his own experience that the railroad system is a failure. Farmers who for thirty years have not been able to obtain a single lump of coal except by bribery, trickery, or plain theft are not likely to be much impressed by all the noisy propaganda about individual miners who have dug so many extra tons of coal. People who for the past five years have been standing in ever-lengthening queues to obtain a slice of meat can scarcely be expected to cheer some heroic farmer who has presumably raised more hogs than his plan had called for.

People keep asking what's become of all the coal, where those quantities of meat have gone to, and where we ship all those goods if the railroad men and dockers are (as we are told) continually overfulfilling their plans. This list of goods now but never previously in short supply grows longer. Matches are in short supply, drugstores don't carry basic medicines, there is no cotton wool, and buying a newspaper is becoming something of a problem. Nobody tries to explain it rationally, and silence begets anxiety and suspicion.

Has no one realized what a fatal error was the explanation of the meat shortage offered by a journalist of *Polityka*—namely, that it was all the fault of retired persons, whose pensions had just been increased? This is the sort of reasoning that, in our propaganda system, earns a reporter promotion to deputy chief editor.

The shortage of reliable information generates gossip, rumors, tittle-tattle. Since disasters, failures, or mistakes are never honestly admitted or explained, they tend to assume fantastic proportions in the eyes of the public. The news that four dead bodies have been found in snowdrifts in Warsaw may swell by tomorrow to the discovery of a stack of bodies. And the number of bodies will grow from day to day as long as the mass media keep silent and there is no official report on this subject.

When disaster strikes again, let us not be surprised to hear those cruel and damning words: "The press is lying!" Everybody knows from personal experience that to lie is easy, but to undo a lie—or to wriggle out of it—is often impossible.

You cannot improve the government structures, and call for sacrifices or patience, if you do not have the slightest confidence in society and do not enjoy the confidence of society in return.

I believe that I have every right to express these opinions—without fear of punishment for criticism of the regime. Today, with our historical perspective, we only have to study the press for the years 1955–57 and 1968–70 to see that the journalists who alerted the ruling team to impending crisis were right to do so. As a journalist, I have lived through and been part of five great political upheavals—September 1948, October 1956, March 1968, December 1970, and June 1976. I am absolutely convinced—and not from reading tea leaves—that we are on the threshold of another and most serious upheaval of all. Loss of confidence in the present ruling team, which has now reached its nadir, goes together with loss of faith that any change at all can truly improve and steer the fortunes of the nation in the direction it wants to take.

These bitter words are dictated not by the spirit of opposition or hostile criti-

cism. Read any historical study of the People's Guard or the People's Army.*
You will find my name there. Or read any postwar anthology of reportage or
fiction, and you will find my work there.

From *Krytyka* (Warsaw),
Winter 1978/1979

Translated by Halina and Harry Willetts

*The People's Guard (later referred to as the People's Army) was organized in 1942, following the
rebirth of the Polish Communist Party (dissolved by Stalin in 1938), under the name of the Polish
Workers' Party.

DYZMA

Jerzy Urban

He came in response to an ad. A large factory was looking for an economist, with five years of experience, to take over its trade department. He brought a copy of his diploma. The letter of recommendation, provided by the Central Office of Foreign Trade, was exemplary. He pointed to the statement in his personal documents that indicated his previous place of employment, and confirmed that he left of his own volition, having been unable to find an apartment.

He placed all the documents on the desk without saying a word. Then he asked:

"What's the salary?"

They told him.

"For an economist with a master's degree?"

"For an economist with a master's degree."

"I never knew that your pay is so wretched. Too little."

He turned to go, but they called him back. It's not easy, after all, to find a man with suitable credentials who wants a job in the provinces. They told him they'd look into the possibility of a higher salary. Did he know any foreign languages? Yes, he did. Then he asked about an apartment. They told him there was one waiting for him. He said, "Raise the pay, and I'll be back next week."

And come back he did. The salary was raised. With special permission of the management.

At the outset, he had a long conversation with the director. The latter was in a quandary. Was he dealing with a con man, or a genius?

He familiarized the new employee with the marketing problems. The people over at Trade demand elasticity, he explained; they provide the factory with short-term agreements and insist that the assortments always be adjusted to the demands of the market. The trouble, however, is that this kind of production

The title of this essay is taken from *Kariera Nikodema Dyzmy* (The career of Nikodem Dyzma), by Tadeusz Dołęga-Mostowicz, a celebrated prewar novel about a Polish con man.

simply doesn't work. For instance . . . And the director pulled out reams of statistics.

The visitor paid them no heed. With an imperious gesture, he shoved the papers aside and said:

"It'll be taken care of."

The director became irritated. "What? What will be taken care of? The deficit merchandise or the change in orders?"

"Either we'll do what Trade wants, or if Trade wants, it will be done. What's the matter—were you born yesterday?"

"We're being smothered by export," the trade genius's chief continued. "To do what they want us to do is impossible—we have neither the raw materials nor the necessary machinery. All these things had already been settled some time ago. According to engineer D., we'll get the stuff for the second quarter of next year. You can't dream of getting it earlier, because it's only by next year that the import orders will be filled. Earlier delivery is ruled out because of the international context."

"Mr. Director!" said the newcomer, "why all this talk? My eardrums are bursting. Everything will be taken care of."

The director's ire was again rising. "How!?"

"Look, this is my third day here, right?" said the economist. "I'm busy with my apartment. I have no head for export. Why don't you put together a delegation, and in two days I'll take them with me to Warsaw. I'll be back in five days, and then I'll tell you how things stand. All right?"

"All right," the director replied. "But aren't you taking it all too lightly? You people from the center ''

"Enough of this talk! When I say it will be done, it will be done."

"Get yourself out of here, but quick!" said the genius of trade to his co-worker. "And don't forget to take the desk with you—and also the plants. They give me a headache."

"Where am I going to work?" asked the new chief's only subordinate dejectedly after being evicted.

"That's not my problem," said the trade expert. Then he tacked a card marked "Jan F., M.A." on the door, closed the door, and left.

For two days no one saw him. On the third day he came to collect his delegation and left for the capital. No sign of him for a week. Then he returned.

"It's been taken care of," he reported to his chief.

The chief nearly jumped out of his seat. "What's been taken care of?"

"Everything."

"What do you mean, everything? What concretely? With whom? How?"

"What's there to talk about? The papers will come, so you will see for yourself. I'm off to Warsaw, to make sure things are in order."

"What things?"

"Look, do you think that those bureaucrats will ever fill the orders if I don't breathe down their necks? Maybe by next year, if we're lucky. . . ."

He left. He telephoned from Warsaw. He asked questions that made the director's flesh creep.

"There he is, wheeling and dealing, yet he's never taken the trouble to learn anything about our production," the director complained to his colleagues.

They waited to see what would come of it. Finally the head of trade returned, his pockets full of orders. Within a few days, letters started arriving at the factory, and things became lively.

The director pressed his trade genius to tell him how he had managed it all. But it didn't seem as if the new man refused to explain, but that he simply couldn't.

Within the next few weeks he kept calling Warsaw, until it became obvious that the man knew everybody in the capital who was in any way connected with that particular industry. And if the management of the factory had no idea of what magic was at work, they could at least overhear snatches of conversations.

"What—no? Have you gone mad? What are you in charge of—peddling herring or foreign trade? No? Well, then, I'll call the minister. You think of nothing except how to destroy our industry. . . ."

And more in the same vein . . .

"Nikodem Dyzma," commented the chief's secretary prophetically. She was very well read.

The head of trade wrought miracles, though naturally the first series of successes was followed by some failures. For a bureaucrat, however, his behavior was bizarre: frenzied trips to the capital followed each other in rapid succession; his office stayed empty for days; papers would be either ignored or signed without reading; everything was settled by word of mouth; and as for meetings, the head of trade avoided them like poison. The opinion of his colleagues was unanimous: the man was strange—and a genius.

One must also admit that he joined no cliques, kept his distance, maintained no relations with his associates. Which is not to say that he had no social life. In fact, every day he bicycled to the inn located in a nearby town, where he spent hours drinking with the locals, returning to the factory apartment complex in the evening well intoxicated. Which is why he was always suffering from a hangover.

Oddly enough, no one in the factory ever discovered that Jan F.—for that really was his name—had no master's degree, was not an economist, had never made it to high school, and hadn't even finished elementary school. Neither the factory management nor their Warsaw associates ever realized that this man—agile, obstinate, and teeming with dynamism—had not even the remotest knowledge of production, of marketing, of economic laws and principles, and that his unique ability consisted, rather, in the skill with which he would seize upon an overheard formulation, some fragmentary phrases, and then appropriate them and inflate them with a dizzying show of confidence, outshouting and driving everybody to exhaustion, until they simply gave up—and gave in. In short—a master of bluff and bluster.

The truth finally came out—though in a most unexpected way.

Jan F. lived with his wife and children, as mentioned earlier, in the factory's apartment complex. Which meant in full view of everyone.

The wives of the engineers, bored and unable to find suitable jobs in the boondocks, took a vigorous interest in the new arrival. In time, the factory's "society salons" were buzzing with fascinating stories: that the wife of Mr. F. is raising a hog in the back room, that she keeps potatoes in their bathtub, that the children are filthy, that Mrs. F. is slovenly, and that when the salary comes in, she and her husband stuff themselves to the gills, so that by the end of the month there's nothing left to eat but potatoes. And so on, ad infinitum.

The rumors emboldened the women secretaries. And so they furnished the director of the factory with a manuscript written by Jan F., which boasted more spelling errors than words.

Things heated up.

No one—that is to say, neither the factory director, nor the hero of this tale, nor the author of these lines—knows who came to the procurator and informed him of their suspicions. Most likely the procurator did something embarrassingly simple—namely, he lifted the phone and called the institutions where Mr. Jan F. had ostensibly been employed. The answer was that no one had ever heard of him.

A brief investigation followed. Yet even when everything was out in the open, the director was still reluctant to fire him.

The procurator's office established that Jan F. had previously worked in some city cooperative. It was a small workshop, and Jan F. was an ordinary worker. In time, he was elected to the managing board and became involved in matters of trade, eventually acquiring some kind of experience. As the future was to show, he successfully parlayed the experience gained in a small shop consisting of a few workers into a grand job in a large government factory.

One fine day Jan F. fell out with his colleagues and was dismissed. He decided to look for a better job. He forged his personal documents and letter of reference, including the statement that he had left his job voluntarily. How he had obtained the official stationery remains a mystery to this day.

He was sentenced to a year and eight months in jail.

At the trial, his former director, appearing as a witness, said:

"There was a lot of unpleasantness, though this was really my fault. The man was a terrific worker. Such trade experts don't grow on trees. I'll be frank: if I could, I'd hire him again tomorrow, with open arms. I never had such an excellent man heading my trade department. I don't now, and I never will."

From *Wszystkie Nasze Ciemne Sprawy*
(All our dark affairs), by Jerzy Urban Kraków, 1974), pp. 114–18

Translated by Abraham Brumberg

ALCOHOLISM IN POLAND

The text that appears below is taken from the book *Poland 2000*, published by the Surveys and Prognoses Committee of the Presidium of the Polish Academy of Sciences. Issued in 1975 as a typescript lecture, it was designed for internal use only, with only a small number of copies in circulation, and it remains to this day unfamiliar to the general public.

We are all aware of the pernicious nature of alcoholism, of its calamitous dimensions, of the danger it poses for the future of the country. We are continuously reminded of it as we gaze at the dismal scenes enacted on the streets of our cities, on village roads, in public places. We are struck by the remarkable speed with which huge quantities of alcohol reach our retail markets, as compared with the sluggish delivery of other products. Our liquor shops are not disrupted by stocktaking or repairs; the delivery of alcohol is never delayed by lack of transportation facilities or by "illness of personnel." The most obscure hamlet, the most dilapidated and forgotten alley in the suburbs will invariably boast a store selling alcoholic beverages—or a kiosk—or, for lack of anything better, some illicit den known to everyone in the neighborhood, police included, and functioning round the clock.

How much is being produced, how much is being sold? How large a share of the national budget is devoted to alcohol production and distribution? What role does alcohol fulfill in our social life, not only as a cause of illness and crimes, not only as a brake on production, but above all as an instrument of rule? For surely it deadens the aspirations of Polish society, clouds its collective consciousness, vitiates its instinct for self-preservation, and stifles its energies. What is the actual role of alcohol in the life of our country?

These are the questions we often ask ourselves when physically confronted with this veritable plague. Any search for answers in the official press and literature is in vain. The authorities keep silent on this subject and compel everybody else to be quiet as well. "It is forbidden to disseminate in the public any statistical information concerning the state and increase of alcoholism in the whole country"—thus the guidelines of the Central Office for Control of Press, Publications and Performances, recently made available by KSS/ KOR (chapter 11, p. 10).

A partial answer to these questions is provided by the paper that we are reprinting here, with some abridgments and editorial changes. We did not ask the permission of the authors—for understandable reasons. We ask their forgiveness for this lapse—and offer them our gratitude as well. We have done so in the firm belief that their work deserves to be read by a wider public.

WORKING COMMITTEE OF THE POLISH LEAGUE FOR INDEPENDENCE

According to the statistical data furnished by GUS,* the average Pole consumed 6.2 liters of pure, 100-proof alcohol in 1974. This figure does not include the consumption of alcohol produced illegally, which—according to police sources—adds another 5 to 10 percent to the total amount. We can therefore assume that in 1974 the average Pole—a statistical unit embracing all drinking and nondrinking individuals, old people and children included—downed over seven liters of pure alcohol.

Compared with the prewar period, the per-head consumption of alcohol has grown fivefold, and has doubled in the last twenty years. The rate of increase in the consumption of alcohol from 1972 to 1973 came to 7.7 percent per inhabitant. This rate of increase is very high in comparison with other countries.

Who drinks?

Surveys conducted in the 1960s showed that over half the alcohol sold is consumed by men. Those who drink excessively are men in the most productive age bracket (twenty-one to twenty-nine years old), who are either about to marry or about to establish families, or are already fathers. These people, whose dependence on alcohol varies, provide our society with distinct behavioral models, and they constitute a high percentage of alcoholics, the number of which is estimated at between 400,000 and 500,000.

It is assumed that the average alcoholic influences and complicates the life of four people, and that there are 2–2.3 million heavy drinkers in Poland. The number of those indirectly engaged in the drinking subculture is about 8 or 9 million—which is to say, over 25 percent of the Polish population.

What do we drink?

Above all, vodka. According to the GUS statistical data, in 1973 65.1 percent of the alcohol consumed by the average Pole was vodka. In 1971–73, the consumption of vodka and spirits increased twice as rapidly as the consumption of wine and considerably faster than that of beer. Part of the reason is to be found in the January 1974 price increase of alcoholic beverages: wine went up, on the average, by 41.4 percent; beer, by 33.3 percent, and vodka, only by 20.6 percent.

How do we drink?

Characteristic of Poles is not only their preference for vodka and other beverages of high alcoholic content but also an excessive one-time consumption. Numerous polls have shown that over 50 percent of vodka-drinking adults consume it in huge quantities, thus markedly crossing the intoxication threshold—that is, by 20 centiliters, or four glasses. It is estimated that over 800,000 people cross this threshold daily.

Who drinks the most?

*GUS (Głowny Urząd Statystyczny)—Main Statistical Office.

Men drink four to seven times more than women, and for many years heavy drinking was widespread mainly among males. At the present time women constitute 7 percent of all medically treated alcoholics. As more women have entered the labor market and as their traditional role in society has altered, the alcohol problem has increased among women and is expected to grow even more in the future.

The most heavily drinking group are young men aged twenty-one to twenty-four. This has occurred within the past few years, inasmuch as national surveys in 1961 and 1962 indicated that the heaviest drinkers were aged between twenty-five and twenty-nine. Subsequent surveys revealed that the age of those who drink for the first time is becoming lower. According to the data, more than one-fourth of schoolboys aged seventeen emulate the drinking habits of adult males ("a fourth [of a liter] per head") [a common barroom expression]. In the course of six to eight years, the amount of drunkenness among the young doubled. Between 1962 and 1972 the increase in alcoholic consumption among teen-agers was considerably greater than among adults.

Alcoholic consumption among most people increases commensurately with wage increases, and decreases in step with prosperity as measured by ownership of durable goods. Adults who own more items such as refrigerators, washing machines, television sets, and so on drink less than those who only own, say, a radio. This, however, does not apply to teenagers.

There is no direct relationship between social background and the amount of alcohol consumed. In fact, it has been proven that young industrial workers with a white-collar family background drink more than those of working-class origin. One study showed that in Warsaw factories the more-educated young people consume more alcohol than the less-educated. The same is true in the countryside: the higher the education, the heavier the drinking.

There is a correlation between drinking patterns and specific family mores. Thus children of heavy drinkers will drink more than others. Palpable contradictions between parents' doctrinaire opinions, on the one hand, and their actual behavior, on the other, are a case in point. Lack of parental control is another, often fostered by the increase of women entering the work force and chronic scarcity of family time available to working parents. The exclusion of children from any family responsibilities, the reluctance to impose any demands on them—on the theory, at least in some sectors of society, that children deserve "a better life"—are other contributing factors.

Many surveys disclose that schools do not exercise any influence on alcohol-related problems, for they view their function as limited exclusively to academic matters. Teachers are generally uninformed about the family background of their pupils, and in cases of broken families this lack of interaction between school and home is especially disastrous.

Youth organizations are similarly at fault: indeed, negative behavior patterns are more frequently in evidence among those who do belong to organizations than among those who do not. What is particularly glaring is the incidence of such behavior in organizations designed to educate and socialize youth—e.g., drunkenness among directors and counselors in camps for children and young adults.

Another disturbing factor is the frequently demoralizing effect of the work-place milieu on the "alcoholic behavior" of young persons. As a rule, a worker is expected to spend his first wages on drinks for all his workmates; this is the price for being accepted as a member of the work force. Polls taken in workers' hostels yield particularly alarming statistics. Workers in positions of authority (foremen, brigade leaders, etc.) are involved in 50 percent of all recorded "alco-holic incidents," more than half of which take place in factories and on construc-tion sites—and it is this element that also inspires others to similar behavior. There is no evidence of any social discipline in places of work: no one is dis-missed for drunkenness, nor are any sanctions applied to those whose excessive drinking jeopardizes the system. The same is true for directors and managers who drink to excess.

Many attempts have been made over the years to combat the rise of alcoholism in Poland. After the war, several laws were passed and various administrative and economic measures were taken in an effort to curb the consumption of alcohol. None of them has been effective. The decree of the Council of Ministers of May 5, 1972, serves as a good example: not only did it fail to curb the consumption of liquor, but one of its unfortunately worded clauses contributed to its increase. According to this edict, any profits from the sale of alcoholic bever-ages that exceeded the 1972 level were not to be added to the assets of the territorial people's councils. What happened was that the people's councils, in an attempt to secure this money, eliminated the last restrictions on the sale of alco-hol in 1972. To this day the regulations for the sale of alcoholic beverages in relation to the sale of other consumer products have not been published. As a result, alcohol is still the most easily accessible commodity on the national mar-ket. There is one liquor store per 840 inhabitants in Poland—as compared, for instance, with one store per 27,000 persons in Sweden.

Actions aimed at removing beer kiosks from the streets of our cities have not affected the population's drinking habits. Police campaigns to clear the streets of drunks and send them to already overcrowded alcoholic clinics were undertaken for appearance' sake only. Such patently superficial measures frequently lead to results opposite of those intended. Such is the case, for instance, with the sim-plistic [antidrinking] propaganda promulgated among young people—as borne out by many polls taken among students.

The failure to provide the market with attractive consumer products or to develop adequate facilities for recreation and amusement, the lack of concerted educational campaigns, the absence of any social discipline—all these factors have had an alarming effect on the use of leisure time and have encouraged the drinking propensities of the population. The single organization created to com-bat alcoholism—the Public Antialcoholic Committee—has proved ineffectual. The mass media (radio, TV, cinema) do not have a well-defined program, and to make matters worse, censorship has prevented the dissemination of adequate information about the extent of alcoholism in Poland.

The above analysis of the problem of alcoholism in Poland, as well as of the lack of any programs for combating its future spread, suggests that the increase in alcoholic consumption will proceed apace. But the situation is so grave that some changes must, after all, occur. A simple extrapolation from recent trends indicates that within the next few decades alcohol consumption [in Poland] will reach proportions exceeding those of any other society. Some of these necessary changes will no doubt be taken by society itself, as it becomes conscious of the perils of alcoholism. The mode of life in a highly urbanized and industrialized society will act as a check on the unrestrained consumption of alcohol. Demographic factors (aging, for instance), as well as economic factors will also play their role. The question is, when will these changes come about? If they are delayed, the price paid by the Polish nation may prove excessive. Assuming that the average yearly rate of increase in alcoholic consumption—7.7 percent—is maintained over the next sixteen years, the 1990 figures of consumption of alcohol would rise to 328 percent per head, of which 21 liters would be pure spirits. In keeping with past patterns, the consumption of vodka would mount to 14 liters.

We reject this eventuality, convinced as we are that the self-protective instincts of the Polish people will not permit it to court self-destruction—indeed, the biological extinction of the nation. Nevertheless, we must remember that this instinct on which we are counting had already failed us once in the past: to be precise, in the eighteenth century.*

From *PPN* (Polish League for Independence) (Paris: Instytut Literacki, 1979), pp. 123–30

Translated by Abraham Brumberg

*The reference here is to the lack of national cohesion in the face of the territorial designs of Poland's neighbors, which resulted in the three partitions of the country (1772, 1793, and 1795–96).

PRIVILEGES

Krzysztof Czabański

This text has a history of its own. For many months it was detained by the censors. The public prosecutor became interested in it—as well as in its author and the editorial staff of the periodical in which it was finally published. Eventually, representatives of the Bureau of the Council of Ministers resolved to respond to the criticism contained in this article prior to its publication. As a result of the information supplied by Minister [Jerzy] Urban and Director Gołaszewski, the author was able to bring some of his statements up to date and make them more precise. This is duly noted in the text.

It is not the author's intention to imply that every member of the power elite, without exception, took advantage of privileges. His intention is merely to describe the mechanism that leads to depravity and that is an integral part of a certain system's *modus operandi.—The Editors* [of *Tygodik Solidarność*].

I collected information about the privileges of the ruling group in Poland in the years 1978–80. One source of information were conversations with so-called well-informed people and with members of the establishment. Some of my informants tried to convince me that the problem was marginal—an old problem, known in all countries and to all systems—and not worthy of attention. Others pointed out that the subject of our conversation was mere gossip, "vulgar rumors," a subject from which no conclusions could justifiably be drawn.

When in the spring of last year I presented a preliminary version of this essay to a dozen or so well-known sociologists and journalists, I was told that I was exaggerating and that I was giving too much credence to "evil tongues" and "slanderers." Now that so much has been revealed concerning the life of the "builders of a second Poland," I can be accused of the very opposite—namely, that the documentation I assembled doesn't do justice to the magnitude of the subject. Let me clarify at once that I am not concerned with criminal operations, corruption, material abuses, and so on. That is a matter for the public prosecutors and the courts. My only aim is to illuminate the system of legal privileges, a system created by the ruling group for its own benefit, a system resulting from

this group's unique position in society, and one which serves to stre
position. Let us begin with a brief look at the types and forms of the

SALARIES AND INCOMES

The Council of State decrees of the autumn of 1972, concerning the salaries of
individuals occupying leading state positions and pensions for those persons and
members of their families are already well known. These decrees have now been
annulled. Let us merely note that the amounts of the pensions were not disclosed
in the decrees, just as they haven't been disclosed in any documents of the Polish
United Workers' Party. The decrees sanctioned the exclusive position of the
members of the upper elite and their families (including grandchildren), and
simultaneously introduced a precise inner-group gradation (the supergroup consisting of the first secretary of the Central Committee of the Polish United Workers' Party, the premier, and the chairman of the Council of State). Moreover, the
premier could, at his discretion, extend the privileges embodied in the decrees to
a person of his choice.

Recently, the amounts of the pensions of the premier, vice-premiers, and
ministers have been divulged. Nevertheless, we still do not know the amount of
incomes received by the ruling group, though we do know that these incomes—
outside of pensions—derive from a whole system of special services, discounts,
and supplies.

The distribution of various types of goods and services is in the hands of the
Bureau of the Council of Ministers (henceforth referred to as the Bureau). The
allocation of automobiles or apartments is a source of considerable financial
income for the recipients, although its extent is difficult to gauge. Other sources
of income are: (a) the so-called envelope system, in which large sums of money
are given to members of the ruling group on state holidays and other occasions;
(b) publication fees—for example, for an official's statement in print; and (c)
gifts—i.e., on the occasion of an official's, or his wife's, name day, when they
are presented gifts (with money taken from state funds) sometimes costing tens
of thousands of zlotys. Likewise, when an official pays a visit to, say, a factory,
its management presents him with a gift, usually one of the factory's own attractive products. Gifts to officials also come from foreign delegations, which in turn
receive gifts from the institutions they visit—all of it paid for by the state treasur-
ies (our own and foreign).

The incomes of the ruling group and its subsidiaries are tax-exempt. Financial
departments do not know the government pay scale, because the so-called R
table has not been published.* The pay scale of the party functionaries is also
unknown. "Employees of the District Council Office," says Teresa Klosińska,
"faced with information sent from various institutions about the honoraria they
pay, must determine by the surname whether or not the person should be asked to
complete an income tax return." ("Compensatory Tax and the Professional
Structure of the District Council of Downtown Warsaw," typescript, Institute of

---

*The R table contains the pay scale for high government officials.

Sociology of the University of Warsaw, 1978). Tax information is withheld on order of the provincial committees of the Polish United Workers' Party. Apparently some party committees collect information concerning the revenues of local administrative bodies.

RESIDENCES

The ruling group resides in villas or high-standard prewar apartment houses. Maintenance costs for these lodgings are covered by the state treasury (according to the Bureau, the state treasury paid for the housing of only three individuals: the party first secretary, the premier, and the chairman of the State Council.)

So far as one can surmise from fragmentary information, the quality of the villas of the top leadership is very high, and not only by Polish standards. Architects estimate the construction cost of one of these villas at 16,000,000 to 18,000,000 zlotys. Some estates have double or triple energy sources (miniature water-power plants, special power lines), artificial waterfalls, miniature botanical gardens, swimming pools, and various athletic facilities. For interior decoration, not only the services of an art expert but also museum resources are utilized. This is called "borrowing." The expert's orders for such items as silver fixtures to hold a carpet in place are filled in special factories.

Increasingly, members of the ruling elite purchase state-owned apartments and villas, at the rate of between 600 and 900 zlotys per square meter (as compared with between 7,000 and 12,000 zlotys per square meter in cooperative houses). Housing cooperatives also offer villas to the select few at bargain prices (for example, 180,000 zlotys) as well as various special terms—e.g., remitted bank credit, long-term payments, and so on. (The Bureau claims that sixteen houses were specially built in Warsaw for persons designated by P. Jaroszewicz.* The cost of each house came to approximately 1,300,000 zlotys. The tenants settled directly with the cooperative.) The cooperative makes up these losses by raising the prices of houses and apartments for other people.

The government can also resell a mansion bought from a private owner to a chosen individual in exchange for repairs and upkeep. State agencies then carry out the repairs with regulation materials for which the chosen person pays, of course—but a minimal sum, even by the lowest standards. A department can also take possession of some village at state expense, then announce an auction but notify only one person—the buyer. The bid is low, but nobody beats his price and everything is done legally. (The Bureau assures us that it no longer buys up and sells back property.)

Special care is bestowed upon the surroundings and access roads to private estates. Unsightly hovels are demolished and unpleasant views are blocked by colored fences. Sometimes television cameras and military patrols guard the villas and often there are signs saying: "Military Area. Entry Strictly Forbidden."

*Piotr Jaroszewicz, prime minister, December 1970–February 1980.

Dachas [villas] are arranged with the help of the mechanisms described above: government (i.e., low) prices for land, special and remitted bank credit, construction materials at "reduced prices," labor performed by prisoners, soldiers or teams of workers from the agencies subordinate to the owner of the lot. (In the agreement of September 3, 1980, signed by Interfactory Strike Committee and the Government Commission in Jastrzębie, there is a clause forbidding the use of mining teams for the construction of private villas.)*

PURCHASING

In Poland, supply methods vary, depending on the type of merchandise. Thus, food supply comprises two elements: food and food distribution. Some food-producing industries are assigned special recipes and health diets; that is where food for the VIPs is produced. Some agricultural institutions are said to manufacture certain products by traditional methods, using natural fertilizers and without chemicals. Foodstuffs produced in this manner are supplied directly to the homes of the ruling group, according to the orders of the lady of the house.

Some factories also provide sale salons for the elite, where attractive articles unavailable to the general public are regularly sold, and where one can outfit oneself from head to toe for a song (that is, at "reduced prices") or purchase furniture and other articles. In exceptional cases the factories produce special merchandise, from clothing to furniture privately ordered by a VIP. (According to the Bureau, this practice has now been terminated.)

People living outside the big cities find it is easy to purchase goods in the PEWEX or Baltona stores† with zlotys (with the permission of the provincial governors; the Bureau knows nothing of this). In the provinces there is actually a whole system of select stores for privileged persons.

AUTOMOBILES

The Bureau has at its disposal sixty Polonezes for use by the ruling group and its subsidiaries. These are automobiles used for testing, and the factory absorbs all operating costs (including repairs and gasoline). When the car is worn out ("tested"), the chosen individual receives the next model free. Several departments other than the Bureau have Polonezes at their disposal on the same basis. (The Bureau admits that such practices were extant but only in other government departments, not those under the aegis of the Bureau.)

*This agreement—one of three signed at the end of the strikes in the summer of 1980—specifies that workers are "forbidden to work in any capacity at all outside their own enterprises," and more specifically, that they cannot be employed "on the personal behalf of enterprise managements."

†The PEWEX and Baltona were stores reserved exclusively for members of the elite, in which articles could be purchased only for foreign currency. The Baltona stores were expressly for diplomatic officials or officials sent abroad, and their prices were even lower than those at the PEWEX stores.

Automobile coupons are available to all members of the ruling group from minister on up. (At present, coupons have been eliminated but "direct sales," based on extremely vague criteria, have appeared in their place.) The executives of the provincial committees of the PZPR have the right to allot an automobile to whomever they like. These can be purchased on installment plans, often without paying any interest.

When prices of automobiles go up, Polmozbyt* receives from the Central Committee or provincial committees of the PZPR lists of people to whom cars should be sold at the former, lower prices.

FOREIGN COUNTRIES AND FOREIGN CURRENCY

I have already mentioned the trips to the West and the availability of foreign currency to members of the ruling group and their families. (The Bureau reports that as of February of this year holders of diplomatic passports wishing to buy foreign currency are subject to regulations that apply to everyone; to which one must add that, unlike the average person, they are assured of acquiring it.) This can be for a personal trip or for an official trip, as part of an official delegation. In the former case, the individual must pay for a part of his foreign currency; in the latter case, he gets it as a "travel allowance." For trips taken by members of the ruling class, whether personal or official, living costs abroad are absorbed by the appropriate embassy. (The Bureau denies that it ever refunded embassies for expenses related to private trips.)

Official delegations are exempt from customs. Even for personal trips, members of the ruling group and their families, and also members of the ruling group's subsidiaries, use special border passages where there is no customs inspection. (According to the Bureau, there are no special border passages; however, individuals occupying responsible positions and their families are exempted from customs regulations.)

RELAXATION

Here, too, trips abroad constitute the greatest attraction, although even the highest officials usually travel only to socialist countries. These trips are free. In Poland, the chosen have at their disposal approximately seventy luxury rest centers, most frequently under the auspices of the Bureau. (These are not to be confused with the more modest houses owned by the Bureau for lower-ranking functionaries.) The holiday houses of the Bureau are located in attractive localities, sometimes in nature reserves. (The Bureau explains that it owns only four rest centers for the highest leaders—as well as residences, reception mansions,

*A central agency in charge of all car sales and distribution within Poland.

and hunting mansions for use of other officials—and that none of these places is located on the territory of a reserve.)

For the purposes of sport and relaxation, the elite have at their command hunting grounds and stables, enclosed and diligently guarded by the military, and yachts formally registered as the property of some institution. (The Bureau reports that it owns no stables or yachts.)

HEALTH CARE

A special system of health services exists for the elite. This includes a government clinic, Ministry of Health and Social Care nursing homes, nursing homes for the Central Committee of the PZPR and the Central Council of Trade Unions, separate medical clinics for adults and for children, separate sanatoria (under the aegis of the Ministry of National Defense of the Ministry of Internal Affairs), special hospital wards, mainly in military hospitals, and also pharmacies not open to the general public.

There is some differentiation within this system. For example, in a government clinic (with medical equipment on a par with the best Western clinics, private rooms for patients, a swimming pool, a hotel for guests, its own food supplies, and so on) there is also a "superward" for provincial governors and up.

The patients have the necessary medicines, including foreign medicine, at their unlimited disposal, as well as individual professional service and, if necessary, foreign consultants as well. They can also travel for treatment at state expense to Switzerland or other countries, though this applies only to the seriously ill and depends on the availability of a given form of treatment. The cost of maintaining a separate system of health service for the elite is entered in the state budget under the heading "social services." (The Bureau explains that there is a special medical system for governing groups the world over.)

EDUCATION

In the 1960s the highest aspiration was a diploma from an institution of higher learning. Now, the fashion in the governing group is for doctorates and professorships. A VIP's doctorate most often is in an area in which he himself plays an important part (for example, as the head of some department). For a professorship a VIP will have to wait a few months.

Subsidiaries and families of the ruling elite also have easy academic careers. They obtain successive degrees and academic titles without much trouble; they direct institutions (sometimes founded especially for them) or scientific committees, which is important when competing for membership in the Polish Academy of Sciences; and they can easily get tenure and foreign stipends. Let us also note the fringe benefits of party scientific institutions, such as special foreign currency reserves and higher pensions.

IMPUNITY AND UNACCOUNTABILITY

Members of the elite also enjoy certain exclusive privileges when they break the law. To arrest and prosecute a party official, the law-enforcing agencies must first get approval either from the secretariat of a provincial committee of the PZPR or, in the case of a higher official, from the administrative division of the Central Committee. As a result of these regulations, even preliminary police investigations are frequently not initiated (e.g., the several fatal auto accidents caused by members of the ruling group) or else prosecution is waived. (The Bureau claims that those at fault for the accidents were not exempt from punishment.)

The ruling group treats the prosecuting apparatus in a purely instrumental way—a comfortable arrangement both for the elite and for the officials of the prosecuting apparatus, who can count on immunity when they themselves commit a crime. In point of fact, there is no crime which cannot be hushed up one way or another. At most, the matter ends in dismissal of the individual from his post (and a transfer to another less public but still executive position).

The various mechanisms described above serve to isolate the ruling group, including its families, from the rest of society. A few additional details are relevant.

The ruling group has at its disposal a special information service, which supplies it with detailed reports on the latest international and domestic developments. Depending on their relative positions in the hierarchy, the members of the elite receive transcripts of foreign broadcasts, bulletins containing data withheld by the censors, special commentaries prepared by various experts, translations of articles in foreign publications (not available to the general public), and confidential statistical compilations.

The ruling group is greatly concerned about its public image and role in history. To this end, special exhibits in museums are arranged, memorial tablets are erected, and history books and encyclopedias are full of details about the lives and activities of our leaders. In addition, state prizes are regularly awarded to them—e.g., the Order of Builders of People's Poland, which is automatically bestowed upon leading members of the hierarchy on their fiftieth birthday. Yet certain data—such as the material status of the leaders—remain shrouded in secrecy.

FAMILIES AND CHILDREN

It must be stressed once more that privileges are granted not only to high officials, but to their families and children as well. Thus the latter attend special schools and receive scholarships to study abroad. (The Bureau denies the existence of special schools.) They advance rapidly, often becoming heads of institutions created especially for them. Until recently the offspring of the elite were concentrated mainly in the academic world, but as of late they gravitate more toward diplomacy, foreign trade, and private initiative. The emphasis is shifting slowly from aspirations for prestige to that of material gain. As for the wives of officials, they, too, often direct various institutions or find lucrative positions in the mass media. What with the widespread practice of intermarriage among children of the elite, the favoritism shown to people who "marry into" the families of VIPs, the institutionalized network of privileges for their various protégés and "wards," nepotism has by now become a dominant element of our contemporary social reality.

From *Tygodnik Solidarność* (Warsaw), October 16, 1981

Translated by Jeff Jarosz

Workers and Peasants

The first of the two articles in this section, which appeared in an independent publication in 1977, examines the history, impact, and efficacy of strikes as an economic and political weapon of industrial workers. The somewhat pessimistic observations of the author, a well-known writer and journalist, are particularly interesting in view of the fact that only a year later the weapon was used on so massive a scale, and so successfully at that. Clearly the sophistication of Polish workers (see chapter 6, by Alex Pravda) had been underestimated even by those—such as the author of this article—who had been directly involved in their daily lives and struggles.

"The Lack of Food in Poland—Reasons and Effects" is both an expression of the militancy displayed by many Polish peasants—traditionally the most conservative social group—in the 1970s and a compelling survey of the catastrophic situation in Polish agriculture during the Gierek period—and earlier. For a discussion of the regime's agricultural policies, see chapter 3, by Włodzimierz Brus.

IN PRAISE OF STRIKES

Józef Śreniowski

Strikes are a particular form of protest against exploitation or social inequality. This definition renders meaningless questions about the right to strike, or the fairness of strikes. One cannot dispute the right to strike without also calling into question the right to protest against injustice or poverty. Anyone who contends that strikes occur without due cause should become acquainted with the demands of striking workers. Given the present conditions and political ban against strikes, people who decide to act collectively at their place of work are, as a rule, aware of the risks involved and do so only as a last resort.

In their political injunctions, the authorities have excised the word *strike* from the official language. So efficacious is this ban that striking workers balk at using the forbidden term and go so far as to petition for work breaks, a right already won by earlier generations of workers. The antipathy to the word *strike* is so powerful that workers treat colleagues fired for participating in a strike as though they had been justly punished for violating the law. Not infrequently the victims, too, share this view and, feeling guilty, accept the correctness of the legal and social sanctions against them.

The provisions concerning strikes in our labor laws and other relevant legal statutes are ignored by the prevailing ideology, which maintains that strikes can exist only in capitalist countries. Because of a peculiar statutory loophole, strikes per se are not illegal, even though the right to strike has not been explicitly upheld in the courts. To get around the legal loophole, the authorities refuse to recognize a strike as collective action; instead, they isolate the individual's participation in a strike and construe it as a severe breach of an employee's obligations (Article 52.1, First Labor Code). Some recent legal decisions argue that "willful or arbitrary work stoppage, assembly during working hours, or the resumption of work on the basis of the fulfillment of specific demands are serious violations of workers' obligations" and conclude that "workers guilty of such activities cannot be tolerated in a socialist factory."

The suppression of the word *strike* and denial of the rights to representation and self-government have made traditional strikes a rarity. Today we are faced with a new kind of strike. Due to the changes in the working community, in society as a whole, and in the political system, contemporary workers are quite different from those who went out on strike at Semperit in 1923, the mine at Mortimer, and the glassworks at Hortensja in 1933. Furthermore, strikes today have new implications. In a capitalist economy or in a democracy, strikes defend group interests. In the centralized economy of a socialist state, they are construed as a political activity that undermines the monopoly of power—the cornerstone of a totalitarian system.

What is the nature of strikes in Poland today? Can one call the various actions in our factories "strikes," even though they are essentially different in scope and character from those that occurred during the prewar period, or in 1956–57 at Poznań, Warsaw, and Łódź, and in December 1970 and June 1976? I am referring to unrest that most frequently takes the form of meetings, work stoppages, or slowdowns. I estimate that this type of strike has occurred in three-quarters of our factories, from gigantic industrial complexes to the smallest plants. In some factories strikes occur with frequent regularity. These strike meetings lack the features of a traditional strike: a chartered organization, a planned course of action, formulation of demands, election of representatives. Without a union structure, demands are sometimes not articulated and at other times represent only a particular group's point of view, such as one shift in a factory. Unrest of this sort frequently lasts no more than a few hours. Seldom do spokesmen for the striking workers emerge.

However, when reprisals threaten even the passive participants in a strike, workers build a safety net by selecting representatives. They frequently turn to the veterans among them: a foreman, the local party representative, or simply a trusted colleague. Acting as spokesmen, these intermediaries dilute the actual demands formulated by the workers. Such "surrogates" act in a dual role, torn as they are between their loyalties to the authorities on the one hand and to their fellow workers on the other.

One can rarely identify the organizers of a strike meeting: they occur spontaneously. People are alerted to get ready, and word goes out to bring a double ration for lunch. Occasionally the elements of an organization surface, in that some workers assume an active role: someone makes the rounds announcing the location of the meeting, someone watches at the door for strikebreakers, speakers take the floor.

An organization formed on such an ad hoc basis dissolves when the meeting ends or when management initiates reprisals. The lessons learned are few. For example, it is questionable whether the participants in the June 1976 events learned from the experiences of 1956 and 1970–71.

As has already been mentioned, the so-called surrogates present the management with a compromised version of the workers' demands. As a rule, whenever demands are not precise, the management responds with stopgap solutions. Even when workers who hold warning strikes know exactly what their grievances are, the confusing system of productivity quotas and compensation hinders the formulation of clear demands. Without the constraint of a union, the management has great latitude to maneuver. When strikers demand additional compensation for hazardous work conditions, the management raises the bonuses; or when strikers protest the arbitrary increase in productivity quotas, it bribes the workers with new fringe benefits.

Social, organizational, or political questions, which go beyond the issue of compensation, are not supposed to concern workers. In fact, workers frequently take up issues other than pay and the supply of goods. Their statements, however, rarely reach the public.

At the present time, strikes are directed against inefficiency, poor planning, mismanagement, waste of human labor and bureaucratic absurdities. Workers protest the managerial practice of increasing the work load in order to win favorable reviews and promotions from the authorities. As the song has it, "by the sweat of their brows, some dig ditches, some make policy switches."

While I've heard it said that strikes disrupt the economy and curtail production, the opposite seems to be the case. Organizational bottlenecks and years of mismanagement result in losses far greater than those caused by any disruption of production during a strike. Strikes are a reaction to our failing economy; they pave the way for reforms and lead to a search for new solutions.

I do not share the fears of those who claim that strikes fuel inflation. Issues of pay are by no means on the agenda of every strike group. When it is a matter of pay, the issue is often not a raise but a cost-of-living adjustment. This was the demand recently at the hospital supply plant in Pabianice, where the monthly pay declined by 500 zlotys as a result of an increase in productivity quotas. It is even more unreasonable to claim that the struggle for pay raises is caused by exaggerated consumer expectations. On the contrary, strikes in Poland simply attempt to maintain the standard of living that has been attained but is now threatened by inflation.

Many crucial problems are solved only by strikes. Deprived of the right to organize, workers cannot negotiate directly with management. Thus grievances brought before management are acknowledged only after the lack of response has led to a strike. Sometimes, of course, management is already well acquainted with the points at issue, but is either slow to respond or unable to redress them. This is precisely what leads to worker action. Strikes force government administrators and political authorities to face and appreciate previously trivialized tensions. Strikes refute the official (if tacit) assumption that working conditions are accepted by workers, who will also not object to the introduction of any arbitrary changes.

After a strike, changes that had been regarded by the authorities as unfeasible suddenly become feasible. Department heads, hitherto distant and passive, move into action. The plant elicits the attention of higher officials—a fact that may redound to the benefit of other plants as well. In fact, a strike in a particular factory may generate desirable reforms throughout an entire industrial sector.

On the basis of such a precedent, officials may develop a blueprint for handling a resurgence of unrest in any economic sector. I suspect that last year's strikes have compelled the authorities, weakened by the June 1976 unrest, to issue new guidelines that call for "elasticity" and "dialogue with workers." The effect has been a policy of partial conciliation toward worker demands and a temporary halt to the use of reprisals as a method of dealing with strikes.

In the long term, a strike may motivate the authorities to move toward modernization of a given industry by upgrading the equipment and the commodities produced, as well as improving work conditions and the system of compensation.

A strike may uncover organizational resources left untapped before its outbreak. It mobilizes the work force, or a part of it, to act as a united body and provides it with an organizational framework. The changes instituted in the wake of a strike may be called "the post-strike intervention" of the authorities. As a rule they are accompanied by the rotation of cadres. There is a shake-up in the factory management, the factory council, the party committee, and the youth organization. Even though these changes rarely extend beyond a given factory, they nevertheless have certain long-range beneficial effects. The striking workers may not be aware of the impact of their actions, because officials are not replaced immediately after the strike, and because some of them even continue to remain at their posts. But once workers realize that even in such cases they have been successful, they will better understand the extent of their power.

Workers' pressure fulfills a vital social role, regardless of its immediate effects on the economy. People are forced to confront publicly expressed demands, and this contributes to the development of a common perspective. The need to formulate demands compels the strikers to take a clear-cut stand on the issues at hand. Protests against exploitation and injustice are translated into concrete concerns such as rates of productivity and pay in real terms. Unless workers' demands are presented in such specific terms, they are not likely to bring about any lasting changes. Formal agreements are useful, for they allow workers to have recourse to rules and regulations instead of being dependent solely on the whims of their superiors. It should be added that striking workers frequently strive only for what they have been entitled to all along, according to existing regulations.

A strike also fulfills an important educational function. This is particularly evident when workers, acting in unison, successfully resist the authorities' attempts at individual reprisals. Victories are, in fact, seldom unaccompanied by reprisals: the authorities are apparently far more eager to discredit the idea of worker solidarity than to fulfill any worker demands.

Strikes are ineffectual whenever demands are not immediately granted and when its participants are fired. Even then, however, favorable changes may well ensue for those who remain at their jobs—and who thus learn something about the efficacy of collective action and realize the shallowness of the authorities' concern for working conditions and for labor relations. They also gain an insight into the machinery of repressions, which selects scapegoats without regard to an individual's productivity or value to the factory, and which descends with equal force on specialists and unskilled workers, on party members and nonmembers, on veterans of many years and on novices. Even when the workers' demands conform literally to the guidelines set at the last party conference, the workers' action is immediately combated by official reprisals.

Strikes also impress upon their participants the close connections between the various organs of power: the management, the national administration, the party, the trade unions, the courts, the military, and the employment bureau. This united front gives lie to the notion that authorities will bargain in good faith when conflicts arise. The workers begin to realize that "peaceful negotiations" are impossible, and that their only recourse is collective pressure.

When I met workers who had been fired after the June 1976 strikes, I often wondered whether their experience had the same significance for them as the events of March 1968 had for my generation. For many it was similar—a kind of shock treatment, a bitter confirmation of the rightness of their cause. But in March 1968 we had not been isolated. The workers pushed out of the factory gate in 1976 often (though not always) found themselves out of their element. Because of the absence of fellow feeling in their own communities (and it must be noted that, as a rule, in most areas one is cut off from one's co-workers), such strikers felt isolated, guilty, and socially ostracized. They found the epithet "hothead"—sometimes used in jest, sometimes not—hard to take.

In my opinion the activities of that period, promoted by the Workers' Defense Committee (KOR), demonstrated that a unified point of view among the working community had emerged. KOR's moral support was of crucial importance to the many people "laid off for distributing leaflets."* Fortified by this support, they would not forget the experiences of June 1976 despite the efforts of propagandists to stifle the memories.

The renewal of a unified point of view has replaced the attitudes of apathy and embitterment among our workers. Some of those who were at the forefront in the June events had also been active in December 1970. Conceivably those who were politicized in the June events will in future promote the idea of free unions through mass action.

From *Glos* (Warsaw), no. 1/13, 1979

Translated by Michael Kott

*That expression has become a part of Polish folklore, because sugar coupons were also introduced in June 1976. In Polish the word *kartki* means both leaflets and coupons.

THE LACK OF FOOD IN POLAND– REASONS AND EFFECTS

Wiesław P. Kęcik

Only he is a slave who does not know how or does not wish to be free.

Wincenty Witos*

As a nation, our position forces us to ask ourselves: what next? The following outline is just one attempt to describe the situation, and to suggest a plan for further action.

I. THE LAND IS UNPRODUCTIVE. Millions of hectares are lying fallow throughout the country. The exact figures are unknown. In 1977 it was disclosed that in the State Land Fund (PFZ—Państwowy Fundusz Ziemi) alone, out of an overall acreage of 19 million hectares devoted to agriculture, over 1 million hectares of plowland were lying fallow. The land is unproductive in the so-called collectivized sector. It is being ravaged by extensive and wasteful exploitation: it is excessively fertilized, salted, overdrained, poisoned by too much manure, and impoverished by too much concentration on one type of farming. This is the picture of one-fourth of potentially productive agricultural acreage, and it is little better on the remaining three-quarters. Lacking stability, without heirs for their land, faced only with the prospect of having to relinquish their farms to the state, a considerable number of farmers want to bleed the land of all it can give and are returning nothing to it. They would in any case be unable to put much into it even if they wanted to, for there is less and less natural and artificial fertilizer to be had. Other farmers are involved in "specialized" farming; their work, too, is wasteful, for there is no crop rotation and the soil is given no chance to rest.

And yet not so long ago in Poland the land was called "our mother, the food provider."

2. THE STRATEGIC AIM OF STATE AGRICULTURAL POLICY is the collectivization of agriculture without diminishing food production. It is therefore not a question of increasing food production. If production can only be kept

---

*Wincenty Witos (1871–1945) was the leader of the Peasant Party (Piast), which was organized before World War I and which was considerably more conservative than the Left (Thugutt) Peasant group. In interwar Poland, both peasant parties frequently collaborated with each other.

at the same level, the land is to be brought under state control. That is the theory, but it goes even further in practice. In 1975 the country's average production of the four cereals was about 26 quintals a hectare; in 1977 it was only 24 quintals, and in 1979, 22 quintals. Yet despite the reduction, this land is continually being brought under state control. The state farms (PGR—Państwowe Gospodarstwa Rolne) receive about 100,000 zlotys for each hectare farmed of the land allocated to them by the State Land Fund. They have all the credits, amortizations, and allowances possible. They have machinery, fertilizers, and fodder. And yet the final product from each hectare is very often inferior. The state creates giant conglomerates with thousands of hectares, thousands of head of cattle, flocks of sheep, and poultry. These then become places where epidemic diseases generate and spread; thieving, bribery, and corruption thrive. There are huge economic losses: the cost of producing a liter of milk, for instance, is 38 zlotys; that of producing a kilo of meat, 150 zlotys.

That is the strategic aim of state agricultural policy. It can be defined even more pithily: hunger and kolkhozes.

3. THE AVERAGE AGE of those who work in individual farming in Poland is about sixty-three years. According to the Retirement Act, which will come into effect in July 1980, women farmers will retire at sixty, men at sixty-five. Because half of the farmers are women, it can be said that the whole peasant village will be in retirement and that four years later the whole village will die. Thank God these are only averages and statistics.

The state, in order to achieve its "strategic aim" peacefully and not to be forced to compete with the peasant in food production, is systematically destroying individual farms. As a result, young people escape to the cities. Almost the only ones who stay on the farms are those who have simply been unable to leave. If a young man stays, he cannot find a wife to join him on the farm, and vice versa. Consequently, only old people are left, and they face two choices: to produce a bit more than the collectivized farms do, or to hand over the land, letting it fall into the clutches of the state under the "strategic aim of state agricultural policy."

Before the war, the peasant would go barefoot if necessary, just so that he could purchase another acre of land. Even twenty years ago, I remember my grandfather taking me over the boundaries in the Grójec region and telling me, "The most important things, child, are land and the wisdom to enable you to get your bread from the land."

4. LIVING CONDITIONS IN THE COUNTRY are incomparably worse than in the town. A farmer's income averages just over 30 percent less than the income of someone from the nonfarming sector. And the farmer must also invest some of that income. In the so-called technical infrastructure, and even more in the communal infrastructure, the damage wrought to the land is frightening. The infrastructure provides the foundation for living and working, and without this foundation there can be no normal activity. Roads, light and power, drainage, gas, trains and buses, shops, cinemas and theaters, schools and nurseries, servicing workshops, medical clinics, facilities for working, learning, and recreation: in all these areas, the village is being terribly maltreated and shortchanged. It is

not surprising that whoever can escape from the countryside does so. The discrimination against the village is even more evident in the various state distribution lists: fewer sugar ration cards are issued, less coal is made available, and the minimum pension is lower. Not until 1972 was the system abolished whereby the farmer was compelled to sell a certain percentage of his produce to the state. Towns and industries were reconstructed after the war at the expense of the villages. When a city dweller travels through the countryside and sees how well dressed the peasant's daughter is, and that his son has a car, he says: "They are having a bad time of it? They've never had it so good!" He fails to understand that when a peasant has put up a cottage instead of a cowshed, when he has bought a car rather than a tractor, when he has invested not in the land but in clothing his daughter, and when he drinks into the bargain, it means that he sees no hope of continuing to farm, that he has opted for consumption at the expense of investment, and that the semblance of wealth in the village in fact indicates the approaching end of the village, the end of the peasant, and the end of food for all.

5. THE UNFAIR PRICE STRUCTURE. When the peasant wishes to buy anything—from nails and hammers to kitchen utensils, not to mention plowshares and machinery—he has to pay considerably more than the actual value of the goods. He is thus directly taxed to help prop up the government and to develop industry. At the same time he is paid for his products considerably less by the state than it cost him to produce them. In order to produce and sell to the state, he must pay out of his own pocket. This may seem incredible, but it is true. He is forced to do this because otherwise he cannot obtain from the state monopoly items that are vital to him for living and working: coal, fertilizer, fodder, building materials—and a pension, which is calculated on the basis of the amount of goods sold to the state. The peasant farmer's balance sheet is helped a little by private sales of fresh produce at farmers' markets, but even on those sales he loses a considerable part of his earnings.

Once a year, after harvest time, the peasant has a comparatively large sum of cash on his hands—tens or hundreds of thousands of zlotys. This is nothing compared to his input and the physical work contributed by all the members of his family, ten to eighteen hours a day throughout the year. It's also nothing compared to the real needs of the family and the farm. It is at this time, too, when cash is lying around, that the real tragedy occurs. Instead of money, the farmer has pieces of paper. There is nothing to buy. There are no tools, machinery, bricks, construction steel, furniture in the shops—only vodka and the outstretched hands of state administration workers, looking for bribes [for the items the farmer needs]. The money can also be put into the National Savings Bank (PKO—Powszechna Kasa Oszczędności), where, in the course of a year, it will lose at least a few percentage points of its real value.

And while we are on the subject of banks, here is an interesting little item: it was decided at a central level to wind up the Cooperative Bank (Bank Spółdzielczy) in 1975. Whereas previously the district leader had decided about the allocation of credits, all decisions are now made at the central office in the new State Cooperative Bank. In other words, money comes from the members of the cooperative, while the decisions come from the state authorities. And the profits also go to the authorities—an example of the peasant road to socialism.

Until recently, the peasant preferred to go without food rather than incur debts; he was afraid of loans because if he defaulted he would lose his land. Today the poor can receive a loan at 8 percent and must repay it in full. Swindlers, in "cooperatives" or as "specialists," irrespective of their debts to date, can receive any amount of credit at 4 percent and largely amortized as well.

It is easy to destroy a sensible price structure, but it will be more difficult to put it together again.

6. THE LACK OF MECHANIZATION. Because of the depopulation of Polish villages, mechanization ought to be introduced to do the work now done by hand. But how can it be introduced when in much of the country there is no electrical power, or if there is any, only enough for light bulbs? How can it be introduced when there are no paved roads, no repair workshops or spare parts; when it is so difficult to obtain oil and gasoline; when a new tractor can only be purchased for dollars,* or only a damaged one from the collectivized sector? Our small, broken-up fields need small, cheap tractors with a complete set of accessories. I have seen such a tractor once in my life: it was standing in a showroom on Puławska Street in Warsaw. There was a label on it that said "Price: 300,000 zlotys," and a second label said "Sold." The girl behind the counter said that it had been made in Poland.

Polish farming mechanization means: a huge tractor on a state farm, with a pitchfork, spade, and rake as accessories.

The peasants themselves have tried to introduce mechanization. Back in the nineteenth century they set up agricultural circles, pooled their resources, and bought machinery. This wealth kept growing until a few years ago, when it was wrenched away from the peasants. On the basis of those peasant machines, the Cooperatives of Agricultural Circles were set up and were assigned directors, land, and money. In order to change the "social structure of the countryside," even government and Sejm [Parliament] officials have not flinched from theft; there has been a horrific waste of land and public money, not to mention [corruption of] people's consciences.

7. THE MONSTROUS GROWTH OF A RAPACIOUS ADMINISTRATION. A man in a raincoat with empty pockets and a book of party literature under his arm is sent out as leader, secretary, manager of agricultural services, or police commandant. Within a year or two he has acquired a villa, a Polonez,† and a little Fiat for his wife. Anyone else, no matter how frugal, would never have been able to save up enough from his earnings in three years to afford a Polonez.

Production is not at all profitable for the peasant, but it must be for everyone else concerned. An entire complex price structure of bribes exists—for every brick bought, every kilo of potatoes sold. Anything is possible, as long as you know whom to go to and how much it will cost. That is the system of agricultural services!

---

*Since Poland imported tractors largely for its "socialized" sector of agriculture, it was exceedingly difficult for private farmers to purchase one, unless they could pay for it with dollars.

†A small Fiat, produced in Poland.

8. THE LEGAL REGULATIONS concerning farming are a legal noose around the neck of the farmer. The peasant has become simply the user of the land, not its independent owner. At any time the supervisor can turn him off his land or move him onto other fields. Each farm is subject, in accordance with the regulations, to an annual inspection by the supervisor, who assesses the state of the farm. He then tells the peasant what is to be done and how he must do it, "for if not, I'll take the land away from you." The peasants have already had enough of this, so more and more frequently the official hears the words: "Well, then, take it away. Then at last I'll have some peace!"

Only the Communists could have thought up such a sentence as, "The changes being made in farming do not therefore pertain to the limitations of farm ownership so much as to a new understanding of it."† They take your land away from you, the land on which your ancestors have sweated for centuries and from which for centuries they have labored to extract the stones, the land that has provided you with food throughout your life—and that is called "a new understanding" of ownership!

The law of ownership is sacred. In my opinion it was absolutely wrong, before the war, to demand agricultural reform without compensation.[2] First, because it infringes on the law of ownership; second, because it thus paved the way for the Communists to take other people's property away from them. There should be a natural system, based on profitability, and not a system of injunctions and prohibitions. Whatever action is rational and wise should be put into effect, and then people will carry it out because it is of benefit to them and not because they have been ordered to do it.

Farming cannot be run like industry (although, as we can see, industry is not doing very well either). But the Communists know best what our needs are: they'll organize our lives and they'll organize us. Yet even now they do not know that farming is not only and not principally a small production plant, but it is also and above all a family that manages a farm—real people with individual consciousness, formed by centuries-long contact with the land. Today scientists are demonstrating that even animals must not be moved to new sheds every two months, that one must respect their habits and the adaptation to their environment that they have made over many generations. If these are not respected, the cow loses weight and its milk-yield drops. If that is how a cow is affected, what about man? A man works, plans, and produces what suits and is profitable for himself and his family. There is no way that it can be any different. If the state insists on changing a man's plans, it must do so in such a way that the changes are even more profitable for him—not with injunctions, inspections, and sanctions. The state is for the people, and not the other way around!

9. THE DECLINE IN EDUCATION IN THE COUNTRYSIDE. Over 40 percent of farmers have not completed elementary school, 50 percent have completed only elementary school, and only 0.5 percent have had any sort of higher education. While the number of agricultural schools and their pupils in-

*Edmund Spirydowicz, *Ziemia i prawo* (Land and the law) (Warsaw: Ludowa Spółdzielnia Wydawnicza, 1977), p. 75.

creases each year, more people are leaving agriculture each year in spite of their education. Proportionally fewer young people of peasant origin are going to college today than before the war. There has been a decline in self-education, in cultural organizations among workers, and in general reading habits. Scientists agree that agrobiology has deteriorated. Given the state of schools today, it can safely be predicted that a considerable percentage of children in the countryside will not receive even an elementary education. The closing of village schools condemns the youngest children to many kilometers and hours of travel: over-tired children sleep through their lessons and they cannot do their homework because they arrive home too late. The level of teaching in village and farm schools is also very low. Under such circumstances no proper education is possible.

10. LACK OF SELF-GOVERNMENT AND DEMOCRACY has created and intensified this deplorable situation in agriculture. The peasants have not had any real influence on decisions that closely concern them. The system is alien: it fails to take into account the dual structure and function of farming—that is, both the farming family and the sphere of its productive activities. Although almost everything depends on the knowledge and skill of the farmer, he is, in effect, deprived of the ability to make choices and decisions. Since almost everything has been forced on the peasant, his reaction has been to throw up his hands, allow his children to leave the farm, and cease to consider the farm his own, wanting only to see the end of his days on it. He is unable to choose his village administrator, nothing is ever accomplished at meetings, his opinion carries no weight. Institutes called "cooperative" are not; the district cooperative Peasant Mutual Aid is dubbed "Mutual Decline" in the country. There is a lack of control over the conduct of state administration, and a lack of openness in public and political life. The Domy Ludowe (People's Clubs), which were once centers of village life and culture, have been abolished. Peasant youth organizations have been disbanded. This path leads to the stifling of all initiative and to the destruction of the farmer. And once the people have become passive, the party can grow, govern, and claim that it provides the impetus for all aspects of public life. The party Mafia can do this because it has all the mechanisms of control, on the one hand, and dispenses the goods that are in continual short supply, on the other. And so one part of the population breaks under the whip and another queues up for its rations. How many have held out against this gang?

The solution, if one is still feasible, must be comprehensive. Cosmetic changes will be of no use. But the solution *must* begin with actual self-government and democracy. Before this becomes a reality, and in order for it to become a reality, the discredited system must go.

11. SELF-DEFENSE is not only and above all a Committee for Self-Defense.

Self-defense is the revival of initiative, self-government, democracy, organization, enlightenment, culture, a cooperative movement, and openness in public life.

Self-defense is the improvement of the price structure, of living conditions, and of the legal system.

Self-defense is the deeper involvement of the Church in the nation's socioeconomic problems.

Self-defense is the liquidation of the state farms' deficits.

Self-defense is productive land, food for all.

But *self-defense* is also:

—your effort, your courage, your greater knowledge

—your level-headedness, integrity, truthfulness

—building good relations with your family, neighbors, and colleagues

—a well-chosen village administrator, councillor, and member of Parliament

—winning public control over the village cooperative (Gmina Spółdzielna), agricultural circle, and agricultural bank

—winning the battle for a church, school, shop, and bus stop

—the participation of all—farmer, teacher, priest, doctor, and forester

—keeping the best of the young people in the village

—straightening up every stooping back.

Today we are treading the best path to collective national suicide. The only way out is THROUGH DEMOCRACY AND SELF-GOVERNMENT—TO FREEDOM!

We are surrounded not only by the chalk circle of ideology, but also by a circle of bayonets, tanks, rockets, and alliances. Slogans are not enough. Caution, courage, and solidarity in the community are also needed.

The system does not function, but it persists. It persists because society has been fragmented. Everyone has been left on his own, and a person on his own can be destroyed or exploited at will. We must uncover the communal instinct in ourselves. We must lose no time in taking a good look at our neighbor and seeing that he has the same problems as we have. We must visit other villages, districts, and regions—the people there also have the same problems. If today you can take your neighbor's best land with a bribe, tomorrow he can do the same to you. You express surprise that people in the town know nothing of your work, of your low earnings, of the lack of food and means of production, or the hours spent at the bus stop or in the queue to see the supervisor. And what do you know of the problems of scientists, students, craftsmen, and factory workers? But look around properly: it really is the same life, and they really are working under the same conditions, for it is the same system. Try to become closer to those around you, for that, too, is the road to freedom, though it certainly is not the shortest road. And perhaps it will turn out that there are more of us that we had thought, that it will be more difficult to crush us than we had thought. Perhaps then we shall begin to regain all the ground we have lost in all areas. . . ? TRY!

From *Placówka*, no. 1 (14),
January/February 1980

Translated by Joanna Gladysz

Church and State

Jerzy Turowicz, for more than thirty years editor of one of Poland's most influential periodicals, the Catholic weekly *Tygodnik Powszechny,* sets forth, in the first of the two pieces that follow, the fundamental demands and grievances of Polish Catholics vis-à-vis the state. Widely respected for his scholarly and editorial achievements, as well as for his moderate views, Turowicz clearly eschews polemics in favor of an appeal to reason. Without in the least obscuring the gravity of his criticism of government policies, he is clearly at pains to establish a genuine dialogue and to seek solutions that would be acceptable to the regime. How difficult it was even for this eminently reasonable man to speak freely is illustrated by the fact that his article, originally scheduled for publication in *Tygodnik Powszechny,* was struck down by the censors and appeared only in an unofficial journal.

"Normalization à Rebours" (normalization in reverse) describes the efforts of the regime to prevent a group of peasants from building a church in their village. It is no doubt a scene that took place in many villages throughout the country, and it provides eloquent testimony to the resilience of Poland's faithful, on the one hand, and the absurd (and in the end, ineffective) tactics of the country's rulers, on the other.

DIALOGUE, PLURALISM, AND UNITY

Jerzy Turowicz

"There are no problems that cannot be discussed by our party and our society," said Edward Gierek in the report of the political bureau of the Central Committee at the Second National Conference of the PZPR.

That being the case, one problem that should be discussed is the question of relations between Church and state, between Catholics and Marxists in our country. An article by Mieczysław Rakowski, "The Basis of Cooperation and Dialogue" (*Polityka,* March 25, 1978), was an invitation to just such a discussion. The author raised important and difficult questions, ones that are not often mentioned and that are of profound interest to all Poles. He showed great objectivity, pragmatism, and public spirit. Although Rakowski stressed that he was speaking for himself, in his capacity as the chief editor of *Polityka,* his opinion can be taken as more or less authoritative, and we may suppose that many Communists would agree with him. In taking part in the dialogue initiated by Rakowski, I would similarly emphasize that I speak for myself, having no mandate to speak on behalf of the Church in Poland or its hierarchy, although I believe that I am expressing the views of many Catholics in our country.

Rakowski puts his comments in the general context of the changes that have taken place in the last few decades in relations between the Catholic Church and socialist states and, more specifically, of recent events affecting relations between Church and state in Poland. My own view differs somewhat from Rakowski's with regard to the international context, but that is immaterial at this point. There is no doubt that the Vatican's "Eastern policy," initiated by Pope John XXIII and consistently carried out by Pope Paul VI, aimed at improving the Church's position in socialist countries and contributing to peace among nations; it did, in fact, create a new situation in the relations between the Church and the socialist world.

Of more importance here, however, are such specifically Polish events as the meeting between the Primate of Poland, Cardinal Wyszyński, and First Secretary Edward Gierek, which took place October 29, 1977, and Gierek's visit to Pope Paul VI in the Vatican on December 1, 1977. These were events of the highest importance. The speeches made by Gierek and Paul VI; several later statements by Gierek, particularly during the Second Party Conference and in the Sejm; several statements by the Polish episcopate, particularly the primate's homily on the Feast of the Epiphany, which Rakowski rightly considers to be very significant—all these bear witness to a new climate in which fruitful dialogue and cooperation could be envisaged.

Of course, verbal declarations, however weighty and authoritative, cannot by themselves change anything. Certain conditions must be fulfilled, certain events must occur before cooperation becomes possible, and this is not a simple process. As Rakowski rightly reminds us, "In the past the Marxist movement as a whole was radically atheistic and declared war upon the Church and religion. Its premise was that religious faiths would soon disappear. Such a premise obviously caused distrust in the Catholic Church and pushed it toward a confrontation."

But Rakowski sees a marked change: "The Marxist camp has long since abandoned its dogmatic-sectarian interpretation of sociopolitical relations"; "socialist ideology has left behind primitive atheism, which saw as its aim the battle against God." It may be doubted whether either theoretical or, particularly, practical changes in the Marxist camp have gone as far as Rakowski would like to believe. Certainly, ideological conflict between Marxism and Catholicism continues, nor can one deny that during the thirty years' relationship between the Church and the state in our country, a dossier of facts and experiences has accumulated that is not easily ignored. This means, in effect, that it is not easy to pass from confrontation to cooperation.

Not that changes for the better have not occurred. A very important result was achieved by strengthening the links between the Apostolic See and the government of the Polish People's Republic: the creation, on both sides, of permanent groups for working contacts, whose final achievement was Gierek's visit to the Vatican. Nor do I forget the process of normalization of relations between Church and state, begun a few years ago: through this process some, though by no means all, of the relevant and difficult problems have been solved. Not surprisingly, the authorities and the Church have different views of what the concept of normalization should involve—which in turn has caused problems.

At this point the state has appealed to the Church for cooperation, on the ground of public good, and the Church, through the Polish Primate, has responded positively. The starting point for this collaboration was the concept of national unity, political and moral, proclaimed by Gierek and the political leadership, and the striving toward positive goals, which is essential if Poland is to overcome its socioeconomic difficulties. The state itself, in the declaration of the Front of National Unity, has stressed the importance of the Church. "Socialist Poland remembers the Roman Catholic Church's contribution toward the preservation of Poland's national values and her cultural heritage. It notes and values the Church's concern for national interests, and the essential part played by Catholics as well as other denominations in the efforts of the people as a whole to develop their country."

Cooperation was expected from the Church mainly in areas of social morality: the upbringing of young people, the strengthening of the family, the inculcation of a positive attitude toward work, et cetera. And if the Church responded to this call for help, it is because—as the above quotation reminds us—the Church has always been deeply concerned for the welfare of the people, while also always regarding as one of its main tasks raising individual and collective moral standards. This has been true in the past and is equally true today, regardless of political conditions or forms of government. Nevertheless, certain conditions must be fullfilled for cooperation fully to occur and further to develop.

After all, the situation is somewhat paradoxical: the Communists have always treated the Catholic Church as a political power whose activities hinder the building of socialism—hence the constant tendency to limit and counter the Church's influence, if not to eliminate it altogether. There is plenty of evidence that this tendency still exists, even though one would expect it to be modified. But how can the Church be expected to collaborate with authorities who are seeking to curtail its influence? How can the Church accept limitation of its mission, its aims, and its means, when at the same time it is being treated like some sort of volunteer (and controlled) rescue squad for certain circumscribed, if important, purposes, such as the fight against alcoholism?

What is at issue is state recognition of the Church's place and role in the life of the Polish people, who have been Christian for a thousand years and an overwhelming majority of whom belong to the Catholic Church. Obviously, the Church's very existence in a socialist country has political importance. But this is not to say that the Church has political aims. Poland's Primate reminded us, in his homily, of Christ's words, "My kingdom is not of this world." The Church does not feel called upon to change political structures; on the contrary, it has a right and a duty to carry out its mission under any political circumstances. Church and state are separate in Poland. Some may oppose this separation, but I think most Polish Catholics not only do not question it but also cannot imagine any other relationship between Church and state under a socialist regime. The interpretation of this separation, however, may give rise to differences of opinion. One would expect these two independent institutions to exist in a state of mutual respect, even amity, agreeing not to interfere in each other's internal affairs. But separation of Church and state cannot mean limitation of the Church's activity solely to matters of ritual, to what takes place within church walls. Nor can religion be treated as a completely private matter, unrelated to general human society. The Church's aim is to lead people toward salvation. But this eternal aim is achieved on earth, by educating people in real, concrete circumstances. A Christian view of life involves a concept of man—the meaning of his existence, his vocation, his rights, and his duties. And such a view rests upon religious faith. The Church, therefore, cannot remain indifferent to civic, socioeconomic, and political conditions. The Church must demand of a political structure that it ensure the best conditions for the full development of human personality; it must demand that man be able to live in peace, to enjoy freedom and justice. For this reason the Church so often protests when human rights are violated.

In all countries of the world the Church acts in the name of justice and freedom, regardless of the politics of their governments. In recent years in Latin America it was precisely the Church that became the main social force fighting for justice and human rights. And although the Church undoubtedly has a political significance in this context, that significance does not necessarily encroach upon internal state affairs or affect the separation of state and Church. The

Church is concerned only with questions of morality, which are binding in public affairs as well as in interpersonal ones.

It must be stressed, then, that the business of the Church cannot be confined to matters of a strictly religious and ecclesiastical character when dealing with our daily sociopolitical reality. It must, certainly, provide religious education, preach the gospel, administer the sacraments, and conduct charitable activities. But it must also participate in the public and cultural life of our country. This is not a matter of Church privileges. As Pope Paul VI said to Gierek, and as our bishops have said many times: it is a matter not so much of the rights of the Church as an institution as of the rights of believers who are citizens of this country, who profess a certain Christian view of life, and who wish, in accordance with their beliefs, to shape their own and their children's lives, to take part in and influence the fortune, life, and culture of their country.

Although one could cite examples showing that Catholics play a part in the life of the country, the Catholic presence is neither quantitatively nor qualitatively sufficient to satisfy the needs or the rightful aspirations of the faithful. The Church is expected to exert a positive influence on youth and to raise its moral standards, yet in Poland there is no regular, customary Catholic youth organization, and [those who participate in] informal activities however strictly religious, in this area encounter various obstructions and difficulties. Culture—in the broadest sense of the word—is now the main factor in shaping views and attitudes, in forming public opinion and expressions. The Church has a right, recognized by most countries in the world, to employ, in its religious and evangelical capacity, the tools of culture—among others, the mass media. But the Church is virtually unrepresented in the "official" culture of our people—in television, radio, the big publishing houses. Catholics as such have no access to state-controlled cultural media. As for the "private" sector allotted to Catholics, it is so small that the number of books, periodicals, and so on [that they can produce] can in no way meet the demands of the faithful.

To give but one example: the weekly *Polityka,* excellently edited by Mieczysław Rakowski in the spirit of Marxist ideology, has a print run of 300,000 copies a week. *Tygodnik Powszechny,* the leading Catholic weekly in a country where the vast majority of the population is Catholic, can print only 40,000, which does not meet even half the demand. We receive daily desperate letters from readers unable to buy or subscribe to the publication.

No less serious are the qualitative restrictions. The Office for the Control of the Press, Publishing, and Public Performances has frequently made it impossible for Catholics as well as for others of independent views to voice their opinions on matters that are sometimes of the utmost national importance.

Rakowski raises the question of the Church's attitude toward atheists, demanding that Catholics, who insist upon tolerance for themselves, should show it to nonbelievers. I see a grave misunderstanding in such an approach to the matter. There are few Catholics in Poland who would reject a nonbeliever's right to his views. It is the privileged position of atheism that believers find unfair. I am not speaking of the Society for Disseminating Secular Culture, or of the weekly *Argumenty* or other similar journals. I have in mind the general question of ideological principles in culture—above all, the ideological coloring imparted to education, and the firm attempt to give it an atheistic hue.

Finally, one of the most painful problems—discrimination against Catholics in their chosen vocations. Professing Marxist views and membership in the party greatly assist promotion and bestow various privileges, while professing Catholic beliefs can make it difficult, if not impossible, to pursue a career. We often hear appeals not to divide society into believers and nonbelievers. The appeals, made by socialists, are justified, but it is not we, the believers, who create this division; rather, discrimination against us often makes us second-class citizens.

It is therefore not a question of privileges, but of justice and equality. Rakowski is quite right when, concluding his article with an appeal to increase the productive and social activity of the whole country, he writes: "It is self-evident that such activity cannot be forced into a schematic framework. The People's government is obliged to ensure that every individual has equal opportunity to work for his country and for himself."

The subject of my remarks, which were prompted by M. Rakowski's article, is the place and role of Catholics in Polish society, as well as the possibility of a dialogue and collaboration between the Church and the Marxist state. But the problem is larger, and its solution lies not solely in recognizing the rights of Catholics. Rather, it should be sought in the real democratization of our sociopolitical life, by creating conditions ensuring greater freedom for the individual to seek truth, to express his convictions, to exert real influence upon the life of the collective. In order to accomplish this, it is necessary to acknowledge the ideological pluralism that exists in Polish society. That pluralism encompasses far more than Catholics and Marxists. I have in mind not only philosophical or religious differences, but also the different views on social, economic, political, and cultural problems. Pluralism does not preclude the moral and patriotic unity of the people—on the contrary, unity can be based only on pluralism. All thinking and honest citizens of our country, regardless of their different views, share a common concern for the welfare of the collective, for the material and cultural progress of the country and its place among nations. We agree with what Edward Gierek said at the Second Party Conference: the solution of basic problems is "a national platform, overriding the differences that exist or could exist in our society and that arise from differences in social or professional position, education, local traditions, and attitudes toward religion."

The real obstacle to this unity is not pluralism itself, but the refusal to recognize it as fact. It is ignored, neglected, not allowed to be seen or heard. The real obstacle is the attempt to create ideological uniformity, spurious at best. The recognition of pluralism as a fact that neither hinders nor excludes unity would make it possible for our citizens to express opinions about ways and means of achieving common aims, and would enable them to attain real instead of false unity. In addition, it would provide the basis for satisfying the demands of the Church, and for a conclusive dialogue between the state and the Church, leading to a constructive collaboration for the good of the whole nation.

From *Spotkania* (Lublin),
no. 3, 1978

Translated by Halina Willetts

NORMALIZATION Á REBOURS

A. B.

It is a truism that Communist power in our country is in a state of permanent crisis. Society has not accepted it, and probably never will. This is proved every time the "crisis" reaches a climax, revealing the utter nullity and impotence of the "rulers of People's Poland"; panic drives them to seek the support of the nation that has "vowed" obedience to them. I use quotation marks because the nation has never in fact promised either loyalty or obedience; rather, discipline and silence were forced upon the people. I therefore regard the frank rejection of usurping powers as heroic.

Whenever a "minor revolution" occurs in Poland, the authorities always try to establish contact with the people through the Catholic Church. In these situations the Church automatically becomes the political spokesman for Polish society and, in the absence of any other, its only genuine representative.

The Communists, well aware of this, prefer to deal with a quasi-political and primarily moral representative of the people than with the people itself. The tired old slogan, "normalization of relations between state and Church," is heard yet again, declarations such as those one heard from Gierek on various occasions, denying the existence of any cause for dispute between the two.

To demonstrate the nature of this "normalization," I should like to record what happened in Jaworzyna (Silesia). The inhabitants of Jaworzyna vainly sought official permission to build a parish church, or at least a number of chapels to cater to the needs of people living in several suburbs. (In Niedzieliska and in Osiedle, state chapels were built without the authorities' permission or assistance.) After many years of fruitless applications, the members of the church-building committee resolved on a course of action whose efficacy had been proven before. The building of a car-repair shop, for which legal permission had been obtained, was begun. No one took much notice, especially since the site was surrounded by a high fence and work progressed very slowly. Sud-

NOTE: Unlike most of the contributors to uncensored publications, the author of this article chose to remain anonymous.

denly, on Sunday, February 5, 1978, the fence disappeared and people saw a church, its wide portals adorned with a picture of Our Lady of Częstochowa. Masses were celebrated until late evening, attended by thousands of people who came in droves from the townships, and soon afterward Cardinal Wojtyła consecrated the new church.

For a while, the authorities did nothing, paralyzed by a state of shock. Then they attempted to close down and demolish the church, but they were frustrated by the faithful, who stood guard day and night. The church-building committee was taken to court, heavily fined, and harassed in the usual way, but owing to legal complexities no conclusive decision was reached. The committee sought permission to legalize the already standing church but met endless bureaucratic difficulties. Finally, just before May Day celebrations, the authorities attempted to hide the church from the adjacent highway by screening it with enormous billboards bearing propaganda material. However, the supports for the billboards and the cement foundation in which they were to be sunk were destroyed the very same day and can still be seen lying outside the offending church.

The whole incident casts light upon two facts: one, the true nature of the "normalization" to which the Communists revert in times of stress; and two, the systemic destruction of Poland's tradition of the rule of law.

From *Spotkania* (Lublin),
no. 3, 1978

Translated by Halina Willetts

Polish Communists:
Two Profiles

The political opposition in Poland in the 1970s consisted almost exclusively of people who had given up any hope whatsoever of reforming communism "from within." Within the ranks of the PZPR, however, belief in a "revisionist" solution of the mounting crisis had not been totally extinguished. One of the foremost proponents of reforms was Stefan Bratkowski—journalist, sociologist, historian, one of the organizers of DiP ("Experience and the Future" club), and long-time party member. The speech reprinted below was delivered in March 1979 at a party meeting, and was not meant to be publicly disseminated. Within a short time, however, it found its way into the pages of a KOR publication, and it became known throughout the country.

In November 1980, Bratkowski was elected chairman of the Union of Polish Journalists and appointed editor of the weekly supplement to the daily Życie Warszawy, a position from which he had been removed several years earlier. He used his authority, as well as the respect he commanded (even among his political opponents), to lash out against the party's policies and especially against the tactics of the hard-liners, which, he felt, would drag the country into an abyss. The latter responded with a bitter counteroffensive and finally succeeded in expelling Bratkowski from the party. Several days after Jaruzelski's coup, Bratkowski issued yet another spirited open letter to his comrades and to the country at large, thus courting arrest and prosecution.

The article by Władysław Machejek introduces us to an altogether different world. Machejek became a Communist before World War II and fought the Germans during the occupation. After the war, he served each successive Communist regime (Bierut, Gomułka, Gierek) with unremitting zeal. As a reward, he was allowed to edit his "own" newspaper, Życie Literackie, which soon became a haven for some of the most retrogressive and obscurantist elements of Polish political and cultural life. A hack writer, he has published a number of thinly disguised autobiographical novels, one of which, Czekam na słowo ostatnie* (I await the last word), is replete with anti-Semitic invective and caricatures of

*For an excellent analysis of the novel, see "Autoportret Faszysty" (A Fascist's self-portrait), by Irena Grudzińska-Gross, ANEKS (London), no. 16–17, 1977.

"liberals," intellectuals, and—for good measure—homosexuals. Another distinctive feature of this multivolume novel is its cult of manliness, power, and authority. Machejek's political journalism is notable for its extravagant praise of party leaders and policies, as well as for its bombastic and pretentiously "literary" language.

The article "And Now—to Work!" is typical of the latter. It appeared two months after the Eighth Congress of the PZPR, which took place in February 1980 and which was remarkable for its failure to come up with any solutions to the acute problems facing Poland. At the congress, the then prime minister, Piotr Jaroszewicz (theretofore lavishly praised by Machejek), was taken severely to task and dismissed from his post. A new prime minister, Edward Babiuch, was appointed several days later, and on April 4 he delivered his first major address to the Sejm—thus providing Machejek with yet another source of inspiration.

During Poland's "renewal," Machejek became a champion of Solidarity, only to turn against it with venom after the military coup on December 13, 1981. Needless to say, he continued to edit *Życie Literackie*.

SPEECH BY STEFAN BRATKOWSKI, March 16, 1979

I take the floor as a rank-and-file party member and hope my words, unexpurgated, reach our leaders and perhaps comrades in other party organizations. While I am not speaking on anyone's behalf, my comments are based upon discussions held over many months with hundreds of the nation's leading specialists. I expect some, if not all, will in time publicly address the issues facing our Commonwealth. But history is bearing down upon us. We have only two months this spring to take decisive action. I am voicing, for the benefit of the party, views that our experts, given the opportunity, would corroborate.

While it is generally believed that the present crisis is primarily political, it originated in the chronic failures of our economy. Economics and politics are inseparable in a country with the eleventh largest economic potential in the world. Our economic crisis requires a series of political solutions. Without them, we will never truly mobilize the heart, mind, and will of the nation.

In the 1970s Poland departed from policies leading to stagnation, technological backwardness, social austerity, and the scarcity of consumer goods. The present party leadership has already taken energetic and sweeping steps toward reform. Unfortunately, the system of administration, management, and organization that worked fairly well in a no-growth economy has gradually broken down. Central planning has become ineffectual. Neither energy use nor the potential of our transport system has been investigated in several years. No accurate data have been compiled on two of the most vital sectors of our economy. Efforts toward coordination have ceased. No one is keeping records of the licenses Poland has purchased or of our major investments. There is no quality control over production. In the last twelve months our debts have accumulated to the point where Poland frequently lacks the liquidity to service its debt repayment.

Therefore it is no exaggeration to say that today our party's greatest adversary is this economic chaos and its consequences. The gravest danger we face is the disenchantment of our workers. We have lost the cooperation of workers who until quite recently were willing to purchase tools with their own money for state-owned factories. Even today workers would be willing to perform the most onerous tasks without pay, provided they were convinced of their value. Instead, dissatisfaction and lack of confidence in the authorities and in our currency are rife. Mobilizing the armed forces and militia would be useless. Not force, but reason, is the way to recovery.

My strong language is not meant to incite you. We're not after scalps; we're after reforms and a guarantee that they will be implemented. The reforms must be both political and economic, for without the former, the nation and economy cannot be revitalized.

What, then, do we expect? Above all, we demand respect—that is, a marked change in attitude toward us. Everyone knows we Poles are open-hearted. Nevertheless, we must be treated seriously. Many Poles drink too much, many scrimp on soap. It is true we have plenty of faults. We make notoriously poor subjects for feudalism, an absolute monarchy, or an oligarchy. Ours is not a feudal era with arbitrary laws. Only a republic based on consistent and binding law is right for us. We are republicans—for the republic and lawful government. That is why we constructed socialism. Otherwise, Poles are tough to govern and a modern economy cannot function.

What at the minimum do we expect by way of reform?

ONE: A party separate from the government, the economy, and the courts, conforming to the party leadership's repeated declarations that the party sets policy and the government carries it out. The administration's and management's subsequent failures or mistakes would no longer be blamed upon individuals who did not make the decisions. This would require the adoption and enforcement of a constitutional amendment prohibiting anyone from simultaneously holding political, administrative, and managerial posts. When a man is solely accountable to himself, irresponsibility ensues.

TWO: Enforcement of the constitutional mandate guaranteeing the legislature's sovereignty over the executive branch, in accordance with socialist theory of the state. The defunct advocacy system, borrowed from ancient European parliamentarism, will not suffice. We must give the legislature the right to summon any administrator or citizen to obtain necessary information and explanations.

THREE: Enforcement of the constitutional mandate curtailing the administration's and management's influence over the mass media. Corruption of mass media employees through special benefits, payoffs with luxury items, part-time posts, or by any other means must be eliminated. The government and management must relinquish their control over what the press prints, the radio broadcasts, and television airs. They should enjoy a positive mass media image solely on the basis of merit—i.e., by presiding over an effective administration and a well-managed economy.

FOUR: A truly autonomous judiciary and the reorganization of our legal system. It is a wise and ancient tradition of the Polish Commonwealth that the judiciary should not be subject to executive control. A flood of bureaucratic regulation, arbitrary law enforcement, illegal acts, and activity that is "above" the law are the bane of our nation and its economy. Better a harsh legal code that is consistently enforced than a reign of quasi-feudal whim. To reiterate, our republic must be governed by universally enforced laws whether they apply to traffic violations or censorship. A government must be bound by the laws it has helped establish. Otherwise, our system will continue to trip over itself.

FIVE: A constitutional mandate transferring control over the law enforcement apparatus from the administration and management to the legislature. Moreover, the work of the Central Planning Commission, the Office of Statistics, and the legislature needs to be coordinated.

SIX: Administrative, judicial, and economic appointments should be made solely on the basis of merit. A government is effective only when its officials can be held accountable and has a mechanism for rectifying false or harmful policies. The feudal system of favoritism, which rewards fealty rather than competence, provides no such safeguards. Parenthetically, it would be advisable to set a constitutional limit on the tenure of administrators and managers. Management theorists recognize that an eight-year term is sufficiently long for a leader and his constituents.

These reforms overstep none of the principles that guided the founders of the socialist state. They represent the application [of these principles] in praxis and therefore are no cause for alarm. They will not undermine but fortify our political system. While they do not guarantee that future mistakes will be avoided, they provide a framework for early detection and correction.

As I have said, our society insists upon respect. We no longer fear the truth, and we demand recognition as fellow citizens, not subordinates; as partners, not pawns for manipulation. We expect an honest and thorough dialogue about the state of the Commonwealth, rather than journalistic histrionics in support of every managerial and administrative mistake. Let me assure you that the nation's serious journalists, who are my professional peers, are not exploiting the free exchange of ideas to cry wolf or to square their personal accounts. And I am not one to paint an overly bright picture of a press that has had no space for my political views for six years running. But let's get back to the more important matters of the Commonwealth. We are painfully aware that our unwieldy system of management and government corrupts even individuals of exceptional integrity.

We are a mature society that has benefited from its own experience and that of others. A genuine national dialogue is required to convince society that its concerns are being heard. Until this conviction is widespread, nothing will change. Attempts at manipulation—giving only to take away—have no place today. Without society's cooperation, our country and its economy cannot be rejuvenated. No amount of wishful thinking, propaganda, or force will obliterate this truth. Talleyrand once said you can accomplish a lot with bayonets, but you can't sit on them. It is common knowledge that the comrades in the coercion apparatus don't want to take the blame for others, and comrades in the army, ready for any national disaster, are not willing to assume responsibility for cotton deliveries to Łódź—let alone for firing upon fellow citizens. By the way, such a harebrained scheme would spell the political suicide of our party.

To corral society's cooperation, we must provide guarantees for the classes that form our nation's backbone. Workers' unions should be exclusively for workers and represent their interests without employer interference. In fact, the concern of Polish workers for their workplace is frequently more genuine than their employers'. They have not derailed this train, and they will not derail the Polish economy. Treated as partners, they will behave as partners.

Our farmers must also be given guarantees if they are to share responsibility for our agriculture. Doctrinaire proposals for rural depopulation to raise agricultural productivity are simply obtuse. They ignore that for every American farmer there are eight industrial workers;* in the present circumstances, these half-baked proposals border upon political provocation.

Guarantees must also be given to the class of private manufacturers and merchants, who have already been officially recognized as part of the work force. Without guarantees, private craft and trade will remain overrun by speculators and petty swindlers. Inadequate regulation produces, on the one hand, large profits for shady dealers; on the other, a shortage of shoemakers, plumbers, carpenters, and producers of parts for large industry. Neither arbitrarily established taxes nor payoffs profit the state.

We do not expect miracles within two months, only a clear and credible program for reform that capitalizes on our strengths. We can rely on the cadres of qualified workers, the talents of our technicians and managers, and, if the right conditions are created, a resurgence of individual initiative, which is the only miracle we are entitled to expect. We have two great assets: an abundance of natural resources and a still-unspoiled agriculture that continues to prune our trade deficit. Owing to chaotic import practices our modernized industrial equipment is less of an asset than its cost would suggest.

In the last ten years, employment and prices have been the recurrent themes of discussions about economic reform. Occasionally "socialist" economists have openly proposed utilizing a reserve work army to increase productivity and fight inflation. Their scheme is ridiculous; an individual worker's output accounts for only 13 to 17 percent of gross industrial productivity. No one disputes that our present employment structure is flawed. The problem is not a surfeit of able-bodied men working in key industries, but the shortage of mid-sized, small, and family-owned commercial and manufacturing enterprises. Disproportionately few people work at this level of enterprise in the nationalized, coop, mixed, and private sectors. We must have incentives to reward capable and creative people for solid work. If we did, the service sector alone would absorb approximately half a million people, thereby significantly reducing inflation. Remember, our flawed employment structure and unmanageable bureaucracy fuel inflation. It is a numerically shocking, though hidden, flaw. The ratio between bureaucrats and workers in an average cooperative employing the disabled is far higher than in key industries. Approximately 200,000 highly qualified people work in this "fluff" sector of our economy. Forming a layer between central planners and

*The ratio in Poland at that time was approximately two and a half industrial workers to one farmer.

regular industrial managers, they paralyze decisions and obstruct the flow of information. They set their own salaries, corrupt others, and produce little but disturbances. We are wasting thousands of excellent experts and managers through such unproductive employment practices.

Some people maintain that to cure our economy the price issue must be resolved. Today, even they realize we must first settle the currency issue before discussing prices or central planning. The several categories of non-cash currencies in circulation are incommensurate and have no direct cash value. Consequently, we never know the true cost of things and cannot ascertain what prices can and should be. How are we to assess our costs and set prices when we are forced to import basic parts and hardware from as far away as Japan because we haven't developed an indigenous light industry; when trains transport gravel to building sites hundreds of kilometers away because shorter freight runs are prohibited; when our system encourages raising production and overhead costs; when profit is calculated on manufacturing costs alone? To resolve the price dilemma we must first tackle the currency and overhead questions. We could attack the currency problem as it's been done in Hungary—decently, openly, without deception, by providing subsidies for those who might suffer as a result. Such readjustments are not a novelty.

A realistic picture of the need for reform emerged from recent discussions at the meetings of the Committee of Organizational Management Sciences and the Polish Economic Society. They recommended revisions in the management and central planning structures of our economy, which would eradicate bureaucratization and encourage individual initiative. Opponents will harken back to the age-old and sacred argument, "Reforms are costly: we have no money and therefore cannot afford them." In fact, the opposite is true. We are paying a premium for the absence of reform through rising costs of overhead, declining productivity, waste, and a ruinous trade deficit. Without reform, even an international moratorium on our national debt could not save us. Each month without reform produces further losses, further waste, and further demoralization.

Experts agree that three problems demand immediate attention. Long-term central planning has simply become incompetent and no longer deserves its name.

It is not my intention to arouse panic or apprehension. Yet I feel compelled to shatter the complacency of those who think "everything will be all right." The screws can no longer be screwed tighter or deeper; their threads have been stripped. Society has more means than ever before to express its dissatisfaction. Imagine, if you will, ten million postcards with the words "Step Down"; imagine the walls of cities and villages plastered with handbills making the same demand; imagine a wave of murderously mocking jokes (at which we excel) or songs in the streets that need only be hummed to convey their scathing message. These are the weapons of the impotent, some may say, but I wouldn't advise anyone to tangle with them. While they are not lethal, they have been known to confound the mightiest authorities. These weapons have not been used because our society continues to wait patiently. But in my view, and in this I am not alone, the reserves of patience are nearly depleted. We have no further excuse to procrastinate.

As a rank-and-file party member, I call upon the party leaders and all of its members: let us prove that we are capable of leading the movement for reconstruction of the Commonwealth; let us strive to make the word—the word, law—lawful, and a Polish zloty—the zloty.

From *Biuletyn Informacyjny* (Warsaw),
no. 3 (29), 1979

Translated by Michael Kott

AND NOW–TO WORK!

Władysław Machejek

If there is one thing that the Eighth Congress of the PZPR has taught us, it is that we have not lost our wings, that we have retained the power to fly. On April 3 we heard from the lips of Edward Babiuch that the [party] program must be carried out immediately. I should like to deal with certain points made in the premier's speech—and to add my own hopes—briefly and concisely.

Edward Babiuch assumed a new high position amid the waves of approval created by the Eighth Congress itself. Edward Babiuch is not a new figure, and his words do not come from any revelation; they are conclusions drawn from long experience, from long practice in a position of great responsibility. He wants, among other things, to renew certain initiatives, as well as to establish control over some activities and evasions that have thus far eluded our control.

Premier Edward Babiuch spoke before the Great Chamber which had just assembled to open the eighth session of the Parliament of the Polish People's Republic. As many as 218 out of 460 deputies became deputies for the first time (the principle of rotation works unimpeded in this area—fortunately, it does make good use of experienced parliamentarians). When opening the previous session, Jarosław Iwaszkiewicz,* towering above Parliament, certainly greeted the "young" delegates eloquently in order to dispel any provincial complexes that would lead to mere mimicry or silence. This time, Jerzy Ziętek, that good-hearted, vigorous Silesian veteran, made reference to that gesture. This does not mean that both great men were encouraging the unleashing of some sort of parliamentary whirlwind; each of them, of course, knows his place. There is no question of playing to the gallery here. Here what matters is mastery over the unsettled issues, how best to liquidate that list—and it was to this point, too, that Premier Edward Babiuch addressed himself in his speech.

Oh, a tear wells up in my eye: I, too, was once a young and perpetually learning deputy. . . . I, too, followed that path faithfully.

---

*Jarosław Iwaszkiewicz (1894–1980), a distinguished Polish novelist, poet, and essayist, was for many years chairman of the Polish Writers' Union and editor of the literary journal *Twórczość*.

Just before the commencement of the eighth session of the Sejm, which was concomitant with the formation of a new government, the second plenum of the Central Committee of the PZPR took place: the proceedings were summed up by Edward Gierek, who, having taken stock of society's approval of the policy of the party and the FJN (Front of National Unity), as expressed by the elections, noted that this approval signifies confidence that the wide-ranging but difficult economic, social, and cultural tasks will be fulfilled. Difficult times are coming—he's been giving us doses of that truth for many months now. There should be no mincing of words when difficult problems have to be dealt with. In turn, Edward Babiuch, in great detail, translated the general issues into their basic elements.

2.

The new premier's speech reveals a logical system, joined by stabilizing links. That was straightforward, though somewhat bitter, news! As I remarked, there is no question of searching for any new road; it is a question of the true rate of development, a question of a more equitable division of the national income and of differentiating between those with pockets that bulge and those who are as poor as the proverbial church mouse, a question of avoiding any limitation on the socialist nature of our system. This is underscored in the passages that discuss curbing excessive increases in the cost of living, so as to maintain, as planned, a proper correlation of the cost of living with wages and other income. Therefore, we must be particularly vigilant about "formation of this relationship, accurate statistics in this area, the analysis of family budgets. . . . We will do everything in our power to maintain the present general standard of living, correcting it where it gives the most urgent indications that basic social needs remain unsatisfied."

One need only applaud—I have been doing just that for a long time, while urging the realization of that which we had been "threatened with" for quite some time now. Of course, simply recognizing the situation of families with limited means or, to be blunt, living at the edge of subsistence (some retired people and families with many children and very low average income) will not fill their pockets. It is, however, a good thing to be aware of the actual social situation of many millions of people, to be aware of how the dynamic growth of wages and income has been distributed, to be aware of the need for more rapid improvement. Now, for a second time, Edward Babiuch as premier is encouraging statisticians (and thus GUS—the Main Statistical Office) to fulfill their true role. It is clear that there are common goals here and that the statistical data should reflect public sentiments. (Incidentally, perhaps we will at last discover how much we have in capital goods, processing plants, medical supplies, etc., in Poland; time after time the press advertises unclaimed property.) Those who have suffered are not promised anything at once; nevertheless, the very desire to act is significant and stands out in bolder relief than ever before. There is an awareness of the increase of inequities in society. It is not only a matter of lowered wages and incomes (for various, often justifiable, reasons); what makes it worse is the widespread recognition that the norms of social justice are being violated—to be frank, that there are some privileged persons who earn a good deal of money or whose wealth is evident from the affluence of both their homes and their life styles, yet who profess to earn average or even wretched incomes. Restraining their ostentation will also have some effect on reducing social gaps. So the premier's speech dealt correctly and realistically with the role of state subsidies which, unfortunately, often "cause a violation of the principle of social equity by granting additional privileges to higher-salaried, wealthier people"— for instance, through differentials in apartment rents, meat prices, electric rates. Also, the "administration of public funds should correspond, more than it has up to now, to the principles of social equity." Such tendencies bolster a sense of revindication of socialist morality, a feeling that Premier Edward Babiuch tried to inspire by announcing "a gradual reduction in the existing spread of income in all cases where it is not justified by real differences in the nature or results of the work performed. We will bear this principle in mind when shaping income policy. In this phase, too, we will improve the system of taxation."

As everyone knows, thus far the state treasury's attempts to calculate excessive income have often run into obstacles, including the proverbial goose that lays the golden eggs. At one point a campaign victimized many homeowners who could not be held responsible for "dachamania,"* for in many cases they had tried to escape bad housing conditions, and had acquired their property by hard work (and often by skimping on meals). These petit bourgeois are not like the owners of BMW limousines or Fiat Mirafloris, which are worth more than those hard-won little houses, earned by sweat. The limousine owners, however, remained pure on paper—socially, and from the point of view of taxation. And while on the subject of "dachamania," I think that one should take into account the real value of any acquisition and delicately inquire where the money for it came from—if, perhaps, from "scraps" and "odds and ends." And let the appropriate response illuminate the moral and social collapse of the policies of that oligarchy; this, too, belongs in a program that seeks to bring social order in a people's state. An excess of money in many hands even overcomes inflated market prices and as a result, production and commerce, as well as gastronomy, are attracted to luxury goods since, for certain groups, nothing is too expensive.

I know that I have been carried away by the social theme that, one felt, the premier fervently emphasized, but, of course, his speech encompassed the totality of relations in our country and was a true report on the state of the nation. I repeat—reliable information.

The functioning of the economy will be the most important concern, especially investment and housing. In contrast with my one-time evaluation of former proposals, I have some reservations about how the current system of planning will work though at other times my appraisal has been different. There is an imbalance in the economy; the greatest difficulty is a lack of coordination—in the supply of materials and in the means of processing and marketing them. This is an area in which a centralized socialist system should demonstrate its superiority, yet it is precisely here where problems are continuously mounting, where the balance of resources bursts and necessitates corrections that tie up resources

---

*The proliferation of private villas (dachas) for the elite.

already invested; in other areas insane haste has led to excesses of power and to the corrupting wages of hastily recruited shock workers. The premier struck out severely at this type of practice.

Furthermore, he declared that we will live on what we produce ourselves, even though things will be tight and we will have to cut back. We learned that the foreign banks are not waiting for our offers. "The conditions for obtaining foreign credits have worsened. Credit is increasingly expensive and increasingly difficult to obtain." We must fully economize on fixed purchased assets, including those that have been imported:

> We must draw conclusions from the fact that a considerable portion of our fixed assets, both productive and non-productive, are not utilized to the full. The total value of our fixed assets has already exceeded nine billion zlotys. One percent of that amount is equivalent to the annual investment outlay for construction in housing. . . . We have a lot of machines and devices, including a considerable portion which have been imported and which wait a long time to be installed. All this has a negative effect on the stability of the economy, causes a justifiable anxiety, and requires fundamental improvement. . . . Anyone who undertakes and profits by investments not performed in accordance with obligatory principles is striking at the vital interests of society.

To the point.

Premier Edward Babiuch wasted no time on empty promises, in chasing rainbows, or on preaching. I am under the impression that realists and Communists have been waiting for words such as these. They will no longer feel like outsiders. No, no one has been promised any "rose gardens." Furthermore, the premier struck out at high-handedness and representational funds (I'm very worried about my 500 zlotys for coffee, tea, and cigarettes for foreign delegations), limousines, especially those of foreign manufacture, for dignitaries. In the complaints and grievances voiced at the stormy discussions before the Congress and the elections a burgeoning critical note was sounded with regard to the attitudes of people in positions of authority, their "private" lives and family situations.

"We will counteract," said the Premier, "instances of abuse of office, corruption, favoritism, and speculation."

3.

I think that the working class, the great majority of the honest, hard-working community, have given their approval to the direction the new government's actions. Trade unions have been consulted. Experience and public knowledge have been met half way without the loss of long-range perspective. We are thus returning to a period of disciplined stabilization of what has already been achieved and are fashioning a new form of dynamism that does not live on pap. To be sure, truthful information will not emerge at meetings where no one speaks his mind. Or where Communists convince other Communists that communism is good and that it will prevail. Of course, it will prevail, but not by talking about it. But I do not believe that the authorities are interested in hindering the flow of reliable information. And so Premier Edward Babiuch revealed the full extent of the reality, thus making it possible for us to counteract it. The time will come for the rest, too. If those in possession of solid information speak bluntly about reality, then society will set store by that information. In turn, well-informed people must be required to take internal and external realities into account. Solid, disciplined, equitable information, that is not all that much, and yet, at the same time, it is everything in the realm of mutual understanding.

From *Życie Literackie*
(Kraków), April 13, 1980

Translated by Richard Lourie

Controversies
(Uncensored)

Vigorous debates constituted one of the most fascinating features of the free, or "uncensored," press that flourished in Poland in the late 1970s. The controversies aired in various unofficial periodicals transcended purely ideological confines. They touched upon matters of history and historiography, Polish national traditions, economic and social problems, literature and the arts. Given the vitality and diversity of Polish intellectual life in the nineteenth century, between the two world wars, and (all efforts of the censors notwithstanding) under Communist rule, it is hardly astonishing that the Polish revolution of September 1980–December 1981 was not only one of the most bloodless, but also one of the most articulate revolutions in contemporary history.

The debate between Piotr Wierzbicki and Adam Michnik is quintessentially within the tradition of the Polish intelligentsia, as it concerns a topic that generations of Poles have had to deal with—namely, how can one preserve one's moral integrity under conditions of foreign occupation? What is the price to be paid for collaborating with a detested regime—and what indeed should be the nature (if at all) of such collaboration? Piotr Wierzbicki is a one-time teacher and well-known writer and journalist. Adam Michnik is a historian who had come of age politically during the events of March 1968 (see chapters by Leszck Kołakowski and Tadeusz Szafar), one of the founders of KOR, and author of *Kosciół, lewica, dialog* (The Church, the left, dialogue) (Paris, 1977), a book that explores the possibility of fashioning an understanding between the traditional values of the left and the new social and political activism of the Catholic Church.

The second controversy is also rooted in one of the historic preoccupations of the Polish intelligentsia—the relationship between "Polishness" and Catholicism. To Father Sroka, the two are virtually synonymous. To his critics—both youthful members of KIK (Clubs of Catholic Intelligentsia)—the national-religious symbiosis is not only false, but potentially dangerous to the survival of Poland as a free and pluralistic country.

A TREATISE ON TICKS

Piotr Wierzbicki

DEFINITION OF THE TICK

Ticks are something between the new masters of Poland and opposition activists; they are, like the majority of the Polish nation, forced into at least passive participation in the socialist-Soviet Vistula spectacular. Is a tick therefore simply a gray citizen of Poland? Is a peasant a tick if he thinks that things were better in Bierut's time, or a worker if he commits himself to labor emulation, or a clerk sent out with a banner into the streets of Warsaw to welcome the beloved leader of the land of the Soviets? Is everyone a tick who bows down obsequiously to the new masters? No, if tickery were simply a synonym for submissiveness, there would be nothing to discuss. Submissiveness is a banal phenomenon, existing in all places and as old as the world. Tickery is something rather special. It is a phenomenon characteristic not of society as a whole but only of the upper intellectual levels. We do not seek ticks among peasant-workers, booking clerks, and charwomen. We seek them among rectors of colleges, journalists, and artists. The tick serves his masters in a highly specific and refined manner. He serves them by the quiet work of his gray matter. A tick stands erect on his two hind legs and thinks. About what? About how to justify the idea that that which is must be. Justification is not the strongest point of the new masters. In the task of justification, the ticks fill in for them. When a rector finds a place for some dignitary's son at the behest of someone on high, this is simply an ordinary case of bowing one's head. When a professor writes a text indicating that from ages past intellectuals have been eager for power for reasons of ambition, and publishes this precisely when the security police are holding discussions with those intellectuals, the situation is more refined. Here it is not the body but the spirit that stands up on its hind legs. Here the gray matter is put into service.

Are they then cynics, refined swindlers, out for profit? Really! A tick a cynic! If a tick were a cynic, then this sketch would have been finished long ago. But the tick does not know how to be a cynic. A cynic is someone who has the courage to lie brazenly. Brazenly, but once only! A cynic does not do and say what he thinks, but he does think for himself. His words and deeds may be called deceitful, but the sphere of his thought is free from deceit. A cynic is in conflict with life. A tick is not. A tick, then, while laboring to find some justification for the various deeds of the new masters of Poland, must also toil at talking himself into these deeds. The tick does violence to his own spirit.

GENEALOGY OF THE TICK

We shall leave to the historians the task of discovering the forefathers of ticks in past ages. Being concerned with the present, we shall point out only their immediate ancestors. The tick directly traces his descent from the "positive nonparty" type who inhabited Poland in Bierut's day. The positive nonparty type was a citizen of People's Poland, concerned with the construction of the country, supporting the general line of the party, sympathetic to the Soviet Union, honest, active, disciplined but having in his ideological ballast small accretions of the "old," a dubious social origin, a certain intellectual way of expressing himself, a certain tendency to fall into aestheticism. Precisely as a result of this small accretion of foreign matter, the positive nonparty type did not belong to any militant organization. But he played a very active role in organizations of a general humanitarian character such as the Polish-Soviet Friendship Society, the League of Women, the Committee for the Defense of Peace, the Popular Front, and the Polish Red Cross.

The positive nonparty type was generally a middle-aged professor who looked with warm sympathy on the execution carried out on Polish learning by the party, security police, and Communist youth, or a gray-haired writer of an aesthetic type who granted the Stalinist activists absolution from the uplands of Bach and Chopin, or a prewar engineer who was an enthusiast for the rationalization movement. The positive nonparty type was a person well known in his own environment. He was distinguished, therefore, by a certain positive character; he diligently approached everyone personally when there was a meeting, and sometimes even sat on the presidium.

The positive nonparty type played rather a passive role in the class struggle then being waged in our country. He did not unmask enemies of the people; only rarely did he speak up sharply at meetings, emphasizing what was humanistic in the new system, rather than its revolutionary character. Obviously there was nothing remarkable in this. And yet it was necessary. The Stalin-Bierutite functionaries valued him and cherished him more than one of their own. Sometimes he even drove a Demokratka.* Every union of creative artists, every academic discipline, every place of work had a very essential educational function; it showed that truly the best Poles were members of the PZPR and employees of the security service, but that the nonparty citizen, if he so wished, could stand, perhaps not in the first but anyway in the second rank.

*A luxury Chevrolet car, bought during the first years of People's Poland for the country's highest elite.

TYPES OF TICK

Ticks live mostly in the capital of Poland or in some of the larger administrative centers. They congregate in the universities and in other types of institutes of higher learning, in the presidium, committees, departmental secretariats, and institutes of the Polish Academy of Sciences, in the scientific institutes of individual ministries, in unions of creative artists and the press, particularly in the editorial boards of literary-social weeklies or monthlies. Ticks appear among the young, the middle-aged, the old, among Aryans and among Jews, Catholics, and atheists. Ticks—from a certain intellectual level upward—appear everywhere, in every generation, in every social, racial, and ideological group. The multitude of their varieties is thus impressive.

But let us consider, first of all, the artistic tick, principally of the literary kind. It seems that there are at least three varieties.

1. The gray-haired creative type, the humanist and aesthete. Ticks of this variety are extremely well known and popular in society; they have received from the new masters of Poland the right to carry on in their old-fashioned, prewar European style. In return, all that is demanded of them is that every so often they should, with an understanding smile, do homage to the socialist-Soviet crudeness flooding into Poland. Their mouths are full of Bach, Chopin, Leonardo, and Tolstoy; sometimes they sit on some presidium or other and utter beautiful speeches to suit the occasion.

2. The young creative type, the avant-gardist. Ticks of this kind are particularly cunning. They know that under Bierut avant-garde creative artists were treated frostily by the *crème de la crème.* And they know quite well, too, that today, (under Gierek), the avant-gardist is treated warmly by the people's government, because, today, the threat for that government is not the form but the content. So let him jabber, screech, and use a donkey's tail as a paintbrush—just so long as he does not describe what is actually going on in Poland. They hope, however, that the public at large will not notice this turnabout in the government's attitude to the donkey's tail. And so, dressed up in the plumage of nonconformists, they soar on the fumes of pure form. The task assigned by their masters is exceptionally modest: not to see what is going on in Poland. And, to the best of their strength and ability, they do not see.

3. The middle-aged creative type, the petty realist. The masters of Poland do allow these ticks to look at the country, but subject to a certain condition, that out of it comes a twisted, trifling, womanish "tut-tut." The petty realist, who in his mind has chopped Poland up into tiny pieces so that the censorship can swallow it, gains from the authorities the right to work, publish, and even to criticize individual errors and shortcomings. In exchange, he supplies the reading public with proof that it is possible to write as he wishes, provided that it is done skillfully, so as not to irritate the censor.

We now have to analyze how the tick reveals himself in his political attitude, in his actions and toward his environment. We can distinguish—from the point of view of political attitude—at least four varieties of tick.

1. Party ticks. There must be some misunderstanding here. A red tick? Not at all. The party, although continually criticized for its dogmatism and rigidity, is nevertheless at bottom extremely elastic and tolerates in its ranks some extremely atypical citizens. If, then, it is possible to be a member of the party while going to church and confirming to a fideist outlook (recognizing, of course, its inferiority to Marxism-Leninism), why should it be impossible to be a member of the party and also a tick? And, in fact, there are quite a few ticks in the party. In the coffeehouse or the literary salon, the party tick is absolutely indistinguishable from the nonparty tick. If he practices the profession of writer or journalist, he becomes increasingly absorbed with cultivating the most enlightened and humanistic traditions of socialism and fighting the most hard-headed groups within the bosom of the party. The party tick rails against any party hard-liner, and, out of his experience, forged by polemics against idiocy, can without fear for his reputation publish every couple of years an article justifying the necessity for successive price rises and how absolutely essential they are for further increases in the standard of living. The party tick functions daily as if certified. He can specialize in criticism and polemics, and is not obliged to write every day about love for the Soviet Union. Once every several years, however, he behaves like a completely normal person; he receives an assignment, he fulfills his obligations, he does his duty. Some party ticks have long since become ripe for the change into nonparty ticks, but they remain in the party organization only out of inertia and fear of the face that the apparatchik will pull when he sees returned to him forever the tickish party card, which is so valuable for the organization.

 2. *Ticks of the center*. These make up a definite majority of the tick population. The tick of the center (nonparty, obviously) is a loyal citizen of the country; except for certain reservations regarding the conduct of current politics, he never comes into conflict with the government; he supports that government with learned works demonstrating the incompetence of the government of prewar Poland and the growth of fascist trends at that time, by articles on the denaturation of the consumer life style in Western countries, reports of Nazi war criminals who have escaped punishment, and books on the positive changes that, in spite of errors, are taking place in our country. It is only rarely that the tick of the center receives an assignment to defend the progressive system, only at difficult moments and in drastic situations. He does not play a fundamental role in political campaigns, he does not write manifestoes; he does only as much as he has to, and so, for example, if he works for a newspaper, he does not on his own initiative write an attack on the workers of Radom and Ursus. If, however, the editor-in-chief asks him to write an anonymous editorial on that subject, he does so—trying, though, to make the text as cultural as possible—and is very proud that, instead of the word "bandits," which someone proposed, he used only the milder designation of "hooligans" to refer to the demonstrators.

 3. *Nonconformist ticks*. The nonconformist tick is encountered only rarely. He is a tick who has won for himself the status of a notorious and incorrigible fighter, battling against the nonsense that surrounds us on all sides. The nonconformist tick does not deliver laudatory speeches; he does not write propaganda; no one proposes to him that he should write some introductory article justifying something or other. He holds views that are honest, bold, and incorruptible. And

these are his texts. There is only one threshold that the nonconformist tick will not cross. He will not associate himself with any opposition activity. Provided that he does not sign protest letters or go to illegal meetings, he is allowed to act and function as a public figure. In fact, not much is demanded of him. But if he wants to remain a nonconformist tick, he will have to work at it systematically, since few people are able to remain such. It is necessary to hold some trump card—for example, an unquestioned talent or an especially influential job. Nonconformist ticks, who are honest, talented, critical of the reality about them, and who do not come into conflict with the government, are valuable to the latter, provided that they stay under control. From time to time a nonconformist tick actually does get out of control, signs a round-robin or a protest letter, and moves on into the category of enemies of the people.

4. *Ticks who are victims of oppression.* This would appear to be a contradiction in terms: a victim of oppression can surely not be a tick; a victim of oppression is surely an undaunted opposition activist, prepared to make the greatest sacrifices. And yet there do exist ticks who are victims of oppression. How? Because a progressive system wages war against the enemy within a very specific manner. In reactionary social systems the state deals with its enemies by striking at them alone. This constitutes a serious breach of the principles of dialectics, forbidding the separation of anything or anyone from their socioeconomic base. Hence in the Soviet Union and later in People's Poland and the other socialist countries the method adopted was to deal with the enemy by striking, when possible, not only at him but also at his children, great-grandmothers, aunts-in-law, neighbors, acquaintances, and anyone else who might know him, and also at those who might not know him, but who independently are enemies, or at least potential ones. Ninety-nine point something or other percent of the tens of millions of inhabitants of the Gulag Archipelago are people who never themselves raised a hand against the land of the Soviets.

In People's Poland this phenomenon occurred on a scale that was incomparably smaller but enough so that, as an additional refinement, there were to be found in prison or simply on the pavement a few random individuals who not only were not enemies of the people (who, say, had fought against the Germans in the Home Army), but, on the contrary, intended merely to honor the people or to offer the people support with advice and a timely word—but of course it is impossible to check this. Thus we come to the circumstances where certain actual or potential ticks did become victims of oppression. In 1956, the ticks came out of prison, were rehabilitated, and began their great careers as ticks. They ran like the wind into collaboration with their masters. Forthwith, too, they began to lead the way in sycophancy, sycophantic intrigue, and semideviationist pretense at opposition. Their busy goings-on would have been suspect to anyone who could see the distinction between liberal-humanist slogans and the moral and political content of concrete actions. But their goings-on were not suspect to everyone. For the ticks had endured suffering in the past. They had been victims of oppression. They had passed their practical examination with flying colors. No one reminded these martyrs why they had been persecuted. Human memory is short. He was in prison, therefore he is a hero.

MECHANISM OF FORMATION OF THE TICK

A citizen of the Polish People's Republic, we may say, is not born a tick. At some period in his life, some process takes place in him or there appears in him some tickogenic element. There are various ways of turning into a tick. We have been able to identify and distinguish four.

1. Bad social origin. A progressive system is so perfect and so morally elevated that it constantly produces complexes in people. In Bierut's time, one such very typical complex was the social origin complex. The social origin of highest renown in People's Poland is obviously a working-class origin. In second place comes a peasant origin, and here it is preferable to be the child of a poor peasant than a rich one (in Bierut's time, this was applied more consistently than today: the children of poor peasants were made much of, the children of middle peasants less so, while the offspring of kulaks—i.e., peasants owning farms of say, 15 hectares—could not even dream of getting into a school of higher education). In third place comes origin from the intellectual class (in Bierut's time, two kinds were differentiated, the "working intelligentsia," a more positive group, and the "intelligentsia," a decidedly suspect group). In fourth place came descent from the "private enterprise" class, which was obviously fatal. And what then? A great big gap, and then came the worst thing under the sun: to be descended from prewar landowners, aristocrats, and factory owners.

If—speaking about Bierut's time—it was difficult to be the child of parents owning more than two cows, how was one to bear the burden of being the child of a banker, a squire, an aristocrat—in short, of an exploiter and enemy of the people who in collusion with foreign capital had pushed Poland toward the calamitous precipice of September 1939? For some people this was past endurance. They created for themselves, against the background of their inappropriate social origin, a guilt complex and made an all-out effort somehow to wipe out their guilt and to beseech the favor of the people's government. A party career was closed to them, but the career of a tick lay open. And they became ticks. A count for hire; a "positive" count is an important sociological element for present-day Poland. He is living proof of the humanitarian tolerance of the proletarian avant-garde which, rather than breaking his bones, cossets him, and also of the patriotic unity of all Poles, rallied, in spite of the differences that divide them, around the party and its leaders.

2. The desire to be someone. This is at once the most universal and most banal tickogenic mechanism. In a country where, in order to become not only a director but even some subordinate boss or department head, it is desirable and usually obligatory to belong to the PZPR, the road to a career and a life of success lies open only to those who rule and those who toady to them. If one is not very gifted or indispensable as an engineer, mathematician, physicist, chemist, astronomer, etc., then to carve out a career for oneself one must either join the party or become a tick. Some jobs are simply closed to other citizens. For example, that of journalist. In a progressive system a journalist is not just an expert in transmitting and commenting on information; he is a "worker on the ideological front," a petty clerk with the task of carrying out propaganda instructions. A journalist in People's Poland has the responsibility of defending and praising the current team of the PZPR to the last hour it holds office, even if (as in December 1970) it deploys machine guns against the workers, and then to criticize it and thunder without mercy the instant that it has been ousted by another PZPR team. Only party members and ticks are fit for this task.

3. *Total loyalty*. A celebrated Polish composer found himself one day (during the 1970s) among a group of his fellow musicians in the presence of one of the deputy ministers of culture and art. During the course of a discussion on the problems of music, someone drew the attention of the deputy minister to the fact that there were two gifted Polish composers living abroad, Andrzej Panufnik and Roman Palester, and that it was many years since their music had been performed on Polish concert platforms. The deputy minister replied: "I don't see any objections: if you want to play them, then play them!" At this the celebrated Polish composer burst out: "But, Mr. Minister, haven't you seen the anti-Soviet implication on the sleeve of the Panufnik record?" (he meant that the composition is dedicated to the memory of the victims of Katyń). The minister had not seen it; he was put out of countenance and said that since the musicians themselves had reservations concerning the matter, he did not want to have to deal with it. Thus the question of the blocking of Panufnik and Palester was deferred for a certain time.

The question now arises: what did the celebrated composer achieve by making this denunciation of his émigré colleague? We would propose the hypothesis: loyalty. The celebrated composer, winner of a state prize, esteemed by ministers and deputy ministers, constantly able to travel abroad, simply does not know how to behave disloyally. If one minister lets him travel abroad, if a second pays him compliments, if a third gives him a prize, if the party accepts his slightly suspect aesthetics, how can he have the right to behave like a Judas? No, from the deputy minister who favored him with his trust he could not hide anything. The deputy minister was quite ready to agree to Panufnik, because he obviously had not seen this anti-Soviet reference. If the celebrated composer did not have the duty to inform the minister, then who did? Obviously, he did have that moral duty.

4. *The truth lies somewhere in between*. There exists a type of character and intellect trained to the formula "the truth lies somewhere in between." These are the compromisers, the people who never clearly commit themselves to any one side because they have a soft character and intellect. In any situation they have a simply infinite battery of arguments for and against. They are of the opinion that the government in Poland is bad, but there are certain positive features, that in Sweden the government is better, but . . . that dependence of Russia is a very bad thing but, on the other hand, however . . . Ticks of the "truth lies somewhere in between" type perhaps lack the essential quality of the tick: they do not have to do much work on themselves to become muddleheaded; they already are muddleheaded, their heads get infected with compromise and halfwayitis already at birth. There are grounds for assuming that if the system changed, these "ticks by birth" would behave in the new anti-Communist system just as they do today—namely, with reserve and hesitation—while all the other ticks would

obviously immediately don the plumage of indefatigable anti-Communists. Ticks from birth, less hypocritical than the rest, nevertheless fulfill the same tickish function and are, moreover, fairly numerous, especially in university circles.

LIFE OF THE TICK IN SOCIETY

The tick is a citizen who is active professionally. Just active? Unusually active, committed, even a fighter. Against whom does the tick fight? He fights against symptoms of evil appearing not somewhere abroad but here in Poland. The tick, generally speaking, cannot come to terms with the fact that roses still do not grow everywhere around the prisons and jails. So the tick fights for flower beds and herbaceous borders. He dedicates his working life to this cause. He speaks out and writes articles and letters to the editor. Just pick up the annual index for any newspaper from 1956, 1968, 1970, and 1976. There we can see numerous ticks in action. One devotes a series of articles to an incompetently restored apartment house in Gdańsk, a second rages about the neglected grave of some poet, a third considers that it would be possible to build a fun fair in Radom, a fourth states that he will not rest until they repaint the fence of the children's playground at Ursus. And so, according to the ticks, the inexorable improvement of our reality continues.

THE TICK AND HIS COMPANIONS

A tick normally associates with ticks. There are obviously exceptions to this rule. These relate to contacts both with party members and members of the opposition. In the case of a party member, the tick generally contents himself with a single representative of this variety, a single one but not a random match. Who is this person? He is the tick's immediate superior, his boss, chairman, or professor. The contact that the tick maintains with the party member, his superior (very cordial, marked by a somewhat intimate respect, but not too frequent), is usually concealed from the rest of his acquaintances. The tick fears that his superior, the party member, might not take the fancy of some of his companions, that indeed this group of companions might think evil of him. What does it mean, "evil"? That he is a red.

To a tick—this must be plainly understood—it matters considerably that those around him should not confuse him with the party riffraff. Some ticks are pre-pared to distance themselves from party members to the extent that they maintain contacts with members of the opposition. Perhaps "members of the opposition" is too strong—such a tick generally has one member of the opposition in his circle of acquaintances. As a result he suffers agonies of fear (when they bundle off to jail the member of the opposition who has the tick's telephone number in his diary), but still it makes him feel heroic, courageous, and antistate. The majority of ticks, however, keep clear of the opposition, and when one of their nonopposition acquaintances becomes a dissident, they sever relations with him.

Ticks congregate in coffeehouses, inciting people against the system, rooting for enemies of the people and intriguers. They read the opposition press, but still, they will never sign any protest letters, never write an antistate text, and never meddle in anything that might cost them their job. If at their place of work—for example, in an editorial office—some conflict of a political nature breaks out in the Union of Creative Artists, the tick tries to settle it. When there is a drive against Solzhenitsyn, Kołakowski, or Sakharov, the tick is bold enough to point out that while it is possible, even necessary, to write polemics against them, this must be done in a skillful and cultured manner; that assaults that are too sharp and unwarranted have the reverse effect. When the party members launch a political attack on some celebrated artist or other, the tick does not join the offensive, but expresses a skeptical or downright negative opinion on the purely artistic value of his work.

THE INNER LIFE OF THE TICK

We now come to the most important part of our text: an attempt to present the tick's system of thought, an attempt to describe his intellectual structure. Let us have a proper look at it.

A. ARGUMENTS FOR NOT SIGNING A PROTEST LETTER. Ding-dong! A visitor he hasn't seen for ever so long; tea, chat, and more chat. The tick's acquaintance from opposition circles has come to see him. Together they wax indignant over some new police roundup, massacre, or amendment to the constitution imbued with warm sentiment toward the USSR. The doors and windows are tightly shut; one can frolic at will. Suddenly the visitor goes to his coat pocket and takes out a sheet of typescript. He gives it to the tick, who quickly skims through the closely typed text of the latest protest letter. The tick stops reading and begins to ask factual questions about the present range of actions. The visitor replies; the tick listens. But only on the surface. In reality, he is busy with another matter, figuring out how to explain that he cannot sign. He must decide, according to the circumstances and the person of his interlocutor, what line of argument to use. This is the repertoire at his disposal:

(a) *Duty to the family*. The tick cannot sign a protest letter because the tick is a person with duties and responsibilities. It is not for oneself, of course; the tick cannot allow that certain definite consequences of signing should affect his family. It is rather a matter of wife, husband, aunt, and grandmother. Most of all, the children. The thought that his children might have to eat headcheese instead of frankfurters, or apples instead of bananas, that they might be expelled from the day nursery, might not be admitted to kindergarten, or won't get exemplary-conduct badges in school is unbearable to him. Protest letters are all right for bachelors and unmarried women, and also for basically irresponsible people. His hands are tied. One day, when the child has his school graduation certificate, his M.A,. and his doctorate, then maybe, maybe . . . providing, of course, that no grandchildren have appeared.

(b) *Love of his job*. The tick cannot join in the protest because his professional work plays a simply enormous role in his life. Without his editorial board, his theater, his film crew, his union of creative writers, without the responsibility of publishing his books, life would be simply unimaginable. Signing a protest would mean dismissal from work, a ban on publication, the end of his career. The tick can't do this to himself. Of course, he would sign at once if he were in as strong a position as N. N cannot be touched. If N signs, no one will do anything to him. In general, it is people like N who should sign, those who cannot be touched. Here the tick calls to mind the millionfold ranks of pensioners. That's who should be the army of the opposition. What can they do to pensioners? They won't cut off their pensions. Why does no one go to the pensioners with protest letters? And the chronically ill—the tick begins to dream—the incurables, the cancer patients, those to whom the Polish People's Republic can do nothing more, why do they not sign? Go and seek your signatories in the hospitals; don't expose people who are already exposed to repression. Go to the hospitals and old people's homes.

(c) *The wrong moment.* The tick has been thinking about taking part in some protest action, but just now it is quite the wrong moment. Why did no one come to him with a protest letter last September? September was the time to protest, and to protest sharply, not now. The action comes simply too late. Too late, and, in another sense, too early. This is too important a question to be played about with in an incompetent matter. Think about what you're doing! I'm warning you!

B. PROVOCATION. The tick possesses an irresistible, powerful and all-embracing tendency to see provocation in everything that goes on around him. Provocation, of course, by the party or the security police. The mouse lashes its tail against the cat. The naive person thinks that this is an anticat action. The tick knows better: it is not an anticat action but a cat action. The cat had a hand in it, inspired it, and lets the mouse come closer, to get its hands on the evidence. Evidence of what? That the mouse doesn't like it. The students have taken to the streets—provocation. The workers of Radom and Ursus protested against the decision to raise prices—provocation. The setting up of KOR—provocation. Setting up the Movement for the Defense of Human and Civil Rights—obviously provocation. How does the tick know that these are all provocations? Why, because if the security police did not have a hand in it, no one would have taken to the streets, no one would have protested against anything, no one would have been able to found anything. The very success of the action is evidence of its provocative character. The security police don't let anything happen without their approval.

For what purpose—according to the tick—does the government of the Polish People's Republic burn down regional party headquarters, get students and workers onto the streets, and induce naive intellectuals to organize protest actions? Obviously, to trap those opponents of the regime who have not yet been trapped and to have an excuse for turning the screw still further.

The tick has seen the authorities' deceit and does not let himself be maneuvered and will not let himself become involved in suspicious goings-on.

C. LIBERALS AND HARDHEADS. The tick is an expert in a certain field of knowledge, to which one would have thought he would not have access. Namely, he has a perfect knowledge of the factional fights within the PZPR. In knowledge on this subject the tick surpasses not only the rank-and-file members of the party but also a great many members of the Central Committee, and maybe even of certain secretaries, not to speak of members of the secretariat. The tick knows the party setup, and nobody knows it better than he, or maybe only the CIA. This knowledge includes the view that members of the Politburo and their deputies, secretaries and members of the secretariat, heads of party sections and first secretaries of regional committees can be divided into two categories of activists: liberals and hardheads (or hard-liners). The liberals try all they can (unfortunately, it is not much) to make the economic policy more rational to have greater freedom prevailing in matters of culture, and to see that the police and security authorities dealing with dissidents use as gentle methods as possible. The hardheads or hard-liners strive (and, unfortunately, they succeed) to tighten the belt of the economy, to turn the screw on culture and to use the sharpest means possible in the struggle against the opposition. To this intraparty front must be added—in the opinion of the ticks—an independent force, which implements its own policies. Some hardheads within the party possess certain contacts with security. However, the party as a whole, its first secretary included, has only a limited influence on the doings of security. The police in Radom tortured the workers—Gierek knew nothing about it. The security hounds the members of KOR, gifted intellectuals and artists—Minister of Culture Tejchma, who is a member of the Politburo, knows nothing about it.* The party liberals in general know very little and can do even less. But why can they do so little? And here we come to perhaps the greatest achievement of the ticks' gray matter: because the opposition has weakened their position.

What this liberal Tejchma builds up, what steps he takes to loosen the screw on culture, is immediately undone by some letter from writers about the fate of Poles in the USSR or on the amendments to the Constitution. For the hard-liners say at once: "You want to loosen the screw a bit, Comrade, you feel sure that they'll be good now, but what does this letter say?"—and Minister Tejchma cannot find an answer, the protest letter has knocked the arguments out of his hands.

The program of action that results from the ticks' diagnosis: the sensible citizen must act in such a way as to enhance the power of the liberal wing of the party. What weakens that wing? Letters, protests, strikes, demonstrations, and uncensored books. What strengthens it? The absence of letters, strikes, demonstrations, and uncensored books. You want liberalization—avoid all ill-considered actions, don't protest, don't make demands, don't take to the streets, don't take part in producing provocative literature—only censor it carefully at home yourself. Be present at the meeting of the Union of Polish Writers. After the meeting, somewhere upstairs, there will obviously be a dogged battle between the liberal Minister Tejchma and the hard-line Secretary Łukasiewicz. The meeting elects an executive committee from writers guided by the party; the opposition doesn't get to vote. "Victory for Tejchma," the ticks say with relief in their voice. In a literary weekly there appears—surely, by chance—a cartoon against anti-Semitism and thus of an antistate nature. The editorial ticks express their profound sorrow: "Something terrible has happened, we have given a pretext to the hardheads; now they will grab our journal, now we shall have to take great

---

*Tejchma was dismissed from the Politburo at the Eighth Party Congress in February 1980.

care that these idiots (the bosses) don't let something through again.'' You want liberalization, you don't want the hotheads to carry the vote, then be on your guard, take action against irresponsible behavior, censor your own work and other people's (for it could happen, by chance, that something could get past the censors, and then the hardheads will notice it). You want liberalization, then fight against freedom. Why? Because otherwise the hard-liners will come and grab you by the throat.

D. SOMEONE WORSE WILL COME. Let us for a moment take a closer look at the soul of a tick in a middle or high position in the social hierarchy—for example, the head of a section of a socioliterary weekly, or the director of a scientific institute. Isn't he full up to the nostrils with these ultraloyal leading articles, this scolding from undereducated apparatchiks from the Central Committee? He's fed up to the back teeth and even higher; ten times over he's been ripe to chuck the job and do anything else. But if he's a true tick, then he'll never actually do it. Why? Because if he leaves, someone worse will come in his place. And that our tick can't allow. Someone will come and will call the workers of Radom not just hooligans, as before, but bandits; someone will come and will attack idealistic scholars not for idealism but for subjectivism; someone will come and throw out the book, standing ready in type, which the censor did not pass, crudely and with insults, instead of sending it back after half a year of delay and smiling conversations. Everyone must—in the opinion of the tick—stick to his job, bear the heavy burden of responsibility, even humiliation, for the sake of higher reasons. Such as? The good of Polish culture, obviously. The good of Polish culture is the supreme value. One must be able to sacrifice one's personal interests for it. The ticks make this sacrifice. They serve, they offer incense to the censor, they kick out, even make denunciations—all for the good of Polish culture.

E. THE WORLD THROUGH THE EYES OF A TICK. How does the contemporary world appear through the eyes of a tick? It is obviously a world divided into two blocs, American and Soviet. Poland is dependent on the Soviet Union, which is obviously a totalitarian state. Indeed, today there are not more than two or three completely independent states in the world. The struggle for the complete independence of Poland is an unreal one. The West is obviously better than the Soviet Union, but it, too, has various deeds on its conscience. Radio Free Europe sometimes gives interesting news but it is generally biased. The BBC is better. Nationalism, national fervor is a bad thing; the best stance is that shown by mildly leftish intellectual centers in the West: humanism, progress, common human values. Liberalization is a good thing. The struggle for the complete independence of Poland smells of must and obscurantism.

F. THE TICKS' AUTHORITIES. Ticks consider themselves to be morally pure individuals, untainted by any dirty or, God forbid, nasty business. They are humanists and moralists. What plays the fundamental role in tick morality and culture? Obviously, the examples of actual people. For a tick to feel good and to be himself, he needs a compass in the person of some individual of renown and moral purity, acknowledged for his higher culture. This is usually a professor, cosseted and promoted by the Polish People's Republic, but for some period subjected to mild repression, prosecuted, or in any case put out of his job, but afterward gloriously restored to favor. Such a professor, armed with the reputation of indomitable courage, afterward delivers innumerable fine speeches, sits on innumerable presidiums, is spoken of as a great scholar, and is quoted in the press by every second journalist. And a great tick or a quasi-tick like this is chosen by the ordinary tick as his compass. Above the tumult of opposition blusterers, he rises like a great statue, imparting spirit, support, and warmth. G. THE TICK WANTS TO BE LOVED. Being related spiritually and socially to the liberal opposition, but a comrade in the flesh to the party masters of the Polish People's Republic, the tick tries to be on good terms with everyone and wants to be loved by everyone. In an opposition milieu, he strives to pass as truly committed to opposition activity, morally pure, indomitably brave, nonconformist. In institutions of the Polish People's Republic, he wants to appear truly apolitical, dutiful, devoted to his work, loyal. From the members of the opposition he looks for acceptance; from the Polish People's Republic, prizes, promotions, awards, and orders. When one side ceases to accept the tick, he raises hell. He mobilizes his acquaintances, who have influence with the opposition; he runs around town offering profuse explanations. His advocates quickly come forward, showing that a righteous man has been wronged, that he is in a very specific situation, that he cannot be put on the same plane as patent conformists, that he has suffered so much. . . . A tick caught *in flagrante* snatches at the most fantastic means of defense. These depend principally on the attribution of hidden antistate intentions to visibly progovernment deeds and actions. For example, a journalist who specializes in praising the world revolution, caught between two fires and driven to the wall, will try to show that, under the guise of criticism of presidents and kings, he is really criticizing the leaders of totalitarian states such as the Soviet Union and the Polish People's Republic.

WHO HAS THE RIGHT TO WRITE ABOUT TICKS?

In concluding this sketch, let us ask ourselves the question: who should write about ticks, who has the right to do so? The answer seems simple—the nonticks should write about ticks. But this answer is simple only on the surface; who can say of himself with a clear conscience that he is not a tick? Who, indeed? It is the tragedy of the Polish intelligentsia, Polish culture, and simply of Poland, and the reason that this study has been written, that all or almost all of us are, in whole or in part, or have been to a certain degree, ticks.

From *Zapis* (Warsaw), no. 9, June 1979; English translation reprinted, with permission, from *Survey* (London), no. 110, 1980

TICKS AND ANGELS
Adam Michnik

Wierzbicki says: "We shall leave to the historians the task of discovering the forefathers of ticks in past ages." Since I feel that I have connections with the profession of historian, I shall allow myself to make a few remarks by way of a supplement.

The genealogy of the "tick" phenomenon must be sought in political situations where foreign domination of the Polish people assumed a chronic character and any hope of armed defense for our national values was totally illusory, when compromise with the conquerer had become inevitable to preserve the very existence of the nation. The problem of the permissible limits of compromise was then a daily challenge to the minds and consciences of people who, in a conquered country, wanted to live and act. Total acceptance of the formula of compromise was the road to becoming morally compromised and to spiritual capitulation; total rejection of the formula of compromise was the road to a more or less heroic isolation. During the years of the partition of Poland, attitudes of compromise and situations of difficult choice were our daily bread.

There were violent disagreements and fundamental differences between the supporters and opponents of accommodation, between the legalists and the conspirators, between those who advocated special betterment and the insurrectionists. The supporters of radical action in the heat of their polemics always glossed over the differences between betrayal of the nation, accommodation, and work for social improvement, but tended to reduce all these different patterns of behavior to a common denominator: a desire for personal gain. Only when time had rubbed off the corners and leveled out the contours did it become possible to evaluate the effectiveness of different forms of resistance to the fate of foreign domination and to see the complementary nature of these opposites.

To put it clearly: there were different ways of fighting for the Polish cause and these were effective in different ways. It was not only those who took part in armed uprisings who fought for the existence of the nation. Sometimes accommodation was effective, sometimes legal opposition, and sometimes society was simply forced to strive for social betterment. If there was some sense (and I myself think there was, though even today it is open to doubt) in resorting to insurrectionary tactics in the time of Kościuszko, the [Napoleonic] Legions or the [1830] "November Night," it quite clearly made political nonsense to plot insurrections in the puppet-kingdom of Poland under the governorship of [the Russian General] Paskevich.

I want to recall that time, now far in the past, because it makes it easier, I think, to master our emotions and to think things over calmly.

We may note, therefore, that an active member of the opposition views reality in one way and an intellectual writing a commentary in another, while a moralist, trying to dispense justice to the "visible world" will view things in yet a third way. Each of these views has its own lights and shades. The perspective of the member of the opposition is inevitably forced to be one-sided. This helps him to reshape the world, but makes it difficult for him to perceive the many dimensions involved. Moralism lets one perceive the snares that lie in wait for everyone who assumes an active responsibility, but fosters the aesthetic cult of "clean hands." The stance of the spectator makes it easier to understand the complexity of the human condition but makes it no easier to answer the question "What is to be done?" or the question "What is good and what is evil?"

One looks upon the world one way if one wants to change it, another if one wants to understand it, and yet another if one wants to pass moral judgment upon it. I am convinced that I will not change this state of affairs by my article. Anyway, that is not my ambition. I simply want to try to convince my opponent that if he totally commits himself to thinking in moralistic or current-opposition terms (which comes to the same thing), then he will lose a certain essential part of reality from his field of vision.

It is important to remember these shamefully banal observations when taking up the question of the attitude of the Polish intelligentsia under the governments of the former regime. The picture drawn by Wierzbicki is clear and unambiguous. At that time, Poland was under the rule of Stalinist-Bierutist functionaries, and Party Young Communist troops carried out the execution of Polish learning. And that's all. Somewhere the whole dramatic quality of social and political reality has been lost; lost, too, somewhere is the whole impassioned picture of the mingling of disaster and hope, understanding and naivety, fear and gallant courage, the dynamism of society and the behind-the-scenes actions of the Soviet advisers. It is as if in answer to the Stalinist primer on which we were reared at the time we had been given a primer *à rebours*, where the colors were equally compressed and glaring and the picture of the world equally infantile.

The reality of the early postwar years was—in my opinion—incomparably more complicated than would appear from the ultrasimplistic formula of the "reds" and their intellectual lackeys, the "ticks."

This period is among the most painful in our history and among the most hypocritical. It may even be that it is because it is so painful that it is hypocritical. Putting aside the general discussion, which cannot but be painful, to another occasion, I shall make only a few fragmentary remarks.

At that time, the country was drained of blood and the fortune of war determined by the Yalta Conference. The form of postwar reality had been determined not by the blood that had been shed and the heroism of the anti-Nazi resistance but by the international balance of power. The Western allies abandoned Poland. What way forward was left to our society?

I have dwelt on this problem many a time. So many times have I striven to find, in the not too far distant history, the point at which an error or false choice in Polish policy sealed the unhappy fate of the Polish nation. And I could not find one. Following through the history of the Polish cause during and after the war, I have the feeling that Clio, the Muse of history, has turned her back on the Poles so as not to give them even the shadow of a chance to break the bonds of misfortune and to find a way out of national oppression. Every direction of Polish policy was a losing one.

Time went by, the Stalinist noose was drawn even tighter around the neck of a nation oppressed and drained of blood. Everyone was faced with the question: where is the limit of permissible compromise? What price can be paid for the chance of lecturing, publishing, pursuing one's profession? For in a totalitarian system it is always necessary to pay an admission fee, and this has become ever more exorbitant. The conditions laid down are always accompanied by more or less veiled threats and blackmail.

I do not remember such times; I know them only from various reports and documents. Today, years later, it is difficult to evaluate the actual choices that were made at that time. It is even more difficult to find a measure, out of the context of that time. He who knows of such a measure is simply to be envied. If Nadezhda Mandelstam is right when she asserts that silence in the face of totalitarian domination is a "true crime against the human race," then almost everyone is guilty of that crime. Even the noblest have been forced into passivity and silence. Only those in the prisons and labor camps are free from this. "Blessed prisons," wrote Solzhenitsyn, "only there can a man achieve freedom from participation in this accursed machine of lies."

Aleksander Wat wrote somewhere that there is only one answer to the question of how intellectuals should behave in the lands where Stalin ruled. It is the Shakespearean answer: "They must die."*

Perhaps this is the true answer. But still, I consider, this answer can be made only for oneself, this measure meted out only to onself, this sacrifice demanded only from oneself. Anyone who demands this answer from another is arbitrarily arrogating to himself the right of determining the life of another. And this, in general, leads to nothing good.

In spite of what we read in the "Treatise on Ticks" no rectors or editors who were outwardly obedient but "pro-Western" and "counterrevolutionary" in the depths of their soul had an easy life, by any means, in Stalin's time. Fingers were constantly pointed at them. They were constantly suspected of the "taint of bourgeois consciousness." Overzealous agitators saw in them camouflaged defenders of the past. To such juvenile agitators the world appeared grossly simple. The capitalist system—the cradle of fascism—was enemy number one of human happiness. Anyone who decided to make even the least compromise with the dying culture of the capitalist West was, for them, the principal adversary.

*Aleksander Wat (1900–1967), Polish writer and essayist, lived in the USSR during World War II and emigratred to France shortly after the war.

The simplicity of this view of the world, the ease of passing judgments, the highly intolerant political fanaticism of these years dictated to a young writer, even if he already had recognized productions to his credit, lampoon-formulae such as "for bourgeois writers the fight against German fascism became an escape from political decision, or even worse, became a cover-up for imperialist ideology! . . . It is necessary to reassess actions which in the years of nationalist deviation were termed 'antifascist' and 'righteous,' thinking that this would suffice forever."

I do not want—that would be demagogy—to assert that Wierzbicki is repeating against the same people the same objections that were once formulated by the most fanatical adherents of the Stalinist line. I am able to distinguish between the text that is an ardent protest against conformism and the distortion of reality.

I really do understand Wierzbicki's anger and his opposition to the process which Miłosz, some years ago, called "moral decay" and "Pétainism." I understand, too, however, the bitterness of people who, through all this, often clenching their teeth and enduring humiliations, created a morsel of our own mental reality, preserved and restored old values, and built up new ones, and now, today, are called "ticks."

It is senseless to demand careful and balanced appraisals from a lampoonist. The very technique of the lampoonist's art makes an opinion more radical. I do not make the claim that Wierzbicki, by employing the definition "tick," is sharpening the outlines of reality, but that his antitick passion makes it impossible for him to understand them. For—although this does not emerge from Wierzbicki's text—the reality of our country differs considerably from the reality of those countries that are our neighbors. We are less receptive to the process of Sovietization. Why?

There are various factors that make us different: historical tradition; the Catholic Church and the brave though so very realistic line taken by the episcopate; the countryside that has defended itself in the face of collectivization; finally, unremitting social pressure. This has manifested itself sometimes in violent explosions (Poznań, 1956; March 1968, December 1970; Radom, 1976), but generally in quiet, daily, dogged resistance. A resistance that is, as it were, incompatible with denunciation. The mental atmosphere of a part of the intellectual environment, lectures and seminars in institutions of higher learning, the carrying out of doctoral research and the publication of learned communications, novels, slim volumes of poetry, essays, meetings of the Union of Writers or the P.E.N. Club, films and theatrical presentations, museums, concerts, and art exhibits. And this comes largely from the work of people who sign no protests and perform no spectacular deeds of opposition. Yet it is equally due to them that we now breathe a different air in Poland. A spiritual air. And this daily creation of an invisible but fundamental strand in the culture and consciousness of the nation is not simply the result of reading *Zapis* or the *Biuletyn Informacyjny** or the publications of the Independent Publishing House, NOWA. It is a result of the totality of Polish achievements.

*Zapis, a literary periodical, and Biuletyn Informacyjny, a news bulletin, were both founded by KOR (Workers' Defense Committee).

This totality is becoming an object of envy to visitors who are citizens of other nations of the "camp." They do not envy us just for KOR, SSK,* and uncensored publications, but also for journals that are published officially. And not only for *Tygodnik Powszechny* or *Więź,* but also for *Twórczość, Pamiętnik Literacki,* and even for *Polityka.*† They envy us our full churches and our fully operational catechetical centers, the theatrical productions of Diemek and the films of Wajda,‡ the appearance of our streets and our attractively dressed girls. Thanks, then, to all this we are preserving our identity and a capacity to keep up a resistance to the Sovietization process.

I should be the last to claim that our situation is satisfactory and that our aspirations have been pacified. Sometimes, however, one must look at our situation, at our ills and misfortunes, not only from the viewpoint of aspirations and misfortunes, but also from the viewpoint of threats. Among those threats I include the picture of the fate of a nation that we see in our Eastern neighbors, the Lithuanians, Byelorussians, and Ukrainians. They have to fight for their existence at the elementary level: it is a struggle for language, religion, the treasury of national culture. Let us evaluate these differences. Let us evaluate how different is the fate of nations under a Communist system. It is also worth considering circumstances that are taken for granted concerning the most essential differences between the Russian and Polish defenders of human rights. In short: although the political police make life difficult for us, we feel that we are strong, since we have the support—moral and material—of broad sections of our society. We have the support of people who are not by temperament either politicians or heroes, who do not want to have to give up their comparatively stable family life, who certainly rarely decide to sign a protest letter, and who—I must say— actually take for granted the success of the campaign in defense of the workers of Radom and Ursus. Without the support of such people, independent publishing work would be hard to imagine.

I have a different outlook from Wierzbicki's concerning the "people between the government and opposition." When a learned professor of sociology reacts to the protests of intellectuals against torture in Radom by writing a refined theoretical study in which the protest of these individuals is depreciated, then my anger resembles that of the author of the "Treatise on Ticks." But when a professor, instead of making a comparative psychoanalysis of the protesting individuals, decides to use his parliamentary immunity and go to Radom for one of the trials, to see for himself how the functionaries were meting out justice, and if then, without in the least involving himself in the cases that were being fought, he makes a report to the government about what he has seen there—why does Wierzbicki call his action "tickish"? I do not consider it so. I would rather

---

*SSK: Student Solidarity Committees, organized in the late 1970s by KOR.

†*Tygodnik Powszechny* and *Więź* are lay Catholic publications; *Twórczość* and *Pamiętnik Literacki* are literary journals; *Polityka* is a socioeconomic and political weekly edited by Mieczysław Rakowski.

‡Kazimierz Diemek is a well-known Polish theater director; Andrzej Wajda is the director of a number of famous films, among them *Ashes and Diamonds, The Man of Marble,* and *The Man of Iron.*

rejoice that in the bosom of the governing elite rational attitudes are beginning to define correctly their own proper interest, that I can recognize in the circle of my opponents at least a shadow of political culture. So far there have not been many such symptoms. I think, however, that if we abandon hope of such an evolution, then the alternative scenario must include a sequence of violent confrontations between the authorities and society. Any one of these confrontations can give rise to a national tragedy. It is our common duty to avoid such situations, since it could turn out that the whole nation and every Pole, not excluding the government, would pay an inordinately high price for their lack of responsibility in this matter.

This conclusion does not mean simply that anyone should be persuaded to take part in intraparty intrigues. On this point I share Wierzbicki's skepticism. It is important, however, to remember that we live in a society where hundreds of thousands of active people belong to the Communist party. Membership is the price that has to be paid for taking part in public life, for the chance of a job at management level, and so forth. Maybe Wierzbicki considers (and I myself am of that opinion) that the price is too high, that it is a price not worth paying and is unseemly. Nevertheless, we live and we shall continue to live among people who think otherwise. We must learn how to coexist with them and to teach them to coexist with us. We must learn the difficult art of compromise without which true pluralism is impossible. Furthermore, we must observe in the face of the authorities the standards of political culture, even when the authorities do not preserve these standards. Only then shall we manage to set dignity against totalitarian brutishness.

I am not an aesthete, and I do not suppose that everybody, one and all, could live in a state of uninterrupted friendship. I do, however, believe in the creative power of our actions. I believe that it is possible to increase or decrease the amount of hatred and intolerance in our public life. I believe, finally, that the shape of an independent and democratic Poland is even now being hammered out. I should wish to see it based on tolerance and political culture, but I know that it will require long years of work to make these values universal. Hence it is necessary to make them universal even today, and not in verbal declarations but in daily action.

That is why I am so afraid of a certain type of reaction to Wierzbicki's essay. For the "Treatise on Ticks" is an extremely evocative text in its passion for unmasking the essential diseases of Polish intellectual and civil life. It is a continuation of the great tradition of Polish lampoons on society. Wierzbicki does not flatter the reader; he accuses and overturns. Such a stance in an author earns respect.

Nevertheless, the "Treatise" will not be a bucket of cold water on the intelligentsia but on a nice, simple reader, confined to cheering the hearts of the dissidents, unless it is supplemented by a "Treatise on Angels." For among us, angels are doomed to criticism, which they are bound to scorn, especially if it comes from the pen of Gontarz or Kłodzinska.* But an angel who is not criticized, an angel confirmed in his angelicness can turn into a devil. You don't

*Loyal party journalists.

believe it? Read that book about the most noble and valiant people in Russia, a book I have hated for years, yet to which I return again and again, like an addict to cocaine, a book that is a curved mirror in which every angel sees his disgustingly distorted face, a book that is antipathetic and penetrating to the point of cruelty. Read *The Devils* by Dostoevsky.

I know that whenever a tick wants to justify his "tickery," he takes down from the shelf this very book, nicely bound in morocco, and reads out to his interlocutor choicer and choicer extracts. I know, too, however, that if the experience of the "devils" is not thought over and internalized by the Polish democratic opposition, then that opposition will be menaced not so much by secret policemen with scarred faces and dead eyes, but by Stavrogins and Verkhvenskys *à la polonaise*.

For a moment that does not perceive what is an unacceptable value in society is not sufficiently mature to reform it.

From *Zapis* (Warsaw), no. 9, June 1979; English translation reprinted, with permission, from *Survey* (London), no. 110, 1980

THE SPIRIT THAT REVIVES
Fr. Bronisław Sroka, S.J.

Our moral standards, our social position, our human values are not, for the most part, determined by biological or psychological conditioning but, rather, by the ideologies with which we come into contact and then assimilate. Our attitude toward religion, our world outlook and our national traditions passed on to us throughout history—all this collective heritage influences our individual decisions and actions, as well as our whole life. This is true not only of individuals but also of social groups and whole nations.

If Polish pilots who fought during World War II in the Battle of Britain were regarded as the best fighter pilots of all, it was not because of their genes, or strength of character, or even training, but above all because of the values of the Polish national tradition. It is true, of course, that the Air Force School in Deblin [in prewar Poland] was one of the first training centers in the world to use psychological tests in accepting their students. It is also true that the level of training of pilots was exceptionally high at that time. Nevertheless, the combat value of our pilots was determined principally by their ideological attitude, one that inspired them with the desire to defend higher values, one that imbued their efforts with sense and with meaning.

Let us take a different example. On the streets of our towns we see, unfortunately, many people who do not understand the meaning of life, people who are lacking in acceptable moral standards and who are incapable of behaving honestly either at home or at work. Their favorite means of recreation are drinking and other similarly unsavory activities. The fault may perhaps lie with the difficult living conditions, or perhaps with the social structures typical of our part of the world. Perhaps! However, the main culprit is the absence of an appropriate ideology that would impel these people to improve themselves. This example, too, proves how dependent we are on ideologies and attitudes—on the spirit that revives.

One other example. The Poles sent to Siberia in the nineteenth century, sentenced to exile and hard labor for participating in national uprisings, were regarded by their foreign fellow-inmates as just, friendly, courageous, honest, and possessed of a high degree of self-respect. Even the Russians noticed it—for example, Herzen, Dostoevsky, Lavrov, L. Tolstoy, and many others, including the Cossack [*sic*] Shevchenko—all praised the Poles for their humanitarianism and for their boundless love of liberty. Herzen admits that Poles "awoke in him the greatest respect and sympathy. Compared with their punishment, which they bore with remarkable stoicism, his own misfortunes appeared very slight indeed. He was friends with many, some of them the source of profound feelings and subjects of an almost religious adoration" (A. Rogalski, *Rosja a Europa* [Russia and Europe] [Warsaw, 1960], p. 41). Russians were convinced that while a Pole could be killed, he could not be broken or brought to his knees. A Pole exiled to hard labor never complained, begged for mercy, or degraded himself—and because of this he was held in esteem by his enemies. This esteem occasionally gave way to a chronic inferiority complex and hatred of all things Polish—as happened, for instance, with Dostoevsky.

The reason for these extraordinary attributes exhibited by Poles is not to be sought in their national character but, rather, in their religion. The Christian concept of man emphasizes liberty, dignity of man, the beauty and value of life lived according to certain ethical principles. It was their religion that taught the Poles to see God in every human creature. In other words, the source of their greatness was their ideology.

Now, ideology can be a source of energy or weakness, a spirit that revives or kills, one that can lift a human being to unknown heights or cast him to innermost depths. Whatever the ideology man embraces, it is bound to affect him. It is the decisive factor in shaping our attitude toward life, the world, ourselves, and others. It constitutes the foundation of our moral and social perceptions. The most influential ideology is the one that will fashion the life of individuals as well as of nations. It is therefore of paramount importance to choose the correct ideology.

Today our country is teeming with various ideological currents. Some are thrust upon us by force, with the help of the media and other forms of social pressure. Some are offered slyly in the guise of forbidden—yet fashionable—fruits. But we Poles need not roam those ideological black markets. As a nation, we are fortunate in having our own ideology, one that is part of our national culture, tradition, and conscience. It was present at the cradle of our history and has sustained us for a thousand years. Its preeminence has been tested and confirmed through the ages. Its existence eliminates the need for choosing among other competing doctrines and settling for the most fashionable one. There is only one ideology for us—our Christian faith!

Catholicism gave us our culture, with its tolerance and love of liberty. It was because of it that during the years of freedom and independence our nation was able to live peacefully and work honestly, and it was that which kept up our spirits during the years of hardship and prevented us from producing any Quislings.

Our society intuitively understands the values in Christian thought. At a time when we are being suffocated by alien ideologies, our nation, in a logical exercise of self-defense, unites with the Church. About 80 percent of our students admit to being Christian. Marvelous! Yet at the same time the question must be posed: how is it that only about 15 percent of them take part in school chapel activities? These centers, after all, are the only means today (with the exception of the family) through which we can spread Christian thought. If we really feel responsible for the future of our nation, we must examine this question in all candor.

Young people today are undoubtedly full of noble impulses. They courageously defend human rights. They have often proved their genuine patriotism. Yet it behooves us to remember the value of consistently fulfilling our duties—and that includes religious duties. This is why participating in student chaplaincies is of such importance. It is there that young people will find the spirit that revives, the spirit that directs the strength, health, and identity of the nation. And it is up to us to make sure that this spirit is passed on to future generations. If we let it slip from our grasp, if as a result of our passivity an alien ideology becomes dominant, our society will rapidly turn into a gray, quarreling crowd of egoists, cowards, informers, and toadies. "Catholicism," according to Roman Dmowski, "is not an addition to Polishness, coloring it to some degree, but is an integral part of it. It is to a large extent Polishnesstself. To separate Catholicism from Polishness, and religion and the Churchrom the state, is to destroy the very heart of the nation!"*

God Almighty, do not let our generation tear our nation away from the Church! Let Poles remain Poles! Amen.

From *Bratniak,* no. 1, 1977

Translated by Joanna Gladysz

*Roman Dmowski (1864–1939) was the founder and principal ideologist of the National Democratic Party, which espoused an ultranationalist, an anti-Semitic, and—on geopolitical grounds—a pro-Russian orientation.

A REPLY TO FATHER SROKA

Wojciech Ostrowski
and Jan Tomasz Lipski

Father Sroka's article deals with subjects of such fundamental importance to our social awareness that we believe our reply, though somewhat late, is still relevant.

It is true that a whole range of current ideological opinions have conditioned our view of society and our role in it, as well as our attitudes to our own and other social groups. These opinions, in conjunction with any professed or well-tried norms of civil behavior, also determine how receptive we are to the nameless evils around us. They enable us to define these evils and to find reasons for reversing, overcoming, or preventing them. Today we are in particular need of carefully formulated ideological guidelines that would help us analyze the present state of our society, its essential nature and processes, the reasons for its shortcomings, and, finally, the means to be employed in altering popular consciousness and establishing a program for the future.

This need is obvious. For the past decade or so, Polish thinking has been dominated by a violent distaste for any matters that do not directly concern the "self," one's possessions or professional status. It has also been dominated by masochistic submission to manipulation at the hands of the official mass media, which blunt society's sensitivity and, consequently, sow mistrust of any independent organized activity. An ideological vacuum and a lack of optimism have pervaded Polish thinking, and standards of civil behavior have eroded with the disappearance of any sense of joint responsibility and of a communal feeling that might provide support and strength to individuals involved in common social activities. Spiritually, in other words, the Pole of today has lost that precious quality that is greater than any selfish attitudes toward career and advancement. The disappearance of fellowship within the community has intensified withdrawal into personal privacy, and the lack of any ideological vision of the present and the future has brought about a mood of pessimism. Thus there is now a need for views that would do away with all timid passivity, a need for such a variety of new ideas as would widen the scope for social activity. These views must be clearly and forcefully spelled out. The time has come to infuse the awareness of fellow Poles with vital new ideological substance; we cannot afford to waste this valuable time, nor—considering the needs of Polish society—should we try to stem the flow of new ideological views in the arduous pursuit of ideological pluralism.

Is Christianity providing the stimulus for positive social behavior? In our opinion, Christianity cannot determine ideological choices, for it is not an ideology in the normal sense of the term. It can only create a basis for putting such choices into practice. That basis—a readiness to work with others for one's fellow man—is embodied in the word "Catholicism," which can be translated from the Greek as "universality," "togetherness," or "brotherhood." And the value of Christianity lies precisely in that spirit of fellowship and communion with all people: man professes his faith in God through his relationships with everyone around him.

The universal quality of the Church lies above all in the way in which it embraces all peoples, regardless of race, sex, or ideology, the color of their skin, or the type of passport they hold. There is no way in which the universality of Christianity can be reconciled with narrow parochialism, xenophobia, and emotional chauvinism. Catholicism should in principle reject any tendencies toward treating external expressions of faith as a collection of symbols dividing people into "one's own" and "aliens." It is the outmoded "ethnocentric" Catholicism, holding "Polishness" in the tight embrace of traditionalist religious societies, nationalistic military emblems, and commercialized folklore, that has surprised and upset us in Father Sroka's article. We hope the Father will try to understand our views as we are trying to understand his. We are all concerned with bringing out the best qualities of Christianity, but the problem is that of its social dimension—whether it should be open to all and not reject either those who are still searching or those who are clearly "outside" the faith yet are surely not "aliens."

Father Sroka's attitude is potentially as dangerous to Christianity as it is to "Polishness." If we were to accept the concept of nation put forward by Father Sroka, and if we were to assume that anything non-Catholic, or which comes from without, is to be rejected, we would in fact deprive ourselves of a large part of our culture. To be consistent, we would have to disown works inspired by attitudes often far removed from Catholicism. We would have to forget about the novels of such "unbelievers" as Prus, Orzeszkowa, and Żeromski, the social ideas of Kelles-Krauz, Abramowski, Krzywicki, and many, many others.* This would be tantamount to destroying the "very essence of the nation," just as it would mean the negation of Catholic traditions.

The Church's influence on the historical shape of our nationhood and on the cohesion of our national ties is indisputable. And it is unfortunate that the Church's contribution—a thousand years of propagating the standards of Christian ethics and the participation of the Church in the creation of many of our

*Bolesław Prus, Eliza Orzeszkowa, and Stefan Żeromski were late-nineteenth-century and early-twentieth-century novelists with pronounced liberal and anticlerical leanings. Kazimierz Kelles-Krauz (1872–1905), Edward Abramowski (1868–1918), and Ludwik Krzywicki (1859–1941) represented different trends of the Polish Marxist movement.

social institutions—is passed over in silence. Such censorship, such manipulation threaten the historical continuity of Polish consciousness. Yet must national consciousness be maintained by upholding and replicating its most extreme manifestations? Poland is no different from any other nation, though perhaps—because of its past—a bit more experienced. But let us exhibit some restraint in assessing our own history. It has no doubt had some luminous moments, yet its dark sides can hardly be denied. We consider it, therefore, in bad taste to extol our nation above all others, and to claim that it is—more than any other nation—imbued with "the spirit that revives," just as it would be in bad taste for any of us individually to cite our achievements as proof of our superiority over others. It is enough for Poles to know that they are capable of being better than they are now. Improvement depends on whether or not the Polish nation can display an open attitude—free of xenophobia—toward the problems of the modern world and toward all modern cultural currents, no matter where they come from.

Polish culture is part of European culture. The most important trends in our literature, social thought, and philosophy would be incomprehensible out of this context. Polish culture cannot grow and develop apart from the culture of the West, a rich culture teeming with often contradictory ideas. Nor could Polish Christianity develop in such isolation. One needs only to glance through any issue of *Znak*, *Więź* or *W drodze* to see how they are all influenced by French, German, or English thinkers.* It is also worth remembering how much Christians have learned through contact and discussion with atheists, or with non-Christians whose thinking was moving closer to that of the Christian philosophy. We cannot ignore Stanisław Brzozowski,† for example, or, for that matter, the still very much active Leszek Kołakowski. And yet Father Sroka would have us dismiss them as uninteresting, as alien products of an "ideological black market."

Father Sroka's views also have political implications. Roman Dmowski spells them out in his work *Kościół, naród i państwo* (Church, nation and state), to which the Father refers. According to Dmowski, the Poles are a Catholic nation. This does not mean that all Poles are Catholic, of course, and Dmowski is well aware of this. He therefore defines a Catholic nation as one that embraces all sections of society with "a deep sense of duty and service to the state. The modern nation believes that the state belongs to it, and that it is responsible for the state; and it tends increasingly to run the state in its interests."

The criterion for that "deep sense of duty and service to the nation" has to be established arbitrarily. For Dmowski, this means embracing a national ideology—that is, the ideology of his own movement. Since Poland, according to Dmowski, is a Catholic nation, the laws of its state must be governed by the Catholic faith. This is how the division into "better" and "worse" citizens comes into being—"better" being those who can guide the destiny of the state, "worse" being those who do not deserve this role. Such a division is the conse-

---

Znak, *Więź*, and *W drodze* are all lay Catholic journals.

†Stanisław Brzozowski (1878–1911) was a Marxist philosopher and novelist who drew close to Catholicism toward the end of his life.

quence of frivolous notions about the "national essence," according a privileged position in society to a particular ideology. Is this not reminiscent of the practices of the present ruling party in Poland? The leaders of the Polish United Workers' Party also bestow civil rights only on those who agree with them.

Is this formulation, then, compatible with civil and human rights? Is making use of the state (and therefore of the state's coercive power) for religious ends compatible with the spirit of Christianity?

We apologize if Father Sroka meant something different. But we believe that one must cite a sentence from Dmowski's book only within the context in which it appears.

To sum up: we are in favor of free and untrammeled contacts and discussions between Christianity and all other philosophies of life; of the concept of a nation that envisions the full use of the nation's entire cultural heritage, and that is open to all cultural influences from without; of the separation of Church and state; and of a secular state that guarantees equal rights for all citizens and places no restrictions whatever on the free development of all contending ideologies.

From *Bratniak*, no. 3, 1977

Translated by Rosemary Hunt

The Enemy Within

"The Campaign," by Anna Chmielewska, and "1968 and All That," by Marek Turbacz, both focus on two of the most noxious aspects of Communist propaganda: the search for scapegoats, and the composite image of "the enemy." The first examines what during the Stalin era was known as the amalgam—that is, the tendency to ascribe numerous features, however fanciful or discordant, to any individual or group of individuals that the party considers its mortal adversary. Thus in the Soviet Union during the 1930s, Stalin's erstwhile, potential, or actual critics, whatever the differences among them, were all lumped together into a single sinister conspiracy: Trotskyites and "right-wing" Communists, social democrats and poets unhappy with the dictates of "socialist realism," liberals and loyal party members who had the misfortune of incurring Stalin's displeasure were all presented as one vast organization plotting, with the help of American, Japanese, or British imperialism, to overthrow the "socialist order."

In the late 1940s, yet another enemy was added to the list—to wit, "international Zionism," or to put it plainly, the Jews. The use of this odious political weapon has become a perennial feature of Communist politics in Eastern Europe, perhaps nowhere more consistently than in Poland, where anti-Semitic prejudices have deep historical roots. In his memoir, Marek Turbacz recalls his experiences with and reactions to the antiintellectual and anti-Semitic campaign unleashed by the factional struggle that raged in Poland in 1968—a campaign that eventually resulted in the exodus of almost all of the remaining Jewish community in Poland.

Anna Chmielewska is a young Polish sociologist, and Marek Turbacz is the pseudonym of a young Polish historian and political writer.

THE CAMPAIGN

Anna Chmielewska

The usual answer to the question of what is the essence of the control of the published word is, "Censorship." However, from official statements we learn that this control consists in "exerting a definite influence on public opinion" and in forming the "state of social consciousness, the verification of long-standing ideas and values originating in previous social structures whose usefulness needs to be examined."* This statement speaks directly of a measure that is perhaps more menacing than censorship—namely, the intentional and purposeful shaping of human minds. Censorship impoverishes us, while propaganda deforms us, though obviously the former is indispensable to the latter's effectiveness.

The influence of propaganda is most palpably evident in the mass media (for simplicity's sake I shall limit myself here to the daily press). As a rule we are almost oblivious to its activity, we have grown accustomed to it, and it is part of our daily existence. Its essential character emerges—brazenly and abruptly—whenever the press launches a campaign.

A press campaign is a phenomenon of uncommon interest. As a rule it accompanies the climax of social or political tensions and becomes their only generally accessible mirror—though to call it a distorting mirror would be putting it mildly. Various causes bring a campaign into being—for example, difficulties and unexpected events whose challenge must be met, or power struggles within the party. A campaign is essentially the authorities' verbal response to a given situation, a response that both hides and reveals its true nature. Thus in 1968 the response was reactionary and policelike; in 1970 and 1976, it was antiworker; and in 1975–76, it was directed at the society's aspirations for greater national sovereignty. This year, the campaigns reveal the authorities' weakness when confronted by economic catastrophes, by workers, and by the opposition. Finally, a campaign elicits a certain spontaneity, providing party journalists with an opportunity to climb the ladder of success, to show their true colors, to demonstrate loyalty. A campaign is a great open competition for bootlicking,

*"Dziennikarze o prasie" (Newsmen about the press), *Miesięcznik Literacki*, 1975, no. 2.

shrewdness, and ruthlessness. At times it can turn into a competition mandatory for everyone.

But this approach is open only to those who have mastered the art of reading between the lines, of deciphering texts, of perceiving the meaning behind a particularly intense passage; in this process the actual content of an article becomes of secondary importance. In fact, the function played by the content of the article is often completely lost sight of.

The more common approach, of course, is to take the articles literally, and it is precisely this approach—the approach of the "consumer"—that I propose to follow. For whatever the writer's aims might be—to participate in a political struggle, to display loyalty to a new policy, to discharge a commission by proving that white is black—his text is always produced with some consumer in mind. What does it matter if he deals in half-truths and outright lies, that the facts are connected in ways that affront common sense, that the motivations and views are ascribed to people who cannot conceivably hold them, or that terms are used that are altogether at variance with their dictionary or even colloquial meaning? The writer is not out to elucidate, explain, or convince, but to rouse emotions and approval.

How is this done? By examining even the tiniest bit of text, we can distinguish three levels:

1. the factual (e.g., there is an organization called KOR, and the foreign press writes about it);
2. the interpretative-evaluative (the organization has hostile intentions and is directed from abroad, which renders it treasonable);
3. the emotional
    a. by appealing to deep-rooted convictions or prejudices (e.g., this is the work of Jews on behalf of German revanchists);
    b. by creating new fusions of feeling and value (to criticize the party is to slander Poland).

This arrangement indicates the stages through which the consumer of such texts should pass in order to become a model citizen, a member of the collective in whose name an author in a propaganda campaign uses the pronoun "we."

But those who possess the ability to read between the lines, the so-called subtexts, will confine themselves to the factual level—in the example used, to the fact that there is a group called KOR—and will satisfy their curiosity by reading the Western press, listening to foreign radio, and seeking information from those they know to be better informed.

In order to accept the interpretive-evaluative level, one must already have certain definite inclinations. By way of illustration, let me review the press's image of the situation in 1976–77.

According to our newspapers, Radom and Ursus were just side issues, the work of troublemakers, matters worthy only of meager press notes "from the courtroom," matters condemned to be expunged from memory. This is what was essential:

1. Poland is thriving and enjoying considerable success.

2. The West is having serious problems.
3. Certain forces in the West are displeased by our development and are doing what they can to destroy it.
4. Those forces have allies in Poland who want to carry out their aims.
5. Why are they doing this? Because they hate People's Poland.
6. Why do they hate it? Because they are connected with foreign ideologies, with the bourgeois world-view, with the concepts of the National Democratic Party and the *sanacja*,* the Christian Democratic Party, right-wing socialism;

> with fascism;
> with liberalism;
> with revisionism;
> with Zionism;
> with Trotskyism;
> with reactionism;
> with opportunism;
> and with NEP.

7. What are these enemies doing? They are scheming, stirring things up, engaging in slander.
8. Do they have any chance of success? No.
9. Then why are they doing it? In order to win the good graces of the people behind them.
10. And what do they get from this? Satisfaction, because all that is ours is alien to them.

> And so on.

Any reader who will accept this construct must be a person for whom the press is a superior authority to be trusted more than his own eyes and his own memory, a person who does not judge a given piece of information by its contents or by whether it conforms with his own knowledge, but by its source. He accepts statements that are mutually contradictory and incoherent. Social psychology would describe this mentality as dogmatic.

The circle of the convinced, however, does not consist exclusively of people inclined to dogmatism. It also embraces those who all their lives have been condemned to one single source of information, and who are thus characterized by blissful ignorance. Certain features of a press campaign are designed especially for them—(for instance, continuous references to things universally familiar, long known, and self-evident. All these references are supposed to induce a sense of humility in the reader, to remove any doubts and questions—such as, what precisely are those "well-known forces"? Since they are presumably clear to everyone, there's obviously something to it.

Yet to deride the intellectual level of a campaign is an easy way of avoiding the issue. Rather, let us see what are the emotions, convictions, and stereotypes that a campaign conjures up, and what are the values it tries to engender.

Sanacja (purification) was the name bestowed upon the military regime installed by Marshal Józef Piłsudski in 1926.

The official language is saturated with military terminology. On various fronts (ideological, production, harvest) battles, struggles, and campaigns are ceaselessly waged (for peace, to fulfill the plan, to achieve a better beet crop). My use of the term ''press campaign,'' however, is related less to the militarization of the Polish language than to its essential ingredient, its most salient component, its ostensible cause no less than its manifest target—THE ENEMY.

As a rule, of course, the newspaper world is one of unremittingly good cheer and festivity, brimming with heartwarming success stories about miners, farmers, students, or what have you. Suddenly, however, THE ENEMY appears. Who is he? Well, to begin with, he must be an outsider. It is not any given activity that turns somebody into an enemy but, rather, his immanent ''otherness.'' Thus, explanations for his behavior are not to be sought in his environment but in his basic character, which is one of *hostility*. On the other hand, one attribute of the enemy is that he is easy to recognize.

In that respect, the situation in March 1968 was ideal. Not only because the enemy's distinctiveness was plainly seen in his own name or his mother's or grandmother's maiden name, but also because the blatant anti-Semitism of that period was perfectly consonant with the image of the enemy. The essence of anti-Semitism is the unquestioned assumption that the Jew is different, alien, hostile; and that each and every act of his is, by the nature of things, tainted by evil or guile.

This, it must be emphasized, was by that time anti-Semitism in its purest form, one that could be rationalized neither by economic factors—as before the war— nor by political considerations, as was the case shortly after the war. It had become an act of faith permeated by hatred and requiring no justification or exemplification. In March the interchangeable nature of the concepts—''different . . . alien . . . enemy''—was drilled into our heads. The antithesis of those and other such qualities formed the platform on which we were to unite. That meant 100 percent Polishness (in the racial sense, purity of descent) and our inherent nobility (no one had ever been burned at the stake in Poland; ours was Europe's oldest tradition of tolerance).

However, not quite three years later, the enemy proved to be that very social group of which the party was supposed to be the emanation—the working class, the source of the charisma that sanctions the party's supremacy. But here, too, a remedy was quickly found. The enemy's distinguishing feature turned out to be its youth. In the newspaper reports that appeared at that time, the youthfulness of those who threw stones, carried off a corpse, or set a car on fire was invariably stressed. At first, age was synonymous with hooliganism, but by January 1971, when the media adopted a more conciliatory tone, the emphasis shifted to that of harmful irresponsibility, impatience, impetuousness, and disregard for material possessions, all of which were the ostensible attributes of youth, so at variance with judiciousness, the desire for harmony and order, respect for property, prized by sober-minded adults. Once again, the fault lay not in objective conditions, but in the quintessential nature of the youthful culprits.

In the years 1976–77 workers, writers, students, clergy, peasants, scholars— representatives of nearly all levels of society—came into opposition with the policies of the regime. The task of propaganda, therefore, was to indicate the common feature uniting people gray-haired and young, religious and nonreligious, intellectuals and workers, those with foreign-sounding names and those whose names were universally familiar. It was a mind-boggling order—but a solution was soon found.

"There's nothing missing in their 'programs,' " wrote Bohdan Roliński about the opposition, "utopia and Trotskyism, remnants of Social Democracy and bits and pieces of NEP, the latest anti-Communist ammunition, a slice of Zionism, a bit of Christian Democracy."* As for Jerzy Andrzejewski,† his sociopolitical fickleness ("a non-Marxist, a non-Catholic") "is only a small part of his biography." Or take another party journalist: "Their concepts contain a surprising cross-fertilization of the ideas of bourgeois liberalism and nationalism, revisionism and anarchism."‡

"Who's taking part in the hunger strike? There's a Catholic, there are those who are probably setting foot inside a church for the first time, and two relatives of the person serving a sentence for common crimes. An odd conglomeration"—thus Dominik Horodyński.§

And Anna Kłodzińska, writing in *Życie Warszawy:*

> Eleven persons of both sexes and various ages organized the hunger strike in the church chapel. Among them Mr. Cywiński, from Kraków, the editor of one of the Catholic monthlies. What did he seek in that group? Whose advantage was better served during those seven days? That of the advocates of Trotskyist theories alien to Mr. Cywiński or of Mr. Cywiński with his own world-view? Could it be that in the "atmosphere of mutual understanding" those world-views moved closer together? Anything is possible in today's world. . . . That was a strange group of people, a hodgepodge of life stories and world-views. ‖

There you have the solution. Is it possible to find a common denominator for our enemies, a uniform source of their enmity, the features that make them different from us? Yes, it is—by calling attention to precisely that multitude of convictions, those evolving world-views, the different personal and ideological experiences—in other words, *their* pluralism versus *our* moral and political unity.

This scheme is effective only in one respect—it invests pluralism with an emotional aura. As a means of distinguishing the enemy by his background or his

---

*Bohdan Roliński, "Miał to być diament" (It was supposed to be a diamond), *Życie Warszawy,* January 8–9, 1977.

†Jerzy Andrzejewski, born in 1909, is one of Poland's most eminent writers, a one-time Communist who left the party in 1957 and became one of its most outspoken critics.

‡Marek Jaworski, "Przeciw socjalizmowi—przeciw Polsce" (Against socialism—against Poland), *Trybuna Ludu,* February 21, 1977.

§Dominik Horodyński, "Ekshibicjonizm polityczny" (Political exhibitionism), *Trybuna Ludu,* May 27, 1977. (The reference here *et passim* is to a hunger strike that took place in a Warsaw church in May 1977; a dozen people participated in it in protest against the government persecution of workers arrested during the disturbances in Radom in June 1976.)

‖ Anna Kłodzińska, "Mistyfikacja i boczne wyjście" (Mystificaction and a side exit), *Życie Warszawy,* June 1, 1977.

youth, however, it won't wash. In fact, then, there is no solution and the attempt is doomed to tautology. The enemies, it turns out, are "those same people again," "the ones who have for twenty years" opposed People's Poland. They are enemies because they hate Poland and they hate Poland because they are its enemies. Furthermore, since society at large is, after all, loyal, the enemies turn out to be a "small group" that cynically manipulates impulsive youth and naive intellectuals.

As far as those latter categories are concerned, the campaign does not neglect to play on antiintellectual moods, to pit the work of the muscles against the work of the mind. Intellectuals don't produce anything, they have no idea of hard work and thus are in some sense isolated from the mainstream of our life. Their task, then, is to put their particular skills at the service of the working people, and no more than that. "Students to their studies, writers to their pens"—that was the slogan in March 1968—to which people added the words, "and workers to their shovels," thus deciphering the essence of the slogan as an attempt to erect social barriers and to dispossess society of its political rights. Everyone should only be concerned with his allotted sector and leave general issues to the special solicitude and protection of the authorities—no more, no less.

At present, the antiintellectual motif is being played more gently, less coarsely, but in a way that is more menacing and more refined. The right to speak up is granted to those who work hard and want to do so in peace. This is in the traditional mold—in the popular view (and it is precisely this that is played on) intellectuals don't work, they only write. Moreover, even their mandate and credentials are attacked, what early in his career Professor Szczepański had defined as a "search for truth and for the laws governing the world of things, life and people," the striving "to create new arrangements for human affairs and to enrich the world with new values." At that time, twenty years ago, he also wrote that the intellectuals' task is "to furnish the rulers and the ruled with bases for making reasonable decisions and for the use of power."*

But all this is for naught, for in our newspapers today the noun "intellectual" is usually accompanied by the adjective "naive." In sum, the tone here is one of tolerant scorn. Intellectuals are not only unable to understand "all the laws of the economy and the laws pertaining to the mechanisms of governing,"† they are "inexperienced people who in the name of humanistic slogans . . . and without giving the matter serious thought, lend their names to activities whose true political meaning they do not perceive."‡ For a long time now they have let themselves be manipulated by crafty operators unmasked long ago, and they are, moreover, subject to the obviously meretricious glamor of the West.

Whatever form the internal enemy takes—Jews, hooligans, "a small vocifer-

---

*Jan Szczepański, "Inteligencja i społeczeństwo" (The intelligentsia and society), *Warsaw*, 1957. (Szczepański is a famous sociologist whose collaboration with the authorities had made him a frequent target of criticism by fellow intellectuals. In 1980–81 Szczepański, as a deputy in the Sejm, threw his support behind Solidarity, and after the declaration of martial law in December 1981 he was one of the few deputies who voted against government measures, including the formal ban on Solidarity, passed in October 1982.)

†Kira Gałczyńska, "Rzeczpospolita Polaków: Rozmowa z Edmundem Osmańczykiem" (The republic of the Poles: conversation with Edmund Osmańczyk), *Trybuna Ludu*, January 7, 1977.

‡Marek Jaworski, *op. cit.*

ous group'' and their paltry supporters—the enemy would be a dull and insipid figure were it not for the fact that whenever he appears, Poland becomes the forward bridgehead of a camp besieged by hostile forces. In such a context the only vaguely familiar activities of our internal enemies deserve a specific label —treason. Treason is an emotionally unambiguous term, which, however, depending on the needs of the moment, embraces a wide variety of human behavior: emigration, personal connections with certain foreigners, publishing an article abroad, an interview with a Western journalist, right up to signing a collective protest or defending strikes, since all these things are grist for the mills of enemy propaganda.

The making of the external enemy is a good example of applying a symbol arousing negative emotions to an area that is neutral, or even positively charged. In the newspaper version, the Western world usually admires our accomplishments and acknowledges our international standing, but when it is time for a campaign, it suddenly turns out that the West is full of hostile and inimical forces. Among them, the pride of place belongs to West Germany. In fact, playing on the anti-German animus is a phenomenon occurring with monotonous regularity. Thus among the currencies not spurned by the supporters of ''hostile forces in Poland,'' only Deutsche marks are mentioned, and among the Western papers slandering our society, it is chiefly German titles that are singled out. (In Roliński's article ''All the Antennae at Poland,'' of the thirteen European publications cited, ten were from West Germany.)*

Thus the general hostility of the West is turned into the unmistakable hostility of the Germans, and the aroused anti-German feelings are supposed to be transferred onto the Western world by virtue of negative association.

Xenophobia, odious attitudes, and social barriers aren't all that our newspapers offer. There are certain other values that merit attention.

First, respect for material possessions, more than for life or health. In 1970, for instance, newspapers excelled in shedding tears for damaged property. There were photographs and descriptions of some wreckage in Gdańsk, a historical building that nearly burned down, broken windows, all of which was meant to arouse indignation; but there was nothing about anyone being killed or wounded. In 1976 the only account to come out of Radom concerned the pillaging of stores, rotting food on the streets, and ruined carpets. The massacre of workers was presumably of no interest to the reader.†

The same sort of mentality is evident in the motives ascribed to the enemies— i.e., self-interest and calculation. What, for example, do those who, after numerous warnings, were arrested for their activities, expect to get out of it? They ''had to spend time in prison for the sake of their credibility—to spend time in a 'Communist prison' is to earn the highest mark of distinction in capitalist propaganda.''‡ And why does Jerzy Andrzejewski flirt with treason? For money, to win the Nobel Prize.

---

*Życie Warszawy, May 28–29, 1977.

†Alfred Los, ''Płakały ale broniły'' (They cried but they defended), Polityka, July 17, 1976.

‡Bohdan Roliński, ''Wszystkie anteny na Polskę'' (All the antennae at Poland), Życie Warszawy, May 28–29, 1977.

Yet another feature of the campaign that merits attention is the appeal to what in academic language would be termed egalitarianism, but which in fact is nothing but sheer human envy. The enemies are always described as enjoying material privileges denied to the average citizen. In 1968, it was the pampered students and the writers who could travel abroad, and in 1970 it was the shipyard workers earning high wages that were the most common targets. The point of all this is not merely hypocrisy—though that is obvious: after all, the authors of those articles in 1968 and in 1970 enjoyed enormous privileges themselves, while the workers singled out for attack earned higher wages in accordance with legal regulations. The main point is that the writers, the students, the dignitaries removed from office, and the shipyard workers have all proved to be ungrateful. The benefits (including workers' wages) are not something they were entitled to by dint of hard work, or because it is natural to want to be dressed better or take a trip to the mountains: the benefits are bestowed by the state, and therefore the state deserves absolute obedience and loyalty. The state, in other words, is the highest value. It is also the ultimate creditor—and the people, in turn, are the debtors. There can be no rights enjoyed by individuals outside the state—they are all indivisible. To quote our party daily: "The goal . . . should be the complete identification of the citizen with the socialist state, the convergence of his most essential interests with the interest of the state."*

And so we have arrived at the simple system of values that governs our sociopolitical life. Some of the characteristics discussed earlier seemed negative but that was because outmoded standards had been applied in evaluating them and now, seen in perspective, they are revealed as virtues.

Dogmatism and ignorance turn into loyalty and confidence in the highest authority; xenophobia becomes unity with the state in a moment of danger; aggression against different ways of social behavior, a reluctance to take pluralistic attitudes becomes the relinquishing of the right to make all decisions to the state; the fetishism of material values becomes a gift for ceding one's rights to the state.

Let me now draw up the image of the common, average man who calls the authorities "they." He is insufficiently informed, does not trust the newspapers, but is uncertain of being right himself ("I'm no expert on that"). Lacking confidence, and reluctant to make gestures of protest and resistance ("You know nothing's going to come of it, things'll be even worse"), he is apt to erupt periodically with generalized aggression ("They make trouble, then they emigrate and we're the ones stuck here." "The young people haven't been through what we have, they can only cause trouble." "Things are bad, but complain to the Germans? They're just waiting for it"). Overworked and anxiety-ridden, he wants peace more than anything ("You've got to live somehow").

His features and those adumbrated above almost coincide. It is only that one

---

*Marek Jaworski, "Wobec państwa. Rozmowa z profesorem Marianem Wojciechowskim" (Vis-à-vis the state: A conversation with Professor Marian Wojciechowski), *Trybuna Ludu*, December 17, 1976.

word, "they," which he uses to defend his individuality and the remnants of his—perhaps illusory—independence that actually cause him to be in continual opposition to the authorities and to be dispossessed of all rights. Which rights are in question here? "Rights that are supposedly inalienable and eternal." But no such rights exist. Though there is one such right and it binds all patriots today: "the inalienable right of every Pole to participate in the development of our country, to surmount the successive obstacles on the road of development, in a word, to realize the programs of the Sixth and Seventh Party Congresses."* He usurps that one right for himself in order to saddle the authorities with the responsibility for all the failures and impossibilities.

The aim of a campaign is to direct his frustration, which gives rise to the hopelessness, dejection, and irritation that are the stuff of our daily lives, onto others—strangers, the young, those who do not want to submit to the impossible. All his activity is to be focused on the private area—the family, career, installment payments for his Fiat. But, above all, the campaign's aim is to force him to enclose everything meant by the word "they" in the word "we," so that he identifies with the state and adjusts himself to its aims and aspirations.

Patriotism, according to the simplest interpretation, is the acknowledgement of the fatherland as a superior value that is worthy of any sacrifice and renunciation. Only one form of manipulation is required: to juggle emotions and contexts so that the three words—party, state, Poland—are identical in meaning. In a given situation any of the three elements in this fusion can predominate—the party, when successes are being tallied (successes are always credited to it, mistakes and shortcomings are the fault of individuals). The state is the dispenser of goods, although in times of tension it is more convenient to cede that position to Poland ("Poland gave them everything"). Poland is the executor of obligations but it is primarily the shield behind which the party and the state vanish immediately when there is a wave of discontent and the voices of criticism arise. The manipulation of patriotism is not confined to the degeneration of the language, to making it unsuitable for criticizing political realities.

The requirements of sacrifice that this concept includes are exploited to impose their own positive program on society and that "one inalienable right" Misiorny speaks of, the right to sweat in rhythm with the party's resolutions and plans. To be sure, this is not a very exciting program. But the complex of Polish provincialism, that sense of insufficient worth that makes Poles unusually sensitive to opinions about themselves is a source of succor here. It is enough for the propaganda instruments to point out the menace—"Poland is being slandered abroad!"—to elicit an emotional response: "They're saying vile things about us!" Precisely—"about us" and not "about them." That's the point here: to reduce people to an inert collective united by injured national pride, so that the paralyzing word "we" common to both rulers and ruled makes its appearance accompanied by a common enemy, and a common goal—peace and discipline.

And just as insipid patriotic platitudes are to lead to an incapacitating identification with the authorities, so do its basic characteristics—intellectual dogma-

*Michał Misiorny, "Obowiązek i odpowiedzialność" (Duty and responsibility), *Trybuna Ludu*, July 21, 1977.

tism, xenophobia, and the parvenu mentality—take root and rouse destructive social emotions.

To what degree does a campaign such as the one depicted here succeed in achieving its desired result, the degeneration of collective consciousness? That question will, for the time being, remain unanswered.

From *Zapis* (Warsaw), no. 4, 1977

Translated by Richard Lourie

1968 AND ALL THAT
Marek Turbacz

Not feeling competent enough to offer a historical assessment, I should merely like to say a few words about what March 1968 meant to me.

I did not participate in the March events. I had no interest in politics, nor did I understand it. I was a student, yet I had never felt impelled to join any organized movement. I was a passive witness to the demonstrations and other incidents [of that time]. Nonetheless, March 1968 proved to be one of those factors that transformed my attitude and my consciousness, and that after eight years led me to make my debut as an oppositionist.*

My parents stem from the prewar intelligentsia. I would characterize their views as moderately Endek.† During the war they belonged to the AK.‡ I think that the atmosphere in which I was brought up was fairly typical for the Polish Catholic intelligentsia of peasant origin. Which is why I should like to dwell on this for a while.

The most powerful "substance" which I imbibed from early childhood on were the memories of the war, particularly of the [August 1944] Warsaw Uprising (an animus toward the Germans is all that I retained from those years). There was never any talk about the current situation—about Stalinism or Russian domination. My parents were evidently apprehensive lest their child divulge something inadvertently—either in school or anywhere else.

My parents had no understanding of politics—its mechanisms and significance. At home I often heard it said that politics was something dirty, that politicians have nothing but their own interests at heart. The word "politics"—in whatever context employed—always had a pejorative connotation. (My

---

*With his essay "Możliwości działania opozycji w Polsce" (Possibilities for oppositionist activity in Poland), which circulated unofficially in Poland in 1976, and then appeared in *ANEKS* (London), no. 16/17, 1978.

†From the initials "ND"—National Democrats, a prewar political party, ultranationalistic and anti-Semitic.

‡AK (Armia Krajowa)—Home Army, the largest underground military force during the German occupation.

mother praised KOR in principle, but at one point she asserted critically that there seemed to be some politics in it). This attitude toward politics is very typical of Poles.

J. J. Szczepański* considers the words of Joseph Conrad as something of a symbol for the AK generation. This remark strikes me as very much to the point. In his novels, Conrad illuminated the most magnificent and most dramatic conflicts taking place in unusual and critical situations, far removed from everyday life—such as the war was for members of the AK. At the same time, however, Conrad had no understanding for politics—an area in which morality is linked profoundly to social life. Bertrand Russell said about Conrad: "Apart from his love for England and hatred for Russia, politics was of little concern to him."

In the vision of reality that was proffered to me, there was no room for struggle, for commitment. Reality was unchanging and unchangeable. Of course, contemporary reality was viewed in a negative and hostile way, yet there was nothing I could learn from it and about its historical roots or essential nature. What affected me most indelibly was the sharp demarcation line between those who belonged and those who did not belong to the party—that is, the division between the bad and the better. (I shed this stereotype only at work, where I found many friends among party members.)

I was taught to dislike the Russians. I was told that it wasn't worth reaching for a Russian book. To be sure, we are inundated with trivia, yet this distaste extended to the whole *oeuvre* of Russian culture, including Dostoevsky. (Conrad, too, despised Russia and the Russians. He simply dismissed Russian literature.) I read a great deal in my youth, yet it was only in my late teens that I threw myself into Russian literature and poetry—and was mesmerized by it.

The one truly revolting thing that my parents tried to imbue me with was anti-Semitism. This cultural attitude, which does not condone pogroms, expresses itself in distaste and contempt—for instance, by putting the ending *"uś"* onto Jewish names.† Polish anti-Semitism lumps us together above all with the Piasecki bands‡ or the March "Hunvaybins."§ But the *endecja* is comprised not only of the Falanga fascists, but also of all those liberal and humanitarian *inteligenty* who wouldn't dream of swinging a club, but who always remember who is a Jew, and who remain passive in the face of pogroms. These people, too, are at least partially responsible for the death of Narutowicz, ‖ for the ghetto

*A prominent Polish writer, who in late 1980 was elected Chairman of the Polish Writer's Union.
†An attempt to caricature a Jewish accent.
‡Bolesław Piasecki, in the late 1930s leader of the fascist organization Falanga and after the war head of the proregime Catholic association PAX, commanded several groups during the war, which fought the Germans, the Communist partisans, and Jewish partisan units alike. Piasecki's "bands" were not associated with the Home Army.
§A pejorative term that derives from the Chinese word for the Red Guards (Hung Uey-Ping) during the "Cultural Revolution" in the late 1960s.
‖ Gabriel Narutowicz (1865–1922), a distinguished scholar of liberal persuasion, was elected president of the Polish Republic in 1922, against the bitter opposition of the right (especially the *endecja*), which considered him a creature of Marshal Piłsudski and of the country's national minorities (which supported his candidacy), especially the Jews. He was assassinated on December 16, only five days after his inauguration, by Eligiusz Niewiadomski, a painter, extreme nationalist, and anti-Semite.

benches at the universities, for the pacification of the Ukraine, and for blowing up Russian Orthodox churches.*

Apart from the various antagonisms I had to get rid of, my home also bequeathed to me a sense of patriotism and an understanding of what constitutes a nation. In addition, I inherited the cult of struggle for values, particularly those embedded in the AK tradition, and to some extent, of the tradition of anti-Russian insurrections.

To read today the works of former revisionists† is to be struck by the fact that they approach problems in social, rather than national, categories. Their principal values are those of human rights, democracy, freedom, and state sovereignty. (This is what distinguishes them, for instance, from the PPN— the Polish League for Independence.) I am far from charging them with lack of patriotism, yet their patriotism is something very private, something that only faintly colors their way of thinking. For that matter this way of thinking is also mine—I, too, do not apotheosize the concept of a "nation." But it seems to me, from my own observations as well as from sociological surveys, that in Poland a political or social movement aspiring for mass support must somehow relate itself to patriotism, and not only the struggle for peace and democracy.

If, as it seems to me, the works of Conrad are emblematic for the AK generation, so for the revisionists the symbol is *Płomienie* (Flames)—the life story of Michał Kaniowski, who, alien to national traditions and values, fought side by side with the [Russian] Populists in the name of freedom and social justice, against despotism.‡

March 1968 came as a shock to me—as it did to most of my fellow students. Until then I had not followed political developments. I had heard next to nothing about the brochure by Kuroń and Modzelewski, and Kołakowski's speech on the tenth anniversary of Gomułka's return to power in October 1956, about the growing ferment.§ It was only the events connected with the closing down of *The Forefathers* that brought me face to face with these problems.

This was the first time that the system impinged itself on my life—and most brutally at that: I was shattered by the impotence of the students, the lies perpetrated by the authorities and the press, the violence and savagery of the police,

---

*The prewar Polish government's treatment of its one million Byelorussian and four million Ukrainian minorities was generally one of hostility and continuous attempts to abrogate their national and cultural rights, guaranteed under the Polish Minority Treaty, which Poland signed as part of the 1919 Treaty of Versailles. In the 1920s, gangs of Polish nationalists would frequently blow up Uniate and Russian Orthodox churches, and Polish troops would frequently burn down entire villages whose Ukrainian inhabitants were suspected of anti-Polish actions.

†See chapter 5, by Leszek Kołakowski, in this book.

‡*Płomienie*, by the Polish Marxist philosopher and novelist Stanisław Brzozowski, was published in 1909. It deals with the heroic exploits of the Russian Populists of the nineteenth century (Narodnaya Volya).

§On October 21, 1966, Leszek Kołakowski, then a professor of philosophy at Warsaw University, delivered a speech on "Polish Culture in the Past Twenty Years," in which he subjected Gomułka's policies to thoroughgoing criticism. He was expelled from the party a day later, against the vigorous protests of most of his party colleagues at the university. Two years earlier, Jacek Kuroń and Karol Modzelewski, at that time still Marxists, published an antiregime brochure for which they were arrested and sentenced to long prison terms.

the cruelty of a political order that could remove each one of us from the university, arrest us, or send us for two years to the army.

For the first time this scum revealed itself to me in all its contemptible nakedness—those gentlemen from television and newspapers, the dedicated fascists and the hirelings that every police system has at its disposal—those in and out of uniform, and those who relished beating up young women—and the same ones who later tortured the workers.

In order to rebel against a system, one must truly come to know it. This happened to me in March 1968. By the same token, March provided me with the first basis for an active struggle against the system, even though at that time my efforts proved in vain. The most active element in my [university] department was comprised of students of Jewish background. While I was relatively unfamiliar with politics, I nevertheless had a feeling that this was a closely knit group, with a grasp of what was going on and of what they were fighting for. They aroused my respect and sympathy. They also opened my eyes to the—at best—paltry nature of the atmosphere in which I had been raised, with its contradiction between the rejection of the system, passivity, and hopelessness on the one hand, and the cult of the Warsaw Uprising on the other. The most noxious form of anti-Semitism came from the other side of the barricades. It presented no dilemma to me, for I have never in my life taken to anti-Semitism. But I remember a fellow student from an Endek family. He was about to join the sit-down strike. He asked me heatedly whether I knew who was stirring up all this trouble—the Jews, of course. They're making us pull their chestnuts out of the fire.

I think that for the overwhelming majority of students March had the same significance as it had for me. They, too, knew nothing. They protested in the name of student solidarity, out of a sense of commonality, in response to the news about the attack on the first student meeting, the beatings of students, the reports (no doubt spread deliberately by the security forces) about fatalities. For them, too, March represented their first encounter with politics and with Soviet communism. March somehow shaped the consciousness of my generation. Even if only a small minority of my contemporaries joined the opposition movement, it was thanks to March that the others, too, will never support the system, and will forever regard it as an enemy. I know the active participants of the March demonstration who later succumbed to passivity but to whom one can always turn with some documents either for safekeeping or to be delivered somewhere.

The year 1968 brought into being a hard core of "professional" oppositionists, whose goal in life is to fight against our system, and who now play a significant part in the opposition. Lenin was absolutely right in saying that the leading role in a resistance movement must be played by "professionals." Even if the movement suffers yet another defeat, there will always remain individuals who refuse to adapt themselves to the system.

In the literature that has arisen in recent years, March is often seen as a colossal defeat. The memoirs of émigrés sometimes convey a sense of calamity. Yet in a war, lost battles also have their use.

From *Krytyka* (Warsaw), no. 1, 1979

Translated by Abraham Brumberg

Censorship

In March 1977, Tomasz Strzyżewski, an official of the Polish censorship apparatus—known officially as the Central Office for Control of Press, Publications,
and Public Performances—defected to the West, bringing with him hundreds of
pages of instructions, guidelines, commentaries, and other documents issued by
the Office, all of them covering the period from August 1, 1975, to March 10,
1977. The documents provide a remarkable and comprehensive picture of this
institution—the extent of its activities, the volume of articles, books, plays,
cartoons that were either eliminated altogether or subjected to frequently petty
(though revealing) deletions, the principles guiding the work of the censors as
well as some of the "mistakes" committed in the course of their labors.
Strzyżewski turned the materials over to KOR, which, after satisfying itself
about the authenticity of the documents, published them in two volumes, totaling
nearly 600 pages. The volumes were subsequently reprinted in England by the
Polish quarterly *ANEKS* under the title *Czarna księga cenzury PRL* (The black
book of censorship of the Polish People's Republic). A small selection of them
appeared in the United States in April 1978 under the title *Official Censorship in
the Polish People's Republic* (Ann Arbor, Mich.: The North American Study
Center for Polish Affairs, 1978); a more extensive translation, edited and anno-
tated by Jane Curry, will be published later this year by Random House.

While everyone in Poland had been perfectly aware of the existence and power
of official censorship, its magnitude, as disclosed by these documents, created a
veritable storm in Polish intellectual circles and no doubt contributed to the
struggle against it—a struggle that found its expression in the demands of the
striking workers in the Baltic shipyards and that continued to be one of the major
issues espoused by Solidarity and all other independent social groups in 1980–
81. By July 1981, the Polish Parliament finally passed a new censorship bill.
While preserving censorship in certain areas (e.g., the military), it nevertheless
provided for a significant liberalization of an institution that many in Poland had
come to view as one of the paramount obstacles to the liberalization of the
political system as a whole. The new law was subsequently "revised" by General Jaruzelski's government.

The excerpts that follow are but a tiny fragment of the available material, but they suffice to illustrate the efforts to muzzle the media, to deprive the population of access to truthful information, to make it impossible—as, indeed, it *was* impossible—to discuss any matters that the government considered to be "sensitive," or that reflected unfavorably upon Polish reality, in a free and responsible manner. It was precisely the regime's obsession with control over freedom of expression that made it so difficult to seek any genuine solutions to the ever-mounting crisis and that led to the erosion of the regime's credibility in the eyes of the entire society.

Part one illustrates the "positive" tasks of the censors—that is, the way the media were to propagate, praise, and "explain" a given policy of the regime. Part two consists of instructions on the kind of information that censors must never allow to appear in print. Part three is an "instructive note" that analyzes the mistakes made by a censor in permitting the publication of two items and how such mistakes can be avoided in the future. The final item is of an altogether different nature. It is a conversation with a former censorship official, which appeared in 1981 in the Solidarity paper *Tygodnik Solidarność*. The interview constitutes perhaps one of the most remarkable insights into the mind of a typical government apparatchik: cynical, moderately shrewd, unscrupulous, yet determined to justify himself on grounds of both a higher morality and political realism.

1. DO'S

The Tasks of the Press, Radio, and Television after the Seventh Congress of the PZPR

The rich achievements of 1971–75 in the socialist construction of our country under the leadership of the party—achievements that confirm the correctness of the development strategy adopted by the Sixth Congress of the PZPR—have met with the full support of our society. The Seventh Congress set new, bold and ambitious goals for national socioeconomic development during the next five-year period, goals that represent the continuation of the strategy of dynamic development realized in the first half of the 1970s. They are aimed at the further rapid development of the socialist economy; the expansion and modernization of production potential; an increase in the social productivity of labor; scientific, technical, and organizational progress; upgraded management effectiveness; an expansion of Poland's contribution to the socialist community; and a strengthening of her position in Europe and the world. The year 1976 will mark the first period in which the resolutions of the Seventh Party Congress will be realized. A great deal depends on getting off to a good start in the implementation of the program of the party and the nation and on achieving good results this year. Hence, there is also a need to strengthen the belief of working people and society as a whole in the correctness of the path on which we have embarked and in the unexhausted possibilities for well-organized and disciplined activity, and the expansion of action and initiative. The growing consciousness of working people, their patriotic commitment, and their increasing belief in their own strength and potential are a guarantee of further success in the building of an advanced socialist society in our country. . . .

I. GENERAL TASKS

1. After the Seventh Party Congress, the basic task of the mass media is to disseminate throughout society the program described in the resolution "On the Further Dynamic Development of Socialist Construction—on Higher Quality of Work and Living Conditions for the Nation," and in the resolution "On the

Further Development of the Forces of Socialism, the Maintenance of Peace, and the Further Strengthening of the International Position of the Polish People's Republic.''

The aim of this activity should be to make every citizen aware of the political, ideological, and socioeconomic foundations for the development of the country over the next five years, and thereby to mobilize the population for the full realization of these goals. It is a question of maintaining a high ideological temperature, productive work, and a sense of commitment from the first few days after the Party Congress.

2. In the substantive activity of the mass media, special attention should be given to the following:

—Continued popularization of the record of achievement in national socioeconomic development during the current five-year plan in general and in 1975 in particular. This should touch upon overall macroeconomic gains and on achievements in specific areas, with emphasis on the correctness of the developmental strategy laid down by the Sixth Party Congress, the high level of participation on the part of the working class, and the leading role of the party.

—An indication of the goals and tasks for 1976–80, especially those for 1976, which follow from the strategy for development adopted by the Seventh Party Congress. In particular, we must strengthen society's conviction of the need for a high rate of national development, increased labor productivity, modernity, and high production quality as preconditions for and guarantees of the building of an advanced socialist society, a rise in the people's material and cultural standard of living, and an increase in Poland's international standing and prestige.

II. THE HUMAN FACTOR

In the effort to inspire society to realize the resolutions of the Seventh Congress and the goals for 1976, a central place should be devoted to the role of the individual, of social groups, and of society as a whole. Therefore, alongside numbers and indices, an effort should be made to emphasize the decisive role of people, of the working class, as implementers of our plans, as the crucial element in guaranteeing success in achieving our quantitative and qualitative goals. In this regard, the concept of the ''open plan'' needs to be fully explained.* It must be stressed that the open plan provides working people and factory crews with the opportunity of shaping and improving it. It is open to initiative, commitment, professional and personal ambition, higher quality, and new creative possibilities and perspectives. It is closed to poor work, extravagance, passivity, and egoistic attitudes, all of which should be condemned. A climate favorable to creative

---

*The ''open plan'' provided for investment initiatives undertaken outside the norms set by the state; it led (as it later turned out) to immense waste and abuses.

initiative of the working people, a climate favorable to innovation and dynamic action, should be created and established on a permanent basis. We must create a model of a man without complexes, courageous in his actions, who supports innovation, who seeks to do what is right and derives satisfaction from well-done work. The pressure of social needs should be confronted with the need for greater efforts toward their satisfaction.

THE FORMATION OF SOCIALIST CONSCIOUSNESS. The mass media must redouble their efforts to popularize and explain the meaning, purpose, and essence of the building of an advanced socialist society in this country. It is necessary to make people aware that an advanced socialist society is not only one consisting of producers and of those who consume an abundance of material goods, but also a society of broadly educated, enlightened people with developed intellectual aspirations, a society based on modern technology, a high level of sociopolitical consciousness, and a profound ideological understanding. More attention should be concentrated on the strengthening of approved social values and on the formation of new attitudes, outlooks, and habits. In particular, it is a matter of encouraging patriotism, a term to be understood in the sense of conscientious, creative work for the nation. It is also a matter of the economic education of society. We must impart greater importance to innovative attitudes, reinforce moral values such as goodwill, human dignity, solidarity, and friendship, and pay more attention to the educational function of the family as the fundamental unit of any society.

Respect and politeness in dealing with other citizens is an essential element of all activities at all times.

Under conditions of ideological confrontation, the mass media must take a more aggressive stance in propagating and promoting socialist ideals and must more effectively combat bourgeois and petit-bourgeois attitudes and ideology, basing its defense on a profound scientific analysis.

Particular emphasis should be placed on an explanation of the crucial importance of fraternal cooperation with the USSR and other socialist countries for the economic development of the country and for the realization of the common goals of peace and social progress throughout the world.

TASKS OF JOURNALISTS. If the tasks outlined here are to be carried out, journalists will have to have a good grasp of the problems discussed by the Congress as well as of the documents and resolutions issued by it. An important role in their study of the Congress documents should be played by party organizations and the Association of Polish Journalists.

In carrying out information and propaganda work, which should be consistent yet varied, it will be extremely important to find an answer to the following questions: How can we reach our audience—readers, viewers, and listeners— with an explanation of the tasks outlined by the Congress? How can we engage them in a dialogue and effectively inspire and mobilize them? How can we make these aims the goal and ideal of every Pole? The specific characteristics of individual enterprises and institutions as well as individual voivodships should be taken into account in the presentation of these materials.

It will be possible to accomplish these tasks if every journalist personally identifies with the goals of the party program and strives each day to make that program a reality. This means that journalists, as activists on the ideological front, must be in daily contact with the working class, the creators of all national successes and achievements.

From *Czarna księga cenzury PRL,* vol. 2

Translated by Jane Curry

II. DON'TS

FOREIGN RELATIONS

—All information concerning diplomatic initiatives or actions taken by the socialist countries (especially Poland and the USSR) can only be released after, or simultaneously with, the appearance of appropriate official communiques in the Polish Press Agency (PAP) or TASS. Under no circumstances can information acquired from other sources either proceed or differ in content from official information. [P. 24, no. 2]

—All material containing sharp criticism of the Albanian Labor Party's leadership and the Albanian government must be approved by the Central Office for Control of Press, Publications, and Performances prior to publication. [P. 25, no. 5]

—In view of the principles governing our foreign policy vis-à-vis countries of the so-called Third World, the following rules should be observed:

(c) because of our relations with Iraq and the evolving nature of this problem, the Iraqui Baath party should not be described as the rightist section of the Baath movement, and materials critical of the controversies between the Baathist factions in Iraq and Syria should not be published;

(d) materials concerning possible limitations on the freedom of action of Communist parties and their leaders in Egypt, Algeria, Sudan, Iraq, Libya, and Syria must not be allowed to appear in print;

(j) no information should be published concerning possible trade relations with Rhodesia and South Africa, or contacts between Polish institutions and South Africa;

(m) terms such as "military dictatorship" or other names such as "gorillas" and "military junta" must not be used with regard to countries with which Poland maintains diplomatic relations. This rule does not apply to Chile, Paraguay, Guatemala, and the Dominican Republic. . . . [Pp. 27–30, no. 10]

—The mass media are not allowed to disseminate information about Poland's purchase of licenses from capitalist countries. This regulation applies to licenses already in operation, newly concluded agreements on licenses and all proposals for the purchase of licenses. Brief mention can, however, be made of widely known products, such as Leyland engines, Jones cranes, Fiat automobiles, Berliet buses or Grundig tape recorders. There must be no disclosure of information regarding the proliferation of such licenses.

This regulation is dictated by the need to avoid excessive information about the purchase of licenses in capitalist countries. The cumulative effect of such information might be to induce a belief in the average reader that the modernization of Poland's economy is predicated on the purchase of licenses from developed capitalist countries. [Pp. 36–37, no. 6]

—It is forbidden to publish independently acquired data about negotiations for the purchase of grain abroad. The publication of statistics concerning the magnitude of specific purchases and speculations about future purchases is prohibited. These directives do not apply to official communiques issued by the Polish Press Agency. [Pp. 37–38, no. 9]

—No information is to be published about the purchase of meat or meat products from the German Democratic Republic. General information concerning the import of meat and specific details of contracts already concluded (outside the GDR) may be released on the condition that other directives are not thereby violated. [P. 38, no. 10]

—Information pertaining to the sale of meat by Poland to the USSR must not be allowed to appear in print. [P. 38, no. 12]

DOMESTIC PROBLEMS

—All commentaries, reports, interviews, etc., concerning increases in average wages throughout our entire socialized economy, retirement and old age pensions, and other benefits, whether already granted or promised during the Seventh Congress of the PZPR, must be confined only . . . to indices appearing in the official releases of the Main Office of Statistics. . . . Decisions concerning wages or current social policies are not to be subjected to criticism. There is to be no mention of any further demands for increases in pay or benefits such as retirement and old age pensions, paid leave, health care, scholarships, and so on. [P. 45, no. 1]

—No information is to be released about the special pensions given to various people by the Chairman of the Council of Ministers. Information concerning such pensions can be published without, however, identifying the grantor. [P. 47, no. 4]

—Without approval from the Deputy Prime Minister or Chairman of the State Price Commission, information relating to reductions and increases in the price of any consumer or durable goods is not to be published. [P. 47, no. 7]

—Articles dealing with the protection of, or threats to, the natural environment in Poland, should not contain information about the direct hazards to human life and health created by industry and by chemicals used in agriculture.

This regulation applies to specific cases in which pollution of the atmosphere, water, soil, and food constitute danger to human health and life.

All information about pollution by pesticides is also covered by this directive.

Eliminate, too, all material and information about hazards to the health of workers employed in the production of PVC (polyvinyl chloride). There is to be no mention of dangers arising from the use of PVC in the building industry or the sale of PVC products on the market. [Pp. 48–49, no. 9]

—Cumulative data on the number of road accidents, fires, and drownings should be eliminated by the Polish Press Agency, the national press, radio, and TV. Alarmist comments on this subject should be toned down. [P. 49, no. 10]

English version from *Official Censorship in the Polish People's Republic* (Ann Arbor, Mich.: The North American Study Center for Polish Affairs, 1978)

III. TO ERR IS HUMAN

CENTRAL OFFICE FOR CONTROL OF PRESS,
PUBLICATIONS, AND PUBLIC PERFORMANCES—
INSTRUCTION, EVALUATION,
AND CONTROL GROUP

Warsaw, July 6, 1976
C O N F I D E N T I A L
Copy No. 48

Censors' Instructive Note No. 2

Życie Gospodarcze, no. 5, July 1, 1976, published two articles in its "Industry—Trade—Consumers" section that were very critical, in their assessment of the market situation in Poland, of the supply of ready-made clothing, and of the quality and prices of available goods: "'Czesia' for 360 Zlotys," by A. Szymańska, and "Raisin Bread," by Z. Długosz.

In her article, A. Szymańska wrote that by far the largest number of goods offered by shops selling ready-made clothing are referred to as "junk," and on top of that often come with a ticket describing them as entirely new products.

In addition to its one-sided criticism of market supply, the article also made extensive generalizations about the policy of introducing dubious "novelties" onto the market. It was also very pessimistic in noting that despite enormous outlays in the knitwear industry, the situation in this field is becoming worse throughout the country.

In the second article, entitled "Raisin Bread," Z. Długosz likewise discussed the clothing available in the stores. In her opinion, most of the items offered are unfashionable or of poor quality. The stores rarely get goods that the customers like, and therefore when they do, such items are eagerly snapped up. According to the author, this situation reflects the fact that industry is largely concerned with its own advantage and convenience. At the same time, Długosz offers the example of some Hong Kong shirts eagerly bought up by shoppers because of their attractive appearance and low price, and asks how it is that a capitalist can produce attractive, inexpensive goods while we cannot. One of the reasons she adduces is that "there are elements that hinder an improved adaptation of the supply of goods to demand."

The gloomy tone of these articles is accentuated by the addition of an unfavorable comparison between the paralysis of "key" investments and the efficiency of local and foreign "private businessmen."

In this context, the photographs accompanying the article should also have been evaluated: those on the first, second, and third pages ("our junk") were compared with the items on the fourth page ("Between Warsaw and New York").

Although the article also contains some positive statements and comments, it is dominated, on the whole, by a negative attitude.

In the light of the above, we feel bound to conclude that permission to publish these articles in their present form was a censorship error, even if the specific character of *Życie Gospodarcze* is taken into account. . . .

The controversial items discussed here concerned very important, difficult socioeconomic problems, and hence should have been assessed with great care both by the editorial board and by the representative of our Office. It must therefore be considered a mistake on the part of the censor to have first offered a number of reservations and to call, appropriately, for deletions and reediting, but then to give in to some extent to the editors' arguments. It is true that two minor corrections were made in the text, and that it was stated that the editors of *Życie Gospodarcze* had decided to publish the questioned items anyway and to take full personal responsibility for this decision. Nonetheless, this decision was incorrect for general social reasons. In accordance with obligatory procedure, the censor should not have given permission for publication and should have made his reservations known to his supervisors, thereby ensuring that the editors would make the necessary alterations and deletions.

From *Czarna księga cenzury PRL,* vol. 2

Translated by Jane Curry

THE LIFE AND HAPPY TIMES OF A POLISH CENSOR

I, the Censor

A conversation with K-62, former functionary of the main administration for the Control of the Press, Publications, and Public Performances

Q.: Tell me, can anyone become a censor?

A: Anyone with a college education and a desire to work in the firm. Particularly people with degrees in the humanities. A colleague of mine, a girl, studied political economy, another specialized in Polish language and literature, and one buddy has a degree in journalism.

Q.: Frustrated journalists?

A.: A lot of young people with diplomas in journalism are interested, because the starting pay is good. I got 4,000 zlotys in 1974, but after that you don't advance much. My pal, who's been there for seven years, gets only five grand.

Q.: Well, you've got to have a certain psychological predisposition, don't you?

A.: Look, I swear to you, there are a lot of honest people in censorship—though I bet this doesn't square with your notions. There are all sorts: drunkards, dedicated fathers, good housewives, and floozies. The idea that a censor is some kind of a PIDE* agent is for the birds. To be sure, I've met such types—maniacs, scrutinizing every single word with an evil gleam in their eyes—but only a few. The profession is feminized, for it offers peace and quiet. On the other hand, there is quite a turnover—I'd say only about one-fourth stay on for more than a couple of years. It's difficult to generalize. I remember, for instance, one censor who left and then came back after two years; but he had the mentality of a mole.

Q.: How would you, then, describe the mentality of an honest-to-goodness censor?

A.: I wouldn't like to give you the impression that there's only one specific type. There are many—for instance, the professional soldier, the guard, the

*Portugese secret police under Salazar.

youth leader. Some think in ideological terms—that socialism and the party's leading role are best protected by censorship. Others regard censorship as a terrific game. Chess players, I'd call them. They get their kicks from outsmarting the journalist.

Q.: Where would you place yourself?

A.: In the most numerous group, those who join the censorship knowing full well that they will quit after a few years. You go through life trying to find yourself. It's easier if you have some special talent. But if you're like me— without any compelling interest in anything—you proceed by trial and error.

Q.: Did you find your calling by working as a censor?

A.: It's not in my nature to look for a calling, or anything like that. Even now I couldn't tell you what I would ideally like to do. I know what I would not do.

Q.: Namely?

A.: I wouldn't like to work for the police or for the army, and I wouldn't like to be a priest. Now I no longer want to be a censor, though at one time I did.

Q.: Why?

A.: Because I wanted to be a journalist, and it seemed to me that there's nothing like a stretch in censorship to sharpen your wits in this business. If you have a fairly good head on your shoulders, and certain radical proclivities, censorship is a most congenial pursuit. Provided, of course, that you're not an all-out cynic.

Q.: And you're not one?

A.: I regard myself as one-third cynic. And as a person with no talent for journalism. For good journalism isn't merely clever ideas, or hard work, but above all, style. So what if I'm a zealot, determined to show everyone what the truth is, if I put everything in wooden and schematic language?

Q.: Did you at least try?

A.: I did. In 1971, I took a degree in sociology.

Q.: Excuse me, why sociology?

A.: Because it was easier to get into sociology than into any other field. Later on I worked in the OHP* headquarters, which published a bulletin called *Youth, Study, Work.* I wrote a couple of pieces for it, but my chiefs were all youth leaders, so I couldn't write what I wanted but had to toe the line. I got the hang of it pretty quickly—nothing mysterious about it, mind you. Otherwise the competition would have been too stiff. I still counted on winning my spurs.

Q.: In censorship?

A.: Actually, the time I worked as a censor was like an intermission. Some censors can make a go of writing, but I can't. It's very difficult to write anything when you work full time. I tried in the evenings, at home, but as soon as I tried to say anything sensible, my censor's antennae came up, and I'd start wondering whether I shouldn't make some changes. In the end, I'd

*Organizacja Harcerstwa Polskiego (Polish Scouting Organization). Before the war, an independent organization, later taken over by the Communists.

just do an occasional report and review—and that's all. Then I became personally acquainted with some newspapermen, and I thought, Good Lord, what a zoo! And that's, after all, where I would end up, not being very outstanding in the field.

Q.: But were you an outstanding censor?

A.: I suppose I wasn't the worst, and they were sorry to see me go; my chief literally wouldn't let me quit. I must tell you that I have nothing but pleasant memories of that time; aside from what it does, I'd say it's the only firm—in my experience, at any rate—that works with superior efficiency. An ideal mechanism.

Q.: No need to convince me.

A.: And the likes of my chief I'll never have again in my life. A marvelous man. If it hadn't been for him, I'd probably never have become a censor. For, essentially, I am a liberal. I went through March with my dignity intact.* And I never had a penchant for repression.

Q.: What drew you to your chief, then?

A.: Direct, no bullshit, no clichés. He said censorship existed throughout recorded time, and that they were in need of people. I agreed.

Q.: Why?

A.: Because it was interesting. It gave me a chance to find out what's happening in Poland, and how the mechanism of repression was functioning. It was a fine observation post, and I regarded my work as a learning experience. I wanted to be able to read newspapers like a normal person—just as one does, say, in Paris. That's all.

Q.: Didn't you want to get promoted?

A.: Absolutely not. I didn't intend to stay there—only to join and look around.

Q.: And what were the motives of your colleagues in the firm?

A.: I don't know. Personal relations during the 1950s were apparently very amicable. There were all sorts of entertainments, people fell in love, went to harvests together. Now things are different. In general, it never occurred to me to ask: why are you working here? Wouldn't be in good taste.

Q.: Why?

A.: Simple: if you don't know your own mind, then why are you here? That's the basic question you must resolve when you decide to take the job. Once you're there, any discussion becomes pointless.

Q.: All right, let's talk, then, about the basic structure of the firm.

A.: There's a chairman, two vice-chairmen, and several departmental heads—books, performances, analysis, and instructions. In all voivodship towns there are parallel structures. There the work is considerably easier—for what is there to do for a censor in Zielona Góra? But in Kraków the work is probably at least as complicated as in Warsaw, if not more so, because that's where the *Tygodnik Powszechny* comes out—the best weekly we have, in my opinion.† In the press department there is a special group that reads

---

*That is, during the student unrest in March 1968.

†A distinguished lay Catholic weekly, edited by Jerzy Turowicz.

the religious press; we call them "the saints." Another—"the amusement group"—attends films, theaters, cabarets. Things are easier in the theater, for it's difficult to improve Musset or Fredro; it's the staging that gets most attention. The poster men have it easy, and the book people are bored out of their minds. The group that deserves the most respect and is called "the aristocracy" are the press people. They're the avant-garde, the backbone of the firm, the brainiest and most numerous of the lot. First-class.

Q.: And what place did you occupy in this system?

A.: I worked in the part dealing with transmission, not repression. More specifically, in the section on instructions and analyses, which publishes a news bulletin on how a good censor ought to act in given situations.

Q.: Can you give me an example?

A.: Come now, you can't expect me to disclose the secrets of the firm! I've never passed on any information to anyone, even though in my days this would have been as easy as taking candy from a baby. It wasn't until that fellow from Kraków absconded with the materials on censorship that things became harder.* I wasn't going to be disloyal to the firm. The bulletin simply carried articles pointing out specific cases of oversight or of gratuitous cuts by the censor, and discussed what writings should have been scrutinized more closely and which should have been treated more gently. Our section, in effect, constituted an appeal to the top brass to take an interest in what the papers said.

Q.: In other words, all that wasn't there.

A.: The people at the top got everything, nothing was omitted. That was precisely my job—to present the texts as scrupulously as possible, as well as to give a full account of all the grievances and problems that inundated our tormented motherland. All that stuff that you people had dug up and we eliminated would be elegantly and carefully presented to the press department of the Central Committee across the street.† Which is to say that it is patently untrue that the authorities had no inkling of what was going on. They knew everything. And if the comrades from the voivodships tried to fudge things, I for my part held back nothing. After all, everything that was banned in the country would land on my desk. I was exceptionally well informed.

Q.: And how did all this affect you?

A.: I was in the know; and I could think and discuss things more intelligently.

Q.: Discuss? What about your loyalty to the firm?

A.: Discretion was necessary, but I could talk about everything except, of course, directives issued for the sole information of the censor. That gave me a considerable cachet at various banquets and social gatherings. The girls' eyes sparkled with excitement—all in all, I couldn't have had it any better. The others, working in all sorts of offices, were out of luck, while I, working for the censorship, had it all on a silver platter.

---

*See page 241.

†The censor often addresses his interlocutor as a representative of the political opposition—hence phrases such as "you people."

Q.: You were really so keen on making friends and going to banquets?

A.: I never concealed my profession. Never. The firm exists, it needs people, and people are there for the taking. I among them. What of it? There'd be something wrong with me if my conscience bothered me. Maybe there is. The fact is, I am ready to defend my work to the hilt, though not censorship as such. I was able to function properly in the firm and I must emphasize that I've always kept up my relations with people whom I've known since my college days, and with whom I participated in the March strikes; none of them has ever seriously reproached me for my work.

Q.: How about in jest?

A.: "Oh, you running dog," they'd say, facetiously. Anyway, let me remind you that I worked in transmission, and not in repression; on the creative rather than the preventive side of things. My favorite personality is Bruno Kreisky, I am a social democrat at heart, and I don't wish to muzzle the press. I did not cut—that wasn't my job. In addition, had I worked in prevention, I'd have been deprived of much information.

Q.: All right, then, tell me how a censor gets started.

A.: At first everyone goes through a rigorous training period, and is thoroughly informed as to what information he is not to pass on to others. This pertains to our contemporary history in the broadest sense of the term, and to a few other things they won't let you print anyway, and which I would find it awkward and disloyal to talk about. The course lasts about two weeks, and is tailored to individual needs. There are practical exercises— you get a text and have to compare your work with the cuts made by an experienced censor.

Q.: And they hire those who cut the most?

A.: Those who cut best. I did my training on *Forum,** and at first I cut like crazy. Then the chief said, "You're way off. This here is *Forum*. The texts have already been approved—they can go." I was shocked. In general, you're not expected to cut much. And in fact there was a good deal of admiration for intelligent journalists who kept writing as they pleased and tried to outsmart us.

Q.: Am I to understand that you liked those people you censored most?

A.: Why, of course, they're the best of the lot. And after all, it was the good things we crossed out, not the bad. Kisielewski, for instance, would always append a little note: "How about letting it go through this time, darling?"† No, we bore them no malice. What gave us a lot of satisfaction was drafting our replies, all the more so since we, after all, always had the last word. But there was never any acrimony.

Q.: And wasn't the rank-and-file censor ever tempted to let something go through?

A.: No, that would have been a professional blunder. A good rank-and-file censor is one who crosses out what's required and who understands what he reads.

*A weekly consisting of translations from foreign newspapers and periodicals.

†Stefan Kisielewski, a distinguished Polish writer, journalist, and music critic. See pages 272–84.

Q.: From our point of view, a good censor is one who doesn't have the foggiest notion what he reads.

A.: Well, that's the opposite approach. In my time, at least, the operational principle was that if the censor didn't understand what he was reading, the article could go without any cuts, because the reader wouldn't understand either. We consider ourselves more intelligent than the average reader.

Q.: There's the rub.

A.: Fools have no place in censorship. If your article was confiscated and you said, "God, what nonsense!" you shouldn't have blamed the censor for it. Now, let me make an explanatory statement about censors. People think that censorship is all powerful; yet it is only an arm of the press department [of the Central Committee], and the harder the times, the less the censors have to say. It's a very fine sieve. An article goes first to the fellow on day duty, then to the department head, and if there's need for more scrutiny, it may go all the way to the chief; sometimes—in particularly tricky cases—even higher, including individual [high-ranking] comrades. So if there was trouble, the chief would have to pay for it, not your rank-and-file censor.

Q.: Well, in that case, why not let things through?

A.: You seem to forget that the firm isn't there to let things through, but to keep things from getting through. Once you're on the job, behave correctly—or, as you'd put it, incorrectly, right? The choice is clear: either you work here, or you don't. If the rank-and-file censor would let something slip through, on the principle of "what the hell, let the people find out," he'd be doing a poor job and he'd be letting down his firm into the bargain. The fact of the matter is that those who work for the firm are concerned about good personal relations, and that the firm in general is characterized by a remarkable sense of *noblesse oblige;* for that is what the work requires. Even if the censor is tempted to close his eyes to something, he's not likely to do it, lest the public conclude that the firm as a whole is shot through with such tendencies.

Q.: Human ones.

A.: These tendencies are more likely to exist on the higher rungs of the ladder. Quite frequently the higher you go, the more liberal it gets. A censor sometimes crosses out something, only to have it restored by the chief. My own chief, for instance, was very favorably disposed toward the outspoken papers, and he'd save as much text as he could. He always spoke highly about *Więź,** saying that it would be a great pity if it got into trouble—for there were those eager to take a crack at it—since no journal writes better about our country's history than *Więź.*

Q.: Tell me, does a censor derive any satisfaction from his work?

A.: I was pleased when I prepared my report, and when my chief complimented me, saying it was good and required no changes. But that's a technical kind of satisfaction. Personally, I think that real satisfaction comes to those who are passionate about their work. It's easier for a journalist to

*A liberal lay Catholic monthly, whose editor-in-chief, Tadeusz Mazowiecki, became editor of *Tygodnik Solidarność* in April 1981. He was arrested and interned on December 13, 1981.

get pleasure than for a censor. A journalist would write something, and though we'd blue-pencil it, he'd still feel that it had been worth his effort. The censor would also think, Right, the guy goes down to defeat with his honor intact. But on the whole, the censor derives his satisfaction merely from doing his job well.

Q.: After crossing something out?

A.: My dear young lady, that's what he's there for! He works for a firm that censors. What do you expect him to do—write instead of censor?

Q.: But frequently the censor would also add something on his own.

A.: Oh, well, petty cosmetics. Phrases like "here and there" or "sometimes." As you know, the censor has no personal contact with the writer. I remember only one case, pertaining to Watergate, when there was so much to be changed that the writer had to come to our office to work on the article jointly with the censor. In general, the attitude toward the more distinguished citizens of our country was—how shall I put it?—more elegant.

Q.: Has there ever been a case of a censor behaving disloyally to his firm?

A.: In my opinion, that fellow from Kraków who went to Sweden with all the censorship materials. Because I am not persuaded about his motives. Later on, he said that the scales fell off his eyes, and that he merely waited for a chance to tell it all to the public. But I have a notion that he simply used the opportunity to make some money while creating a bit of trouble for the firm.

Q.: A bit?

A.: This is a sturdy institution, miss, and I don't recall more than a ripple of laughter when the materials were published. Perhaps at the top there was pencils, thought the whole incident amusing, that's all. Still, I must admit he did bring out a handful. In the old days, in the 1960s, he'd have had a harder time taking anything out. Censorship was much less bureaucratized. A lot of things were settled by word of mouth, by a simple telephone call, so there were fewer records, less evidence.

Q.: Surely you can't tell me that during the 1970s there were no word-of-mouth instructions?

A.: In my time, if a minister wanted to get something settled, he had to go through the chairman of the press department. Then we'd get a memorandum. The memo would go to the appropriate unit with a number and date, so that it could be located and canceled if necessary. If there were some oral instructions, I knew nothing about them. Various ministries, such as the Ministry of Foreign Affairs, issued instructions on special occasions. For example, Amin built a monument to Hitler, and nothing could be said about it, because we had good relations with Amin.

The censor's basic text is a thick volume containing general formulations about the principles of censorship. Each week the "pressmen" would have a conference at which instructions for the forthcoming week were received and gone over. For instance, if a student festival was approaching, or when [Wajda's] film *Man of Marble* was about to be shown. And so the word was out: Attention, look out, consult, verify, don't trust yourself too much, act collectively! For you see, the censor has his own intuition, but it's damned individualized. A kind of inner voice tells you—hey, there's something fishy here, I'd better see the chief about it. Then the chief says, "Yes, indeed, there is," or, "Don't worry, let it go."

Q.: Did you ever come across a text so excruciatingly positive that you couldn't stand it and simply threw it out?

A.: If a journalist wrote it in good faith, that is to say, out of stupidity—and there are lots of stupid journalists around—then the censors didn't feel obliged to teach him wisdom. But if he wrote it in order to ridicule, or to make himself look good, then he'd get rapped over the knuckles. We could always tell what's what.

Q.: Did you, or any of your colleagues, ever stop to consider the premises of any instruction or directive?

A.: I'd take things for granted, for any consideration is pointless. What's so mysterious about banning information on poisonous substances in building materials in Tomaszów Mazowiecki—a town so wretched it's astonishing anyone still lives there? Do you expect me to damn censorship on the one hand, and work for it on the other? One simply lets it pass. You can't think too much about it, for it interferes with work. A newspaperman whose heart isn't in it isn't worth much. A censor, however, risks a trip to the insane asylum.

Q.: Has that ever happened?

A.: Perhaps someone or other had a nervous breakdown, but I'm not aware of it. I didn't relish my work, but neither did it turn me off.

Q.: Didn't you ever feel you'd like to quit?

A.: Never. What kept me going was the fact that I wasn't crazy about those times we were living through, anyway. In my opinion, there's something Kafkaesque about a censor, something unreal.

Q.: Nothing unreal about the results of his work.

A.: Try as you may, my dear lady, you'll not get me to confess to any pangs of conscience, moral scruples, or catharsis. Essentially I am a decent man who was doing something subjectively and objectively ugly.

Q.: Something on the order of schizophrenia, in other words.

A.: Do I look like a schizophrenic? I treated censorship as yet another episode in my life, and not the most shattering one, either. I never lost any sleep over it.

Q.: Nevertheless, it seems to me that someone working as a censor must rationalize what he is doing. For instance, you told me that your activity on the "creative," as you put it, rather than "preventive" side provided the authorities with solid information about the situation in the country.

A.: You won't get me to say it. I never thought that by working as a censor I served a noble cause. That just wasn't so.

Q.: So how was it?

A.: I had a yen for information. And the more I worked, the more banned information came to my desk—not because there was suddenly an escalation of instructions, but because the journalists were getting more combative.

Consequently, we had to come to grips with the essential operating principle of censorship—which is that the rulers should rule, while the nation should remain convinced that everything is for the best. More and more texts were expunged in their entirety, thus providing me with marvelous reading material.

Q.: Marvelous? Was your attitude really so dispassionate?

A.: I suppose I became a bit cynical. I even had on my desk a text written by a girl from my old sociology department. She worked hard on it, I worked hard, and in the end the whole thing had to be thrown out. It was an article on the language of official party documents—truly an excellent piece of work. Personally, I was particularly distressed by the things you people wrote about Kraków; you kept writing, and we kept cutting—for, after all, the initiative didn't come from us.*

Q.: So you were shocked most by the articles on Kraków?

A.: I like that city. It wasn't pleasant for me to cross out articles about old women dying of hunger; my own mother lives on a retirement pension.

Q.: Here we are, using mostly the past tense in our conversation, yet censorship is still in existence and is still functioning.

A.: But it's more liberal, you'll have to admit. Apparently the fellows are working differently these days. Nonetheless, I am absolutely convinced that censorship is indispensable. The model may change, things may become more liberal still, but the institution as such is remarkably resilient.

Q.: Were the recent events a shock to the censors?

A.: I visited them last September [1980] and asked whether they felt the breath of history. They said, "Of course we feel it—in the street, in the newspapers, but not in the firm." It wasn't shaking in its foundations. What shook up the censorship was the year 1956, when there was actual talk among the censors themselves about dissolving the institution; also in 1968, when many Jews left the censorship. I don't know what the impact was of December 1970. As for 1976, nothing special happened, and I don't remember any state of alert. The press struck a chord of unanimity, condemned the troublemakers, meetings were held. You did the job for us, although we were vigilant and ready.

Q.: How did the censors react to the emergence of an unofficial press?

A.: In no way whatever. It wasn't a subject for discussion.

Q.: All right, now tell me, please, why did you actually leave the censorship?

A.: Certainly not because the scales suddenly fell from my eyes—as that fellow from Kraków would have it. It wasn't that I knew nothing at first and then was shocked to learn the truth. Perhaps I might have been shocked at the very beginning; as I told you before, I simply became bored.

Q.: Have you found more interesting work?

---

* In the late 1970s, many uncensored publications featured articles about the growing decline of Kraków—Poland's ancient capital and best-preserved medieval city; not only did the authorities allow historic buildings to fall into decay, but they ignored the gradual deterioration of the inhabitants' living standards, the lack of medical facilities, and known cases of starvation.

A.: I came to the conclusion that I wouldn't be able to make a go of it in journalism, so I tried a number of other things, and finally went to the United States for a few months.

Q.: Did you admit, while you were there, that you had worked as a censor?

A.: No, but not because I was ashamed of it, but simply because my English wasn't up to snuff, and I would have had to go into elaborate explanations about who I was and why I had worked where I did. I came back in September and again I am in limbo. I have even heard the following—I quote: "My dear sir, you may be a decent person, your references are pretty good, but under the circumstances it would be careless of us to offer you a job. Mind you, we have nothing against you personally, but if your co-workers learned the truth, you'd be in trouble and so would we." I had to agree that made sense. And I told this chum of mine, who wants to quit—and for a reason that will, no doubt, delight you: "Stay put, unless you want to retool yourself completely." Another friend opened a vegetable store, and now he's in plastics. And doing very nicely, too.

Q.: And other censors, how are they making out?

A.: One is a director of a sanatorium, another joined a publishing house, some have gone into editing. As for me, I frankly don't know what to do with myself.

Q.: And your parents, how do they see your future?

A.: We haven't talked about it. But I bet they're pleased with my brother and me. My brother is into tourism.

Q.: And you?

A.: I decided to put my trust in friends. I'm getting married in three days, and we'll have 120 people at the wedding. It may not be much of a goal in life, but I haven't come up with anything better.

Q.: May I use your name in this interview?

A.: Well, it wouldn't bother me too much, you could even print my name in boldface and publish a large picture of me on the front page. But the wife asked me to be discreet, and I don't want to cause her any grief. Anyway, don't you think it would be neater to use my number? In the firm, you see, they don't use names—only numbers.

Q.: Why did you actually agree to be interviewed?

A.: I like to oblige. Besides, I want people to know how the censorship functioned, or more accurately, how I thought it functioned. A lot of myths have grown up around it—that it's omnipotent, superpowerful, diabolical.

Q.: The question is: will they now learn the truth? What do you think, as a professional?

A.: I talked it over with my chum, who's still working as a censor. He had a good laugh. Said if it were up to him, he'd let the whole thing go through.

Q.: But what would he delete?

A.: Miss, this interview just doesn't lend itself to deletions. You can only throw out the whole thing, lock, stock, and barrel.

November 1980
K-62 was interviewed by
Barbara N. Łopieńska

From *Tygodnik Solidarność,*
no. 6, May 8, 1981

Translated by Abraham Brumberg

Geopolitics: Poland and the USSR

While the efforts of most Polish dissidents in the 1970s were aimed at achieving greater freedom, democracy, and pluralism, the question of Poland's sovereignty as a state and its relationship with the USSR were never far from the surface, and after August 1980 these became two of the most contentious issues of the day. To some (few) political oppositionists, the struggle for Polish independence was as important as—if not more important than—the struggle for internal democracy. To most Poles, however, Poland's alliance with the USSR, its membership in the Warsaw Pact, and the resulting limitations on its sovereignty were a given, dictated by geopolitical considerations.

Yet how to reconcile the aspirations for true independence with the political and military interests of Poland's powerful neighbor? Was it at all conceivable for two countries with so long a history of animosity ever to achieve greater understanding, if not amity? Could the Soviet Union be expected to tolerate the democratization of Poland, and if so, to what extent? Assuming that democratization and a redefinition of the Soviet-Polish alliance would take place, what would be its impact on the ruling party? These are some of the questions to which the following item addresses itself. It appeared in 1980 in *Res Publica,* an uncensored publication.

REALPOLITIK—
THE POLITICS OF REALITIES

J. T.

In Poland all political thought and action must begin with the problem of Russia.
For us that problem has three dimensions.

The first dimension has a strictly political character and concerns the present
state of relations between the Soviet Union and Poland, and may be formulated
in two fundamental questions: 1. How will the Soviet Union react to deeper
changes in our internal situation? 2. Is there any possibility of influencing Big
Brother's attitudes and decisions?

The second dimension of the Russian problem has a historical character and
relates to the question of the possibility and directions of any conceivable internal
evolution with the USSR and the consequences of that evolution for us.

Finally, the third dimension—let's call it the future dimension—bears on
Polish-Russian relations in the world order that could arise, in place of what has
hitherto existed, as the result of profound structural and historical changes.

In this article I will be exclusively concerned with the first issue.

I.

Today Poland faces the real possibility of deeper internal changes. These
changes can be achieved by evolution or by violent upheavals. But in both cases,
quite apart from the form the process of change will take, the question of Soviet
intervention remains a recurrent question.

I think that this question needs to be approached with maximal rationality, for
it is here especially that we lack a clear and lucid evaluation of the situation. For
some, the "certainty" of intervention has become part of the ideology of fear,
which simplifies things greatly but settles very little. They point out the enormity
of the risk entailed by every attempt to force through deeper internal changes.
And there is much in what they say. What they forget is that risk is an integral
part of life, in politics and in history. Nations, like people, take risks and they
have to do so. It is only harmful when they do it blindly and without calculating
the odds.

Others, especially the young, seem on the whole not really to take the possibility of intervention into account. Some people actually believe that a sudden national effort could give Poland her complete sovereignty. Fascinated by the tradition of independence, they forget that independence did not so much bring about inner growth as world war. Others raise the idea of the moral significance of uprisings for maintaining national identity, in turn forgetting that uprisings possess such significance not because they were empty gestures but because independence was always their calculated goal. However mistaken those calculations were, however insane the hopes, it was those very hopes that inspired the command to rise up in arms. Without that glimmer of a chance for success—though it existed only in their imagination—the uprisings would have been entirely acts of absurd stupidity.

If it is to exist and develop, the nation must know how to dream, desire, struggle, but also how to plan ahead. It must be capable of analyzing situations soberly.

Let us begin our considerations with the obvious statement that intervention is a tried and acknowledged instrument of Soviet policy in regard to the countries of the ["socialist"] bloc. This is "acknowledged" in some sense by the West. For the Soviet Union the use of intervention carries no threat of any external armed conflict nor that of a continuing deterioration of relations with the West. The bases of détente between the USSR and the United States were laid down in 1969, one year after the intervention in Czechoslovakia. By so acting, the West demonstrated conclusively that its own relations with the Soviet Union do not depend on the means by which Moscow regulates things within its own sphere of influence.

This does not mean that interventions have no international consequences. On the one hand, interventions have a stabilizing influence on relations within the Soviet bloc. On the other hand, outside its borders, interventions may precipitate the disintegration of the Communist movement and the decline of its dependence on Moscow, as well as the erosion of that moral-ideological support on which, until quite recently, the USSR could count from intellectual circles and those of the intelligentsia of the left. All told, then, interventions play an essential role in the formation of a negative image of the Soviet Union in the public consciousness in the West.

The Soviet leaders seem to have a clear understanding of this way of reckoning gains and losses, and they do not resort to political interventions with undue haste.

Let us first ask under what conditions in the past the Soviet Union did intervene.

The Hungarian intervention in 1956 was undertaken in a situation in which (1) the process of destalinization in the USSR had only just begun, and it was hard to exclude the possiblity of it suddenly assuming a spontaneous character; (2) it could have been assumed that the October movement in Poland would not be confined to the stage achieved but would show tendencies to further development while the ability of the new team to bring things under control seemed problematic; (3) the Hungarians found themselves on a road that led directly to a complete break with the Soviet bloc.

Under those conditions the decision to intervene was the only decision politically possible if the desire was to maintain the integrity of the bloc and avoid an uncontrolled chain reaction within the USSR.

The intervention in Czechoslovakia in 1968 could at first glance seem to be devoid of such deeper strategic dimensions. The Czechoslovak leaders were in control of the situation and had still not damaged the very basis of the party's monopoly on power. The example of the Polish October, however, indicated that if the monopoly on power remains untouched, the changes are apt to be of a transitory and illusory nature and that, after a while, virtually everything will return to normal.

Then why the intervention?

The year 1968 may have been a disquieting one for the USSR. Albania had been outside the Soviet bloc for a few years. Under Ceausescu's leadership Rumania had, since 1964, been displaying a worrisomely high degree of state and party independence. Finally, during the March 1968 events in Poland, a greatly weakened Gomułka took a defensive position against the aggressive Partisans group. The nationalistic ideology of that group could have been only a smoke screen, a purely tactical move. But was that really the case? Could not a new Ceausescu have emerged from the ranks? In no case could that have been risked.

The intervention in Czechoslovakia was thus not an operation with local significance but had wider strategic implications. It eliminated the worrisome "renewal movement," definitely isolated rebellious Albania, put a ceiling on Rumania's separatist impulses, and made it impossible for the nationalistic orientation to take over in Poland. After August 1968, the Partisans ceased to count as a real force in the stuggle for power.

Historical analysis thus indicates that the USSR uses the weapon of intervention sparingly and, it seems, after having made fundamental political calculations. This is attested to by the fact that no attempt was made to intervene in Albania or Rumania, although both those countries had displayed, at the very least, a disturbing degree of insubordination. There were also no signs indicating an inclination to intervene in Poland in 1970 and 1976.

What were the decisive deterrents to intervention [on these two occasions]?

First, intervention is not as a rule an act directed at one country only; it has international ramifications, too. Presumably it is preceded by a serious weighing of losses and gains relative to the entire system of relations within the bloc as well as in the European and world arenas.

Second, the Soviet leaders seem not to exhibit any excessive nervousness when no structural changes are occurring, but solely a change of direction in policy, even of a markedly anti-Soviet nature. I think that the reasons for such behavior are twofold. The first is the role of symbolism in the Soviet mind, the emphasis on form. As long as it is a socialist country, then, in spite of all the "errors" and "deviations," it is still a member of the community; the prodigal son does not cease to belong to the family. The second reason is the purely pragmatic calculation that the prodigal son can return to the bosom of the family, since, as long as he is socialist, his complete assimilation by any other system is impossible. The zigs and zags of Soviet-Yugoslav relations, or the most recent evolution of Albania, seems to indicate that these calculations are not useless. A socialist country never fully and completely falls out of the Soviet orbit—such seems to be the premise behind the pragmatism of Soviet policy. Perhaps only the further development of the Sino-Soviet conflict will bring a radical change of perception here.

What conclusions for the Polish situation flow from these reflections?

Let us begin with the truism about Poland's key significance for the USSR. Although neither the Hungarians nor the Czechoslovak interventions were aimed directly against Poland, Poland, in both cases, was part of the framework of the decision and one of its indirect targets.

Poland occupies too crucial a position in the European system of relations for the USSR to be able to renounce effective control over it. Consider the following: against no other country but Poland has Russian expansionism been so persistent, and over no other country has it attempted to exercise control so long and so consistently as over Poland. Whether we like it or not, control over Poland is central to the Russian sense of its status as a world power.

Second, for the USSR, control of Poland is of fundamental strategic importance. Poland is the point of departure on the route to Europe. If, in one form or another, the specter, not so much of "Finlandization," but of the "Austriazation" of Germany is kept alive, then one condition for realizing it is for Moscow to retain effective control of Poland, strategically and politically. In a broader context, then, control of this sort is a key condition for an effective Soviet policy toward Europe.

Third—and finally—we must take into account the size of our country, its traditional ideological and cultural influence on Russia, and its direct proximity to it: deeper structural changes in Poland could seriously complicate the USSR's own internal situation.

All these considerations point to the conclusion that Poland is the last country in the Soviet bloc that would cause Moscow to hesitate about undertaking an intervention if it ever concludes that its vital interests are truly at stake.

Such a conclusion would also have its costs: an intervention in Poland is likely to assume a violent character, perhaps an extremely violent one, evoking the nightmare of war in Europe. Social shocks, incomparably larger than those following the previous interventions, could be expected. The result would be a powerful increase in the power and influence of the enemies of détente and of cooperation with the USSR, the formation of a patently negative image of the USSR in the West, and, finally, a drastic shift by Western Communist parties into active anti-Soviet positions as a condition of their continued political existence. The internal consequences would be equally if not more threatening: the complete and long-lasting collapse of the Polish economy (especially dangerous in the context of the bloc's critical economic situation), as well as a weakening of the Western flank in case of a potential conflict with China. A Poland ruled exclusively by Communists or co-ruled with other groups ensures the Soviet Union the necessary minimum of stability in that part of Europe. A Poland pacified by intervention only assures the growth of restlessness, enmity, and a desire for vengeance.

There is yet another position on the cost side that might perhaps be ignored (alas!) by the Soviet general staff: intervention can open the ultimate historical abyss between the Polish and Russian nations. And nations endure longer than governments or empires.

I do not doubt that all these costs will, at the appropriate moment, be calculated with all the careful deliberation that seems to characterize Soviet foreign policy.

2.

It is precisely the high costs of intervening in Poland that incline one to be cautiously hopeful that the Soviet leaders will not undertake such a decision hastily. Perhaps they will even agree to accept the internal changes in Poland within limits. Which leads us to the absolutely paramount problem of what those limits are.

Taking into account the categories of Soviet political thinking as they have been until the present, one can assume that all the internal changes in Poland can be described either as the "Polish road," a "deviation," or a "counterrevolution." The first signifies conditional approval; the second, a warning or condemnation but without resorting to the ultimate forms of pressure; the third, intervention.

What can we do to avoid that last possibility?

It seems there must be at least two fundamental conditions. Undoubtedly, it is the Soviet Union's vital state interests—political, military, and economic—that determine the ultimate and impassable border of Soviet concessions. We cannot define precisely either the exact nature or the range of those interests, although we are well aware of their existence and weight.

The first fundamental condition that can influence the option not to intervene is the existence in Poland of sufficiently broad and representative forces genuinely respecting vital Soviet interests in Poland. This would provide a guarantee or at least create a distinct possibility that the development of events in Poland would not move toward a complete break with the USSR but would be kept at a certain acceptable level.

To be brutally direct, all those who consider themselves part of the Polish opposition, if they desire to pursue a real policy in realistic conditions, must be ready to display such readiness.

I want to be clearly understood; I am not calling for political camouflage, for a mere declaration of intent to suit the circumstances. I simply think that a real policy can be pursued only when one is thinking realistically. Poland was, is, and will be Russia's neighbor. Any realistic political concept must take that obvious fact as its point of departure. Anyone utterly blinded to that simple truth by resentment or the memory of tragic experiences would be better off pursuing political activity in New Zealand or Peru.

Thus, the necessity [for co-existing with the USSR] exists—but there is more than that. I personally think that it is arrant political naiveté to be certain that Poland can only lose in an alliance with the USSR. Here I would like to touch on at least two points.

We do not know what is the actual nature of our economic relations with the

USSR. The aura of secrecy favors the conjecture that Poland is an exploited country. Perhaps. However, it seems possible—and this would be profitable for both countries—that our mutual relations could be so arranged that both the USSR and the Soviet market would become a powerful source of an economic boom. Poland's economy could be complementary to the Soviet economy. That is at least a possibility. However, it is highly probable that the Polish economy will be neither complementary to nor competitive with the countries of the West. Today we are not yet thinking in those categories. Tomorrow perhaps we will have to.

The second point concerns culture. Our presence in the Soviet cultural market is beyond any comparison with the influence of Polish culture in any other part of the world. Perhaps we are gladdened by the success of the Polish theater in Paris or of a Polish book in the United States, but these are events of utterly marginal significance for the cultural lives of those countries. In the USSR, on the other hand, the presence of Polish culture carries real weight. And even if that is only a temporary phenomenon—sooner or later that large country will begin to draw directly from the main sources of world culture—it is nonetheless bound to leave an enduring mark on the Soviet public. Those whom you view as your own cultural predecessors elicit a different sort of respect from those whom you view solely as cultural petitioners and traveling salesmen insistently hyping their own handmade wares. There is no question here of curing any political complexes, but it is a simple fact that cultural and political questions are more closely connected than is generally thought. Drawing up a balance sheet of the influences of one's own culture is part of political praxis.

In sum, I do not think that Polish-Soviet relations ought to be viewed exclusively in the context of geopolitical necessity. Does the relationship contain a chance of a genuine realization of our nation's current and historical interests? Here is the question I consider to be of fundamental importance for contemporary Polish political thought. To think this problem through will be a great intellectual task for independent minds. The task is to form a realistic contemporary Polish political doctrine, not one invented and pasted together from colorful swatches of the past.

3.

Let us now move on to the second condition.

In the independent press, the term "Finlandization" is often used to define the model postulated for Polish-Soviet relations. Taking the term literally, it means: (1) a state of Polish dependence on the USSR in the sphere of international relations as well as on the military level; (2) basing mutual economic policy on a purely "commercial" basis; (3) the independence of Poland in forming its own internal system up to and including a multiparty model of democracy.

The first point does not cause the Soviet leaders to have any reservations. I think that even the second point would be acceptable to them; the possible losses resulting from Poland's economic independence would no doubt be offset by the more dynamic development of our reformed economy and the chance of its achieving—within the limits of possibility—those tasks to which the Russians so warmly summon the capitalists of the West, just as Finland does now on a smaller scale, and not so badly, either.

However, it is the third point that is less clear.

It is safe to assume that an attempt to bring about any form of a multiparty democracy would, at the present time, appear to Soviet eyes as (1) a direct threat to the situation within the bloc; and (2) an inadmissible historical regression, a reversal of the evolutionary trend that has the stamp of Lenin's authority and that of sixty years of practice in the Soviet system. In a word, it would be considered a "counterrevolution."

The probability of such a Soviet reaction puts us in an exceptionally difficult situation; for on the one hand, the inability of the PZPR to cope with the country's problems becomes increasingly obvious and, on the other, to retain the principle of one-party rule in any shape or form seems to be a condition imposed by external necessity. A perfect paradox.

This is not the place for an analysis of the ways out; in general, let us say only that the solution may lie in the kind of *modus vivendi* that is established between authentic social forces and the party, a *modus vivendi* making possible real participation by those social forces in the solving of the country's problems without encroaching on the formal bases of the existing system's structure.

This does not at all mean any idyllic "treuga dei" [armistice] but, rather, a state of constant pressure and "mutual enforcement" between society and the party. A state of struggle, but not one of war. Struggle, but also cooperation, working together. A model for similar situations began to emerge during Pope John Paul II's visit to Poland, when a measure of real cooperation between the Church and the state came about.

I think that the Soviet leaders' ability to accept the changes that are headed in that direction and that are brought about in that way will be greater the better the first condition is fulfilled—a far-reaching readiness on the part of our society for real cooperation with the USSR.

Having, then, discussed the limitations, let us now turn to the problem of what constitutes a margin of safety.

4.

Once again I would like it to be clearly understood that I am not propagating any "policy of compromise" with the USSR but only a policy of realities. Here is my understanding of that policy:

(1) To broaden the zone of internal independence is a necessity for us today. The alternative can only be a gradual slide into chaos or a dramatic social shock.

(2) If the USSR understands that necessity and will accept the genuine broadening of freedom in Poland's social, cultural, religious, and economic life, an organized Polish society should display an authentic readiness to respect fundamental Soviet state interests in Poland and the actual limits, *hic et nunc*, of its state sovereignty as the present historical situation demands.

(3) A stable and calm Poland is in the USSR's interest, a Poland with broader internal independence than has hitherto existed is in our interest, and our com-

mon interest is a Poland economically strong, and, in part, complementary to the Soviet economy. That is the obvious basis for a mutual "unspoken accord" and a policy of realities.

That is not a policy that can be conducted in the privacy of cabinets. Stefan Kisielewski's assertion ("Have Geopolitics Lost Their Meaning?" *Res Publica,* no. 1) that the opposition should try to reach the Russians directly seems devoid of any realism to me. There will be no communication. Today, and for a long time to come, that sort of situation is simply not psychologically possible. Moreover, I do not think that such "diplomatic" attempts at defining relations with the USSR would be necessary or even to the point. Talks are made of words, and the wind bears them away easily. Treaties are written on paper, but paper is a highly inflammable material. What matters is not mutual declarations but facts and actions. Not in direct contacts with Russians but by anticipating and shaping their reactions—that and the movement for change in Poland provides the only real possibility of political "dialogue" with the Russians at the present time.

If it is to be a successful dialogue, its opening positions must be clearly defined. Our number one national obligation is the preservation of our national identity. We cannot withdraw from the level of spiritual and social independence we have already achieved. And we cannot cease to develop it further. The only thing we can do is to proceed carefully. For its part, the USSR can accept or reject this state of affairs. The result of rejecting it would be intervention, with all its consequences. The result of accepting it would mean a strengthening of the influence and significance of those groups and individuals in Poland who believe that "one can live" with the Soviet Union and, in the longer run, of the development of genuine cooperation between our peoples.

Today a great historical game is again being played between Poland and Russia. We have only one advantage in that game—the high cost that the Russians would have to pay for an intervention. And we have only one chance—if we are careful and skillful in determining the limits to which we can go. That limit is not static; it is shaped by the international situation, by the bloc's economic state, and finally by the political climate on both sides, which can worsen and stir up feelings but can also, with labor and patience, allay resentments and dispel suspicions. It depends, at least in part, on ourselves, on the wisdom of our collective behavior.

5.

I consider this the only path for us—caution, but also dignity and strength. What will we do if that path is blocked to us?

That is a tragic question. A question for which we have no answer. Apart from that one path, there is also perhaps faith in the durability of the nation for which more than one generation has perished.

From *Res Publica* (Warsaw), no. 7, 1980

Translated by Richard Lourie

A Voice in the Wilderness: Stefan Kisielewski

It is difficult to imagine the history of Polish journalism under Communist rule without Stefan Kisielewski. Essayist, novelist, music critic, composer, and one-time deputy of the Sejm (Parliament), Kisielewski, who embarked upon his multifaceted career in the 1930s has since World War II become a permanent fixture of the Polish political landscape. Associated with the liberal Catholic group *Znak,* and a regular contributor to the distinguished weekly *Tygodnik Powszechny,* he has also written extensively for other publications both in his country and abroad—sometimes under a nom de plume, often without any disguise whatsoever. Kisielewski is above all master of that venerable genre of European journalism, the *feuilleton*—a genre that has allowed him to roam over a seemingly inexhaustible range of subjects, from politics, economics, and international relations to philosophy, literature, theater, and the arts. His eye is that of a satirist, forever alert to the absurdities, oddities, and hypocrisies around him. Irrepressibly witty and (like all satirical writers) given to deliberate flamboyance, he has made himself thoroughly unpopular with the authorities and has waged more battles with the censors than probably any other contemporary Polish writer. Yet so immense is his stature that until December 1981 he had been allowed to publish, occasionally to travel abroad, and—despite the petty official harassments—to remain utterly true to himself.

The three *feuilletons* that follow were all taken from the émigré Polish monthly *Kultura* (Paris), where for many years Kisielewski's essays had appeared in a regular column entitled "A Voice in the Wilderness" and signed "Kisiel"—a distinctively sour (and eminently tasty) Polish fruit dish.

WARSAW'S FALL PASTIMES

It is rainy and cold in the capital; the evenings are dark, recalling blackouts just before the war. The lights are off because of the energy crisis; the Katowice mill is sucking up all the country's electricity. On television there are predictions of partial blackouts even in factories (!)—someone has clearly made an error in figuring the "energy balance." There are lines in front of the stores, the buses are packed, legions of obvious drunks stagger down the streets. Yet at the same time there are more and more private automobiles, and the stores are full of the most expensive goods. I have in mind, of course, the hard-currency stores and the "high priced" stores, those catering to Warsaw's upper crust, the elite, the locals with hard currency at their disposal, the operators, and the higher function-aries with "pull." The worst thing is to work normally—it doesn't pay. Warsaw and Warszawka* are pulsating with lively consumer greed; there is money, even a lot of it, but things are worse as far as food is concerned: even in the most expensive hotels they just serve whatever's around. Socialism knows how to awaken mass appetites—that's its propaganda specialty; it's satisfying those needs that is the problem—but obviously, you can only do one thing at a time.

Besides, there are even problems with propaganda, because after ten o'clock in the morning, there is no way you can get hold of a copy of *Trybuna Ludu* or *Życie Warszawy*. Truly things are in a mess if even propaganda is in short supply. And if you want to deposit hard currency in the PKO† bank, you must also stand in two lines for an hour and a half, which is really the height of organized ineptitude, for, after all, hard currency is what the state needs most. People curse but they also laugh, saying there hasn't been a mess like this for years: just try going to the post office—in the end, even the Warsaw press had to start writing about how overworked the post office is. Obviously there are too

*The ironic diminutive for Warsaw's high society.

†PKO—Polska Kasa Opieki, a bank established in 1929 to facilitate transfer of funds from persons living abroad. In Communist Poland, the PKO has made it possible for many Poles to obtain hard currency, such as dollars, and there exchange it at a special—that is to say, a higher—rate.

many people in Poland, and they hinder the state in the performance of its important functions. Perhaps, as Brecht suggested, the nation should be disbanded?

An old monument to Paderewski has been placed on the grass in front of the Music School: the master, after years of exile and silence, is suddenly back in favor and has at once been promoted to the rank of great patriot and "activist" (his premiership is passed over in silence).* In general many old political figures were recalled on the sixtieth anniversary of the rebirth of Poland; even Piłsudski has been written up here and there. As everyone knows, when there is no bread you have to supply more circuses . . . of patriotism. But the visit of our cardinals to the Federal Republic [of Germany], hitherto almost ignored, was dismissed in a short, ridiculous note that contained more about the Polish officials attending court than about the Primate himself and the progress of his trip, which is of utmost importance to Poland (probably they were afraid of what our Neighbor [Russia] would think and didn't know what else to write). On the other hand, the papers are full of news about the visit here of the Minister of Foreign Affairs of the Republic of Benin, the only problem being that no one has any idea where that country is.

People use foul language and say terrible things but, in compensation, the press is euphoric, superlative, and full of the obligatory, daily photos of dignitaries on the front pages, so much so that you wonder when they actually work if they are constantly having their pictures taken. Yet if you read carefully, you can learn something. To be sure, not in the news from abroad, which is picked and chosen strictly with the policy and propaganda needs of Big Brother in mind. Still, in Poland every newspaper or periodical has the right from time to time (certain weeklies more often) to run a critical piece—obviously, not critical of the system as such but of errors in execution. It amounts to the same thing, because even those accounts are hair-raising. What they come down to is: (a) power engineering is flat on its back; (b) apartment construction is flat on its back; (c) railroad transportation is flat on its back; (d) river transportation is flat on its back; (e) communications—the postal and telephone systems—are flat on their backs; (f) cattle breeding and purchasing are flat on their backs; (g) airline passenger traffic is flat on its back; (h) boat transportation is flat on its back; (i) forestry is flat on its back; (j) paper production is flat on its back; (k) book production is flat on its back; (l) crop cultivation is flat on its back, etc., etc.

What, then, isn't flat on its back? Coal export and the Katowice mill (our *Wirtschaftswunder*, but who thought that up?†) And censorship. The production and per capita consumption of alcohol are also up, the latter barely mentioned in spite of the recently introduced antidrinking campaign. But how can the state combat drunkenness if it makes a living off it, efficiently and copiously draining excess zlotys from the market. That's a *contradictio in adiecto!*

There was also a good deal of merriment occasioned by the revelations about Egon Bahr's "project" to unite Germany at the price of its neutralization. *Trybuna Ludu* quietly condemned these rumors as "harmful" (to whom?), obvi-

---

*The famous pianist Ignacy Jan Paderewski was the first president of Poland after World War I.
†The Katowice Steel Mill was the largest steel factory built in Communist Poland.

ously without a word about the fact that everything had begun with the flight of the chief of Rumanian intelligence (only *Forum* reported that). Quietly, because nobody knew what the hell was going on. Probably someone on the editorial staff of *Trybuna Ludu* still remembered how, in the 1950s, the Stalinist thesis on the need to unify Germany changed into the thesis of the two German states from one day to the next. Perhaps it might happen the other way around—if the Krauts were Finlandized, people in Warsaw say, that might be better for us, too. We would cease being the transit route to the FRG; we might even be able to haggle with this wretched system.

At the same time I found in a priceless issue of *Le Monde* (9/13/78) a letter to the editor by a French journalist who writes that it is necessary to unite the two Germanies within the boundaries of the Weimar Republic: only then will we succeed in having a Europe from the Atlantic to the Urals. As usual, the poor Frenchman forgot about the existence of Poland: Poland was thus to be minus Wrocław, Szczecin, and Gdańsk; it would have a "corridor" but, to compensate, it would also not receive Wilno and Lwów, which those wise gentlemen, Roosevelt and Churchill, eagerly and without haggling gave to Russia as a present. Indeed, everyone who wants to do something in Europe usually begins with a partition of Poland, transporting Poles a few hundred kilometers left or right, certain that no progressive outcry will arise as it did, say, with the Palestinians; the Poles, clearly, never had a good press. I showed that letter to my fellow Warsovians. Damn it, they said, "if the Rooskies'd just support us until that Finlandization happens, then we'll do a little Finlandizing ourselves." But would they allow it? Maybe by now the old sclerotics are dying off and some young man with brains will take over in the Kremlin! Bah. Hopes, hopes . . . Well, but after all, there are the Chinese, and the Japanese aren't stupid, either.

Another special Warsaw pastime now is reading the press backwards, especially the articles by its foreign correspondents, such as Łodziński, Boniecka, Ramotowski, Kedaj, Broniarek, Kołodziejczyk, Hoffman (Rudolf), and a host of others. They write only and exclusively about unemployment in the West, or possibly about inflation and strikes. The latter three specialize in Scandinavian unemployment. They have already written 723 pieces about it, passing over everything else in those countries—e.g., the standard of living, apartment construction, health care, services, social services, communications, and so on. They simply ape Soviet propaganda, except that over there they write for customers who buy everything, never go abroad, and have no opportunity to make any comparisons while we . . . People troubled and enraged by daily shortages and hardships have to read nonsense about Swedish or Danish unemployment or about suppression of strikes in other countries. To read this sort of thing in a country where the right to strike does not exist and strikes end in bloodshed is an absurdity that screams to high heaven. The result is often bizarre, because people who read the papers backwards end up not believing there is any unemployment in the West, only to be subjected to unhappy surprises when they go there.

At the same time, unemployment in capitalist countries is a highly curious phenomenon, resulting as it does from the high development of technology and organization; physical labor is becoming superfluous, which contradicts Marx's theory about the leading historical role of the proletariat. In essence, the proletariat in the highly developed countries is disappearing and the problem of free time and unemployment will have to be dealt with in one way or another—none of which, of course, is discussed by the Kołodziejczyks and Broniareks, whose task it is to blah-blah-blah as much as possible about the horrors of life under capitalism. However, they could not be more willing to live there themselves, and to stay there as long as possible, and so they zealously parley the propaganda as dictated from above—there's the paradox. The point is that our propaganda chiefs issue such orders because they want to be left alone by Russia, but the "correspondents" dutifully execute them because they want to maintain their comfortable status as "locals with hard currency," while living pleasant and interesting lives abroad. Both sides are satisfied with the arrangement and are not the least concerned about the GREAT MUTE, the reading public, who have, after all, been educated and are hungry for knowledge but who are forced to read and to listen to everything backwards, an activity as stupefying as taking the propaganda straight.

And how long will the GREAT MUTE remain mute? Warsaw's underground rumors announce it won't be for long: the unofficial newspapers have given the first signal, and now, in turn, the peasants are revolting. Peasants are revolting in Grójec and, before that, in Lublin, which we learned not from our press but from radio station Warsaw IV—as Radio Free Europe is called here.* The power of the peasants is sufficient, so don't lose hope. God will bless and save our fatherland. So let's drink to the peasant—

And thus ends an autumn evening in Warsaw.

KISIEL
Warsaw,
end of September [1978]

From *Kultura*
(Paris), November 1978

Translated by Richard Lourie

*Warsaw has three radio stations—hence the reference to Radio Free Europe as "Warsaw IV."

BATTLE FOR A TIME
THAT WAS DEAD BUT IS NOW
RETURNING TO LIFE

I have heard it said that we have lived to see Orwell's prophecies come true, while failing to recognize their amazing accuracy. For example, the one concerning the Ministry of the Archives, whose function is to correct history, to remove old, inconvenient documents, and publish new versions of old writings. History, like almost everything else, is a political instrument, and politics is a means of maintaining power. Hence the most important tool for influencing society in a Communist country is censorship, since the authorities retain their power by misinforming the public; and so the censored version of history is at once constantly fashioning the minds subjected to it and disarming them.

We lived through all this in Poland and in a form condensed to improbable absurdity during the fortieth anniversary ceremonies commemorating September 1939. It was a highly peculiar September, though, leaving out one day, the seventeenth, and its consequences. Until recently television and film have made allusions to the Ribbentrop-Molotov Pact and the tragic odyssey of the Poles from the east, but now it has been most emphatically decided that the time has come for that to disappear entirely from the historical record. The September ceremonies were conducted with solemnity and with an eye for detail; every battle and skirmish with the Germans was discussed with precision and objectivity; the heroic Polish army and many of its commanders were praised; eyewitnesses to and participants in various battles appeared on television; historians swore that they would tell the whole truth and nothing but the truth; Professor Włodzimierz T. Kowalski, the leading selector of the newest histories of Poland, peered out at us from television screens looking gloomier than ever; and all of them to a man passed over in silence the date of September 17, 1939, as well as its ominous results for the entire Polish campaign and for Poland's military fortunes. Apparently it was decided that after forty years the time is ripe to erase the date from memory, although not long ago it still managed to appear here and there. Now the silence will be complete, since some people know nothing, others have died, and still others wish to hold their tongues and forget. A commendable ex-post-facto rectification of history's errors.

The question is, how did Orwell know that things would happen this way? Evidently the Marxism applied by the Russians (which he knew from Red Spain) contains a philosophical need to agree with history, which is to say that incorrect history must therefore be changed. This is how the correct version runs: the capitalist imperialists in the person of Hitler attacked Poland, and Poland was saved by the working-class socialist democrats (the Russians). The two years from August 23, 1939, to June 21, 1941, did not exist; there was no secret clause concerning the division of Poland along the Narwa, Vistula, and San rivers; September 17 and the battles and the internment of the Polish army never existed; Molotov's speech never occurred; the deportation of the officers and hundreds of thousands of civilians—and Katyń—never took place; there was no Soviet aid to Hitler for two years in the form of oil, grain, and friendship. Those two shameful years were a nuisance; they are no longer of any use to anyone, and a useless truth is no longer the truth!

In September 1979 I scrutinized our press with a detective's thoroughness and found only two tiny echoes of those long-gone events. *Polityka* discreetly quoted the (Soviet) journal *Krasnaia Zvezda,* which, refuting "imperialist falsifications," maintained that the pact with the Germans in 1939 was necessary to give Russia time to "strengthen and complete the defenses of the country" (about the conditions of the pact not a word). Also in the magazine *Radio i Telewizja,* dated September 18, the chronicle of Polish broadcasting reported: "Monitoring has picked up an official Polish government communiqué that 'in view of the USSR's taking a neutral position in the Polish-German war, the Polish army is not conducting military actions against Soviet troops.'" The falseness of this communiqué could not be more obvious, yet there is not a word to that effect in the accompanying note. . . . *Sapienti sat.*

For a long time none of us "old men" have protested (besides, there was no place one could) against the rewriting of history; for thirty-five years writers, journalists, and professors, not to mention politicians, have agreed to a PARTIAL TRUTH and to the convention of self-censorship; universal self-censorship is a sign of the psychological success of a censorship applied with persistence. It is said that at one point Khrushchev, himself a culprit in the mass deportations of Poles, wanted to explain the Katyń matter as yet another of Stalin's crimes but Gomułka would not agree to it. I understand Gomułka: how many other things would have to be set straight, how much trouble it would cause everyone, how many questions would arise (had they known or hadn't they?)! How many shocks would shake that psychological edifice of ours, so masterfully constructed by the censorship over the years! Silence is better, a conspiracy of silence. "We must forget about all that!" a Polish government minister once said to me at the première of the film *October Night*—he was thinking in terms of *raison d'état.* Forgetting seemed to be favored by the fact that the youth of school age is embarrassingly ignorant of most recent history—something our press has frequently and hypocritically deplored. Thus, no one will inquire about the past. "Where are the snows of yesteryear?"

And meantime, it was precisely the young who inquired! The illegal youth, the tiny elite, the little-known secret periodicals—but a flame lit by a single match may never go out and may at some point even turn into a large fire. There was a prelude to this a couple of months ago in the journal *Głos* in an article splendidly documented and written by a Mr. Jarzewski who charged the *sanacja* government* for having taken no position on the Red Army's invasion on September 17, an act that sowed enormous confusion among the troops and in the whole country, as well as in the world. Which is God's honest truth. I experienced the Russian invasion between Kowel and Włodzimierz while serving in the Ninth Infantry Regiment of the Zamość Legions. There was absolute confusion and disarray; only Colonel Czajkowski managed to reassemble his troops, assuring us that the war with the Germans was continuing and asking us not to prejudge "the nature of the Russian invasion." Thus leaving us a scrap of hope, he led his detachments west through Chełm and Hrubieszów, in the direction of the "front." It was only near Hrubieszów, constantly observed by Soviet airplanes and fired upon from the forests by Ukrainian peasants, that the regiment broke up and dispersed. Whereupon Colonel Czajkowski changed into civilian clothes and headed for Warsaw, thanks to which he is in Canada today and not in Kátyń.

Jarzewski's article caused an underground but passionate dispute. On September 17 there were demonstrations of young people in Warsaw, graffiti were scrawled on the Soviet Trade Mission, ROPCiO organized a demonstration in front of the monument to the Unknown Soldier, and KOR issued a proclamation on the necessity of branding and punishing *all* war crimes in the West and in the East. The authorities trembled at the wrath of their Ally and arrested many young people for the ritual forty-eight hours; one demonstrator was even sentenced to two months for "hooliganism." But an enduring document also emerged: the Independent Publishing House [NOWA] issued a collection of speeches by Molotov and Hitler, as well as Soviet military communiqués from September 1939.

Incredible reading, though none of it was any secret. We will skip the triumphal list of the Polish soldiers taken prisoner "in heroic liberation battles" and the arms captured; we will skip Molotov's joy that Poland, the "monstrous child" (*"urodlive dietishche"*) of the Versailles Treaty had ceased to exist. But when that same Molotov reprimands the Western social democrats for supporting their imperialist governments, which had declared a CRIMINAL ideological war against Hitler, while Hitlerlism is depicted as a healthy movement of the German people that had been unjustly treated at Versailles, a person starts pinching himself to make sure he isn't dreaming. It is perfectly clear that Molotov BELIEVES what he is saying, which means that the Marxist-Russian shaping and interpretation (censorship) of history not only warps the minds of those who read it but the minds of the warpers as well! What, one wonders, did Molotov think when Hitler struck at Russia? What was he thinking while negotiating with the British and Americans for aid? And what were *they* thinking? Nothing, probably—they were used to liars from the East.

The Russians consider the lie a normal political method. The noble Americans condemn the lie but often forget this in practice. The English neither censure lies nor praise them: they do what they have to but they don't forget anything. And have we not been conditioned by the lies, especially here in Poland? Someone

*The *sanacja* ("purification") government came into power following Piłsudski's coup of May 1926.

told me that had General Sikorski been an Englishman, he would have let the Katyń affair go right by him in 1943; would not have reacted, but would not have forgotten, either (which was Churchill's advice). Just the reverse occurred: we reacted, but today in Poland we are forgetting because of the silent accord of the "old men"—some because they want to forget, others because they must, still others because they do not know. It is clear why the Russians have still not expunged Molotov's September proclamation from their history; that's in keeping with their conception of politics. But we, what are we to do? Are the young people right or are the old men who prefer to forget? It has been said of Djilas that he went to extremes because he preferred truth to politics. *Politique d'abord.* "I lied to live." Can an entire nation lie? And ought it to, sometimes? And when exactly? They say that the English, although they remember everything, also pass over in silence or beautify certain portions of their history for pedagogical purposes. What is more important: life or truth, the present or history, *raison d'être* or *raison morale?* Who is to choose? And can the choice be made for us or must we all do it ourselves?

I know that the readers of *Kultura* will shudder at these questions. I shudder at them, too, but I live in Warsaw and I am, after all, friendly with the groups of young people hungry for history—I am disgusted by the old men. But these questions oppress me even though I do not expect any answers. Besides, who would furnish that answer, shoulder the responsibility?

KISIEL

Warsaw, September 1979

From *Kultura* (Paris),

November 1979

Translated by Richard Lourie

THE SCHOOL OF
MORONISM OR GTM

The reading of our press, an activity to which I devote myself with an absurd, masochistic thoroughness, fills me with rage. I am sometimes even ashamed that the ceremonial, perfectly empty blather of our ruling dignitaries does not provoke similar feelings and that instead I fly into a fury at the hired, will-less lap dogs of the press who simply follow orders. But what can you do? We do not choose our hatreds any more than our loves.

Besides, hatred is neither a constructive nor a commendable emotion, especially for a man rooted in his own country who, while engaged in fundamental criticism and opposition, would still wish to remain an organic part of that country, an appreciable component of it, even if the relation be that of the corn to the foot (for the time being, the heart is silent on the subject of corn removal). My hatred, however, has its basis and is not only a matter of nerves. It stems from the conviction that our statistics, ecology, planning—all amount to a gigantic SCHOOL OF MORONISM whose goal is to break people of the habit of thinking clearly and dialectically, so that they will not notice that the emperor has no clothes, that Polish Marxist socialism is meaningless. And what will happen to a nation when people lose the habit of thinking and reaching conclusions independently, and when public life becomes a complete lunatic asylum? What will happen then to the holy Polish nation so fondly cherished by the various uprooted and shipwrecked émigrés?

Censorship is the instrument of the school of moronism. It keeps careful watch to make sure people lose their memory, their ability to connect causes with effects, and that they examine everything separately, out of historical context, criticizing details, of course, but avoiding like the plague any generalizations or overall evaluations. I once wrote about a tribe of Africans that had not observed the connections between sexual intercourse and the birth of children. Now the press of the school of moronism wants to turn Poles into a similar tribe and—there's no denying it—they frequently succeed. Sad, gentlemen, but true.

For example, our press and television have succeeded in making a division in the public's consciousness between economic problems and political action (which is simply never mentioned). Yet the unity of those two sides of the question is the very heart of Marxist dialectics. Whoever does not understand the heart of the matter will not be able to come out against it; and if certain definitions and words are removed, the corresponding concepts will disappear in time—as, for instance, in regard to the authorities' responsibility to society. The elimination of words and concepts causes a change in thinking—precisely as described by Orwell.

Our home-grown Orwellism—that is, moronism—intrudes itself every day, through every crack in our souls, and thus it is no longer noticeable, stupefying us invisibly and painlessly like that medicine that purges you without interrupting your sleep. For example, an enormous self-congratulatory brouhaha is being raised about the "revitalization " of Kraków so as to divert attention from the fact that the old quarters of several dozen historical cities are rotting—this the result of thirty-five years of socialism, which made the state the owner of everything, blocked the possibility of repairs, both private and municipal, and in addition, in the course of the "ideological struggle," destroyed the priceless strata of individual construction-work craftsmen. And so what can one say? The most erudite and highly respected professors let themselves be duped, and they crowed with delight over the magnanimity of the government and the party that had graciously deigned to concern themselves with the "revitalization" of Kraków—that is, to put it in plain language, to retard the process of destruction for which they themselves are responsible and which, considering that a steelworks is located in Kraków, is bound to be a Sisyphyean labor. But the act of diverting attention from their own errors by making fools of the professorial elite was carried out to perfection. GTM—the Great Triumph of Moronism!

GTM is also achieving great success in the above-mentioned matter of the crafts. On April 11, a plenum of the Communist party was called, which was devoted to the mouthing of platitudes, absolutely devoid of content, on the theme—familiar even to rats and mice—of the need to develop the crafts. Yet it occurred to no one on this occasion that this was, after all, a session of the same party that for thirty-five years had been consistently uprooting those very crafts in Poland, calling a halt to this process only when its nonsensical character had become as obvious as an elephant in a zoo—for example, when there was a shortage of small parts for the huge machines whose design, estimated [altogether] in the millions of tons, was carried out with a triumphal hullabaloo, but which stand idle without spare parts. At that point, they hit on the idea of getting help from craftsmen—and guess what they found out? There weren't any! But what happened to them all? Who destroyed them? There were no culprits here, either.

A lack of memory, of linking effects with deeply rooted causes—this is the GTM over a (once) thinking society. Under Bierut, craftsmen and small manufacturers were persecuted as class enemies because there weren't any other class enemies to be found at that time in that war-ruined country, and, according to Marx, class enemies *had* to exist. Under Gomułka, a battle was again waged against excess profits and abuses. In the course of this struggle, the laws regulating the crafts were made so complex that they could be used against everyone. Finally, the few remaining craftsmen threw in the towel and vanished into the state enterprises. "Services" performed on the sly, clandestine acts, go on, of course, but that's all right—after all, we're no longer dealing with class enemies.

Such is the history and overall picture of this particular case, but GTM depends precisely on isolating every issue from its general and temporal context, which is the exact opposite of what dialectics prescribe. The economy is an especially dangerous sphere, because to understand it you must consider economic development no less than profits and losses. Here, too, in the central economic institutions, economists are retired and engineers taken on; engineers see the part, not the whole, and thus are more suitable from the point of view of GTM. Ignoring the whole picture has become a national psychosis, reinforced by censorship; not even reporters and otherwise eminent economic critics are spared. Thus, for example, Andrzej K. Wróblewski* has written a great deal on how our coal is exported and on the ruined northern port in Gdańsk, but he skips entirely the most interesting issues of all—namely: how much do we sell a ton of coal for and in what hard currencies? how much is sold? what are our own costs? what are the profits? do we pay fines and, if so, what sort? A reader in the days of GTM ought not to know about that. Even highly placed intellectuals do not know these things. For example, two leading cultural publicists debating publicly on the question of higher learning in Poland and abroad assert, among others, that the national per-capita income in Japan in 1960 was 510 dollars where it was 570 dollars in Poland. These people, who are never fully informed, do not realize the absurdity of comparing incommensurable statistics of this sort. In a Marxist country the national income is the value of all goods produced as measured by those goods sold or put into storage. In capitalist countries, on the other hand, besides real profit, the national income also includes all services that affect the standard of living. To compare one with the other is like comparing a horse with a rabbit, but how can uninformed people know this, people who have lost the habit (or who, rather, never acquired it) of looking at the whole picture and evaluating the features of their own system as a whole?

Nowhere is GTM more conspicuous than on television. I offer one small example—a series about the building of a steel mill where the workers are making extraordinary efforts, replete with tragedies and heart attacks, so that the mill would begin operation on the appointed day. As far as I know, none of the millions of viewers asked what economic reasons (aside from the scheduled ceremonies and banquet) made it imperative for a steel mill, calculated to run for decades, to open at just that particular minute and second. If there are such complications, wouldn't it be better to postpone it for a couple of days or weeks, and do a better job to boot?

Polish foreign correspondents have fallen victim to GTM in a special way. They have been 'dedialectized'' unconsciously, without being aware of it. As we know, the laws of dialectics teach that one must take into account all elements in every case—not only what is said is important, but where, when, by whom, and to whom. Dialectics, however, have been entirely forgotten by that foreign correspondent reporting to the folks back home about the hard lot of the "gastar-

*A Polish journalist on the staff of the weekly *Polityka;* he resigned after the imposition of martial law.

beiters'' or foreign workers in Western countries. He forgets that he is addressing people in Poland who know that foreign workers went to the capitalist countries *voluntarily* and have no desire to leave, and that, on the other hand, no one had ever heard of any foreign worker coming voluntarily to earn his living in a socialist country. Another correspondent, reporting to Poles in detail and with considerable knowledge of the monetary and customs difficulties of the states belonging to the Common Market, completely forgets that he is addressing people who have trouble buying money for a trip to East Germany or Hungary and who are searched at customs like smugglers. Quite a point to overlook!

Incomplete, incomprehensive information—that is, disinformation—the lie, really, perpetrated on a daily basis, enters our blood and becomes our second nature, even sometimes a moral or a national obligation. People who have accepted the convention of the lie consider lying a patriotic and historical duty. This is a crucial factor in our national GTM! A person from the West, even if he had read Orwell, would have no idea about any of this when speaking with us privately. He does not even suspect that when talking with him, without even knowing it ourselves, we are speaking Newspeak, which is already ingrained in us.

I direct my final words to Gustaw Herling-Grudziński,* who in issue number five of this year's *Kultura* calls on the writers of Poland to renounce all lies, their own included. My friend, in view of GTM, that is no easy task! Millions of people in Poland no longer know what is and what is not the truth, and what it means to be a ''sincere witness.'' For decades, not only our language has been changed but our mental criteria—we are different now, though if you speak with us in the West you will think we are the same as you. We do a great many things without being forced to, instinctively, and that's the whole tragedy, worse and more painful than you in that Naples of yours can imagine. No one forces us now, we do it ourselves, for holy peace and daily order we earn our daily GTM. And hence, perhaps, my hatred for those lesser perpetrators who know not what they are doing!

KISIEL
Warsaw, May [1979]

From *Kultura* (Paris), July–August 1979

Translated by Richard Lourie

---

*A distinguished Polish writer and one of the principal contributors to *Kultura* (Paris), who has lived in Naples since the end of World War II.

APPENDIX
The Gdańsk Agreement, August 31, 1980

This protocol was signed on behalf of the strikers by Lech Wałęsa (resident of the MKS), Andrzej Kołodziej and Bogdan Lis (vice-presidents), Mr. and Mrs. L. Bądkowski, W. Gruszewski, A. Gwiazda, S. Izdebski, J. Kmiecik, Z. Kobyliński, H. Krzywonos, S. Lewandowski, A. Pieńkowska, Z. Przybylski, J. Sikorski, L. Sobieszek, T. Stanny, A. Walentynowicz, and F. Wiśniewski.

It was signed for the governmental commission by: Chairman Mieczysław-Jagielski (vice-prime minister); M. Zieliński, member of the Secretariat of the Central Committee of the PZPR; T. Fiszbach, president of the Party Committee of Gdańsk Voivod and the mayor of Gdańsk, J. Kołodziejski.

The governmental commission and the Interfactory Strike Committee (MKS), after studying the twenty-one demands of the workers of the coast who are on strike, have reached the following conclusions:

On Point No. 1, which reads:
"To accept trade unions as free and independent of the party, as laid down in Convention No. 87 of the ILO and ratified by Poland, which refers to the matter of trade unions rights," **the following decision has been reached:**

1. The activity of the trade union of People's Poland has not lived up to the hopes and aspirations of the workers. We thus consider that it will be beneficial to create new union organizations, which will run themselves, and which will be authentic expressions of the working class. Workers will continue to have the right to join the old trade unions, and we are looking at the possibility of the two union structures cooperating.

2. The MKS declares that it will respect the principles laid down in the Polish Constitution while creating the new independent and self-governing unions. These new unions are intended to defend the social and material interests of the workers, and not to play the role of a political party. They will be established on

the basis of the socialization of the means of production and of the socialist system that exists in Poland today. They will recognize the leading role of the PZPR in the state, and will not oppose the existing system of international alliances. Their aim is to ensure for the workers the necessary means for the determination, expression, and defense of their interests. The governmental commission will guarantee full respect for the dependence and self-governing character of the new unions in their organizational structures and their functioning at all levels. The government will ensure that the new unions have every possibility of carrying out their function of defending the interests of the workers and of seeking the satisfaction of their material, social and cultural needs. Equally it will guarantee that the new unions are not the objects of any discrimination.

3. The creation and the functioning of free and self-governing trade unions is in line with Convention 87 of the ILO relating to trade unions rights and Convention 98, relating to the rights of free association and collective negotiation, both of which conventions have been ratified by Poland. The coming into being of more than one trade union organization requires changes in the law. The government, therefore, will make the necessary legal changes as regards trade unions, workers' councils, and the labor code.

4. The strike committees must be able to turn themselves into institutions representing the workers at the level of the enterprise, whether in the fashion of workers' councils or as preparatory committees of the new trade unions. As a preparatory committee, the MKS is free to adopt the form of a trade union, or of an association of the coastal region. The preparatory committees will remain in existence until the new trade unions are able to organize proper elections to leading bodies. The government undertakes to create the conditions necessary for the recognition of unions outside of the existing Central Council of Trade Unions.

5. The new trade unions should be able to participate in decisions affecting the conditions of the workers in such matters as the division of the national assets between consumption and accumulation, the division of the social consumption fund (health, education, culture), the wages policy, in particular with regard to an automatic increase of wages in line with inflation, the economic plan, the direction of investment, and prices policy. The government undertakes to ensure the conditions necessary for the carrying out of these functions.

6. The enterprise committee will set up a research center whose aim will be to engage in an objective analysis of the situation of the workers and employees, and will attempt to determine the correct ways in which their interests can be represented. This center will also provide the information and expertise necessary for dealing with such questions as the prices index and wages index and the forms of compensation required to deal with price rises. The new unions should have their own publications.

7. The goverment will enforce respect for Article 1 of the trade union law of 1949, which guarantees the workers the right to freely come together to form trade unions. The new trade union will not join the Central Council of Trade

Unions (CRZZ). It is agreed that the new trade union law will respect these principles. The participation of members of the MKS and of the preparatory committees for the new trade unions in the elaboration of the new legislation is also guaranteed.

On Point No. 2, which reads:

To guarantee the right to strike, and the security of strikers and those who help them," **it has been agreed that:**

The right to strike will be guaranteed by the new trade union law. The law will have to define the circumstances in which strikes can be called and organized, the ways in which conflicts can be resolved, and the penalties for infringements of the law. Articles 52, 64, and 65 of the labor code (which outlaw strikes) will cease to have effect from now until the new law comes into practice. The government undertakes to protect the personal security of strikers and those who have helped them and to ensure against any deterioration in their conditions of work.

With regard to Point No. 3, which reads:

"To respect freedom of expression and publication, as upheld by the Constitution of People's Poland, and to take no measures against independent publications, as well as to grant access to the mass media to representatives of all religions," **it has been added that:**

1. The government will bring before the Sejm (Parliament) within three months a proposal for a law on control of the press, of publications, and of other public manifestations, which will be based on the following principles: censorship must protect the interests of the state. This means the protection of state secrets and of economic secrets in the sense that these will be defined in the new legislation, the protection of state interests and its international interests, the protection of religious convictions, as well as the right of nonbelievers, as well as the suppression of publications which offend against morality.

The proposals will include the right to make a complaint against the press control and similar institutions to a higher administrative tribunal. This law will be incorporated in an amendment to the administrative code.

2. The access to the mass media by religious organizations in the course of their religious activities will be worked out through an agreement between the state institutions and the religious associations on matters of content and of organization. The government will ensure the transmission by radio of the Sunday mass through a specific agreement with the Church hierarchy.

3. The radio and television as well as the press and publishing houses must offer expression to different points of view. They must be under the control of society.

4. The press, as well as citizens and their organizations, must have access to public documents, and above all to administrative instructions and socioeconomic plans, in the form in which they are published by the government and by the administrative bodies that draw them up. Exceptions to the principle of open administration will be legally defined in agreement with Point No. 3, par. 1.

With regard to Point No. 4, which reads:
"To reestablish the rights of people who were dismissed after the strikes in 1970 and 1976 and of students who have been excluded from institutions of higher education because of their opinions, (b) to free all political prisoners, including Edmund Zadrożyński, Jan Kozłowski and Marek Kozłowski; (c) to cease repression against people for their opinions," **it has been agreed:**

(a) to immediately investigate the reasons given for the sackings after the strikes of 1970 and 1976. In every case where injustice is revealed, the person involved must be reinstated, taking into account any new qualifications that person may have acquired. The same principle will be applied in the case of students.

(b) the cases of persons mentioned under point (b) should be put to the Ministry of Justice, which within two weeks will study their dossiers; in cases where those mentioned are already imprisoned, they must be released pending this investigation, and until a new decision on their case is reached,

(c) to launch an immediate investigation into the reasons for the arrests of those mentioned (the three named individuals).

(d) to institute full liberty of expression in public and professional life.

On Point No. 5, which reads:
"To inform the public about the creation of the MKS and its demands, through the mass media," **it has been decided that:**

This demand shall be met through the publication in all national mass media of the full text of this agreement.

On Point No. 6, which reads:
"To implement the measures necessary for resolving the crisis, starting with the publication of all the relevant information on the socioeconomic situation, and to allow all groups to participate in a discussion on a program of economic reforms," **the following has been agreed:**

We consider it essential to speed up the preparation of an economic reform. The authorities will work out and publish the basic principles of such a reform in the next few months. It is necessary to allow for wider participation in a public discussion of the reform. In particular the trade unions must take part in the working out of laws relating to the enterprises and to workers' self-management. The economic reform must be based on the strengthening, autonomous operation, and participation of the workers' councils in management. Specific regulations will be drawn up in order to guarantee that the trade unions will be able to carry out their functions as set out in Point No. 1 of this agreement.

Only a society that has a firm grasp of reality can take the initiative in reforming the economy. The government will significantly increase the areas of socioeconomic information to which society, the trade unions, and other social and economic organizations have access.

The MKS also suggests, in order that a proper perspective be provided for the development of the family agricultural units, which are the basis of Polish agriculture, that the individual and collective sectors of agriculture should have equal access to the means of production, including the land itself, and that the conditions should be created for the recreation of self-governing cooperatives.

On Point No. 7, which reads:

"To pay all the workers who have taken part in the strike for the period of the strike as if they were on paid holiday throughout this period, with payment to be made from the funds of the CRZZ," **the following decision has been reached:**

Workers and employers participating in the strike will receive, on their return to work, 40 percent of their wages. The rest, which will add up to a full 100 percent of the nominal basic wage, will be calculated as would holiday pay, on the basis of an eight-hour working day. The MKS calls on workers who are members to work toward the increase of output, to improve the use of materials and energy, and to show greater work discipline, when the strike is over, and to do this in cooperation with the management of the factories and enterprises.

On Point No. 8, which reads:

"To increase the minimum wage for every worker by 2,000 zlotys a month to compensate for the increase in prices," **the following has been decided:**

These wage increases will be introduced gradually, and will apply to all types of workers and employees and in particular to those who receive the lowest wages. The increases will be worked out through agreements in individual factories and branches. The implementation of the increases will take into account the specific character of particular professions and sectors. The intention will be to increase wages through revising the wage scale or through increasing other elements of the wage.

White-collar workers in the enterprises will receive salary increases on an individual basis. These increases will be put into effect between now and the end of September 1980, on the basis of the agreement reached in each branch.

After reviewing the situation in all the branches, the government will present, by October 31, 1980, in agreement with the trade unions, a program of pay increases to come into effect from January 1, 1981, for those who get the least at the moment, paying particular attention to large families.

On Point No. 9, which reads:

"To guarantee the sliding scale," **the following decision has been reached:**

It is necessary to slow down the rate of inflation through stricter control over both the public and private sectors, and in particular through the suppression of hidden price increases.

Following from a government decision, investigation will be carried out into the cost of living. These studies will be carried out both by the trade unions and by scientific institutions. By the end of 1980, the government will set out the principles of a system of compensation for inflation, and these principles will be open to discussion by the public. When they have been accepted, they will come into effect. It will be necessary to deal with the question of the social minimum in elaborating these principles.

On Point No. 10, which reads:

"To ensure the supply of products on the internal market, and to export only the surplus,"

and Point No. 11, which reads:

"to suppress commercial prices and the use of foreign currency in sales on the internal market,"

and Point No. 12, which reads:

"to introduce ration cards for meat and meat-based products, until the market situation can be brought under control," **the following agreement has been reached:**

The supply of meat will be improved between now and December 31, 1980, through an increase in the profitability of agricultural production and the limitation of the export of meat to what is absolutely indispensable, as well as through the import of extra meat supplies. At the same time, during this period a program for the improvement of the meat supply will be drawn up, which will take into account the possibility of the introduction of a rationing system through the issue of cards.

Products that are scarce on the national market for current consumption will not be sold in the PEWEX shops; and between now and the end of the year, the population will be informed of all decisions that are taken concerning the problems of supply.

The MKS has called for the abolition of the special shops and the leveling out of the price of meat and related products.

On Point No. 13, which reads:

"To introduce the principle of cadre selection on the basis of qualifications, not on the basis of membership of the party, and to abolish the privileges of the police (MO) and the security services (SB), and of the party apparatus, through the abolition of special sources of supply, through the equalization of family allowances, etc." **we have reached the following agreement:**

The demand for cadres to be selected on the basis of qualifications and ability has been accepted. Cadres can be members of the PZPR, of the SD (the Democratic Party, which draws its membership from small private enterprises), of the ZSL (the Peasant Party—these three parties make up the National Front), or of no party. A program for the equalization of the family allowances of all the professional groups will be presented by the government before December 31, 1980. The governmental commission states that only employees' restaurants and canteens, such as those in other work establishments and offices, are operated.

On Point No. 14, which reads:

"To allow workers to retire at fifty years for women and fifty-five for men, or after thirty years of work for women, and thirty-five for men, regardless of age," **it has been agreed that:**

The governmental commission declares pensions will be increased each year, taking into account the real economic possibilities and the rise in the lowest wages. Between now and December 1, 1981, the government will work out and present a program on these questions. The government will work out plans for the increase of old age and other pensions up to the social minimum as established through studies carried out by scientific institutions; these will be presented to the public and submitted to the control of the trade unions.

The MKS stresses the great urgency of these matters and will continue to raise the demands for the increase of old age and other pensions, taking into account the increase of the cost of living.

On Point No. 15, which reads:

"To increase the old-style pensions to the level paid under the new system," **it has been agreed:**

The governmental commission states that the lowest pensions will be increased every year as a function of rises in the lowest wages. The government will present a program to this effect between now and December 1, 1981. The government will draft proposals for a rise in the lowest pensions to the level of the social minimum as defined in studies made by scientific institutes. These proposals will be presented to the public and subject to control by the unions.

On Point No. 16, which reads:

"To improve working conditions and the health services so as to ensure better medical protection for the workers," **it has been agreed that:**

It is necessary to increase immediately the resources put into the sphere of the health services, to improve medical supplies through the import of basic materials where these are lacking, to increase the salaries of all health workers, and with the utmost urgency on the part of the government and the ministries, to prepare programs for improving the health of the population. Other measures to be taken in this area are put forward in the addendum below.

Addendum to Point No.16:
1. To introduce a "Charter of Rights for Health Service Employees."
2. To guarantee supplies for sale of an adequate amount of protective cotton clothing.
3. To reimburse health service workers for the purchase of work clothes from the material expenditure fund.
4. To provide a guaranteed wage fund that would make possible rewarding all those who have performed outstanding work in accordance with the theoretically existing possibilities.
5. To set up funds for additional payments upon the completion of twenty-five and thirty years of work.

6. To establish additional payment for work under difficult or harmful working conditions, and to introduce additional pay for shift work by nonmedical employees.

7. To restore additional payment to those attending patients with infectious diseases or to those handling contagious biological material and to increase pay for nurses on night duty.

8. To recognize spinal diseases as occupational for dentists.

9. To allocate good-quality fuel to hospitals and nurseries.

10. To recognize additional payment for years of service to nurses without secondary school diplomas, to bring them up to the earnings level of graduate nurses.

11. To introduce a seven-hour workday for all skilled workers.

12. To introduce free Saturdays without the requirement of making up the time otherwise.

13. To pay a 100 percent increase in wages for Sunday and holiday duties.

14. To make medicine available free of charge to health service workers.

15. To make it possible to make a partial refund of housing loans from the social fund.

16. To increase the allocated apartment space for health service workers.

17. To make it easier for nurses living alone to be allotted apartments.

18. To change the award fund into a thirteenth monthly salary.

19. To give a six-week vacation to health service workers after twenty years of service and to make it possible for them to receive an annual paid vacation for health reasons, as is enjoyed by teachers.

20. To give people working for their M.D.'s four-week vacations and those working for specialized degrees two-week vacations.

21. To guarantee a doctor the right to a day off after night duty.

22. To give workers in nurseries and kindergartens a five-hour schedule, as well as free board.

23. To introduce allocation of cars for basic health service workers and a mileage limit or a lump sum refund for business travel.

24. Nurses with higher education should be recognized and paid the same as other workers with a higher education.

25. To create specially trained repair groups in the ZOZs (factory health centers) to protect health service buildings from further deterioration.

26. To increase the per-capita standard allowance for medicines for hospital patients from 1,138 zlotys to 2,700 zlotys, since the latter is the actual cost of treatment, and to increase the nutrition allowance as well.

27. To set up a system of food vouchers for the bedridden.

28. To double the number of ambulances—this being a real need today.

29. To take steps to guarantee purity of air, soil, and water, especially coastal seawater.

30. To provide citizens with health centers, drugstores, and nurseries, along with new housing developments.

On Point No. 17, which reads:
"To ensure sufficient places in day nurseries and playschools for the children of all working women," **it has been agreed that:**

The government commission is fully in agreement with this demand. The provincial authorities will present proposals on this question before November 30, 1980.

On Point No. 18, which reads:
"To increase the length of maternity leave to three years to allow a mother to bring up her child," **it has been decided that:**

Before December 31, 1980, an analysis of the possibilities open to the national economy will be made in consultation with the trade unions, on the basis of which an increase in the monthly allowance for women who are on unpaid maternity leave will be worked out.

The MKS asks that this analysis should include an allowance that will provide 100 percent of pay for the first year after birth, and 50 percent for the second year, with a fixed minimum of 2,000 zlotys a month. This goal should be gradually reached from the first half of 1981 onward.

On Point No. 19, which reads:
"To reduce the waiting period for the allocation of housing," **the following agreement has been reached:**

The district authorities will present a program of measures for improving the housing situation and for reducing the waiting list for access to housing accommodations, before December 31, 1980. These proposals will be put forward for a wide-ranging discussion in the district, and competent organizations, such as the Polish Town Planners' Association, the Central Association of Technicians, etc., will be consulted. The proposals should refer both to ways of using the present building enterprises and prefabricated housing factories, and to a thoroughgoing development of the industry's productive base. Similar action will be taken throughout the country.

On Point No. 20, which reads:
"To increase the traveling allowance from 40 to 100 zlotys, and to introduce a cost of living bonus," **it has been agreed that:**

An agreement will be reached on the question of raising the traveling allowance and compensation, to take effect from January 1, 1981. The proposals for this to be ready by October 31, 1980.

On Point No. 21, which reads:
"To make Saturday a holiday in factories where there is continuing production, where there is a four-shift system. Saturday work must be compensated for by a commensurate increase in the number of holidays, or through the establishment of another free day in the week," **it has been agreed that:**

The principle that Saturday should be a free day should be put into effect, or another method of providing free time should be devised. This should be worked out by December 31, 1980. The measures should include the increase in the number of free Saturdays from the start of 1981. Other possibilities relating to this point are mentioned in the addendum, or appear in the submissions of the MKS.

Addendum to Point No. 21:

1. Change the Council of Ministers' decree concerning the method of calculating vacation pay as well as sickness benefits for those working under the four-shift system. At present, an average of thirty days is used (while they work twenty-two days in a month). This method of calculation decreases the average day's wages during short sick leaves and lowers the vacation equivalent.

2. We demand regularization, by one legal act (a Council of Ministers' decree), of the principles governing calculation of earnings for periods of absence from work in individual cases. The obscurity of the rules at the moment is used against workers.

3. The lack of Saturdays off for workers on the four-shift system should be compensated for by additional days off. The number of days granted in the four-shift system is higher than anywhere else, but they serve as additional periods of rest after exhausting work, not as real days off. The administration's argument that such compensation should be granted only after the number of working hours in both systems have been made the same does not seem justified.

4. We demand all Saturdays off every month, as in the case in other socialist countries.

5. We demand removal of Article 147 from the Labor Code, which permits extending time to nine hours a day in a week preceding additional days off, as well as Article 148. At the moment, we have one of the longest working weeks in Europe.

6. Upgrade the importance of agreements concerning remuneration by introducing appropriate changes in the Labor Code. These should specify that changes in both individual salary grading or in other components of pay, and also a change in method of payment (from daily wage to piecework) require notification by the employer. One should also introduce the principle that the system under which individuals are classified for purposes of setting piecework rates be made to cover basically all types of work performed by the worker. It is also necessary to systematize the ways in which young workers are made use of, in keeping with their qualifications, so that the above settlement does not become an additional obstacle to their professional advancement.

7. Employees working night shift should be granted up to a 50 percent supplement if under the daily wage system and 30 percent more real pay if under the piecework system.

After reaching the above agreement, it has also been decided that:

The government undertakes:

to ensure personal security and to allow both those who have taken part in the strike and those who have supported it to return to their previous work under the previous conditions;

to take up at the ministerial level the specific demands raised by the workers of all enterprises represented in the MKS;

to publish immediately the complete text of this agreement in the press, the radio, the television, and in the national mass media.

The strike committee undertakes to propose the ending of the strike at 5:00 P.M. on August 31, 1980.

List of Polish Acronyms

ChSS   Chrześciańskie Stowarzyszenie Społeczne (Christian Social Association)
CRZZ   Centralna Rada Związków Zawodowych (Central Council of Trade Unions)
DiP   Doświadczenie i Przyszłość (Experience and the Future [club])
FJN   Front Jedności Narodowej (Front of National Unity)
GUS   Główny Urząd Statystyczny (Main Statistical Office)
KIK   Kluby Inteligencji Katolickiej (Clubs of Catholic Intelligentsia)
KOR   Komitet Obrony Robotników (Workers' Defense Committee)
KPN   Konfederacja Polski Niepodległej (Confederation of Independent Poland)
KPP   Komunistyczna Partia Polski (Communist Party of Poland [1926–38])
KPRP   Komunistyczna Partia Robotnicza Polska (Polish Communist Workers'
            Party [1918–26])
KSS/KOR   Komitet Samoobrony Społecznej KOR (Social Self-Defense Committee,
            KOR)
MKS   Międzyzakładowy Komitet Strajkowy (Interfactory Strike Committee)
MO   Milicja Obywatelska (Citizens' Militia)
OBOP   Ośrodek Badania Opinii Publicznej (Center for Public Opinion Studies)
ODiSS   Ośrodek Dokumentacji i Studjów Społecznych (Center for Social Documen-
            tation and Studies)
PAP   Polska Agencja Prasowa (Polish Press Agency)
PAX   Stowarzyszenie PAX (PAX Association)
PEWEX   Przedsiębiorstwo Eksportu Wewnętrznego (Domestic Trade Enterprise)
PGR   Państwowe Gospodarstwo Rolne (State Agricultural Farm)
PPN   Polskie Porozumienie Niepodległościowe (Polish League for Independence)
PPR   Polska Partia Robotnicza (Polish Workers' Party [1942–48])
PPS   Polska Partia Socjalistyczna (Polish Socialist Party [1892–1948])
PZKS   Polski Związek Katolicko-Społeczny (Polish Catholic Social Union)
PZPR   Polska Zjednoczona Partia Robotnicza (Polish United Workers' Party)
RMP   Ruch Młodej Polski (Young Poland Movement)
ROPCiO   Ruch Obrony Praw Człowieka i Obywatela (Movement for the Defense of
            Human and Civil Rights)
SB   Służba Bezpieczeństwa (Security Service)
SD   Stronnictwo Demokratyczne (Democratic Party [or Movement])
SDKPiL   Socjaldemokracja Królestwa Polskiego i Litwy (Social Democracy [or So-
            cial Democratic Party] of the Kingdom of Poland and Lithuania [1898–
            1918])
WOG   Wielkie Organizacje Gospodarcze (Large Economic Organizations)
ZBoWiD   Związek Bojowników o Wolność i Demokrację (Union of Fighters for Free-
            dom and Democracy)
ZSL   Zjednoczone Stronnictwo Ludowe (United Peasant Party [or Movement])

NOTES

Introduction

1. The Polish League for Independence, founded in May 1976, was the only prestigious group that subscribed in its program to "the regaining of genuine national sovereignty" and "the introduction and continuous existence of a multi-party democracy" (see Peter Raina, *Political Opposition in Poland, 1954–1977* [London: Poets and Painters Press, 1978]; pp. 468–84). The Confederation of Independent Poland (KPN) was a conspiratorial group set up in September 1979 by Leszek Moczulski, formerly a member of ROPCiO, but this underground party, which proclaimed its intention of abolishing the Communist system altogether, gained few if any followers before the advent of Solidarity. Only in late 1981, as Polish society became radicalized and as the confrontations with an increasingly hostile and recalcitrant regime proliferated, did the KPN begin to acquire more support.

2. See "Readings," pp. 263–71.

3. See Peter Raina, *Independent Social Movements in Poland* (London: Orbis Books, 1981), pp. 183–310.

4. See "Readings," pp. 151–55.

5. See Raina, *Political Opposition in Poland,* pp. 485–96, and Raina, *Independent Social Movements,* pp. 311–25.

6. See chapter 4, by Aleksander Smolar, in this book.

7. See *Poland Today: The State of the Republic,* compiled by the "Experience and the Future" Discussion Group, trans. by Michael Vale et al., with an introduction by Jack Bielasiak (Armonk, N.Y.: M. E. Sharpe, Inc., 1981).

8. *Focus on Eastern Europe* (London), vol. 5, nos. 1–2 (Spring 1982).

1. IN SEARCH OF HISTORY

1. For relevant examples of Polish censorship, see pp. 241–51 in this book—*Ed.*

2. Józef Piłsudski (1867–1935), originally a socialist, gained fame as a military leader and organizer of armed opposition to Russia, and then to Austria during World War I. Elected chief of state at the end of the war, he retired from public life in 1923. In 1926, apalled by what he considered to be the rampant factionalism and corruption of the parliamentary system, he staged a coup and installed himself in power. Until his death, Piłsudski was the virtual dictator of Poland, though he refused to do away with the representative system altogether, and in fact restored many democratic freedoms. To the extent that Pilsudski may be credited with any coherent political philosophy, it was that of the primacy of the state and of Polish independence. Roman Dmowski (1864—1939) was the founder of the National Democratic Party, a right-wing conservative movement that by the 1920s and '30s had come to resemble, in its ideology and political strategy, the fascist and Nazi movements in Italy and Germany. One of the axioms of the National Democrats (or *endecja,* as it became known) was that Poland must become an ethnically homogeneous country and that the Jews represented the greatest obstacle to the realization of that goal.—*Ed.*

3. See Jan Tomasz Gross, *Polish Society under German Occupation: General Government, 1939–1944* (Princeton: Princeton University Press, 1979), chapters 1 and 10.

4. The Polish Legions were established in northern Italy in January 1797 by General Jan Henryk Dąbrowski (1755–1818). Their song, entitled "Dąbrowski's Mazurka," was later adopted as Poland's national anthem. Dąbrowski's Legions fought alongside French Napoleonic armies in numerous campaigns, mostly against Austria.

5. Adam Mickiewicz (1798–1855) was Poland's greatest poet, a friend of Pushkin, and an ardent revolutionary. Forced to flee Poland after the November 1830 Uprising, he taught Slavic literature at the Collège de France for four years, and during the 1848 revolutions he organized a Polish Legion in Italy and in 1849 founded an international journal in Paris, called *La Tribune des Peuples.* He died of cholera in Constantinople, where he had gone to organize a Polish army to fight against Russia. Mickiewicz's most famous works are the narrative poem *Pan Tadeusz* and the play *Dziady* (The forefathers).

6. Juliusz Słowacki (1809–1849) is considered by some to be equal if not superior to Mickiewicz in poetic genius. He left Poland in 1831 but kept apart from the rest of the so-called Great Emigration. Zygmunt Krasiński (1812–1859) is considered, with Słowacki and Mickiewicz, to be one of the three greatest Polish romantic poets. He spent most of his life abroad, became a prolific epistolarian, and died in Paris. Cyprian Kamil Norwid (1821–1883) was an innovative poet and painter. He left his country in 1842 and died in poverty in Paris, largely unappreciated by his contemporaries.

7. See Maria Janion and Maria Żmigrodzka, *Romantyzm i historia* (Romanticism and history) (Warsaw, 1978), p. 340.

8. "Ode to Youth," one of Mickiewicz's early poems, was a passionate call to young people to abjure egoism and serve humanity's struggle for progress.

9. Janion and Żmigrodzka, p. 313.

10. Tadeusz Kościuszko (1746–1817), soldier, statesman, and (to this day)

symbol of Polish military romanticism, led an insurrection in Kraków in March 1794, that soon spread throughout Poland. Though he scored some remarkable victories against both the Russians and the Prussians, the nationwide uprising was finally crushed by superior Russian armies in November of that year. A democrat in the tradition of Jefferson and Lafayette (he had offered his services to the Continental army in 1776 and was eventually appointed by Washington as his adjutant), he was the co-author of a manifesto granting personal freedom to Polish peasants and reducing their dues in the way of serf labor by one-half; in 1817, shortly before his death, he granted full emancipation to his serfs.

The Constitution of May Third was passed by the Polish Diet in 1791. It established a parliamentary system with considerable freedoms altogether lacking in Poland's earlier constitutions. The document enraged Empress Catherine the Great, who a year later, in collusion with a group of Polish traitors meeting in the town of Targowice, launched an attack on the Polish army that led to the Second Partition of Poland (1793). The term *targowica* has since then come to stand for treason.

11. In November 1830 a group of Polish cadets staged an uprising in Warsaw, which marked the beginning of yet another war against the Russian occupier; the Polish armies were finally defeated in October 1831. As a result, the "Kingdom of Poland," established by the Congress of Vienna in 1815, became even more of a dependent of the Russian tsar.

12. The second most famous Polish insurrection against Russian domination began in January 1863, with a decree by the revolutionary Central National Committee offering unconditional and permanent emancipation to peasants and enfranchisement of every person in the Polish realm without regard to race, religion, or previous condition of bondage. It lasted eighteen months, and was followed by wholesale reprisals and the elimination of the final vestiges of Polish autonomy.

13. George F. Kennan, *Memoirs* (New York: Bantam Books, 1967), pp. 209–10.

14. Ibid., p. 213.

15. In March 1945, sixteen leaders of the Polish anti-Nazi underground were invited to a conference by the commanding general of the Red Army that liberated Warsaw. The group, including some high-ranking officers and statesmen, was assured of safe conduct and received a promise to be sent to London to consult with the Polish government before engaging in full-scale negotiations with Soviet military authorities. When they appeared for the first meeting, they were arrested and flown to Moscow. After three months of intensive interrogation they were put on trial on the trumped-up charge of having conspired with Nazi Germany against the Soviet Union. All but three received long prison sentences. For a personal account of one of the accused, see Zygmunt Stypuł-kowski, *Invitation to Moscow* (London, 1951).

16. The Treaty of Riga, signed on March 18, 1921, ended the Polish-Soviet border war—called the 1920 War. It established a new Polish-Soviet frontier and regularized the relations between the two countries.

2. THE PARTY: PERMANENT CRISIS

1. For a discussion of the *nomenklatura* system, see chapter 4, by Aleksander Smolar—*Ed.*

2. The reader will find extensive treatments of the history of Polish communism in M. K. Dziewanowski, *The Communist Party of Poland* (Cambridge, Mass.: Harvard University Press, 1959); Jan B. de Weydenthal, *The Communists of Poland: An Historical Outline* (Stanford, Cal.: Hoover Institution Press, 1978); and Adam Bromke, *Poland's Politics: Idealism vs. Realism* (Cambridge, Mass.: Harvard University Press, 1967).

3. The workers' demonstrations in Poznań in June 1956 were provoked by decisions taken by the management of a local machinery plant, which affected the workers' standard of living. The general discontent of the workers was pervasive, however, and soon led to a series of violent protests by workers demanding "bread and freedom." The suppression of the revolt by the military and police resulted in 54 dead and 300 wounded.

4. See "Partia w liczbach" (The party in numbers), *Nowe Drogi* (Warsaw), June 1956; *Rocznik polityczny i gospodarczy* (Political and economic yearbook) (Warsaw), 1958–79.

5. These difficulties manifested themselves above all in low productivity, poor quality of manufactured goods, bureaucratic mismanagement, and growing consumer shortages.

6. See chapter 5, by Leszek Kołakowski, herein—*Ed.*

7. For a discussion of this period, see chapters 5 and 8, by Kołakowski and Tadeusz Szafar, respectively, in this book—*Ed.*

8. For more details, see chapter 4, by Aleksander Smolar, herein—*Ed.*

9. *Poland Today: The State of the Republic* (Armonk, N.Y.: M. E. Sharpe, 1981), p. 55. The "Experience and the Future" group consisted of more than one hundred eminent intellectuals, many of them party members, who between 1978 and 1980 published several devastating analyses of the country's political, economic, and social system, and urged the authorities to take specific remedial action.

10. The only sounding of public opinion on this issue involved party members who were isolated from mainstream opinions and who basically told the leaders what they wanted to hear.

11. See Jane Cave, "Local Officials of the Polish United Workers' Party, 1956–75," *Soviet Studies* (Glasgow), January 1981.

12. See chapter 7, by Christopher Cviic, in this book—*Ed.*

13. See chapter 6, by Alex Pravda—*Ed.*

14. Edward Ochab had stepped down as secretary-general of the party to make room for Gomułka and remained in his entourage until the late 1960s; he remained firmly committed to a "reformist" position well into the period of the "renewal."

15. For the text of the speech, see pp. 187–92 in this book—*Ed.*

3. ECONOMICS AND POLITICS: THE FATAL LINK

1. Data computed from the *Economic Survey of Europe in 1980, Part I*, (UN Economic Commission for Europe, N.Y., 1981) Chapter 3; B. Askanas, *Die Wirtschaft der RGW-Lander an der Schwelle der achtziger Jahre* (Wiener Institut für Internationale Wirtschaftsvergleiche, Reprint-Series No. 53, May 1981); and from J. Stankovsky, *Ost-Westhandel 1979 und Aussichten für 1980* (Wiener Institut für Internationale Wirtschaftsvergleiche, Forschungsberichte, no. 58, March 1980).

2. *Kraje RWPG. Ludność, gospodarka, kultura* (CMEA countries, population, economy, culture), published by the Polish Statistical Office (Warsaw, 1972), table 12 (p. 103). Data for East Germany computed from *DDR-Wirstschaft: Eine Bestandsaufnahme*, German Institute for Economic Research (Frankfurt/Main: Fischer-Verlag, 1973), table 62.

3. See, for instance, Z. Fallenbuchl, "The Polish Economy in the 1970s," *East European Economies Post-Helsinki* (Washington, D.C.: U.S. Congress Joint Economic Committee, 1977), and R. Porter, "East Europe's Debt to the West," *Foreign Affairs* (New York), July 1977. Also my own 1977 paper "Objectives, Methods and Political Determinants of the Economic Policy of Poland 1970–76" (published in German as *Berichte des Bundesinstituts für ostwissenschaftliche und Internationale Studien*, No. 49, 1978). There have also been a number of important studies in Polish published in the West, written both by Polish economists in the West (e.g., several articles by Stanisław Gomułka in the London quarterlies *Trybuna* and *ANEKS*), and by Polish economists unable to publish their works officially in their own country: e.g., Jerzy Bartecki (pseud.), *Gospodarka na manowcach* (The economy led astray) (Paris: Institut Literacki, 1979). The book *Po wielkim skoku* (After the great leap), by Waldemar Kuczyński, who after September 1980 became one of the advisers to Solidarity, was published unofficially in Warsaw in 1979 by the independent publishing house NOWA. It provides an extremely interesting analysis of the decision-making processes in the Polish economy in the 1970s.

4. The *nomenklatura* is the list of positions filled by the party. See essay by Aleksander Smolar—*Ed*.

5. The scheme was meant to link the wage-fund of the enterprise with the improvement in results over the preceding year. The criteria for measuring the results, however, were so complicated as to make them incomprehensible to the workers. Other provisions included a 16 percent ceiling on increases of the wage-fund over a five-year period and no payments until the results for the preceding year were fully evaluated, all of which doomed the new incentive scheme (presented as the backbone of the reform) from the very start.

6. Gregory Grossman, "Gold and the Sword: Money in the Soviet Command Economy," in H. Rosovsky, ed., *Industrialization in Two Systems: Essays in Honor of Alexander Gerschenkron* (New York: John Wiley, 1966).

7. *Rocznik statystyczny* (Polish statistical yearbook), 1976 (Warsaw, 1976), table 13 (p. 332).

8. The Massey-Ferguson deal concerned the complete modernization (that is,

sweeping overhaul) of the Polish tractor industry. Its flaws, according to knowledgeable critics, were well-nigh staggering: it was inordinately costly, it neglected existing (local) design capacities, it led to long delays, production setbacks and the like, and the types of tractors produced under that license were on the whole too large (and therefore too costly) for an individual farmer anyway. A curious feature of the deal was that the Polish negotiators, presumably in order to "save" on the price, agreed to a production line based on the British imperial measure, instead of metric—the only such line-measure in Poland. That meant, of course, that there would be no tools and no spare parts immediately available, and that everything would have to be delivered either directly from the factory or from abroad—hardly an attractive prospect for the potential peasant-buyer.

9. See the Export/Import Supplement to the Polish weekly *Polityka* (Warsaw), no. 10 (October 1980), p. 102, and W. Kuczyński, *Po wielkim skoku,* chapter 9.

10. See the second version of the government's report on the state of the economy, *Trybuna Ludu* (Warsaw), July 6, 1981. No figure was given for the share of imported equipment in the frozen assets.

11. *Rocznik statystyczny,* 1979, table 25 (p. 197).

12. Henryk Flakierski, "Income Distribution in Hungary and Poland since 1965," in St. Antony's College, Oxford, "Papers in East European Economics," no. 60, July 1980 (mimeographed).

4. THE RICH AND THE POWERFUL

1. Jacek Kurczewski, "W oczach opinii publicznej" (In the eyes of public opinion), *Kultura* (Warsaw), March 1, 1981.

2. "Where patrimonial authority lays primary stress on the sphere of arbitrary will free of traditional limitations, it will be called 'sultanism.'" Max Weber, *The Theory of Social and Economic Organization* (London, 1947), p. 318.

3. *Życie Literackie* (Warsaw), March 22, 1981.

4. K. Słomczyński, W. Wesołowski, "Zmniejszenie nierówności społecznych a rozbieżności czynników statusu" (The decline of social inequities and the divergencies in the status factors), *Studia Socjologiczne,* no. 1, 1975.

5. K. Szafnicki, "Oceny płac indywidualnych i dochodów rodzin" (Evaluations of individual wages and family incomes), in K. Słomczyński and W. Wesołowski, eds., *Struktura i ruchliwość społeczna* (Structure and social mobility) (Wrocław, 1973).

6. *Czas* (Gdańsk), March 23, 1981.

7. *Życie Literackie,* February 22, 1981.

8. Taken from a collection of texts marked "for internal use" (Warsaw, 1977), and reprinted in part in the uncensored journal *Głos,* no. 6, 1977.

9. According to the testimony of T. Stankiewicz, member of a commission appointed by the University of Warsaw to examine charges of unjust personnel decisions during the years 1968–80, *Kurier Polski* (Warsaw), April 22, 1981.

10. *Polityka* (Warsaw), March 3, 1971.

11. The speech, delivered at a closed session of Szczepański's co-workers, was printed in its entirety in *ANEKS* (London), no. 16/17, 1977. (In late 1981, Szczepański and one of his associates were put on trial on charges of mass embezzlement and bribery—*Ed.*)

12. These statistics were finally released in 1981. See *Życie Partii* (Warsaw), no. 4, 1981, and *Życie Warszawy* (Warsaw), March 18, 1981.

13. *Gdańsk—Sierpień 1980, Rozmowy Komisji Rządowej z Miedzyzakładowym Komitetem Strajkowym w Stoczni Gdańskiej (August 23–31, 1980), (Warsaw, 1981), pp. 48 and 62.*

14. *Prawo i Życie* (Warsaw), October 5, 1981.

15. The speech appeared in a Solidarity newspaper, *Wolny Związkowiec* (no. 13, 1981), and was reprinted in *ANEKS*, no. 24/25, 1981.

16. *Nowe Drogi* (PZPR theoretical monthly, Warsaw), no. 4, 1976.

17. According to information provided by the first secretary of the party in Radom, Janusz Prokopiuk, *Życie Warszawy*, June 25, 1981.

18. Danuta Zagrodzka, "Jak rządzić żywnością" (How to regulate food supplies), *Polityka*, December 20–27, 1980.

19. *Krytyka* ("uncensored" quarterly, Warsaw), no. 6, 1980.

20. *Dziennik Ustaw* (a journal, published by the State Council, listing all government laws and decrees), no. 42, October 7, 1972.

21. Interview with Klasa in *Gazeta Krakowska* (Kraków), April 24, 1981.

22. A heating duct 800 meters long was installed in the apartment of party leader Józef Kępa, at a cost of 6,500,000 zlotys. At an order of a provincial notable, a road was constructed with armor plates and covered with asphalt twice at a cost of 500,000 zlotys. This case was actually reported in the press, and punishment meted out, before the summer of 1980. (Most of the other data mentioned in this essay come from the spate of revelations that came in late 1980 and after.)

23. As many as eight agencies were involved, for instance, in the house built for Minister Adam Glazur (*Trybuna Ludu*, December 22, 1980).

24. According to the newspaper *Słowo Powszechne*, for instance (April 14, 1981), Z. Nadrakowski, provincial governor of Wrocław, caused the displacement of thirty-one people, with the state paying for the eleven apartments assigned to them.

25. *Argumenty* (Warsaw), July 19, 1981; *Prawo i Życie*, July 12, 1981.

26. *Trybuna Robotnicza*, April 28, 1981.

27. *Trybuna Ludu*, March 17, 1981.

28. *Czas*, March 15, 1981.

29. *Prawo i Życie*, May 24, 1981.

30. *Trybuna Ludu*, April 9, 1981.

31. For further treatment of the subject of parallel economy in Poland, see Irena Grosfeld and Aleksander Smolar, "Economie parallèle en Pologne," *Futuribles* (Paris), no. 40, January 1981.

32. Tadeusz Żarski, *Polityka*, August 29, 1981.

33. *Walka Młodych*, May 17, 1981.

34. *Polityka*, March 21, 1981.

35. *Rocznik statystyczny* (Statistical yearbook) (Warsaw), 1976, pp. 360–61.

5. THE INTELLIGENTSIA

1. An interesting discussion of this subject can be found in *Geneologia polskiej inteligencji* (Genealogy of the Polish intelligentsia), a booklet written by the Polish sociologist Józef Chałasiński, published in 1947.

2. The SDKPiL has sometimes been called—with some exaggeration but not quite without reason—the first Communist party in the world. Even though it did not elaborate a theory of the "vanguard party" in the sense Lenin would subsequently do, it was unqualifiedly committed to the principle of the class struggle and for this reason vehemently opposed the concept of national self-determination. It considered the restoration of an independent Polish state as nothing but a dream and rejected the very idea of national culture. Rosa Luxemburg was among the founders of the party; Feliks Dzierżyński (who was to become the founder of the Soviet security police, the Cheka) is counted among its stars.

3. Ludwik Krzywicki (1859–1941) was one of the most prominent sociologists in Poland and a great figure in the history of the country's progressive intelligentsia. In his early years he contributed more than anyone else to the spread of Marxist theory in Poland, but later on, during the interwar period, his works had only a remote connection with Marxism. Stanisław Brzozowski (1878–1911), a philosopher, novelist, and literary critic, exercised considerable influence on young intellectuals before World War I and later. For a few years of his short and feverishly active life he considered himself a Marxist and elaborated a highly idiosyncratic and interesting version of Marxism that he called "the philosophy of labor." He died a Catholic. Kazimierz Kelles-Krauz (1872–1905) was, among Poles, the closest to the ideas of the Orthodox German school of Marxism that dominated the socialist movement in the late nineteenth century, yet even his version of Marxism deviates in some important respects from the principles propounded by, say, Karl Kautsky.

4. Recently republished by Octagon Books (New York, 1981).

5. See chapter 8, by Tadeusz Szafar, in this book—*Ed.*

6. See chapter 3, by Włodzimierz Brus—*Ed.*

7. See chapter 7, by Christopher Cviic—*Ed.*

8. See chapter 6, by Alex Pravda, for a discussion of KOR's influence on the workers—*Ed.*

6. THE WORKERS

1. For a description of "premature consumerism," see p. 69.

2. According to Lenin, workers, if left to themselves, tend to forfeit political demands in favor of purely economic issues and grievances; it is up to intellectuals to imbue workers with genuine political consciousness.

3. A number of informative articles on this subject appeared in the weekly *Polityka* (Warsaw)—e.g., "Co sądzisz o wydarzeniach?" (What is your view of the events?), no. 37, 1980; and Z. Sufin, "Nadzieje i obawy społeczeństwa" (The hopes and fears of society), no. 3, 1981.

4. See *Dissent in Poland—Reports and Documents in Translation* (London, 1977), pp. 50–79.

5. *Rocznik statystyczny* (Statistical yearbook) (Warsaw), 1979.

6. See, e.g., A. Wajda, ed., *Klasa robotnicza w społeczeństwie socjalistycznym* (The working class in a socialist society) (Warsaw, 1979), p. 210, and J. Kurczewski, "W oczach opinii publicznej" (In the eyes of public opinion), *Kultura* (Warsaw), March 1, 1981.

7. See Władysław Machejek, "A teraz—do pracy!" (And now—to work!), "Readings," herein, pp. 193–97.

8. These emerged as the most clearly perceived benefits of socialism in a September 1979 national poll conducted by the OBOP (Center for Public Opinion Studies) entitled "Idea demokracji w opiniach społeczeństwa" (The idea of democracy in the opinion of society).

9. *Trybuna Ludu* (Warsaw), May 8, 1981.

10. Sufin, "Nadzieje i obawy"; Stefan Nowak et al., "Ciągłość i zmiana tradycji kulturowej" (Continuity and change in cultural tradition), University of Warsaw, mimeograph, 2 vols., July 1976, p. 318, table 11–4. (Stefan Nowak, who has visited and taught in the West, is one of the most eminent Polish sociologists.)

11. J. Rosner, *Polityka społeczna w pracy socjalnej* (Social policy in social work) (Warsaw, 1979), pp. 18–20; Kurczewski, "W oczach opinii publicznej."

12. For a summary of the measures, see A. Sabbat, "End of Bonanza for Polish Party Officials?" *Radio Free Europe Background Report*, no. 58, 1981. (See also chapter 4, by Aleksander Smolar, in this book—*Ed.*)

13. See discussion with members of the Szczecin Interfactory Workers' Committee, *Polityka* (Warsaw), no. 42, 1980, p. 6.

14. Insight into the attitudes of younger workers can be found in W. Wesołowski, ed., *Młodzi robotnicy* (Young workers) (Warsaw, 1975).

15. See, for example, J. Loch, in *Polityka*, no. 51/52, 1975, p. 5.

16. A study of two foundries in the early 1970s found that only one-fifth to one-half of all workers took this view. M. Strzoda, *Aktywność zawodowa i społeczna hutników* (Professional and social activity of miners) (Katowice, 1977).

17. See *Labour Focus on Eastern Europe* (London), May–June 1978, pp. 21–22.

18. For instance, a party survey in Katowice in 1971 revealed such an unfavorable picture of the party's performance in the enterprise that the results were kept under lock and key until 1980. See R. Fedorowski in *Trybuna obotnicza*, January 10–11, 1981, p. 3.

19. For results of this poll, see O. Macdonald, "Party, Workers and Opposition," *Labour Focus on Eastern Europe*, May–June 1977.

20. J. Kołodziejski, "Władza uczyła się pokory" (The authorities learned humility), *Kultura* (Warsaw), no. 46, 1980, p. 9.

21. According to J. Staniszkis, a Polish sociologist, one-third of the Gdańsk Interfactory Committee were party members; see "Evolution of Forms of Working-Class Protest in Poland: Sociological Reflections on the Gdańsk-Szczecin Case, August, 1980," *Soviet Studies* (Glasgow), April 1981.

22. Interview with B. Walker, BBC Television, August 26, 1980; reprinted in *August 1980—the Strikes in Poland (Munich: Radio Free Europe, 1980).*

23. *In a September national poll, 89 percent of those surveyed supported the strikes. See Kurczewski, "W oczach opinii publicznej."*

24. *See Polityka, April 25, 1981, pp. 6–7.*

25. *See essay by Leszek Kołakowski, chapter 5 herein—Ed.*

26. *For details, see Denis MacShane, Solidarity—Poland's Independent Trade Union (London: Spokesman, 1981); also the chapter "Free Trade Unions," in Peter Raina, Independent Social Movements in Poland (London, 1981).*

27. *See Biuletyn Informacyjny KSS–KOR, no. 26, 1980, pp. 27–29.*

28. *For Wałęsa, see "Notes on Biography," by Edmund Szczeciak, in The Book of Lech Wałęsa,* introd. by Neal Ascherson (London: Allen Lane, 1982); and "Lech Wałęsa: Symbol of the Polish August," by Michael Dobbs, in *Poland—Solidarity—Wałęsa,* by Michael Dobbs, K. S. Karol, and Dessa Trevisan (New York: McGraw-Hill Book Co., 1981).

29. A minor caveat: shared earlier experience does not satisfactorily explain the action of the Silesian miners, who had taken no active part in the protests of 1956, 1970–71, or 1976. For one thing, they had always been the highest-paid workers in Poland; for another, Silesia was Gierek's own bailiwick and had been favored with a better and more varied supply of consumer goods than the rest of the country. The strikes by Silesian miners in 1980—which so surprised and chagrined party leaders—stemmed, rather, from local grievances, such as dissatisfaction with lack of safety measures and existing shift arrangements, and even more from the miners' general sympathy with the shipyard workers, their concern lest inaction be seen by workers everywhere as the passivity of a privileged group, and their eagerness to demonstrate their loyalty to a common cause.

30. See Appendix—*Ed.*

31. In a national poll conducted in mid-September 1980, four out of five respondents thought that prices had risen faster than wages. See summary of OBOP Poll No. 16, 1980, p. 3.

32. For the situation in the mid-1960s, see Kazimierz Słomczyński and Tadeusz Krauze, eds., *Class Structure and Social Mobility in Poland* (White Plains, N.Y.: M. E. Sharpe, 1978), pp. 154–55. For 1979, see Sufin, "Nadzieje i obawy społeczeństwa."

33. Sufin, "Nadzieje i obawy społeczeństwa."

34. See Nowak et al., "Ciągłość i zmiana tradycji kulturowej," p. 318 (table 11-4).

35. See Raina, *Independent Social Movements in Poland,* pp. 375–80.

36. See *August 1980,* p. 379.

37. See Wajda, *Klasa robotnicza,* p. 316, for the workers' view of the party.

38. On earlier workers' councils and their demise, see Neal Ascherson, *The Polish August—the Self-Limiting Revolution,* (New York: Viking Press, 1981), pp. 83–84; and chapter 5 in Jan B. de Weydenthal, *The Communists of Poland: An Historical Outline* (Stanford, Cal.: Hoover Institution Press, 1978).

39. Article 6 of the "Solidarity Rules," *Głos Pracy* (Warsaw), November, 17, 1980, p. 3.

40. See Ascherson, *The Polish August,* pp. 150–51.

41. See, for instance, W. D. Connor, "Dissent in Eastern Europe: A New Coalition," *Problems of Communism* (Washington, D.C.), January-February 1980.

42. The studies by Nowak showed, in fact, that Catholic workers supported civil liberties more staunchly than their nonbelieving colleagues; see "Ciągłość i zmiana tradycji kulturowej," p. 307.

43. Ibid., pp. 290 and 318.

44. Address by Stefan Bratkowski at the party meeting of the Warsaw branch of the Polish Journalists' Association, *Biuletyn Informacyjny KSS/KOR* (News bulletin of KSS/KOR), no. 40 (August 1980). For the English text, see "Readings,' pp. 187–92, herein—*Ed.*

45. See chapter 9 in this book, by George Schöpflin—*Ed.*

46. For a fuller discussion of this phenomenon, see Alex Pravda, "Industrial Workers: Patterns of Dissent, Opposition, and Accommodation," in Rudolf L. Tokes, ed., *Opposition in Eastern Europe* (Baltimore: The Johns Hopkins University Press, 1979).

7. THE CHURCH

1. Perhaps the most shocking evidence of the Church's anti-Jewish animus was contained in a pastoral letter by Cardinal Hlond, the primate of Poland, read from the pulpits of most churches in February 1936: "It is a fact that the Jews fight against the Catholic Church; they are freethinkers and constitute the vanguard of atheism, of the bolshevik movement, and of revolutionary activity. It is a fact that Jewish influence upon morals is fatal and their publishers spread pornographic literature. It is true that the Jews are committing frauds, practicing usury, and dealing in white slavery." The Primate urged his flock not to yield to hatred, "not even of Jews," and not to assault Jews physically, for that would be "contrary to Catholic ethics." On the other hand, he approved of the campaign "to avoid Jewish stores and Jewish stalls in the markets," to "fence oneself off against the harmful moral influences of Jewry," and "especially to boycott the Jewish press and the demoralizing Jewish publications." (Cardinal August Hlond, *Listy pasterskie* [Pastoral letters] [Poznań, 1936], pp. 192–93.)

2. According to the concordat between the Polish state and the Vatican, ratified in March 1925, the Church was given full freedom to conduct its affairs, its vast landholdings were exempted (with some minor exceptions) from the Land Reform laws, the government agreed to pay the salaries of the priests, and religious instruction on public school premises was made mandatory. Both under the constitution of 1921 and again under that of 1935, the Church was accorded a preeminent position among the other faiths in Poland. (See Richard M. Watt, *Bitter Glory—Poland and Its Fate* [New York: Simon & Schuster, 1979], pp. 256–57; Kazimierz Kumaniecki, *Odbudowa państwowości polskiej—najważ niejsze dokumenty, 1912–styczeń 1924* [The reconstruction of Polish statehood—principal documents, 1912–January 1924] [Warsaw: Czernicki, 1924], p. 519; and Wacław Komarnicki, *Ustrój państwowy Rzeczypospolitej Polskiej* [The government structure of the Polish Republic] [London, 1943], pp. 231–34.)

3. Present-day Church dignitaries in Poland have taken a clear-cut stand on the principle of Church-state relations, and have in effect criticized the prewar links with the secular authorities. Thus in an interview published in the September 25, 1981, issue of *Tygodnik Solidarność*, the Polish primate, Archbishop Józef Glemp, stated that "today there is much less of a threat of an alliance between the Church and the state," thanks largely to "the teachings of the last Vatican Council, which wants no privileges, but demands freedom for the Church. Without those teachings, we could easily become dependent on the authorities, on the system, as has happened, after all, in the past."

4. R. F. Leslie, ed., *The History of Poland since 1863* (London, 1980), p. 285. Despite the fact that Poland had become the graveyard for millions of Jews, the poison of anti-Semitism still affected large parts of society (see Paul Lendvai, *Anti-Semitism in Eastern Europe* [London, 1971]). Unfortunately, this was true of many Catholic clergymen as well. During the notorious "blood-libel" pogrom in June 1946, which claimed the lives of over forty survivors of the Holocaust (see chapter 8, by Tadeusz Szafar, in this book), the local bishop, Czesław Kaczmarek, refused to provide any assistance to the town's tiny Jewish community, and subsequently the primate, Cardinal Hlond, issued a statement that deplored the "painful incident" but went on to place the blame for it on "Jews who occupy leading positions in the alien government and endeavor to introduce a political structure that most Poles do not want." In recent years, the Catholic Church in Poland has taken various steps to remove the stain of anti-Semitism from its record. In June 1981, for instance, a special mass was held in the Kielce cathedral to commemorate the victims of the Kielce pogrom.

5. Hansjakob Stehle, *Eastern Politics of the Vatican, 1917–1919* (Athens: Ohio University Press, 1981), p. 271.

6. On Piasecki and PAX, see Lucjan Blit, *The Eastern Pretender* (London, 1965).

7. For the full text, see Hansjakob Stehle, *The Independent Satellite* (London, 1965), pp. 306–9.

8. Ibid., pp. 309–10.

9. Ibid., p. 64.

10. Peter Raina, *Political Opposition in Poland, 1954–1977* (London, 1978), pp. 137–38.

11. Ibid., pp. 144–45.

12. Ibid., pp. 406–7.

13. Adam Michnik, *Kosciół, lewica, dialog* (The Church, the left, dialogue) (Paris: Instytut Literacki, 1977).

14. Raina, *Political Opposition in Poland*, p. 407.

15. See Alex Tomsky, "Poland's Church on the Road to Gdańsk," in *Religion in Communist Lands* (Keston College, Kent, England), 1–2, 1981.

16. *Dissent in Poland—Reports and Documents in Translation (periodical)* (London, 1977), pp. 20–23.

17. *Op cit.*, p. 151.

18. *The Times* (London), December 8, 1976.

19. *Dissent in Poland*, p. 160.

20. Reuters, February 29, 1980.

21. *Strikes in Poland—August 1980* (Munich: Radio Free Europe Research, October 1980).

22. Denis MacShane, *Solidarity—Poland's Independent Trade Union* (London, 1981), p. 96.

23. *BBC Current Affairs Research and Information Section Report*, no. 49/81, November 12, 1981.

8. ANTI-SEMITISM: THE TRUSTY WEAPON

1. "Wiece w Warszawie" (Rallies in Warsaw), *Trybuna Ludu* (Warsaw), March 9, 1981.

2. Political anti-Semitism is defined as the deliberate exploitation of certain traditional popular prejudices by a political party or movement for its own goals, which intrinsically have nothing to do with Jews as such, or with the so-called Jewish question. Political anti-Semitism, therefore, feeds on, but cannot be wholly identified with, such widespread (and irrational) sentiments as parochial xenophobia, religious intolerance, social discrimination, economic competition or jealousy, or nationalism and chauvinism. Modern political anti-Semitism in Europe first appeared about a century ago. In Poland it became the favorite weapon of the right-wing *endecja* (National Democratic Party).

3. The accusation that either all Jews in Poland were Communists and/or worked for the Stalinist apparatus of terror or that most security officials and other prominent members of the Communist establishment in the 1950s were Jewish is simply too absurd to be taken seriously; even a superficial comparison of the sets of data proves there simply were not enough Jews to fulfill all these functions. Nonetheless, the myth still lingers on and even finds its way into respectable but uncritical Western studies. The American historian Richard V. Burks obviously did not bother to check the respective figures when he light-heartedly claimed that in Warsaw (as in Bucharest and Budapest) "virtually every important police official was Jewish" (*The Dynamics of Communism in Eastern Europe* [Princeton: Princeton University Press], p. 160); neither did M. K. Dziewanowski, approvingly repeating this nonsense and adding that the role Jews had played in the Soviet subjugation of Eastern Europe was "not unlike [that of] the Greek *phanariotes,* an oppressed minority of the Ottoman Empire who were used as a tool of the imperial system" (*The Communist Party of Poland: An Outline of History* [Cambridge, Mass.: Harvard University Press, 1976], pp. 297–98).

4. The preliminary research done by Michael Checiński, one-time senior officer in the Polish military conterintelligence ("The Kielce Pogrom: Some Unanswered Questions," *Soviet Jewish Affairs* [London], no. 1/1975, pp. 57–72), while far from conclusive, indicates that certain high-ranking officers of the Polish Security, acting on orders of their superiors in the Soviet secret services, may well have instigated the massacre on the sly, or at least had created conditions favorable for its "spontaneous" outbreak, and then had shifted the blame on right-wing opponents of communism in Poland. Until 1981, the subject was

taboo. But on the thirty-fifth anniversary of the pogrom, the Solidarity chapter in Kielce commemorated the victims with a mass in the local cathedral. Interestingly enough, a letter to the editor of the union's newspaper referred to the surprising impunity of the mob: "part of the Militia, as described by the contemporary Polish press, instead of regaining control over the situation, joined the murderers—see, for example, *Dziennik Polski,* July 10, 1946"—*Tygodnik Solidarność* (Warsaw), June 26, 1981, p. 15.

5. The trial of the Czechoslovak Communist Party's First Secretary Rudolf Slánský and other party leaders, in November 1952, had a pronouncedly anti-Semitic character. Of the fourteen defendants, eleven were Jewish, and all were accused of working for the "Zionist conspiracy." The "doctors' plot" involved the arrest, in January 1953, of a number of Soviet doctors, most of them Jewish, who were accused of plotting the assassination of prominent Communist Party leaders. The charges were withdrawn and the doctors released shortly after Stalin's death in March 1953. In the opinion of most observers, the Slánský trial, the "doctors' plot," and other similar developments were all steps preparatory to the arrest and deportation to Siberia of hundreds of thousands of Soviet Jews.—*Ed.*

6. The most comprehensive, though by no means satisfactory account of the 1956 intraparty factional struggle is still the essay "Chamy i Żydzi" (Boors and Jews) in Witold Jedlicki, *Klub krzywego koła* (The crooked circle club) (Paris, 1963), chapter 1. The Crooked Circle Club was an informal discussion group that arose in the mid-1950s in Warsaw; tolerated by the authorities for a few years, it was finally closed down by Gomułka in 1959.

7. "We consider it intolerable to provoke racial hatred and to exploit the tragedy of individuals or of a nation as a whole [to attain] the improvised goals of political struggle." Quoted from *Polityka* (Warsaw), no. 16, April 18, 1981, p. 2.

8. *Polityka,* no. 15, April 11, 1981, p. 2.

9. The English text of Gomułka's speech can be found in *Radio Free Europe Situation Report,* Munich, June 22, 1967.

10. For a detailed analysis of these writings, see Tadeusz Szafar, "Endecized Marxism: Polish Communist Historians on Recent Polish Jewish History," *Soviet Jewish Affairs* (London), vol. 8, no. 1, 1978.

11. Jerzy Topolski, ed., *Dzieje Polski* (The history of Poland) (Warsaw, 1976).

12. In 1976, the party succeeded—over considerable opposition from various groups in society—in passing two amendments to the 1952 constitution. The first recognized the "leading political force in society at the time of socialist construction," and the other defined one of the country's goals as that of "strengthening its friendship and cooperation with the Soviet Union and other socialist states." The second amendment was a diluted version of the original proposal, which stressed Poland's "unshakable fraternal bond with the Soviet Union." (See Jan B. de Weydenthal, *The Communists of Poland: An Historical Outline* [Stanford, Cal.: Hoover Institution Press: 1978], pp. 156–61).

13. For details see Łukasz Hirszowicz and Tadeusz Szafar, "The Jewish Scapegoat in Eastern Europe," *Patterns of Prejudice* (periodical). (London, 1977), vol. 2, no. 5.

14. *KOR Communiqués* (Warsaw), no. 1 (September 29, 1976) and no. 5 (December 21, 1976). (For a discussion of KOR's activities, see chapter 5, by Leszek Kołakowski.)

15. *Aktualne zagadnienia walki klasowej* (Topical problems of the class struggle) (Warsaw, 1977), pp. 12–13, 15 et passim.

16. "Although one's feelings are an extra-religious affair, it is a good thing that the cradle of the Christian religion was Galilee, at that time a Syrian province shunned by the Orthodox Jews because it was considered unclean and international; among the Hellenes and Levantines of Galilee, on the other hand, the need for love and sacrifice was very great" (*Życie Literackie* [Kraków], April 10, 1977).

17. Władysław Machejek, *Czekam na słowo ostatnie,* (I wait for the last word), 4 vols. (Kraków, 1976). For a detailed analysis of this work, see Irena Grudzińska-Gross, "Autoportret faszysty" (Self-portrait of a fascist), *ANEKS* (London), nos. 16–19, 1977. See also Machejek's article in this book—*Ed.*

18. *Kierunki* (Warsaw), August 7, 1977.

19. *Krytyka* (Warsaw), no. 1, Summer 1978 (mimeographed). Reprinted in London by *ANEKS,* 1978. (For an example of one of the contributions, see "1968 and All That," by Marek Turbacz, in this book—*Ed.*)

20. See, for example, *Spotkania* (Lublin), no. 3, April 1978 (mimeographed), reprinted in Great Britain (C.C.P.W., 26 Pout St., London S.W.1), *Kosciół i totalitarianizm* (The Church and totalitarianism), esp. pp. 53–84.

21. For positive appraisals of the *endecja* traditions, see, for instance, articles in *Bratniak* (Gdańsk), no. 1/15, 1979 (mimeographed), and *Opinia* (Warsaw), no. 2, 1978 (mimeographed). (See also the two articles from *Bratniak* translated for this book, "The Spirit That Revives" and "A Reply to Father Sroka"—*Ed.*)

22. In 1967–68 Kania was secretary of the party Warsaw voivodship committee, at that time one of the most active centers of anti-Semitic propaganda, openly peddled in its press organs (see Łukasz Hirszowicz, "The Current Polish Crisis and the 1968 Anti-Semitic Campaign," *Institute of Jewish Affairs Research Report* [London], no. 23, December 1980.) When Kania was promoted to the Central Committee apparatus and put by Gierek in charge of the purge of Moczarite elements in the security services, he tried, in some individual cases at least, to help victims of the 1968 witch hunt.

23. *Trybuna Ludu,* November 4, 1980.

24. A journalist, himself Jewish, and a frequent critic of the independent unions, tried to make the most of this lapse; cf. Jerzy Urban, "Racja istnienia" (Raison d'être), *Polityka,* March 7, 1981. Because of Urban's close association with *Polityka,* whose editor-in-chief, Mieczysław Rakowski, became deputy premier in February 1981, General Jaruzelski appointed Urban as the government's press spokesman in August 1981. Urban stayed on in this post after martial law was declared on December 13, 1981.

25. A striking illustration of the level of these publications is provided by a pamphlet called *Marzec 1968—nieudana próba zamachu* (March 1968—a failed attempt at a coup d'état) (Warsaw; no publisher, 1981). The "name" of the author is Dr. hab. Ida Martowa—that is (in deliberately quixotic Polish), Associate Professor Dr. Ides of March (!). An examination of this work clearly indi-

cates that the author had access to police archives, and tends to confirm a Warsaw rumor that the author is Ryszard Gontarz, a notorious anti-Semitic writer and recently a filmmaker, who in 1968 was party secretary in the Ministry of Internal Affairs. According to the pamphlet, both Jakub Berman, the former Polish Communist *éminence grise*, and the Georgian Lavrenti Beria, late head of the Soviet secret police, "had grown up in rich bourgeois Jewish families and had been prominent leaders of the Zionist movement."

Another mimeographed publication, signed "Poles-Patriots," claims that the Katyń massacre of Polish prisoners of war in 1940 had been ordered by the "Russian Jew Beria," entirely without Stalin's knowledge, and that President Kennedy had been assassinated by an "American Jew, Jack Rubinstein (Ruby), a bordello owner," acting on orders from the "International Trotskyite-Zionist Organization."

26. See, e.g., Krystyna Kersten, "Kielce—4 lipca 1946 roku" (Kielce—July 4, 1946), *Tygodnik Solidarność*, no. 36, December 4, 1981. The article had originally been banned by censors but was later released by a court of law.

27. Mimeographed anonymous appeal, "To all Polish women—our mothers, wives, and daughters—who wait in lines!" (Warsaw, July 1981) (in my private collection).

28. According to Politburo member Stefan Olszowski, "the attitude of Grunwald is correct," in that it "accepts socialism" and "defends people unfairly accused of nationalism" (*Polityka*, April 11, 1981).

29. According to Solidarity's organ, *Tygodnik Solidarność* (no. 13, June 26, 1981), it took its correspondent a long time to locate Stanisław Szkutnik, chairman of the Grunwald branch, presumably located at the Warsaw Steel Plant, where "neither workers, nor managers, nor party and union activists have ever heard of Grunwald." The telephone conversation between Szkutnik and the Solidarity reporter is worth quoting: *Q*.: "Who can belong to the Grunwald Union?" *A*.: "Every Polish woman and man." *Q*.: "What does it mean?" *A*.: "But surely you know what it means." *Q*.: "Can a Jew be a member?" *A*.: "If somebody is of Jewish origin, it is strictly up to him, but I think that such a man, after two or three meetings would give it up of his own volition." (Ibid.)

30. *Gazeta Krakowska* (Kraków), May 20, 1981.

31. *Kierunki*, May 17, 1981. In the fall of 1980, PAX executed an about-face, embraced the "renewal," and firmly disassociated itself from its founder's anti-Semitic legacy. But after the December 1981 coup, it reverted to its old "loyalist" character.

32. See, for instance, *Literaturnaia gazeta* (Moscow), April 16, 1981.

33. Waldemar Stelmach, "Trzy grzechy" (Three sins), *Rzeczywistość* (Warsaw), no. 13, April 16, 1981. The campaign against Professor Geremek became especially noxious after Jaruzelski's coup. (The name Geremek came from his stepfather, a Gentile, who married his widowed mother after the war—*Ed*.)

34. The publication of "The Protocols" was reported and criticized in *Polityka*, nos. 35 and 37, August 29 and September 12, 1981. (For a fascinating study of the "Protocols"—a document concocted by the tsarist secret police, the "Okhrana," and purporting to prove the existence of a "world Jewish conspir-

acy"—as well as of their origins and uses, see Norman Cohn, *Warrant for Genocide* [New York: Harper & Row, 1967]—*Ed.*)

35. The one salient exception was the leader of the Szczecin Solidarity chapter, Marian Jurczyk, who in a widely quoted speech combined lusty attacks on the Communist party with gross anti-Semitic slurs. An ardent nationalist, Jurczyk in effect accepted Grunwald's claim that all of Poland's troubles were caused by "Jewish Stalinists." It was denounced by *Tygodnik Solidarność* and, on the fateful day of December 12, 1981, by Wałęsa himself (see the Washington Post, December 14, 1981).

36. Andrzej Żabiński at the Ninth Plenary Session of the PZPR Central Committee (*Trybuna Ludu,* June 6, 1981).

9. POLAND AND EASTERN EUROPE

1. Marcin Król, "Pologne: une révolution différente," *Commentaire* (Paris), no. 12, 1980–81.

2. Paying of stipends by the state made the churches more dependent on the state, without subordinating them completely.

3. The Roman Catholic Church had extremely close ties with the Hapsburg rulers.

4. Gierek's regime collapsed on September 5, 1980, less than a week after the signing of the Gdańsk agreement. (See appendix—*Ed.*)

5. According to Ceausescu, the Polish Communist party had committed a grievous error by permitting the establishment of a free union not directly under its control.

6. Since the early 1960s, the Rumanian Communist leadership has been promoting Rumanian nationalism as the principal means of securing the loyalty of the population. The greatness of Rumania's past and the superiority of the Rumanian nation have been extolled both in popular media and in scholarly journals. These writings have also been imbued with an anti-Soviet and an anti-Hungarian slant (regarding Bessarabia and Hungarian Transylvania, respectively), and, increasingly, the campaign has become intertwined with the cult of Ceausescu as the embodiment of Rumanian national grandeur.

7. In February 1907, a major peasant uprising broke out in a Rumanian village and soon spread throughout the entire country. The major demand was that of redistribution of large estates to poor peasants. The uprising was eventually suppressed.

8. There is considerable—though indirect—evidence that in the aftermath of the Polish crisis East German workers have come to perceive their regime as the guarantor of their relatively high standard of living and security, likely to be imperiled by the growing Polish unrest.

9. In August 1980, the town of Tîrgovişte was swept by massive strikes of workers protesting food shortages and low living standards. The strikes were settled by economic concessions.

10. "Magyar hangok a lengyel esemenyekrol," *Magyar Fuzetek* (Paris), no. 7, 1980.

11. The reference here is to the dog, in Arthur Conan Doyle's Sherlock Holmes story *Silver Blaze,* that did not bark in the nighttime as it had been expected.—*Ed.*

12. The decision to build the Katowice Steel Works was strongly criticized by various groups in Poland, which felt that the project would prove an economic and environmental disaster. As it turned out, the critics had been right. (See chapter 3, by Włodzimierz Brus, in this book—*Ed.*)

13. The second wave of terror had as its aim the final destruction of claims to autonomy made by various groups in society—workers, peasants, and intelligentsia—during the 1956 revolution and the decisive assertion of party supremacy.

14. Poles did not need visas to visit East Germany. In consequence, many of them would cross the border to buy large quantities of East German products, unavailable in Poland.—*Ed.*

15. In early 1981, there appeared a number of articles in East German periodicals whose aim was clearly to present the history of the Kingdom of Prussia in a favorable light. Given the fact that Prussia had competed against Poland for power and territory, and that the Prussian *Drang nach Osten* (drive to the east) was directed against Poland, the new campaign was bound to arouse anti-Polish feeling. Ironically, while Moscow's loyal German ally was thus enlisting history and nationalism in an effort to discredit Poland's "bloodless revolution," the Soviet Union launched a campaign claiming that West German "revanchists" supported Solidarity in the hope that a victory over "socialism" would result in the return of the Polish "western territories" to the Federal Republic of Germany.

INDEX

CONTRIBUTORS

JACK BIELASIAK is Associate Professor in the Department of Political Science and the Russian–East European Institute at Indiana University, and author of *Poland: The Politics of Crisis* (Boulder, Colo.: Westview Press, in press).

ABRAHAM BRUMBERG is a former editor of the bimonthly journal *Problems of Communism*. He has also edited *Russia under Khrushchev* (New York: Praeger, 1962) and *In Quest of Justice—Protest and Dissent in the Soviet Union Today* (New York: Praeger, 1970), and was the U.S. editor of *Communism and Democratic Society—a Comparative Encyclopedia* (in German and English) (Freiburg: Herder, 1966–70). He is a contributing editor of *The New Republic* (Washington, D.C.) and has contributed to *Foreign Affairs* (New York), *The New Republic* (Washington, D.C.), *Dissent* (New York), *The Economist* (London), and other American and British publications.

WŁODZIMIERZ BRUS, a Polish-born economist formerly at the University of Warsaw, left Poland in 1972 and is presently teaching at Wolfson College, Oxford. Among his books are *The Market in a Socialist Economy* (London, 1972) and *The Economics and Politics of Socialism* (London, 1973).

CHRISTOPHER CVIIC is a specialist on Eastern Europe at *The Economist* (London), a BBC commentator, and author of numerous articles on political and cultural developments in Eastern Europe.

JAN TOMASZ GROSS, a sociologist and historian, is Research Associate at Yale University. He is the author of *Polish Society under German Occupation: The General Government, 1939–1944* (Princeton: Princeton University Press, 1979) and (with I. Grudzińska-Gross) of *War through Children's Eyes: The Soviet Occupation of Poland and the Deportations, 1939–41* (Stanford, Cal.: Hoover Institution Press, 1981).

LESZEK KOŁAKOWSKI, for many years Professor of the History of Philosophy at the University of Warsaw, was expelled from Poland in 1968 for political reasons and is now a Fellow at All Souls' College, Oxford. He is the author of numerous articles and books, among them *Main Currents of Marxism,* 3 vols. (New York: Oxford University Press, 1980).

ALEX PRAVDA is Lecturer in the Department of Politics of the University of Reading, England. He is contributor to A. Kahan and B. A. Ruble (eds.), *Industrial Labor in the USSR* (Elmsford, N.Y.: Pergamon Press, 1979), and author of many articles on labor problems in Eastern Europe.

GEORGE SCHÖPFLIN is Joint Lecturer on East European political institutions at the London School of Economics and Political Science and the School of Slavonic and East European Studies, University of London. He is also the author of numerous studies on political institutions in Hungary and other East European countries.

ALEKSANDER SMOLAR, a sociologist, left Poland in 1968, and is presently Chargé de Recherche, Centre National de la Recherche Scientifique, Paris, and editor of the Polish quarterly *ANEKS* (London). His articles on the Polish social and political system have appeared in various French publications.

TADEUSZ SZAFAR, a Polish-born journalist and historian and author of numerous books and articles, left Poland in 1975. He is now a Fellow at the Russian Research Center, Harvard University. He has contributed to *Survey* (London), *Soviet-Jewish Affairs* (London), and other publications in Great Britain and the United States.